Programming UCSD Pascal

Seymour V. Pollack

Department of Computer Science
Washington University
St. Louis, Missouri

Holt, Rinehart and Winston

New York   Chicago   San Francisco   Philadelphia
Montreal   Toronto   London   Sydney   Tokyo
Mexico City   Rio de Janeiro   Madrid

Library of Congress Cataloging in Publication Data

Pollack, Seymour V.
    Programming UCSD Pascal.

    Includes index.
    1. PASCAL (Computer program language)   I. Title.
II. Title: Programming U.C.S.D. Pascal.
QA76.73.P2P646   1984   001.64'24   84-3732
ISBN 0-03-069393-4

Printed in the United States of America
Published simultaneously in Canada

4   5   6   7   039   9   8   7   6   5   4   3   2   1

CBS College Publishing
Holt, Rinehart and Winston
The Dryden Press
Saunders College Publishing

Contents

Preface

Pascal is the first major programming language based on a preception of programming as a systematic process. While earlier languages include features that offer varying opportunities for structured programming, the presence or absence of such features is more a matter of circumstance than design. Most of these languages were conceived and implemented prior to the emergence and crystallization of structured programming concepts. Subsequent extensions to these languages have been constrained by the necessity to remain compatible with their original syntactic rules.

Pascal, on the other hand, has no such ancestral restrictions. It reflects an explicit concern with structured programming. In fact, a major design objective is to encourage the use of constructions and practices that are associated with the production of clear, reliable programs. This is done, to a large extent, by incorporating language features that facilitate structured programming and by erecting barriers that make structured programming more awkward or difficult to avoid.

Given this orientation, it is useful to view Pascal as the beginning of a new generation of programming languages. This book reflects that view since it accepts structured programming as a rational approach to program development and it presents Pascal as a reasonable vehicle for supporting this approach. There is no need, at this stage of the discipline, to defend structured programming and argue against the ad hoc approach that preceded. Nor is there any payoff in describing the (earlier) unstructured approach only to point out its shortcomings. Consequently, this book presents the subject as if people always sought to write well-structured programs.

Since Pascal was originally designed to be used primarily as a teaching vehicle, its initial version encompassed a range of facilities that appear to be modest when contrasted with the more elaborate programming languages used in production environments. As a result, numerous versions of the language have appeared, each with a set of enhancements and supporting software designed to enrich the range of facilities available to the programmer. A particularly attractive set of enhancements is provided by the p-System, an operating environment that is helpful both in educational and production settings. Within this environment, programs can be prepared, modified, stored, retrieved, and executed without elaborate and complicated interaction between the user and the system. Thus, when the student is learning to write programs in a clear and orderly way, he or she receives an additional bonus by learning about the nature and effective use of an interactive operating system. Although these additional operating skills are acquired almost incidentally, they serve as a useful foundation on which additional knowledge can be built. Moreover, the p-System has been implemented on a wide variety of computing machinery including most types of personal computers. Consequently, the skills and techniques learned on one computer are immediately transferable to many others, and Pascal programs developed under a particular p-System implementation are directly transferable to numerous other such installations.

Although this book concentrates on teaching the features of UCSD Pascal (the version of Pascal implemented under the p-System) and their use in developing well-structured programs, it includes sufficient information about the p-System so that its contents can be used effectively without additional documentation. (However, students are expected to develop some familiarity with the screen editor prior to or during the early part of their work. Some suggestions in this regard are given at the end of Chapter 2.)

This book is designed for students who have not had previous experience with either Pascal or the p-System. Its extensive use of examples makes it equally suitable for a class or for self-study. If the student has worked with another programming language (on any system), it may be appropriate to bypass the first chapter. Students acquainted with another version of Pascal may find that Chapters 3 and 4 require only a light going-over, but Chapter 2 still will be essential.

There is no intent to present UCSD Pascal in its entirety. Several specialized features have been omitted in favor of well-illustrated discussions of sound programming principles and practices. However, the groundwork for learning to use these features is provided by including a detailed explanation of units (Chapter 17). This material may be included as part of the instruction if students are to deal with complex programs involving separately compiled modules. Otherwise, Chapter 17 can be omitted without loss in continuity. The foundation built throughout the rest of the book ensures that the students will have the skill and understanding to learn this additional material whenever such a need might arise.

I would like to thank Brete Harrison and Paul Becker of CBS College Publishing and Cobb/Dunlop Publisher Services for their help in preparing the book and seeing it through its various developmental stages. Special thanks are due to Dr. Jerome R. Cox, Jr., Chairman of Washington University's Department of Computer Science, for his foresight in discerning the appropriate direction for computer-related education, and for his adventurous spirit in choosing to lead rather than follow in that direction. Finally, my continuing gratitude and love go to Sydell, Mark, and Sherie Pollack. I consider myself fortunate indeed to have such a wonderful family.

Seymour V. Pollack

Chapter 1

Introduction

In this book we shall learn the features of the Pascal programming language and techniques for using them to develop effective programs. The particular version of Pascal that we shall use is the one developed at the University of California at San Diego and known, therefore, as UCSD Pascal. This name does not refer to the language alone; rather, it implies an entire programming environment in which Pascal is designed to function efficiently. The entire environment is called the *p-System* because it is built around a hypothetical computer called the p-machine. The p-System is installed on a wide variety of computers, and it includes facilities that make it convenient to prepare, store, and use programs written in Pascal as well as several other languages. Our focus will be on UCSD Pascal itself, with occasional references to the p-System.

Unlike the names of most other languages, Pascal is not an abbreviation for anything. The language is named in honor of Blaise Pascal, a brilliant French mathematician of the seventeenth century (Figure 1.1). He is generally credited with building the first successful mechanical adding machine. Although there is no direct historical connection, Pascal's device (Figure 1.2) is considered the starting point in a long line of arithmetic machines preceding today's electronic digital computers.

The Pascal programming language, developed by Dr. Niklaus Wirth, was introduced in 1971. Although there already were several hundred programming languages in existence at the time, Pascal is not just another one to add to the list. Pascal is important because it explicitly seeks to support a view of programming as a systematic, orderly activity. The earlier major programming languages represent ideas and attitudes about programming that date back to the early 1950s. Accordingly, these languages place primary emphasis on making it convenient to specify certain kinds of computations. With few exceptions, these languages pay only incidental attention to the organization of these computations and to the data on which they are performed.

Over the years, the programming process has been the subject of extensive study. As a result, we now appreciate the importance of treating a program as a manufactured product. While it is not a physical item (we do

Figure 1.1

Blaise Pascal (Courtesy of Science Museum, London)

not think of a program as something that can be carried around in a bucket), it shares many attributes with a physical product: It consists of several parts (called *modules*), each of which is designed for a particular purpose. Moreover, these modules must work with each other in certain predefined ways in order for the overall assembly to function properly and effectively. The programming process lends itself to the same orderly, systematic approach underlying the design and development of any other product. Structured design and structured programming, both of which are still evolving, stem from this recognition.

In this context, Pascal is significant because it is the first major programming language in which program design and organization are central concerns. Therefore, its primary features are arranged so that they encourage good structure by making it easy to specify. Pascal goes even further by

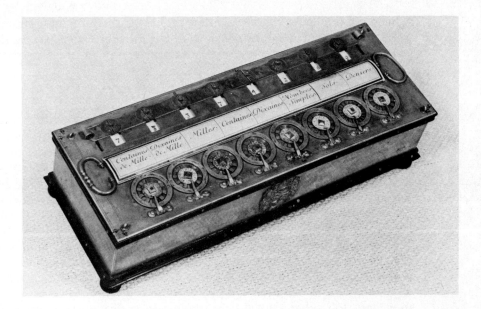

Figure 1.2

Mechanical calculator (Courtesy of Smithsonian Institution)

imposing requirements that make it awkward or difficult to avoid good structure. The result is a powerful tool that can be of great help in using the computer to solve problems effectively.

1.1 SOLVING PROBLEMS SYSTEMATICALLY

The computer does not know all the answers. Strictly speaking, it does not "know" anything. Its circuits are designed to move information around in certain ways so that particular elementary operations can be performed on that information. However, it is up to us to combine these operations so that the overall effect is to produce results that are useful. Thus, when we use a computer to solve a problem, we are the ones who determine how the problem is to be solved, and the computer carries out the solution by following our directions. The programmer knows how a certain problem is going to be solved before he or she calls on the computer to help out. The method of solution, called an *algorithm*, is worked out beforehand and is expressed as a series of steps, each of which brings us closer to the final result. We bring the computer into the picture by restating the algorithm as a *program*. This is the same series of steps, described in the precise vocabulary of a programming language.

Before we can write a program, it is necessary to develop an algorithm and describe it so clearly that its conversion to a correct program is relatively uncomplicated. It is at this stage that problem solving takes place; not when the program is written. Although there is no exact, foolproof recipe for solving problems, there are orderly steps that help increase the likelihood of a successful solution. We shall outline these steps briefly in the next few sections.

1.1.1 Identifying the Problem

It is difficult to imagine the amount of time, money, and effort spent on developing extensive, ingenious solutions to the wrong problems. Common sense would indicate that this can be avoided by making sure the problem is clearly defined before one plunges ahead and starts solving. Yet these situations continue to arise more frequently than we would hope. Recently, administrators of a hospital in a certain city observed that their patients were staying one or two days longer than those admitted to other hospitals for the same types of operations or treatments. The problem was spotted immediately (or so they thought): Obviously, the physicians kept the patients too long after surgery. The hospital launched an extensive and vigorous campaign aimed at encouraging the doctors to get their patients up and moving as soon as good practice allowed. The physicians insisted they were doing that anyway, but promised to pay particular attention to this issue. Nothing changed. Finally, the real problem was discovered: A patient could not be discharged until the bill was ready, and it was taking the accounting department a day or two longer to prepare the bill than it did at other hospitals.

Because of situations like this, many organizations have made it a rule to develop and agree upon a precise, written statement of the problem to be solved before any work is started on a solution.

1.1.2 Finding a Suitable Solution

It is easy to say, "Now that we know exactly what the problem is, the next step is to find an effective way to solve it." Sure. Nothing to it. Of course, there is no step-by-step procedure that leads us from problem to solution. In fact, we cannot be sure that there *is* a solution just because we know what the problem is. Because of these uncertainties, this step is usually the most difficult one in the entire process. It is the one in which much of the creative effort and ingenuity is concentrated. Entire libraries can be filled with writings examining the nature of this process. Several are given as references at the end of this chapter.

For our purposes, the solution to a problem takes the form of an *algorithm*. We can define an algorithm as a sequence of steps or rules that meets certain requirements:

1. An algorithm must be *finite*. That is, it must come to a stop sooner or later. For instance, suppose we were faced with the problem of producing a particular shade of blue paint. Our proposed solution is as follows:

Get a can of base paint and a can of blue coloring.
Open both cans.
Add blue coloring to the base paint until the color is right.

While this procedure seems harmless enough, it might not be finite. For example, there could be a case where the base color is too blue to begin with. According to the instructions, this is not the right color. But the procedure says to keep adding till the color is right. So, in goes more and more blue, indefinitely. This is not as ridiculous as it sounds. Remember that computers cannot exercise judgment. It is up to us to provide a specific mechanism that will guarantee a stopping point regardless of the conditions under which the algorithm operates. For this little procedure, we might specify the following revision:

Get a can each of base paint, white, and blue color.
Open the three paint cans.
IF
     the base paint is too blue
THEN
     Add white paint, a little at a time, until the color is right.
ELSE
     Add blue paint, a little at a time, until the color is right.

We may be able to think of situations for which this revised procedure will not be finite, but we shall not belabor the issue. The basic point is that there must be a way to bring our procedure to a successful conclusion if the procedure is to be useful.

2.   An algorithm should be *precise*. This means that each of the steps must be described in such a way that it can be performed by whoever (or *whatever*) will be carrying out the process. In our little example, which lacks precision, we would have to specify the amount of blue or white to add (how much is "a little?"), and we would have to describe how to determine when the right color is produced. For a skilled colorist, this might be as simple as saying, "When the mixture matches this color sample, you have the right color." For someone who is less sensitive to color, the directions might be quite different: "When the mixture gives a reading between 407.5 and 423.3 on the Schmugelsky Coloramic Pigmentovacutron, you have the right color." If the algorithm is to be transformed into a computer program, the requirement for precision means that each step must be expressed in such a way that it can be carried out on a computer.

3.   An algorithm should be *general*. This means that the procedure should not be so limited that it solves only one specific problem for one specific case. Instead, it should be capable of producing satisfactory solutions for a variety of cases. For example, our little color mixing procedure does what we need it to do as long as we want that particular

shade of blue. We could generalize it by expanding its capabilities to include other shades of blue, or even other colors.

There are many instances where we can come up with several different solutions for a problem. For instance, suppose we are driving along and suddenly the ride becomes much bumpier without any noticeable change in the road. Moreover, steering becomes more difficult. After stopping the car and inspecting it, we find that one of the tires is flat. Before discussing possible solutions, we must agree on what the problem is. In this instance there is little difficulty on that score: Our journey has been interrupted, and we wish to resume it as soon as we can. When we state the problem that way, we can think of numerous potential solutions. Here are just a few:

1. Abandon the car and continue on foot.
2. Buy another car and continue in that one.
3. Reinflate the tire and continue the trip.
4. Get in touch with a service station and have one of their mechanics replace the tire.
5. Flag down a passing motorist and persuade that party to transport us to our destination.
6. Flag down a passing motorist and persuade that party to replace the tire.
7. Call home and get a loved one to come out and replace the tire.
8. Replace the tire ourselves and continue on our way.

Sometimes we can narrow down the choices by rejecting some as being clearly unsuitable. In our example, solutions 2 and 3 are in that category. We probably would not need much convincing to reject solutions 5 and 6 as well. After that, the choice of the most "appropriate" solution may become more complicated because what is "appropriate" will depend on the circumstances. For example, solution 1 may be best after all if we are close to our destination and we must get there promptly.

1.1.3 Decomposition of a Problem

Once we identify a problem, it is often impossible to solve the entire problem all at once. More likely than not, the problem is too complicated for us to be able to keep track of all its possible twists and angles at the same time. When this happens, it is useful to break up the problem into a collection of interrelated subproblems. Each of these is small enough so that we can handle it comfortably, as a complete entity.This process of *decomposition* makes it easier to develop a solution for each little problem. As a result we can produce a complete, precise definition of what each piece is supposed to do and how it fits with the connecting pieces. The stage is set, then, for each of these components to be developed separately.

To illustrate, let us return to our disabled automobile. Suppose we decided that the best solution under the circumstances was to replace the flat tire with the spare tire. When we look at the solution more closely, we can identify several steps, each of which embodies a little problem of its own:

1.   Remove the spare wheel/tire and the necessary tools from the trunk.
2.   Remove the wheel on which the flat tire is mounted.
3.   Install the wheel on which the spare tire is mounted.
4.   Place the wheel removed in step 2 in the trunk, along with the tools.

The activities required to carry out a given step become increasingly clear as we focus even more closely. For example, let us consider step 2 in more detail. The actual removal of the wheel cannot occur without some preparation.

2.   Remove the wheel on which the flat tire is mounted:

2.1   Remove the hubcap and retaining nuts from the wounded wheel.
2.2   Find an appropriate place for positioning the jack.
2.3   Set up the jack.
2.4   Raise the car by means of the jack until the wheel no longer touches the ground.
2.5   Remove the wheel.

If necessary, decomposition continues by dissecting each of these subproblems in turn, until each activity has been reduced to a series of simple steps, each of which is completely understood.

The same process applies to a problem solution involving a computer. Eventually, the result will be a program, but we know nothing about that program's details at this point. Rather, the decomposition process tells us how that program divides into pieces and what each of these pieces needs to do. This information is expressed as a detailed description for each part of what eventually will be a computer program. These parts are called *program modules* or, simply, *modules*, and we shall use the term in that context. Note that we haven't written any programs yet. That comes in the next step.

1.1.4 Coding

We are ready to express our solution as a sequence of program statements so that a computer can be used to carry it out. If we did a reasonable job during the previous stages, this part of the process will be like translating from one language to another. Writing such program modules is called *coding*. It is important to understand that we are not developing a solution method at this stage. That has been done already in previous stages. We know what we want to do, and we know how we want to do it. We also know what we want to tell the computer. When we write the code, we convert the description of our intentions from a form that the computer cannot use to a form with which it can work.

As we shall see, Pascal itself is organized to make the coding process particularly convenient.

1.1.5 Testing

After we have expressed a module in terms of Pascal statements, there is no guarantee that the program will be correct. Even the most careful decomposition and analysis cannot always prevent us from overlooking something or just making a mistake. Consequently, each module, once coded, must be perfected by systematically testing it for errors, tracking them down, and correcting them. Then, the pieces are put together and the result is tested some more to make sure that the pieces work together properly.

Many organizations have implemented mechanisms for using and enforcing some type of systematic process for developing computer programs, and some of the related literature is listed at the end of this chapter.

1.2 COMPUTERS AND PROGRAMS

Before a program can produce useful results, it must be installed in a computer so that the machine's operations can be guided by the program's instructions. This section reviews that process briefly.

1.2.1 A Glance at Computer Architecture

The term *computer architecture* is used to characterize the computer's major components, what they do, and how they are interconnected. We are interested in the types of major operations that the computer performs and the way information is moved to support these operations.

Computers operate by executing instructions, each of which does something specific, such as adding two numbers, comparing two numbers, or moving an item of information from one place to another. In most machines, instructions are executed one at a time, but an increasing number of computers (called *multiprocessors*) are being designed to perform several operations simultaneously.

The major functional components of a computer system are shown in the basic architectural diagram of Figure 1.3. Note that the individual boxes do not necessarily correspond to separate physical components. In a personal computer, the components typically are packaged into four physical units, i.e., the central processing unit (which also contains the disk drives), the keyboards, the video monitor, and the printer. In other types of machines they may be packaged differently.

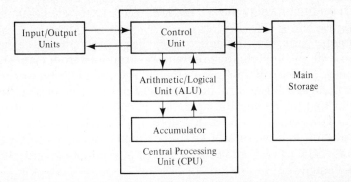

Figure 1.3

Basic Functional Components of a Digital Computer

The Central Processor   The heart of a computer is its *central processor*. For many modern machines, the processor is packaged in a tiny chip about the size of a commemorative postage stamp. Processor chips that are widely used in today's computers include the 8080, 8086, and 8088, all manufactured by the Intel Corporation; the 6802, 6805, and 68000, all manufactured by the Motorola Corporation; the Z80, Z80A, and Z8000, all manufactured by the Zilog Corporation; and the LSI/11, manufactured by the Digital Equipment Corporation. Much of the system's computing is done by the processor, and those activities performed outside the processor are (ultimately) directed by it. The instructions that the processor executes are stored in the *main storage* component (sometimes called *main memory*). Data on which these instructions are to operate are stored there as well.

Main storage is divided into individual units or cells *(bytes)*, each of which is physically capable of holding a single character of information, i.e., a letter, numerical digit, punctuation mark, etc. Each byte has a unique *address* that defines the byte's physical location. This provides a basis for storing information, finding it, and moving it around. Such movements, then, can be considered in terms of addresses. For example, a typical activity might be described as follows: "Make a copy of the information currently stored in address 784 and store that copy in address 1077, erasing what was there before." Pascal provides bookkeeping services that make it unnecessary for the programmer to deal with these details, but it is helpful to understand that somebody (or something) has to deal with them.

When the processor executes an instruction, the actual computations are done by a group of circuits called the *arithmetic/logical unit* (ALU). This component is equipped with a special memory unit (the *accumulator*). When a data item is to be used for a computation, it is brought from main storage to the accumulator, where the computation takes place. The result, then, may be transported from the accumulator to a designated location in main storage or it may be left in the accumulator for further computations.

The *control unit* runs the entire show. For a program to be executed, the control unit must obtain the program's instructions from main storage, one at a time. Each instruction is examined to determine the type of activity being specified, and the control unit activates only those parts of the ALU required for that job. When the operation is completed, the control unit repeats the process for the next instruction. Thus, the processor's main storage and ALU can be viewed as supporting components that provide instructions, data, or computational services in accordance with the control unit's demands.

Peripheral Components   A computer is equipped with several devices (*peripheral components*) for transporting information to or from the central processor. There are various devices covering a wide range of data forms, capacities, and operating speeds. Some (like your keyboard) are capable only of sending information to a processor (*input devices*); others (like your monitor or printer) are designed strictly for receiving information from the processor (*output devices*); still others (like your disk or cassette units) can be used for information transfer in either direction (*input/output devices*).

Many peripheral units have considerable computing capabilities built into them. They include processors of their own, so that they can direct some of their own operations. However, these activities still are subsidiary since they are started by signals from the central processor's control unit.

1.2.2 Machine Language

The kinds of machine instructions that can be specified for a computer are defined as part of the processor's design. Thus, if a program is to be properly executed, its instructions must be drawn from the set of instruction types (i.e., the *machine language*) "recognized" by the processor.

Machine language instructions are expressed as strings of 1s and 0s (i.e., *binary strings*). Each machine language instruction specifies a basic operation such as simple addition or multiplication. (Some instruction types perform more extensive processing.) Consequently, it is likely that any algorithm of interest to its users will require a lengthy sequence of machine instructions for its expression. For example, a program to compute the logarithm of a number may require a couple of dozen machine language instructions. Thus, the idea of having to write such programs in machine language is not an appealing one. Fortunately, languages like Pascal automate this tedious work. In the next section, we examine the basic mechanism that makes this convenience possible.

1.2.3 UCSD Pascal and Machine Language

In spite of the spectacular advances in computing equipment, machine languages have not changed much. Instructions still must be presented to the control unit as a series of binary strings. Relief for the programmer, then, did not develop in the form of more "human-compatible" machine languages. Instead, such help has evolved in the form of increasingly convenient programming languages that enable the programmer to communicate with the computing system on his or her terms rather than those imposed by the machinery.

Programming languages like Pascal are called high-level languages because they make it possible for programmers to describe complicated computations as if they were single operations. For instance, a chemical engineer wishing to compute the temperature drop in a certain type of cooling system under a given set of conditions may need to set up a complex formula involving a number of separate computations. The entire formula could be expressed in Pascal as if it were a single computational step, even though the computer eventually will have to execute 40 or 50 individual machine instructions to produce the result. In effect, the programmer can pretend (or can be fooled into believing) that the computer is designed to handle the formula directly. The thing that makes it possible to sustain this illusion is a *compiler,* a translating program designed to shelter the programmer from the minute details of the machine language. The UCSD Pascal compiler examines the original program (called the *source program*) to determine its computational requirements. Based on the information it finds there, it produces an equivalent set of instructions in a language for a specially designed hypothetical machine called the *p-machine.* The language is called *p-Code.* These instructions are "executed" by the p-machine (which is really a program that converts p-Code to actual machine instructions). Although this sounds complicated (it would seem to be more desirable to go directly from Pascal to machine language), it turns out that the use of the idealized p-machine actually simplifies the process of transforming the programmer's original Pascal statements into a functionally equivalent computational process.

In general, each Pascal statement produces several simpler p-Code instructions. This relationship is shown in the diagram of Figure 1.4. The Pascal programmer is unaware of the existence of the p-machine.

1.3 SYSTEMATIC DESCRIPTION OF ALGORITHMS

The transformation of a Pascal program to one expressed in p-Code and ultimately executed by machine language instructions is handled without human intervention. However, it is up to the human programmer to pro-

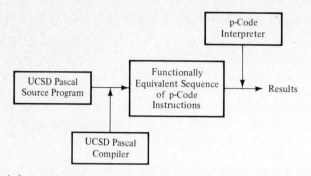

Figure 1.4

Preparation of a UCSD Pascal program

duce a proper sequence of correct Pascal statements. This is not so terrible. We can help ourselves considerably by making sure that there are specifications to guide a program's construction, and that these specifications provide the clearest possible description of what the program is to do.

A number of methods are used for expressing these specifications systematically. One popular descriptive vehicle is *pseudocode*. (Do not confuse this with p-Code. We talked about p-Code briefly in the previous section to provide some insight into what happens behind the scenes. From here on, there will be no need for us to deal with p-Code.) The idea is to present an algorithm's specifications in a form that imitates the final program. Computations and other processing activities are expressed as narrative sentences rather than precise program statements. The exact words and phrases for these descriptions are not strictly defined. Instead, emphasis is placed on the structural framework within which these descriptions appear. The basic idea, though simple, is an important one because it is the cornerstone of structured programming:

> There are certain processing tasks that serve as fundamental building blocks for all programs. Accordingly, it is possible to express any series of computations solely as a combination of these building blocks. When a program is constructed using only these components, it is considered to be a well-structured program. The reason is that such programs tend to be clearer, easier to analyze, and easier to perfect than those in which these structural concepts are not followed.

Pseudocode imposes a standardized way of expressing each of these building blocks. This makes it convenient to prepare a "well-structured" description of an algorithm. One of Pascal's great strengths is that some of its statements correspond directly to these building blocks. Consequently, conversion from pseudocode to Pascal is straightforward.

There are many versions of pseudocode. However, the differences among them are relatively superficial, and primarily concern the exact form for the structured components. The version selected for this book is widely used; in any event, adjustment from one form to another takes but a few minutes, with no painful side effects. We shall build our acquaintance with pseudocode by examining each of the basic structured components and seeing how it is expressed.

1.3.1 The Sequence

The simplest activity is one in which we perform a succession of tasks, one after the other. In concept, it does not matter how many tasks there are or how complicated they may be. The point is that a sequence has a beginning and an end. When we perform a sequence, we start at its beginning and come out at the end. If we choose to avoid a sequence, we avoid it entirely.

The pseudocode representation of a sequence consists simply of a list of activities:

> Do this.
> Then do this.
> Then do this.
>   .
>   .
>   .
> Finally, do this.

For example, suppose a person returned a rented car and the rental company wanted to compute the bill. Charges are based on a fixed rate per day, a fixed rate per mile, a flat fee for insurance, a charge for the gasoline needed to fill the tank when the car is returned, and a discount applied to the total. Data submitted for processing include the car's identification number, the renter's name, number of rental days, number of miles driven, gasoline charge, and discount rate. The pseudocode sequence for the process might look as shown below. (We shall use the word "read" to indicate the process of obtaining data, i.e., bringing information into the processor, for use in our computations and "write" to indicate the display or delivery of data from the processor to the outside world.)

> Read car i.d., name, no. of days, miles, gas charge, discount.
> Compute daily charge.
> Compute mileage charge.
> Add daily charge, mileage charge, gas charge, and insurance fee to
>   obtain total charge.

Compute net charge by applying discount rate to total charge.
Print car i.d., name, individual charges, total charge, discount, and net
charge.

1.3.2 Simple Selection: The IF-THEN-ELSE Component

Not all activities inevitably follow each other. Algorithms often require us
to make a choice between two activities depending on the outcome of some
test. This basic process is described by the IF-THEN-ELSE component:

IF
    the condition described here is true
THEN
    Perform this activity.
ELSE
    Perform this other activity instead.
ENDIF

(ENDIF is a signal to indicate the conclusion of the IF-THEN-ELSE structural component.) Either or both activities can be single tasks or arbitrarily
long sequences. To illustrate, we shall modify our car rental example so
that not every renter gets a discount. Accordingly, we now include a test to
determine whether a discount applies:

Read car i.d., name, no. of days, miles, gas
    charge, discount.
Compute daily charge.
Compute mileage charge.
Add daily charge, mileage charge, gas charge,
    and insurance fee to obtain total charge.
IF
    the renter received a discount
THEN
    Compute net charge by applying discount
        rate to total charge.
ELSE
    Compute the net rate = total rate.
ENDIF
Print car i.d., name, individual charges,
    total charge, discount (if any), and
    net charge.

It is often necessary to set up a situation in which a particular test lets us
make a choice between doing something and doing nothing. The pseudocode for this construction looks like this:

```
IF
      the condition described here is true
THEN
      Perform this activity.
ELSE
ENDIF
```

In cases like this, it also is acceptable to omit the ELSE. For instance, suppose we made insurance optional in the example used before. As a result, part of the sequence would be changed as follows:

```
      . . .
Compute mileage charge.
Compute total charge by adding daily charge,
      mileage charge, and gas charge.
IF
      driver signed for insurance coverage
THEN
      Add insurance fee to total charge.
ENDIF
IF
      the renter received a discount
THEN
      . . .
```

As seen in these examples, the IF-THEN-ELSE can be included as part of a sequence. In concept, it is simply a single step in that sequence. We are saying, in essence, "Now, in this next step, perform the indicated test, see how it comes out, and do the appropriate thing."

1.3.3 Cyclic Activities: The WHILE-DO Component

A third fundamental component of a well-structured program is a *loop* in which an activity (a single step or an entire sequence) may be performed over and over under control of a logical mechanism that is there to make sure the process does not run away with itself by repeating endlessly. There are several ways in which such control can be exercised, and each can be described in pseudocode. The one we shall discuss here is the WHILE-DO construction. This is the most general type of cyclic control, in that any kind of loop can be described as a WHILE-DO construction. The other types of loop constructions are included in the pseudocode for convenience rather than necessity. These will be discussed later.

The general form for the WHILE-DO construction is as follows:

WHILE
   the condition described here is true,
DO:
   Perform this activity.
ENDWHILE

As is true with the other types of structured components, this represents a single conceptual activity that begins with the indicated test being performed for the first time. If the condition described by the test turns out to be false, the entire loop is skipped and the next activity (the one following the ENDWHILE) is started. On the other hand, if the test's outcome is true, the entire activity inside the loop is performed once. ENDWHILE conveys the idea of a control mechanism that forces the process back to the beginning of the loop, where the test is performed again. The point is that the activities inside the loop would be designed to include something that might change the outcome for the test when it is performed again. Otherwise, the outcome always would be the same, and the loop would be repeated forever. As long as the test's outcome is true, the loop's activity is performed one more time, and the process goes back to test the condition once again. As soon as the outcome becomes false, the loop is bypassed and activity continues after the ENDWHILE.

Use of the WHILE-DO component can be illustrated by expanding the car rental example so that the sequence for computing a bill can be applied to a succession of customer's data. We shall make the process general by assuming that we do not know how many returned cars there are. Instead, we shall place the previously developed sequence inside a WHILE-DO component that allows the loop to operate as long as there are data values to process:

WHILE
   there still are renters requiring bills,
DO:
   Read car i.d., name, no. of days, miles, gas
      charge, and discount for the next renter.
   Compute daily charge.
   Compute mileage charge.
   Compute total charge by adding daily charge,
      mileage charge, and gas charge.
   IF
      driver signed for insurance coverage
   THEN
      Add insurance fee to total charge.
   ENDIF

```
IF
    the renter received a discount
THEN
    Compute net charge by applying discount
        rate to total charge.
ELSE
    Compute the net rate = total rate.
ENDIF
Print car i.d., name, individual charges,
    total charge, discount (if any), and
    net charge.
ENDWHILE
Print a terminating message indicating the end of the run.
```

This pseudocode description tells us that the sequence inside the loop will be performed once for each set of renter's data, however many sets that may be. Then, when all of the bills have been computed and printed, the ENDWHILE brings the process back to the test. This time, the test fails (i.e., there are no more renters to process), and the entire loop is bypassed. As a result, the process enters the next activity, and the terminating message is printed *once*.

Problems

1. State whether you think each of the following processes qualifies as an algorithm. If it does not, indicate why it does not:
   (a) Baking chocolate chip cookies by following a written recipe.
   (b) Driving home from work.
   (c) Selling encyclopedia sets door-to-door.
   (d) Curing the hiccups by holding your breath and counting to 36.
   (e) Brushing your teeth.
   (f) Computing the value $9 \times 6 \times 4$.
2. Develop an algorithm for changing an automobile tire in accordance with choice number 6 given in Section 1.1.2. Write a pseudocode description of your algorithm.
3. Many people make a good living by telling others how they can make money in the stock market. See if you can find four or five of these "sure-fire" methods. Write a pseudocode description for each one. Is it possible to write a pseudocode description for something that is not an algorithm?
4. This problem is for those of you who are interested in jogging. Every jogger or runner has his or her own extra special this-is-it method for warming up. Write a pseudocode description for your favorite warm-up routine.

5. Take a look at the car rental example in Section 1.3.3. One of the assumptions in that process is that every renter will have a gasoline charge as part of the total cost. However, it could happen that some renters may fill the tank just before returning the car. Modify the pseudocode description so that the algorithm handles this possibility.

6. The pseudocode in Section 1.3.3 describes an algorithm that prepares bills for any number of returned cars. If we wanted to find out how many bills are prepared during a run, we would have to include a way of keeping count. An easy method for doing this is to set up a counter and include a step in the processing loop that adds one to that counter every time a bill is produced. Modify the pseudocode from Section 1.3.3 or from Problem 5 so that the algorithm prints the number of returned cars processed along with the terminating message.

7. Starting either with the description in Section 1.3.3 or the one produced for Problem 5 or Problem 6, modify the algorithm (and the pseudocode) so that the algorithm computes the total charges billed for the run. This amount is to be printed once, just prior to the terminating message.

8. Modify the pseudocode in Problem 7 so that it describes a process that computes the average amount billed during that run (along with everything else computed in previous versions). This average amount is to be the last thing printed just before the terminating message.

9. Devise an algorithm (and describe it in pseudocode) that computes and prints the sum of the first 30 positive odd integers.

10. Modify the pseudocode description in Problem 9 so that it describes the following algorithm: Instead of computing the sum of the first 30 odd integers, it reads a positive integer named THISMANY and computes the sum of the first THISMANY integers.

11. The process in Problem 10 is based on the assumption that the value THISMANY being read in is a positive integer. Suppose we cannot make that assumption: That is, THISMANY is an integer, all right, but it may not be positive. Revise the pseudocode description from Problem 10 so that the algorithm produces the sum of the first THISMANY integers if THISMANY is positive, as before. Alternatively, if THISMANY is not positive, the algorithm prints the offending value along with a message saying, "THIS VALUE IS NOT VALID FOR MY COMPUTATIONS."

12. Expand the pseudocode description from Problem 10 or 11 so that it produces a sum (or the error message) for each of a succession of input values.

13. Revise the pseudocode from Problem 12 so that, after the last input value has been read and processed, the algorithm prints the number of values read, the number of sums produced, and the number of error messages printed.

14. Devise an algorithm and write a pseudocode description for the following process: We would like to read a succession of (however many) English words. For each word, we would like to print the word, the number of letters in that word, the number of consonants, and the number of vowels. After all the words have been processed, we would like to print the number of words read, the longest word, and the shortest word. If more than one word tied for the greatest length, the *first* word having that length is the one printed. If more than one word tied for the shortest length, the *last* word having that length is the one printed.

15. *Special Challenge:* The American Association for the Promotion of the Use of Blue Paint in Residential Environments (good old AAPUB-PRE) has taken a survey: Senior Room Observers, Room Observers, Associate Room Observers, and Apprentice Room Observers have been hired to observe rooms and report on what they find. For each room observed, the Room Observing Person records his or her Official Observer i.d. number, a preassigned room number, the kind of room it is (living room, kitchen, bedroom, bathroom, dining room, hall, library/den/study, office, laboratory/workshop, laundry/utility, family room/game room/playroom, or other), and the wall color (carmine, light green, royal blue, Hawaiian Sunset, antique white, September Mist, Azure Capri, etc.). Devise an algorithm (and its pseudocode description) that reads and processes these findings. After all the room observations have been processed, the algorithm reports the number of rooms observed, the number painted in some shade of blue, and the number using a color that (alas) is not a shade of blue. Then, the algorithm is to report the i.d. number of the observer who observed the most rooms, along with the number of rooms observed by that observer. Assume there will be no ties. Lastly, the algorithm is to report the total number of living rooms and kitchens (one number) whose colors are shades of blue.

Suggested Reading

Problem Solving

Ackoff, R., *The Art of Problem Solving,* John Wiley & Sons, New York (1978).

Banerji, R. B., *Theory of Problem Solving: An Approach to Artificial Intelligence,* American Elsevier, New York (1969).

Polya, G., *How to Solve It,* Doubleday Anchor Books, Garden City, N.Y. (1957).

Systematic Program Development

ACM Computing Surveys, Vol. 6, no. 4, Association for Computing Machinery, New York (December 1974).

Gillett, W. D., and Pollack, S. V. *Introduction to Engineered Software*, Holt, Rinehart and Winston, New York (1982), especially Chapters 1, 2, and 4.

Ramamoorthy, C. V., and Yeh, R. T., "Software Methodology," Catalogue No. EHO 142-0, Institute of Electronic and Electrical Engineers, New York, 1978.

Computer System Architecture

Nievergelt, J., and Farrar, J. L., "What Machines Can and Cannot Do," in *ACM Computing Surveys*, Vol. 4, no. 2, pp. 81 ff (June 1972).

Tanenbaum, A. *Structured Computer Organization*, Prentice-Hall, Englewood Cliffs, N.J. (1976), especially Chapters 1–3.

Programming Languages

Glass, R. L., "An Elementary Discussion of Compiler/Interpreter Writing," *ACM Computing Surveys*, Vol. 1, no. 1 pp. 55 ff, March, 1969.

Chapter 2

The UCSD p-System Environment

Today's computers offer their users powerful resources for the support of information processing. These resources are so extensive that they cannot be used effectively without some framework for managing them and making them available conveniently. Such management duties are performed by a collection of programs called an *operating system*, and the p-System is the operating system in which UCSD Pascal is designed to work. The p-System provides:

1. services to make it easier to do computational tasks ranging from word processing to program development and execution;
2. a set of simple, convenient mechanisms for requesting these services and/or adding new ones.

This chapter introduces the p-System and focuses on those features that support the preparation and use of UCSD Pascal programs.

2.1 OVERALL SYSTEM ORGANIZATION

The p-System is constructed so that the user obtains and works with its resources by "holding a conversation" with the system: At each stage of the proceedings, the system displays a set of available commands, thereby letting the user know what he or she could do at that point. Such a list is called a *menu*. When the user makes a selection from the menu and issues the appropriate command, the system responds by performing the activity requested by that command and then asking the user what he or she wants to do next. There are numerous possibilities. Often the activity consists of running a program written previously by the user; a different command causes the system to bring stored information from a disk to the user's screen for further work; for certain commands, the system produces a secondary menu of commands, as if to say, "because of the command you just gave me, you have the opportunity to request any of these additional activities listed on your screen. Which one do you want?"

This section introduces some of the p-System's basic components. A little later we shall see how these are used in the development of UCSD Pascal programs.

2.1.1 The p-System File Manager

Many of the p-System's structural characteristics are organized around *files*. A file (in our context) is a collection of information that has been gathered together for some reason. There is no restriction on the kind of information that a file may contain. As far as the system is concerned, a file is a file. To us, the information in a particular file may represent a Pascal source program, a letter to a valued client, a table showing our collection of stamps and their values, our favorite poem, a collection of recipes, or anything else we decide is worth putting in a file. (Much of the p-System's software is organized and stored as files.) The existence of a file is established by giving it a name and letting the system know about it. For the most part, we shall be working with files that are stored on magnetic disks or diskettes, or in main storage.

Since files are important organizational components within the p-System, a substantial part of the system's processing is devoted to the care and feeding of files. These activities are organized around the *file manager* (or *filer*). This operating system program provides the user with a set of commands that enables him or her to perform a variety of file-related operations including:

1. Preparation of new files *(file creation)*. This process enables the user to establish the existence of a new file by submitting a collection of information and giving it a name. In response, the system adds that name to its *directory* of names (after assuring itself that there is no other file with that name in that collection of files), and finds a place to store it.
2. Removal of a file from the system's collection *(file deletion)*.
3. Retrieval of a file for further processing. By issuing a simple command along with the file's name, the user can cause the system to bring that file into a special area called the *workspace*. Oddly enough, the file currently sitting in the workspace is called the *workfile*. The idea of a workfile is a convenient one: Unless told otherwise, the p-System assumes that all file-related activities center around the workfile. This means that once a file has been brought into the workspace, it automatically is available for subsequent processing without further ado. Incidentally, when a file is created, the process takes place in the workspace, and the new file becomes the workfile.

4. Replacement of a file with a newer version (*updating*).
5. Organization of files to form collections. Such a collection is called a *volume*. Each volume can be given a name (i.e., *a volume identifier*), and the system can look for and work with that volume.
6. Transfer of files from one diskette to another.

Detailed discussion of these and other file processing operations can be found in the manual for your particular system. The reference manual will serve as an important companion to this book as you progress in your use of UCSD Pascal on your computer.

2.1.2 The p-System Editor

Working closely with the file manager is a general purpose *editor* whose facilities enable the user to perform a variety of manipulations on a file's contents. (In a typical situation the file being edited is the workfile.) As far as the editor is concerned, a file consists of *text* (i.e., a sequence of letters, numbers, blanks, punctuation marks, and other *characters*). The system attaches no intrinsic meaning to that text. Operations available through the editor include:

1. Addition of information to the file (*insertion*). This may take place at any point in the file. The system's internal bookkeeping makes it appear to the user that the file "opens up" to accommodate the new text. Starting a new file is just a special case of insertion. (In effect, we are adding text to an empty file.)
2. Removal of text from a file (*deletion*).
3. Replacement of text with other text. At the most elementary level, this type of operation can be viewed as a deletion followed by insertion. However, the p-System editor automates this process by providing a single convenient command for the entire task.
4. Searching a file to find a specific place where editing is to be done. Simple commands enable the user to "move through" a file easily so that a specific area can be pinpointed. Each movement is accompanied by an immediate display of the pertinent part of the file.

The p-System's editor is a *full screen* editor. As the name implies, the user is given the ability to move freely around the display screen, making desired changes to the text displayed on any line of that screen. If he or she is through with the text currently being displayed, a simple command quickly fills the screen with text from another part of the file.

Although we shall refer to the editor from time to time, the book will concentrate on UCSD Pascal itself, the assumption being that basic skills have been acquired in the use of the editor. Here again, the reference manual will provide valuable aid.

2.1.3 The UCSD Pascal Compiler

Between the editor and the filer, we have the capabilities for preparing a UCSD Pascal program, storing it away as a file, and bringing it back to the workspace for subsequent revision. Remember, however, that neither of these system components recognizes the file as a program. The part of the system that fulfills that purpose is the Pascal compiler. Consequently, if we want our file treated as a Pascal program, we have to let the p-System know of our intent. This is done with other commands that activate the Pascal compiler (rather than the filer or editor). Depending on the particular command, the user can compile a program (usually the workfile) and store the resulting p-Code (as a new file) for future use, or he or she can run the p-Code right away, without issuing additional commands. Once the compiler has been brought in by the p-System, the programmer can communicate directly with the compiler, thereby exercising some control over what it does. The nature and extent of this control will be part of our discussion in this and subsequent chapters.

2.2 GETTING STARTED WITH UCSD PASCAL

One of the p-System's attractive features is that it is easy to use some of it without having to learn all of it at once. We shall take advantage of this attribute by preparing a simple Pascal program and taking it through the system.

Example 2.1   The program we shall use is shown in Figure 2.1:
Since this is a simple program, this is a good time to explain some of the conventions used to show programs in this book:

1. Words appearing in uppercase letters are parts of Pascal's vocabulary. The ones used in this example are PROGRAM, WRITELN, BEGIN, and END.
2. Words appearing in lowercase letters are defined by the programmer. In this example, the only such word is greeting, the name of the program.

```
PROGRAM   greeting ;
BEGIN
  WRITELN ('Hello there.') ;
  WRITELN ('This is a good start.')
END.
```

Figure 2.1

Program for Example 2.1

3. Text enclosed in apostrophes is called a *literal* and is taken by Pascal at face value. In this example, each of the two literals in the third and fourth lines is a message to be displayed by the program. A literal may include uppercase or lowercase letters, numerical digits, blanks, and/ or any other symbols that can be recognized and displayed by the computer.

4. A letter enclosed in quotation marks refers to a particular key when that key is used to issue a command to the p-System. Thus, when we ask you to type an "L," it refers to the key with the letter L on it.

When the program is executed, it will respond to the first WRITELN statement by displaying the message

```
Hello there,
```

on the screen and going to the end of that line. The second WRITELN statement produces the message

```
This is a good start,
```

on the next line, and the program moves to the end of that line, ready to display on a third line. Since the program ends at that point, there is nothing else to display, and the processing is over.

2.2.1 Preparing the Program

As indicated in Section 2.1, our program must start out as text that eventually assumes an identity as a p-System file. Consequently, we shall activate the system. To do this, we shall use a copy of the System4 diskette. *The master diskette that came with your system package should not be used for programming purposes. Always work with a backup copy.* This copy should *not* be write-protected because the system expects to store the workfile on it. If you have not prepared a backup copy yet, do so by following the procedure given in your p-System reference manual. You also will need a backup copy of the Pascal diskette. This may or may not be write-protected, depending on whether you intend to store your Pascal programs on the p-System diskette or on the Pascal diskette. (If your computer accommodates only single-sided diskettes, you will not have enough room on a single diskette for the p-System and Pascal, in which case Pascal will need to be placed on a separate diskette as described; when this is the case, it is likely that you will have more room for your programs on the Pascal diskette than you will on the p-System diskette. On systems with double-sided diskette capabilities, you can reduce the amount of diskette handling by placing Pascal and the p-System on a single diskette.

Under such conditions you will have the entire second diskette available for your programs. Check with your instructor or in your reference manual to determine your particular situation. Alternatively, you can try it and see what happens.)

Now, insert the System4 backup disk in disk unit #4 (the left-hand drive) and bring in the p-System. This is done by turning the computer off, waiting 10 seconds, and turning it on again, or you can follow the *bootloading* procedure in your p-System manual. The process takes a little time, and at one point it may seem as if the machine has gone away and died. Be patient. After a while, the command line

```
Command: E(dit, R(un, F(ile, C(omp, L(ink, X(ecute, A(ssem,? [IV.03 B3n]
```

will appear. This is the p-System's basic command menu, a list of the system's major resources. (The version number, shown in square brackets, may vary from one installation to another.) The system is said to be in *operating system mode* or *executive mode*. For our immediate purposes, we need the editor, and it is activated by typing the command "E" (the ⟨ return ⟩ or ⟨ enter ⟩ key is not used here). (Some computers have a key that says RETURN, while others use ENTER for the same purpose. We shall refer to this key as the ⟨ return ⟩ key, meaning the oversized key to the right of the letters used for sending information from the video display to the computer.) This brings the editor into main storage from the System4 disk. The system is said to be in *edit mode*. As pointed out earlier, the editor assumes it will be working on the workfile. Since we are just starting, there is no workfile, and the editor calls this to our attention by its initial display:

```
>Edit:
No workfile is present, File?[<ent> for no file]
```

(If a workfile had been available, its first few lines would have been displayed as part of the editor's response.) Being an eternal optimist, the editor offers an opportunity to bring a file into the workspace; however, we cannot take advantage of the situation at this time because we have no such file. Instead, we press the ⟨ return ⟩ key to inform the editor that we are about to start a new file. In response, the editor displays the menu of its basic commands:

```
>Edit:
A(djst C(opy D(lete F(ind I(nsrt J(mp K(ol R(plc Q(uit X(ch Z(ap[E.7h]
```

The Insert command (issued by typing "I") produces the following prompt:

```
>Insert: Text{<bs> a char, <del> a line} [<etx> accepts, <esc> escapes]
```

This tells us that the editor is ready to accept new text. The message in braces offers helpful advice: The < b a c k s p a c e > key deletes a character, and the < d e l e t e > key deletes an entire line. Additional information is provided in square brackets: We are told that when we are finished working on the text, we signal completion by the < e t x > (end-of-text) indicator. (The signal that the p-System uses for < e t x > is produced by holding down the < c o n t r o l > key and typing "C." We shall refer to this signal as < c n t r l >C.) In addition, the < e s c > key gets us out of the text insertion process (without any insertion taking place) and brings us back to the editor's basic command menu.

These are good things to know, but right now we are ready to begin typing the program. Note that after we indent the first WRITELN statement and end that line by pressing the < r e t u r n > key, the editor automatically starts the next line beneath the previous indentation. This will continue to happen until you change it. The < s p a c e b a r > indents further, and the < b a c k s p a c e > key moves the margin back to the left. (As is true in all conversations with the system, the cursor lets you know where you are on the screen.) Thus, after completing the second WRITELN message and pressing the < r e t u r n > key, we move back to the original margin by pressing the < b a c k s p a c e > key twice. Then, we can type END. followed by < r e t u r n > to finish the program. To tell the editor that we have concluded the text, we hold down the control key and type a "C," as explained before. This is < e t x >, the end-of-text signal, and we are brought back to the initial menu of editor commands.

Now, our program can be organized as the workfile. To do this, we issue the Quit command (by typing "Q"), and the editor asks us how we want to quit:

```
>Quit:
U(pdate the workfile and leave
E(xit without updating
R(eturn to the editor without updating
W(rite to a file name and return
```

By pressing "U," the Pascal program is saved in the workfile. (You will notice the activity on disk unit #4.) As part of the process, the system tells us what it is doing:

```
Writing..
Your file is XXX bytes long.
```

By the time the process is completed, the editor and filer are (temporarily) retired, and the p-System's basic command menu is displayed once again. That is, we are back in operating system mode.

The workfile is not a particularly safe place to keep a file, since the next editing session may produce another workfile, thereby destroying this one. The next section shows how to add a newly created file to the system's file library.

To summarize the activities so far, we can prepare a new program and store it in the workfile as follows:

1. Load the p-System from a backup copy of System4 that is not write-protected. The system will display its menu of basic commands.
2. Type "E" to bring in the editor. The editor will display *its* basic command menu.
3. Type "I" to prepare the editor for text insertion. The editor will respond with an >Insert: prompt.
4. Type in your program, ending it with < cntrl >C. The editor will come back with the same menu it showed for step 2.
5. Type "Q" to leave the editor. Its response will offer several ways to exit.
6. Type "U" to store the program in the workfile. After the storage operation takes place, the p-System's basic command menu (the one in step 1) returns automatically.

2.2.2 Saving the Program as a Regular File

We can make a more permanent copy of the workfile by giving it a name and adding it to the p-System's file library. This is done as follows: Suppose we have completed the sequence of activities summarized in steps 1 through 6 at the end of the previous section. Now, from the executive level, we can activate the file manager by typing "F.". In response, the p-System brings in the file manager, and the latter displays its basic command menu. (The system now is in *file mode*.)

```
Filer:
G(et, S(ave, W(hat, N(ew, L(dir, R(em, C(hng, T(rans, D(ate,? [C.11]
```

Type "S." The file manager will respond with the prompt

```
Save on what file?
```

This provides an opportunity to name the file we want to save. Select a name and type it in. (We shall use the program name for the file name.)

```
GREETING < return >
```

The file manager will add the name GREETING to its directory, find space for the file on the diskette, and save the file. When this is completed, the file manager will display the message

```
Text file saved
```

and its basic command menu will appear again. To check whether the operation was completed successfully, type a List command ("L"). The file manager will ask you to identify the volume of interest by displaying the prompt

```
Dir listing of what vol?
```

(The file manager enables each diskette to be associated with a unique volume identifier.) Since we saved GREETING on the diskette currently installed in disk unit 4 (which is the one assumed by the system unless otherwise specified), we indicate this by typing a colon (:) followed by < return >. This produces a display showing the contents of the diskette's directory, and GREETING now will be on that list, along with SYSTEM .WRK.TEXT (the workfile) and the others on the System4 diskette. The file manager redisplays its basic command menu. At this point, we are done with the filer. To bring us back to executive mode, we quit (by typing "Q"), and the file manager beats a rapid but gracious retreat.

Now, we have our program in a separate file that we could retrieve at any time for further editing, or for any other purpose. (In addition, the program still is in the workfile.) The next section will carry the process further by treating the file as a program. Meanwhile, to summarize, we can save the workfile as follows:

7. With the screen showing the system's basic command menu (from step 6 of Section 2.2.1), type "F," thereby bringing in the file manager and displaying its basic command menu.
8. Type "S," indicating your wish to save the workfile. The filer will ask for the name under which the file is to be saved.
9. Type the name you have selected, followed by < return >. The file manager will save the file, issue a message to that effect, and redisplay its basic command menu.
10. Confirm the addition of the file to the directory by typing an "L" to get a listing of the directory. Once the file names are displayed, the filer's basic command menu appears again.
11. Type "Q" to remove the editor and bring back the system's basic command menu.

The same procedure is followed if you happen to be storing your programs on a separate diskette, i.e., on unit #5. Make sure you specify the proper unit number. To see how this works, we shall go through the steps required to store our example program in a file named GREETING on a separate diskette. We shall assume that we are starting with a brand new diskette. This will give us a chance to outline the procedure for converting the blank diskette to a formatted *volume* suitable for holding a collection of p-System files:

1. We start by executing the p-System's DISKFORMAT program to pre-pare the diskette. With the system in executive mode, type "X." The system will ask for the name of the file containing the program you wish to execute. If DISKFORMAT is on your system diskette, type `DISKFORMAT` and ⟨ `return` ⟩. If it is on a separate diskette, place that diskette in unit #5 and type `#5:DISKFORMAT` and ⟨ `return` ⟩.

2. DISKFORMAT will ask for the drive number (i.e., the unit number) on which the new disk will be found. Remove the diskette containing DISKFORMAT from drive 5 (if that is where it was), install the new diskette, and then type 5 and ⟨ `return` ⟩. DISKFORMAT (which is now in control) may ask you to type ⟨ `return` ⟩ again, after which the formatting process will take place.

Now, the formatted diskette is ready to be converted to a p-System volume. This is one of the tasks that the filer does. So, with the new diskette in drive #5 and the system in executive mode, type "F" to bring in the filer.

3. Type "Z." This command causes the filer to set up a new volume. (The "Z" comes from the fact that this command also is used to "zero" an existing volume so that the diskette can be redefined under another name.) The filer will ask you where the diskette is (drive 4 or 5). Type the appropriate drive number and ⟨ `return` ⟩.

4. The filer will ask if you want a duplicate directory. As its name implies, a volume's directory will list the names of the files in that volume, along with information that helps the filer to locate each file. If the directory is damaged or destroyed, the volume is of little use even though the information in the files still may be intact. It is the same type of situation in which a book is physically in a library but we do not know its call number. Consequently, the p-System gives you an opportunity to let the filer build a second directory that will be used in case something happens to the first one. Since this is a new disk, the directory (or directories) will be empty.

5. Next, the filer will ask you to name the volume. We shall use MYVOL for this example, so simply type `MYVOL:` and ⟨ `return` ⟩. (The colon must be included.) The filer will report that the volume has been zeroed, and it will redisplay its command menu.

We are ready to store the workfile.

6. Type "S" (as in step 8 of the previous example). The filer will ask you for a file name. Suppose we want to store our little program as a file named GREETING on the volume named MYVOL:. To do that, type

MYVOL:GREETING followed by < return >. The filer will find the volume (we left it on drive 5 after the zero operation), copy the file onto the diskette, prepare an entry for that file in the volume's directory (or directories), and redisplay its command line.

7. The process is complete. You may wish to perform steps 10 and 11 from the previous example to prove that the file is there, and then bring the system back to executive level.

2.2.3 Running the Pascal Program

The p-System is set up to compile the program in the workfile and execute the resulting p-Code automatically. We shall follow this process here, after which we shall examine a more involved sequence of activities.

Since our previous activities have not affected the contents of the workfile, it still holds our Pascal program. Consequently, we can ask to run it directly. We start by inserting a write-protected backup copy of the Pascal diskette in disk unit #5 (the right-hand drive). (If the Pascal compiler is already on your double-sided system diskette, we do not have to do this.) Step 11 from the previous section left us in operating system mode. Consequently, we simply type "R." The p-System will look in the workfile, recognize the contents to be a Pascal source program, and bring in the Pascal compiler from disk unit #5. Messages will begin to appear on the screen:

```
Compiling...
Pascal compiler - release level IV.0 c3s-2
<     0>..
GREETING
<     2>..
    4 lines compiled
GREETING .
```

The name of the program followed by the period tells us that the compilation process is complete. (The cryptic numbers and dots are indicators of the compiler's progress as it works its way through the program.) As a result, the p-Code thus produced is placed in another file, this one named SYSTEM.WRK.CODE. Execution of these instructions now begins, the screen clears, and the new display says

```
Running...
Hello there.
This is a good start.
```

The instant the program concludes, it returns control of the machine back to the p-System, which goes into executive mode and displays the basic command menu, thereby concluding the episode. Now, if we were to type the Run (R) command again, the system would see that there we already have a file with p-Code in it (namely, SYSTEM.WRK.CODE). Consequently, it would skip the compilation and run the p-Code again. Try it and see what the resulting display is.

2.3 AVOIDING THE WORKFILE

Under certain conditions, it may be advantageous to abandon the use of the workfile. Although the p-System's automatic use of the workfile is convenient, its maximum size may impose severe limitations because of its dependence on the amount of available space on the system diskette. In fact, when a Pascal program gets to be large enough, it may be impossible to use the workfile. This section outlines the procedural steps for editing, storing, compiling, and running UCSD Pascal programs without involving the workfile for the source statements or the compiled code.

2.3.1 Preparing the Source Program

The first thing to do is to save a copy of the current workfile (if there is one, and if you want it) and then destroy it. (We can delete the workfile by bringing in the file manager and issuing an "N" command.) Then, by quitting the file manager, we are back in executive mode, and we are ready to bring in the editor (by typing "E"). We can type in our Pascal source program as described before.

2.3.2 Saving the Source Program

When the editing process is complete, type "Q" (as usual) to signal the desire to quit editing. The display will offer a choice of four actions, as we saw in Section 2.2.2. Instead of typing "U" as you did earlier, type a "W." In response, the p-System will ask you to name the file in which the text is to be stored:

```
>Quit:
'$'<ent> writes to filename
Name of output file(<ent> to return) -->_
```

Type the volume's name and the file's name, followed by < return >, and the storage process will take place. For example, if we were to edit the file MYVOL:GREETING and we asked to store it by typing "W," the system would say

```
>Quit:
'$' <ent> writes to filename MYVOL:GREETING
Name of output file (<ent> to return)
```

2.3.3 Retrieving a Textfile for Further Editing

If editing is to be performed on an existing textfile and there is no workfile, that file can be brought into the workspace without direct involvement of the filer: Making sure that there is no workfile, bring in the editor. When the display informs you that there is no workfile, simply type the name of the file to be edited, followed by < return >. (Make sure you include the volume's identifier.) The designated file will be moved to the workspace and editing can proceed.

When you finish editing (by typing < cntrl >C and "Q"), you can store the newly edited version in place of the previous one by typing "W". As we saw in the previous section, the display includes an opportunity to type "$" " followed by < return >, in which case the file is stored in its previous home, i.e., under the same name from which it was brought in. The second line of the display tells you in which file your edited text will be stored in response to your "$" command. (Of course, you still can type in the file name instead of the dollar sign.)

2.3.4 Compiling and Running without the Workfile

A Pascal program does not have to be in the workfile for it to be compiled and/or executed: After making sure there is no workfile, and with the system at its executive command level, type "C." Since there is no workfile, the system will ask which file to use:

```
Compiling...
Compile what text? _
```

Type the name of the textfile representing your program, followed by < return >. If you do not include the .TEXT suffix, the p-System assumes it. The display will ask you to name the file in which the compile code is to be stored:

```
Compiling...
Compile what text? MYVOL:GREETING
To what codefile? _
```

MYVOL is the volume identifier and GREETING is the textfile on that volume that contains the Pascal program to be compiled. Type the name of the codefile (the system automatically assumes .CODE), followed by < return >, and the compilation process takes place as described before. (Many programmers like to use the same file name for the source and object versions of a given program. This is acceptable, since the p-System assumes the proper suffix, i.e., .TEXT or .CODE, for the appropriate file. For example, if you specify MYVOL:GREETING for your Pascal source program, the p-System will look for a textfile—not a codefile—named MYVOL :GREETING when it is asked to edit or compile.)

To run a compiled Pascal program other than the workfile, make sure the system is in its executive mode, and type "X." The system will ask for a file name:

```
Execute what file? _
```

Type the volume name and file name (followed by ⟨ return ⟩) and the system will look for a codefile by that name. If there is one, it will position it, and the program will begin executing.

Problems

The following problems, though not specifically concerned with UCSD Pascal, are intended to help strengthen skills in the use of those p-System features that relate directly to Pascal programs. In doing these exercises, you may want to refer to your p-System reference manual:

1. Destroy the current workfile and replace it with a copy of GREETING.
2. Add a third line of display to GREETING that says "THIS IS A THIRD LINE.", change the name of the program to prog2, and run the program.
3. Save the program from Problem 2 in a file named PROG2.
4. Using PROG2 as the workfile, change the word PROGRAM to PROGRAN and run the resulting program to see what happens.
5. Starting with the correct version of prog2 from Problem 3, remove the period after END, run the program that way, and report on what happens.
6. Starting with the correct version of prog2 from Problem 3, change the second WRITELN to WIRTELN and try to run the program that way. Then, repair the program and try it again.
7. Format a blank diskette on unit #5 and set up a new directory named MYVOL1: on that diskette. Then copy PROG2 onto the new volume using the name MESSAGE.
8. Change the name of PROG2:MESSAGE to PROG2:EX201.TEXT.
9. Run the program in PROG2:.EX201.TEXT.

Chapter 3

The Pascal Program

One of Pascal's primary advantages is that it compels its users to write highly organized programs. This chapter introduces the language's basic structural features and shows how they are used.

3.1 DESCRIPTION OF PASCAL

Like every other language, Pascal has a grammar, i.e., a set of rules describing the parts of the language and how they can be used to build larger components. Pascal's grammar is particularly precise because preciseness was one of the design objectives. This makes it possible to describe Pascal's syntax easily and directly, as we shall begin to see in the next few sections.

3.1.1 Description of Pascal's Syntax

A convenient way to describe Pascal's structure precisely is to have a special language for this purpose. Such descriptive languages are called *metalanguages*. The metalanguage we shall use in this book is the *syntax diagram* (also called a *railroad diagram* because of the descriptions' general appearance). Each diagram defines a particular Pascal component by showing the legal way(s) in which that component may be constructed. A simple example from English will illustrate the idea behind a railroad diagram and the symbols used for it.

Figure 3.1(a) shows a diagram for something called a *word*. We see that the diagram starts at its upper left-hand corner with the name of the component being described. The line leading from the component's name, and the items found on that line, define the legal ways in which a word may be constructed. Thus, we see that a word can be constructed from something called a *letter*. By enclosing the name *letter* in a rectangular frame, the diagram indicates that *letter* is another component, defined by a separate syntax diagram. The definition for a letter appears in the diagram of Figure 3.1(b), which shows that a letter can be either a *vowel* or a *consonant*. The fact that this is a choice (either but not both) is indicated by a branch in the line. Since *vowel* and *consonant* are in rectangular frames themselves,

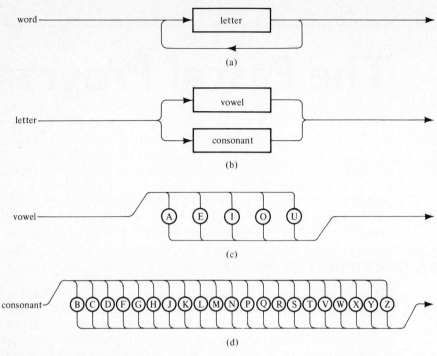

Figure 3.1

Syntax Diagrams

there must be further definitions. Sooner or later, every component has to be defined in terms of elementary items: things that are what they are, rather than being built up from other things. Such items are called *terminal symbols*. In a syntax diagram a terminal symbol is enclosed in a circular frame. For example, the diagram in Figure 3.1(c) defines a vowel as something that may consist of one of the five terminal symbols A, E, I, O, or U. (Notice the five alternative line branches.) Similarly in Figure 3.1(d), a consonant is seen to consist of any one of the terminal symbols B, C, D, F, G, H, J, etc.

Referring again to Figure 3.1(a), note that the line coming out of the *vowel* designation splits into two branches. One of them brings us nonstop to the end of the diagram while the other loops back around. The first branch indicates that a word may consist of a single letter followed by nothing. On the other hand, if we take the return branch, we have a single letter followed by another letter. Having picked up a second letter, we are faced with that choice once more: If we take the nonstop route, we have constructed a word out of two letters; if we loop around again, we attach yet a third letter. Consequently, Figure 3.1(a) is a graphical way of saying that a word may consist of a letter followed by zero or more letters. "Well," you ask, "why go through all this when you could say the same thing so clearly in English?" Now wait a minute. For simple definitions, this may be true. However, as soon as the structure becomes more intricate, the complexity of a precise and complete English description grows rapidly, and the advantages of a precise metalanguage become increasingly dramatic.

One other type of item will appear in Pascal's syntax diagrams: When a symbol is enclosed in an oval frame, it means that the symbol is a *reserved word*, i.e., part of Pascal's permanent vocabulary (like WRITELN in Example 2.1). As such, it serves a specific purpose in Pascal statements and may not be used in any other context. A complete set of syntax diagrams for Pascal is given in Appendix A, and many of these will be discussed individually as we work our way through the language.

The use of a syntax diagram does not guarantee that the definition being portrayed is a correct one. For instance, constructions like *can't* or *well-worn* would be considered to be illegal words according to the definitions in Figure 3.1. Similarly, something like GGZUXD would be a legal word. If it is really our intent to define a word as consisting only of the 26 English letters in any combination, fine; if not, it would be necessary to change the definitions.

3.1.2 Description of Pascal's Semantics

The syntax of a language, no matter how it is expressed, does not describe the language completely; it defines only the structural aspects. Additional factors relating to the meaning of the various components establish how these components can and cannot be used. For example, let us say we are willing to accept the definition of a word given by the diagrams in Figure 3.1. That still leaves us with no information about how letters are used to form a word. As far as the structure is concerned, we start with any letter and keep adding letters till we stop. However, we know that certain combinations of letters simply are not used to form English words while others are used only under certain conditions. For instance, one would not expect to see the letter *x* following an *f* or a *k* (or quite a few others, once you start thinking about it). This kind of information, and many other items like it, make up a language's *semantics*. Unhappily, semantic information is likely to be considerably more voluminous and complex than that defining the syntax, even for small, carefully designed artificial languages like Pascal. The problem of providing complete, precise semantic descriptions continues to resist a satisfactory formal solution. Consequently, we shall have to content ourselves with semantic descriptions in narrative form. To help build familiarity with Pascal, the syntax diagrams will be coupled with appropriate semantic information so that proper structure and proper usage will be unified wherever possible.

3.1.3 Representation of Pascal Programs

Throughout the text, many of the concepts and language structures will be illustrated with Pascal statements, parts of programs, and complete programs. These will be produced as computer printouts in which reserved words will be in capital letters and programmer-defined names will be lowercase. (This has already been seen in Example 2.1.)

3.2 OVERALL PROGRAM STRUCTURE

Every Pascal program is organized in the same basic way. As Figure 3.2 indicates, the program consists of an *identification section*, a *block*, and a concluding period. The period is not part of the block.

3.2.1 The Identification Section

The identification section is a bookkeeping item that establishes the name of the program. As a result, any Pascal program can be identified as an entity that can be made a part of some larger structure (such as a program library) or manipulated in some other useful way. There is not much to an identification section (Figure 3.3): The reserved word PROGRAM is followed by the program name. After a separating semicolon, the program name is followed by zero or more unit definitions and an optional USES clause. (Neither of these components will concern us for some time.) Since the interpretation of syntax diagrams still may be a little unfamiliar at this stage, we shall examine these early ones more closely than will be our practice later on.

The program name is any identifier that the programmer wishes to attach to the program as a whole. Thus, Figure 3.3(b) defines the program name as being an identifier, and Figure 3.3(d) shows simply that an identifier may consist of a letter followed by any number of letters or digits in any combination. However, there are all kinds of places in Pascal where identifiers may appear. An identifier is constructed as shown in Figure 3.3(d) regardless of where it appears, but the meaning associated with each type of usage is a matter of semantics. Thus, when an identifier is used to name a program, we also must know that this name cannot be used anywhere else in the program.

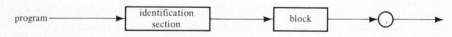

Figure 3.2

Overall Syntax of a Pascal Program

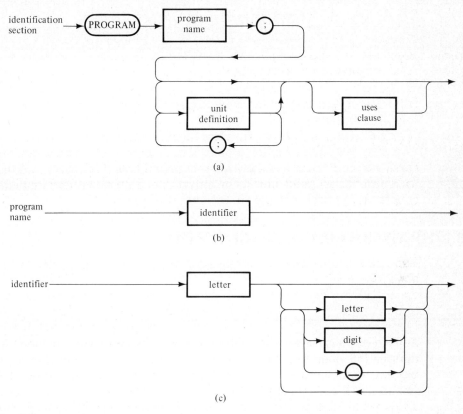

Figure 3.3

Syntax for a UCSD Pascal Identification Section

3.2.2 The Block

The remainder of any Pascal program is organized as a *block*. Because of its versatility, a block may be constructed in so many ways that it would be impossible to illustrate them all. Instead, it will serve us better to learn the block's syntax so that we understand its structure without having to examine each possible combination of ingredients. There are two principal components: a *declaration section* followed by a *processing section*. As Figure 3.4 makes clear, both sections must appear, and they must be in the order shown.

The declaration section presents a complete definition of the data used in the block. Each item must be described in terms of the values it can have. When several items are to be treated as a collection, their organization must be described as well. The ways in which data descriptions are constructed

Figure 3.4

Syntax of a Pascal Block

will be examined in detail later on. Right now, it is important to know that every block starts this way.

The processing section specifies the block's computational activities. As a start, we shall examine a block's basic construction by acquainting ourselves with Pascal's major structural ingredients. This will enable us to become familiar with a block's organizational pattern without immediate concern about each detail.

3.3 FUNDAMENTAL LANGUAGE COMPONENTS

We shall examine three types of major organizational elements within a block.

3.3.1 The Declaration

A *declaration* is used to describe some aspect of data usage in a block. The information given in it enables Pascal to set up storage allocations, bookkeeping, and other support activities facilitating the computations specified in the block's processing section.

One type of declaration is the *variable declaration*. This is the mechanism whereby Pascal reserves storage and associates it with a programmer-defined name. Thereafter (throughout that block), the program can refer to that storage location by using that name. This is called a variable declaration because the value stored in the location reserved under that name is likely to change during the program's execution. As part of the declaration, the programmer also specifies the kind of data to be assigned to that variable (i.e., the *data type*). This becomes part of Pascal's description of the association. The information then is available for Pascal's use in making sure that a value to be assigned to a particular variable is of the same type as that declared for the variable.

The general syntax for a variable declaration is shown in Figure 3.5. As an example, let us look at the following declaration:

```
VAR
    numunits  :  INTEGER
```

This follows the most basic syntax: The reserved word VAR is followed by our variable name (numunits). As required by the rules (Figure 3.5), the

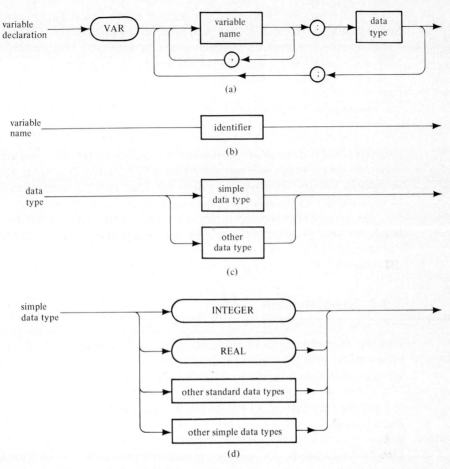

Figure 3.5

Syntax for a Variable Declaration

name is followed by a colon, after which we specify the data type. `INTE-GER` is one of the standard types recognized by Pascal. It indicates that the only kind of value that can be stored in `numunits` is a number with no fractional part. (The reserved word `VAR` is shown on a separate line and to the left of the rest of the declaration to make the declaration easier to read.)

We shall expand the variable declaration by following the inner loop of Figure 3.5's syntax diagram. This enables us to declare several variables of a given type. Thus,

```
VAR
     numunits, branches  :   INTEGER
```

reserves storage for two variables named `numunits` and `branches`, respectively, with each being designed to accommodate an `INTEGER` value. Further expansion can take place by following Figure 3.5's outer loop and declaring variables with different data types:

```
VAR
    numunits, branches    :    INTEGER    ;
    cost                  :    REAL
```

Now, our declaration reserves storage for three variables: The new addition is named `cost` and it will accommodate a `REAL` value (i.e., a number that includes a fractional portion). As Figure 3.5 indicates, a semicolon is used to separate declarations of one data type from those of another.

The variable declaration is just one kind of declaration that may appear in a block's declaration section. Now that we are acquainted with this one, the characteristics and usage of the others will easily be learned when we get to them.

3.3.2 The Statement

The *statement* is Pascal's basic unit of expression in somewhat the same way that the sentence is in a natural language. The contents of the processing section in a program's block consists of some number of statements which, when taken together, describe that block's processing activities.

A Pascal statement can be as long as it needs to be in order to express the desired processing. As Figure 3.6 shows, the statement either is *simple* or *compound*.

Simple Statements   A simple statement represents a single step in a computational process. As Figure 1.4 indicated, the work expressed by a single "step" in Pascal eventually may require several p-Code instructions. Thus, we cannot establish any specific relationship between a simple statement and the "amount of computation" it specifies. Moreover, Pascal's syntax allows great flexibility in the length of a simple statement and the number of operations it can describe.

Organizationally, there are less than a dozen types of simple state-

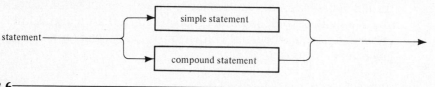

Figure 3.6

General Classification of Pascal Statements

ments in Pascal. The one we shall introduce here is the *assignment statement,* Pascal's vehicle for expressing an explicit computation. For example, suppose the names `cost` and `numunits` refer to variables that were declared with numerical data types. Then, the following specification:

```
numunits := 327
```

is an assignment statement in which the variable `numunits` is assigned a value of 327. The operation being performed is *assignment,* and := is the symbol for the *assignment operator.* Some people find it convenient to interpret this statement as follows: "*The value in* `numunits` *is replaced by 327.*"

Having thus given a value to `numunits`, we can write

```
cost := 32.84 * numunits
```

As a result, `numunits`' value (327) will be multiplied by 32.84 and the value thus computed (10738.68) will be assigned to `cost`. (The asterisk (*) is used in Pascal to denote multiplication.) This still is a simple statement even though it requires more processing than the previous one shown. When we examine the assignment statement's syntax in detail, it will be clear that the specified computations can be extended almost indefinitely without changing the basic structure.

Compound Statements   Although Pascal allows great flexibility in the extent of a simple statement, its syntax imposes certain limitations. For example, the assignment statement can specify an enormous string of computations, but when all the smoke clears, the result must be a single value assigned to a single destination. There are many occasions when we would like to consider several such assignments as parts of a single conceptual activity. (This, of course, is the essence of the sequence described in Section 1.3.1.) We prepare such activities simply enough, by writing statements sequentially. Thus, the two assignment statements from the previous section form the following sequence:

```
numunits := 327 ;
cost := 32.84 * numunits
```

The semicolon is used to separate the two simple statements and is not part of either statement. If we had shown a third statement in the sequence, another semicolon would have been used, this one placed between the second assignment statement and the additional statement.

For us, then, the recognition of activities formed by sequences of simple statements is an easy matter. However, in many situations Pascal has to be able to recognize such sequences as well. One common circumstance, for example, is a simple selection (Section 1.3.2) in which the activities associated with either or both of a test's outcomes require several simple statements for their respective descriptions. The way this is handled in Pascal is to write such a sequence as a *compound statement*. This is nothing more than an arbitrarily long sequence of statements separated by semicolons, starting with the reserved word BEGIN and concluding with the reserved word END (Figure 3.7). For instance, suppose we wanted to test the value in variable yval. If yval is found to be less than 17.4, we want to add 3.6 to it, double the value in zval, and display the two values. These actions would be specified as a compound statement:

```
IF  yval < 17.4
   THEN
     BEGIN
       yval := yval + 3.6 ;
       zval := 2 * zval ;
       WRITELN (yval,'    ',zval)
     END
   ....................................
   ....................................
```

Note that BEGIN and END are not parts of the compound statement; they are brackets that define the statement's boundaries. Since END is not a statement, we do not need a semicolon between the WRITELN and the END.

Note that the syntax diagram specifies a *statement*, rather than a *simple statement*, as the component of a compound statement. At first glance, this seems innocent enough, but a look back at Figure 3.6 reminds us that a statement may be either simple or compound. Thus, we have a situation in which a compound statement legally can contain a compound statement. In fact, the syntactic rule of Figure 3.7 appears to allow a compound statement consisting of nothing but compound statements. How can this be?

The feature that makes it come out all right is an escape hatch that prevents the definition from being circular: Since a simple statement is an acceptable statement (it is one of the available choices in Figure 3.6), then a sequence of simple statements meets the requirements for a compound

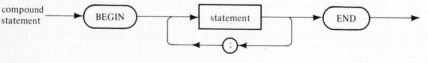

Figure 3.7
Syntax for a Compound Statement

statement (Figure 3.7). The fact that we are able to build a compound statement using only simple statements gives us something that can be used as an ingredient in another compound statement.

When a set of apparently circular definitions is provided with this kind of loophole, it is known as a *recursive definition*. We shall run into this situation repeatedly as we continue to discuss Pascal's syntax. Whenever any doubt arises, convince yourself that the definitions are not circular by finding a specific route through the diagram that meets the definition's syntactic requirements without using itself.

The compound statement forms the basic framework for a block's processing section. In structural terms, the part of a Pascal program that describes the actual algorithm is really a single statement. We saw this in Example 2.1, and it is illustrated again in Figure 3.8, where some details have been added to the organizational picture of Figure 3.2. Note the use of semicolons between the identification section and the block, and between the sections within the block.

3.3.3 Subprograms

When a sequence of statements is perceived by the programmer as a single activity that has uses in several places throughout a program, it is beneficial to implement that sequence as a *subprogram*. This is a separate program that can be attached to another program or installed inside it in such a way that only one copy is needed regardless of the number of times it is used or the number of different places from which its services are requested. Since a subprogram is much like an independent program, it offers additional

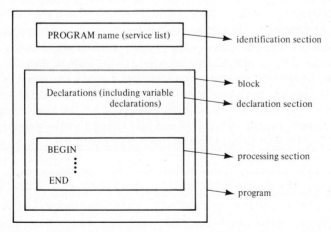

Figure 3.8

Role of a Compound Statement in a Pascal Program

conveniences: It can be developed and perfected separately. Often, this enables the programming work to be divided among several people without having the entire undertaking end up in chaos. Then, once the subprogram is known to be working, it is a simple matter to incorporate it into a larger program. Moreover, if the processing embodied in a subprogram is generally useful, it is just as easy to make it a part of many different programs as it is to install it in the program for which it may have been intended initially. In fact, UCSD Pascal has a standard library of subprograms available (automatically, through the compiler) for inclusion in any program. In addition, there are convenient facilities for writing and installing programmer-defined subprograms in the library.

Types of Subprograms   There are two types of subprograms in Pascal. The *function* provides a facility that enables its users to treat a sequence of activities as if it were a single operation. For example, Pascal has a standard function that computes the square root of a number it is given. Although it takes several Pascal statements to express the computations necessary to produce a square root, the user is unaware of this; he or she simply provides a value (an *argument*) and "asks for" its square root as if the process were as elementary as addition or subtraction. (The way this takes place is outlined in the next section.)

The *procedure* is a more comprehensive type of subprogram in that the processing described in a procedure is treated as if it were a single statement rather than merely a single operation. For example, Pascal's standard subprogram library includes a procedure whose job it is to read the next line of input data. Although the underlying process is rather intricate, the programmer uses the subprogram by writing a single statement each time he or she wants a line of data brought into the processor from the outside.

Subprogram Definitions   When a programmer uses one or more subprograms from Pascal's standard library, there is no need to specify what these subprograms do. The *subprogram definitions* are part of Pascal itself. Consequently, when a programmer requests the use of a standard subprogram, Pascal recognizes the subprogram's name and automatically makes a copy of it from the library for inclusion as part of the new program. However, if the subprogram is one defined and written by the programmer for that program, its definition must be included explicitly as part of the program.

The structure of a subprogram definition bears a close resemblance to that of a program: It consists of a subprogram identification section and a block (Figure 3.9). The subprogram identification section serves the same general purpose as does the program's identification section, and you already know what a block is. These two components provide a complete description of the subprogram's algorithm and its internal data requirements.

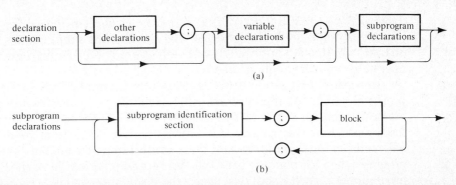

Figure 3.9

Placement of Subprograms in Pascal Programs

Earlier, it was pointed out that only one copy of the subprogram needs to be included with a program, no matter how many times it is requested from different places in the program which is using it. Now that we know how a subprogram is organized, there still is a question with regard to where the single copy is installed in the program. In keeping with Pascal's emphasis on good, straightforward program structure, there is one legitimate place for subprogram definitions: They are part of the program block's declaration section. More specifically, they are the last items in the declaration section, after the VAR declarations. This is indicated in Figure 3.9 as an additional detail in the program's overall organizational picture. (We shall defer discussion of *externally compiled subprograms* which may be used by programs but are not defined within the program using them.)

Here is another example where recursion shows up in our syntactic definitions: Any subprogram (regardless of whether it is a function or procedure) consists of a subprogram identification section and a block. The subprogram is installed in a program so that it becomes part of the program's block. As a result, we can have an acceptable situation in which a block may consist of a number of components, and at least one of those components is itself a block.

A Pascal program may have any number of internally defined subprograms in it. All of them are placed at the end of the declaration section (after the VAR declarations) and just prior to the processing section. If there are several subprograms, their order is not important. Furthermore, functions and procedures may be intermixed. The next section explains why this is possible.

Invocation of Subprograms   Although a subprogram resembles a program, it is distinctly different in the way that it is executed. The only way a subprogram can be executed is by being activated by the program in which it is installed. This is why it is called a subprogram. When a program activates a subprogram, the process is known as a *call* or an *invocation*, and the program doing the activating is known as the *calling* or *invoking* program. Consequently, the physical placement of the subprogram's statements has nothing to do with its execution; the only time a subprogram can operate is when a program calls it.

In a sense, invocation turns control of the computer over to the subprogram. When the subprogram finishes executing, it returns control to the invoking program at a point immediately following the place from which the subprogram was called, and processing continues from there. The mechanisms for keeping track of these control transfers are built into the program when it is compiled and therefore are automatic as far as the Pascal programmer is concerned. As a result, the installation and use of a subprogram is independent of the number of places from which it is called.

Since a function's processing is intended to be viewed as a single operation, it is invoked as part of a computational statement. For example, SQR is the reserved word for the Pascal function that multiplies a numerical value by itself. Assuming that side1, side2, and vsum have been declared as INTEGER variables, and side1 and side2 have respective values of 11 and 14, the statement

```
vsum := SQR (side1 + side2)
```

computes the sum of the two values in side1 and side2. Then, the function SQR is invoked and the sum is delivered to it as an argument on which to operate. In response to the invocation, SQR executes and, when it is done, it delivers a numerical value equal to the square of side1+side2. (In this case, that value would be 625.) The value is assigned to vsum and the computations specified in this statement are completed. As far as the programmer is concerned, the computations appear to consist of three operations: addition, squaring, and assignment.

A procedure is invoked by a separate statement. For example, the WRITELN statement that we used in Example 2.1 called upon a standard Pascal procedure named WRITELN whose job it is to display information on the screen. Once that job was finished, the procedure returns control to the program at a point just after the invocation (i.e., the next statement). Using the same variables from the previous paragraph, the sequence of statements

```
WRITELN ('SIDE1 = ',side1,' SIDE2 = ',side2) ;
vsum := SQR (side1 + side2) ;
WRITELN ('VSUM = ',vsum)
```

describes three activities: The first calls on the procedure WRITELN to prepare and display a line consisting of two literal messages and two variable values. Assuming the previous values, the display would say

```
SIDE1 = 11 SIDE2 = 14
```

After the WRITELN is finished (i.e., the line is displayed), the program continues with the second activity, namely, the computation of the value for vsum. The third activity consists of another invocation of WRITELN, this time to produce the line

```
VSUM = 625
```

(i.e., the square of 11 + 14).

Another of Pascal's standard procedures is READLN, whose job it is to bring input data into the processor (usually from the keyboard). For example, using side1 and side2 as before, the statement

```
READLN (side1, side2)
```

accepts two numerical values from the keyboard, stores them in side1 and side2, respectively, and displays them on the screen. (This display is called an *echo*.)

Thus, assuming we wanted to read the values 11 and 14 into side1 and side2, respectively, and we said

```
WRITELN ('TYPE IN VALUES FOR SIDE1 AND SIDE2.') ;
READLN (side1, side2)
```

here is what would happen: First, the program would display the message on the screen asking for the two input values. (We shall think of such messages as *prompts*.) When we type the two values, they appear on the screen. This is shown below:

```
TYPE IN VALUES FOR SIDE1 AND SIDE2.
11      14
```

3.3.4 Example 3.1

To reinforce the organizational principles discussed in the previous sections, we shall write a little program to meet the following requirements: The program is to read a line of input data containing two integer values to be stored in num1 and num2, respectively. These values are to be used to compute a third value, bigsum, by adding the smaller of the two input values to three times the larger of the two. Finally, the program is to display a line showing num1 and num2, a second line showing bigsum, and a final line of output with the message END OF RUN. We have no advance

Declare integer variables num1, num2, and bigsum.
Read num1 and num2.
Compute bigsum = min(num1,num2) + 3*max(num1,num2).
Display num1 and num2.
Display bigsum.
Display "END OF RUN."

Figure 3.10

Pseudocode for the Algorithm in Section 3.3.4

knowledge as to which input value is larger, but we are guaranteed that they are different.

There is no great difficulty in devising an algorithm for this problem. The solution method is described by the requirements, so that we can move directly to a pseudocode representation of the solution (Figure 3.10). Since the data requirements already are clear at this stage, they are described in the pseudocode, along with the processing. The expressions min(num1,num2) and max(num1,num2) are used to denote the larger and smaller of the two values, respectively. Note that there is no indication as to how these will be determined. That particular problem is simple enough so that its details need not be worked out in the pseudocode. Inclusion or omission of such details in the pseudocode is a matter of judgment; there are no precise rules. As a reasonable guideline, bear in mind that the step from pseudocode to program statements should be as straightforward as possible.

The complete program is given in Figure 3.11. Before we look at the details, a quick comparison with Figure 3.10 will point up the strong relationship between the pseudocode and the Pascal code. We shall make this correspondence work for us as we go on.

Several new things appear in the program. All of them are fairly self-evident, so the commentary will be brief: The material preceding the program's identification section is not part of the program. Any text enclosed by (* ... *) or { .... } is a *comment*. As such, it is displayed along with the code, but is not processed by the compiler. The practice of using comments to provide a narrative description is recommended as an aid to legibility, and we shall follow it throughout the text.

The program finds the larger of the two input values simply by comparing them and providing two alternative computations. One of these will be used depending on the outcome of the comparison. This decision structure is implemented by using Pascal's IF statement. The basic form used here is so close to the pseudocode representation of the IF-THEN-ELSE structural component (Section 1.3.2) that its action is self-evident. (The only thing missing is the ENDIF; Pascal has no ENDIF. Instead, the BEGIN and END brackets around the compound statement help establish the boundaries of the IF-THEN-ELSE component. We saw this structure earlier, in Section 3.3.2 under *Compound Statements*.) We shall explore more features of this

```
(***************************************************)
(*                 PROGRAM EX301                 *)
(***************************************************)
(*   THIS PROGRAM READS TWO INTEGERS NUM1 AND NUM2*)
(*   AND COMPUTES BIGSUM, THE SUM OF THE SMALLER  *)
(*   OF THE TWO PLUS 3 TIMES THE LARGER OF THE TWO*)
(*   INPUT VALUES, THE RESULTS ARE DISPLAYED,     *)
(*   ALONG WITH A TERMINATING MESSAGE,            *)
(***************************************************)
PROGRAM  ex301  ;
VAR
    num1, num2, bigsum  :    INTEGER   ;
BEGIN
  WRITELN ('TYPE IN VALUES FOR num1 AND num2,') ;
  READLN (num1, num2)  ;
  IF
   num1 < num2
  THEN
   bigsum := num1 + 3 * num2
  ELSE
   bigsum := num2 + 3 * num1;
  WRITELN ('NUM1: ',num1, ' NUM2: ', num2)  ;
  WRITELN ('BIGSUM: ',bigsum)    ;
  WRITELN ('END OF RUN,')
END,
```

Figure 3.11

Pascal Code for Example 3.1

powerful statement later on. Meanwhile, Figure 3.12 shows the syntax diagram for the IF statement and the relationship between this statement and its pseudocode representation. Compare the diagrams in Figure 3.12 against the statement in Figure 3.11 to make sure the structure is clear.

The first WRITELN statement is a prompt, asking the user for input values. Once these are taken in (by READLN), the display of the computed result is produced. Figure 3.13 shows a sample run for this program.

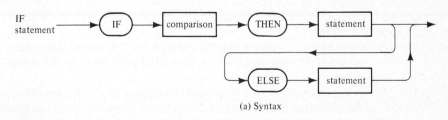

(a) Syntax

Figure 3.12(a)

Syntax for Pascal's IF Statement

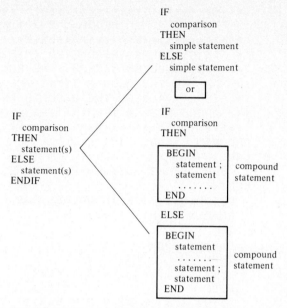

(b) Relation between the IF-THEN-ELSE component and Pascal's IF statement

Figure 3.12(b)

Relation between the IF-THEN-ELSE Component and Pascal's IF Statement

```
TYPE IN VALUES FOR NUM1 AND NUM2,
22      41
NUM1: 22 NUM2: 41
BIGSUM: 145
END OF RUN,
```

Figure 3.13

Sample Run for Example 3.1

Problems

1. Look at Figure 3.11 and explain why there is no semicolon just before the reserved word END.

2. An unsigned integer consists of at least one digit, and a digit may be any of the characters 0 through 9. Prepare a set of syntax diagrams for these definitions.

3. A signed integer can be a positive integer or a negative integer. Using the material from Problem 2 as a basis, prepare syntax diagrams for a complete definition of a signed integer. (Remember that +36 and 36 mean the same thing.)

4. We shall use the term *number* to refer to a general numerical value. For example, 0, −36, 184.507, −0.00743, +44., .208, and +300.003 all are numbers. Prepare a set of syntax diagrams to convey this definition. Use as much of the material as possible from the previous problems.

5. Modern science has made it possible for us to dial a long-distance telephone number directly. Prepare a syntax diagram for such a number.

6. The Peerless Floogle Company identifies each type of manufactured part with a part number consisting of one or two letters followed by a three-digit integer followed by a vowel. The first of the three digits is used as a category classification and ranges from 1–5. Prepare a syntax diagram for such a part number. (If you do not know what a Peerless floogle is, you are cautioned against buying one.)

7. In the land of Fneh, accountants are held in high esteem. Thus, when a person becomes a certified accountant there, he or she is given a new name as part of the ceremony. All accountants' names are hyphenated. On the left side of the hyphen are three consonants (any three can be used) followed by two vowels. On the right side of the hyphen are two digits. Depict this syntax diagrammatically.

8. Referring to Problem 7, suppose the authorities in Fneh decided to modify the rules for constructing highly esteemed accountants' names so that the two vowels have to be the same. How would you handle that in the definition?

9. Prepare a syntax diagram for an automobile tire size. (This will require a little research.)

10. Write the Pascal code for each of the following declarations:
    (a) Three INTEGER variables named COUNT1, COUNT2 and COUNT3.
    (b) Two REAL variables named velocity and time.
    (c) Combine (a) and (b) in a single declaration.

11. Assuming that v1, v2, and v3 are declared as INTEGER variables, specify the value stored in v3 as a result of each of the following sequences. Treat each sequence independently:
    (a) v3 := 404 ;
        v3 := 17
    (b) v1 := −897 ;
        v2 := 61 ;
        v3 := v1 − 4
    (c) v1 := −200 ;
        v2 := 16 ;
        v3 := v1 + 2*v2
    (d) v3 := 688 ;
        v2 := 31 ;
        v3 := v3 − v2 − 43 (remember that := means "is replaced by")

12. Supply the necessary semicolons for each of the following sequences:

(a)
```
BEGIN
    statement
    statement
    statement
    statement
    statement
END
```

(d)
```
statement
BEGIN
        BEGIN
            statement
        statement
            BEGIN
            statement
            statement
            END
        statement
        END
        statement
END
```

(b)
```
BEGIN
    statement
    statement
    BEGIN
        statement
        statement
    END
END
```

(e)
```
PROGRAM prob12e
VAR
        bk,                 m5,
str : INTEGER
        arcs, sides : REAL
subprogram definition
BEGIN
    statement
    statement
    statement
END.
```

(c)
```
statement
statement
BEGIN
    BEGIN
        statement
        BEGIN
            statement
            statement
        END
    END
END
```

13. The Pascal compiler uses a variety of signals (such as colons, semicolons, and parentheses), along with reserved words, to aid in its analysis of source programs. Consequently, the physical placement of the statements is of no concern to Pascal as long as they are in proper sequence. It is of concern to us, however, since legibility and clarity are important programming objectives. This is why we have been using an indented format (as exemplified in Figure 3.11), and shall continue to do so. In light of this introduction, reformat the following program so that its appearance follows this practice:

```
PROGRAM writedown;VAR orig,pct,valuenow:REAL;numyrs
:INTEGER;BEGIN READLN(orig,pct,numyrs);WRITELN(orig,pct,numyrs);
valuenow:=orig*(1.00-0.01*pct*numyrs);WRITELN(valuenow)END.
```

14. Show the output that would be produced by the program in Figure 3.11 for each of the following lines of input:

   (a) 348   27   (c)   30   −56

   (b) −41   6   (d) −303 −32

15. Modify the program in Figure 3.11 so that the first line of output is displayed immediately after the input values are read.

16. Prepare a pseudocode description and a Pascal program to meet the following requirements: We would like to read three integer values num1, num2, and adjuster. These values are to be displayed immediately after they have been read. Then, the program is to compute bigval as follows: Add adjuster to the larger of the two values num1 and num2 and multiply that sum by 4. The value thus obtained is to be added to the smaller of the two values num1 and num2. Display a second line of output showing bigval. Then, display a final line of output saying RUN COMPLETED.

17. Prepare a Pascal program from the following pseudocode description:

   Declare integer variables num1, num2, num3, smallest, largest and range.
   Read values for num1, num2, and num3.
   Display a line with num1, num2, and num3.
   Assign num1 to smallest.
   IF
        num2 is less than smallest
   THEN
        Assign num2 to smallest.
   ENDIF
   IF
        num3 is less than smallest
   THEN
        Assign num3 to smallest.
   ENDIF
   Assign num1 to largest.
   IF
        num2 is greater than largest
   THEN
        Assign num2 to largest.
   ENDIF
   IF
        num3 is greater than largest

THEN
    Assign `num3` to `largest`.
ENDIF
Display the values of `smallest` and `largest` on a line.
Compute `range` = `largest` − `smallest`.
Display a line showing `range`.
Display a final line saving RUN COMPLETED.

    (Expectedly, > is Pascal's symbol for "greater than.") Using no more than two simple sentences, describe the process presented above. Show what the output would be for the following line of input:

−27   40   12

Chapter 4

Preparation of Programs

Pascal's emphasis on program clarity is seen both inside and outside the language itself. By now, we have examined enough of the syntax to establish the idea that there are intentionally close ties between the structural components of a well-constructed program and their expression as Pascal statements. This chapter explores that relationship further.

Proper use of Pascal's features takes us only part of the way toward the production of a "good" program. It is not enough for the program to compute correct results efficiently. One of the most predictable aspects of computer applications is that they are likely to change. A program, seen as being good and wonderful at first, often becomes a bothersome obstacle in the way of progress in a surprisingly short time. The message is clear enough: An important quality of a good program is that it is easy to change.

This places the program's listing in a central position. After serving as a reference document during the program's development, the listing continues to act as a focal point for changes. Whenever a program is modified, the change is denoted by altering the most recent version of the listing to produce a new one reflecting the change. In this chapter we shall establish coding conventions that emphasize clarity and enhance the listing's usefulness.

4.1 THE UCSD PASCAL PROGRAM LISTING

In addition to the Pascal statements and comments, UCSD Pascal source programs can include directives that influence the compiler's activities. Of interest in this section are facilities for producing a program listing.

Directives to the UCSD Pascal compiler are submitted as *pseudocomments*. A pseudocomment looks like a comment except that a dollar sign appears immediately after the left delimiter. Thus, the following constructions

{$compilerdirective}   or   (*$compilerdirective*)

are legal forms for pseudocomments. To produce a program listing, the directive is

{$L+}   or   (*$L+*)

This pseudocomment is placed before the PROGRAM statement, thereby requesting a listing for the entire program. Selected parts of the listing can be suppressed by the pseudocomment

{$L–}   or   (*$L–*)

placed at some subsequent point in the program. If the L+ directive does not appear, UCSD Pascal automatically assumes L–.

When the UCSD Pascal compiler encounters the L directive, it sets up a file named SYSTEM.LST.TEXT in which to store the program listing. From there it is available (like any other p-System file) for subsequent display. If we want to see the listing as it is produced, directly on the screen, the L directive is specified as follows:

{$L CONSOLE:}   or   (*$L CONSOLE:*)

Similarly, the directive

{$L PRINTER:}   or   (*$L PRINTER:*)

produces the listing on the parallel printer.

4.1.1 Example 4.1

We shall produce a listing for the program in Example 3.1 by adding the pseudocomment {$L CONSOLE:} just before the PROGRAM statement. As a result, the compiler will display the listing shown in Figure 4.1. (We have temporarily deleted the comments for convenience.)

Our primary interest is in the statements themselves. The additional columns to the left of the program statements provide information that can help analyze larger, more complex programs. We shall just indicate the general characteristics here:

1. The leftmost column simply shows the line number.
2. The second column, irrelevant here, is used to distinguish among independently compiled modules (called *segments*) that form a larger program.

```
Pascal Compiler IV.0 c3s-2
    Page 1
 1  0  0:d   1   $L CONSOLE:
 2  2  1:d   1   PROGRAM   ex401 ;
 3  2  1:d   1   VAR
 4  2  1:d   1     num1, num2, bigsum  :   INTEGER  ;
 5  2  1:0   0   BEGIN
 6  2  1:1   0      WRITELN ('TYPE IN VALUES FOR num1 AND num2.')  ;
 7  2  1:1  20      READLN (num1, num2)  ;
 8  2  1:1  45      IF
 9  2  1:1  45         num1 < num2
10  2  1:1  46      THEN
11  2  1:2  50        bigsum := num1 + 3*num2
12  2  1:1  52      ELSE
13  2  1:2  59        bigsum := num1 + 3*num1  ;
14  2  1:1  66      WRITELN ('NUM1: ',num1, ' NUM2: ',num2)  ;
15  2  1:1 117      WRITELN ('BIGSUM: ',bigsum)  ;
16  2  1:1 146      WRITELN ('END OF RUN.')
17  2   :0   0   END.
End of compilation.
```

Figure 4.1

UCSD Pascal Listing for Example 4.1

3. The third column helps identify a program's structural components. (For instance, the d's mark the extent of the declaration section.) Other information given by the column becomes more important in complex programs that include numerous subprogram definitions and intricate compound statements.

4. The final column helps the programmer determine the size of the compiled program.

More detailed information about these supplementary columns is given in your reference manual.

Another useful directive is the P directive. This causes the compiler to format the listing so that each page fits nicely on a sheet of 11-inch-long paper. P– deactivates the automatic pagination. In addition, we can force the start of a new page at any point in the listing by including the pseudo-comment {$P} or (*$P*) at that point. Several directives can be included in a single pseudocomment, e.g., {$L+,P}. Note that only one dollar sign is needed.

4.2 STRUCTURAL COMPONENTS AND PASCAL CODE

In this section we shall concentrate on building the relationship between a program's basic structural components and their expression in UCSD Pascal. Once the Pascal representations have been defined, we shall look at convenient ways of writing (typing) them so that their intended meaning is easy to see.

4.2.1 Sequences and Compound Statements

The direct correspondence between a structural sequence and a compound statement (Section 3.3.2, *Compound Statements*) needs no further elaboration. In general, it is a good idea to use a separate line for each simple statement. When a sequence of statements is gathered inside the BEGIN...END brackets, the resulting compound statement is easy to represent clearly when we write it down. As Figure 4.2(a) indicates, legibility is enhanced when the body of the statement is indented two or three spaces in from the BEGIN and END. The indentation, and the fact that BEGIN and END are on separate lines by themselves, make the sequence's structure conspicuous.

There can be reasonable exceptions to the practice of placing each simple statement on a new line. A typical case is one where there are related elementary statements, each of which performs the same kind of activity (e.g., a group of variables being set to zero). In this situation, placement of several statements on the same line [as illustrated in Figure 4.2(b)] does not detract from the statements' clarity.

4.2.2 The IF-THEN-ELSE Component and the IF Statement

Figure 3.12 established that there is a close correspondence between Pascal's IF statement and the pseudocode representation of the IF-THEN-ELSE component. This resemblance is emphasized by writing the IF statement with the same kind of indentation used in the pseudocode. To illustrate, we shall show part of Figure 3.10's pseudocode in more detail. Specifically, the computation of bigsum will be broken down more minutely to include a description of how the minimum and maximum values are determined [Figure 4.3(a)]. The corresponding Pascal code in Figure 4.3(b) shows how clearly the indented form conveys the statement's intent.

```
BEGIN                          BEGIN
  statement        ;             statement
  statement        ;             a := 0 ; b := 0 ; c := 0;
       .                         statement                  ;
       .                              .
       .                              .
  statement                           .
END                                  statement
                               END
  (a)
                                    (b)
```

Figure 4.2

Representation of a Compound Statement

```
IF                                      IF
   num1 is less than num2                  num1    <num2
THEN                                    THEN
   Compute bigsum = num2+3(num1)           bigsum := num2 + 3 * num1
ELSE                                    ELSE
   Compute bigsum = num1+3(num2)           bigsum := num1 + 3 * num2
ENDIF
```

    (a) Pseudocode representation   (b) Pascal specification

```
IF   num1 < num2   THEN
   bigsum := num2 + 3 * num1
ELSE
   bigsum := num1 + 3 * num2
```

(c) Alternative layout for Pascal representation

Figure 4.3

The IF-THEN-ELSE Component as a Pascal IF Statement

Another, more compact way sometimes is used to write the IF statement. Figure 4.3(c) shows the same mechanism as the one in Figure 4.3(b) with the reserved word IF, the comparison, and the reserved word THEN all on the same line. As far as the Pascal compiler is concerned, the statements in 4.3(a) and 4.3(b) are syntactically and semantically identical. Usually, we restrict Figure 4.3(c)'s format to those IF statements in which the comparison is small and simple enough so that everything fits on the same line without crowding. The structure of such a comparison is seen in the test following the word IF in Figure 4.3: Two values are compared against each other. The rule under which the comparison takes place is specified by a *relational operator*. For instance, the < operator in Figure 4.3 represents a rule that says, "If the first of the two values currently being compared is less than the second one, the outcome is true; otherwise it is false." The symbol < is one of Pascal's six basic relational operators. These are shown in Table 4.1. (Other types of comparisons are possible and will be explained later; meanwhile, we shall have plenty to do with just these six.)

Since the processing associated with a comparison's outcome is expressed as a Pascal statement, there is complete freedom with regard to how simple or extensive that processing can be: When a task cannot be expressed as a simple statement, the programmer merely specifies it as a sequence (i.e., a compound statement), and the syntax rule for the IF statement still is obeyed. This was seen in Figure 3.12. To explore this

Table 4.1 Relational operators.

Operator	Meaning
<	Less Than
<=	Less Than or Equal To
=	Equal To
<>	Not Equal To
>=	Greater Than or Equal To
>	Greater Than

decision structure further, Figure 4.4 shows a representation of an IF statement in which a variable named velocity is compared to another value named criticalv. If the two values are equal (i.e., if the outcome of the comparison is true), the program will execute the entire sequence specified within the compound statement. If not, that statement will be ignored and the program will execute the alternative simple statement instead. Indentation of the compound statement emphasizes the fact that, in concept, it is a single task related to one of the two possible outcomes of the true-or-false test.

4.2.3 Example 4.2

We shall illustrate the use of these features by developing a program to meet the following requirements: Real values val1 and val2 are to be compared to a third value cutoff. Those values smaller than cutoff (this may be true for neither of them, one of them, or both of them) are to be used in computing the following results:

1. sum1, the sum of the eligible values
2. prod1, the product of the eligible values
3. sumsqr1, the sum of the squared eligible values

Those values not smaller than cutoff (this may be true for neither of them, one of them, or both of them) are to be used in computing the following values:

1. sum2, the sum of the eligible values, each multiplied by a real adjustment value named adjust
2. prod2, the product of the eligible values
3. sumsqr2, the sum of the squared eligible values

sum1 and sum2 are to be displayed on a separate line, followed by a second line for prod1 and prod2, and a third line for sumsqr1 and sumsqr2. The input value for cutoff is on a separate line, followed by

```
IF
   velocity = criticalv
THEN
   BEGIN

         statement    ;
         statement    ;
                .

                .

         statement

      END
ELSE

         statement
```

Figure 4.4

Pascal IF Statement with a Compound Statement as a Consequent Activity

val1, val2, and adjust in that order, all on the next input line. If no values appear in a particular sum, product and sum of squares, their respective values are to be displayed as zero. val1 and val2 always will be positive, their values never falling below 0.005. adjust's value also will be positive, never less than 0.25.

The heart of the solution method lies in a comparison to determine whether a value is less than cutoff or not. Once this comparison is set up, it can be specified for val1 and val2 in turn, along with the appropriate actions. (Later, we shall examine more efficient ways of doing this.) Specification of the comparison is handled easily enough as an IF-THEN-ELSE component, as shown in the pseudocode of Figure 4.5. Since sum1, sum2, sumsqr1 and sumsqr2 all are quantities to which values may be added, we shall give them starting values of zero so that the additions will make sense. prod1 and prod2 need initial values for the same reason, but in those cases a value of 1 is used, In accordance with the problem's requirements, then, we must remember to change prod1 or prod2 to 0 if its final value is 1. (What conclusion would you draw if you were told that prod1 or prod2 had a value of 1 after val1 and val2 were processed?)

Since the actions required for each comparison's outcome cannot be described by single statements, they must be formulated as compound statements. The resulting program is shown in Figure 4.6.

4.2.4 The WHILE Component and Pascal's WHILE Statement

Pascal's WHILE statement (Figure 4.7) presents a direct representation of the processing for the WHILE-DO component: The test with which the statement starts determines whether the rest of the statement will be ex-

Declare real variables val1, val2, cutoff, adjust, sum1, sum2,
     prod1, prod2, sumsqr1, and sumsqr2.
Set sum1, sum2, sumsqr1 and sumsqr2 to 0.
Set prod1 and prod2 to 1.
Read cutoff, val1, val2, and adjust.
Display the input values.
IF
     val1 is less than cutoff
THEN
     Add val1 to sum1.
     Multiply prod1 by val1.
     Add the squared value of val1 to sumsqr1.
ELSE
     Multiply val1 by adjust and add the result to val2.
     Multiply prod2 by val1.
     Add the squared value of val1 to sumsqr2.
ENDIF
IF
     val2 is less than cutoff
THEN
     Add val2 to sum1.
     Multiply prod1 by val2.
     Square val2 and add the result to sumsqr1.
ELSE
     Multiply val2 by adjust and add the result to sum1.
     Multiply prod2 by val2.
     Square val2 and add the results to sumsqr2.
ENDIF
IF
     prod1 or prod2 has a value of 1
THEN
     Assign it a value of 0.
ELSE
ENDIF
Display sum1, sum2, prod1, prod2, sumsqr1, sumsqr2.
Stop.

Figure 4.5

Pseudocode for Example 4.2

ecuted or skipped over. If it is executed, its conclusion is followed automatically by a return to the test and the possibility of repeating the activity.
Thus, the WHILE statement gives us a framework for a loop controlled
automatically by a test at its beginning. Typically, the test is a comparison
like those used in the IF statement. An outcome of "true" enables the
program to do the processing described by the simple or compound statement attached to the WHILE.

   For instance, suppose we wanted the sum of the first 24 odd integers.
(You'd be surprised; there has been a growing demand for this lately.)
sum24 will be the variable in which the sum is accumulated and count

```
(***************************************************************)
(*                        EXAMPLE 4.2                        *)
(***************************************************************)
(*   THIS PROGRAM COMPUTES SUMS, PRODUCTS AND SUMS OF SQUARES *)
(*   FOR INPUT VALUES VAL1 AND VAL2 THAT MEET CRITERIA WITH   *)
(*   RESPECT TO A THIRD VALUE (CUTOFF). VALUE(S) BELOW CUTOFF *)
(*   ARE USED TO COMPUTE SUM1, PROD1 AND SUMSQR1, AND THE     *)
(*   OTHER(S) IS (ARE) USED TO COMPUTE SUM2, PROD2, AND SUMSQR2.*)
(***************************************************************)
(*$L CONSOLE:*)
PROGRAM    ex402  ;
VAR
    val1, val2, cutoff, sum1, sum2, prod1, prod2,
    sumsqr1, sumsqr2, adjust   :   REAL  ;
BEGIN
    prod1 := 1 ; prod2 := 1 ;
    sum1 := 0 ; sum2 := 0 ; sumsqr1 := 0 ; sumsqr2 := 0   ;
    WRITELN ('ENTER A VALUE FOR CUTOFF.')  ;
    READLN (cutoff)  ;
    WRITELN ('ENTER VALUES FOR VAL1, VAL2, AND ADJUST.')  ;
    READLN (val1, val2, adjust)   ;
    WRITELN ('cutoff:  ', cutoff)   ;
    WRITELN ('VAL1:  ', val1, '  VAL2:  ', val2,'  ADJUST: ',adjust)  ;
    IF
        val1 < cutoff
    THEN
        BEGIN
            sum1 := sum1 + val1    ;
            prod1 := prod1 * val1    ;
            sumsqr1 := sumsqr1 + SQR(val1)
        END
    ELSE
        BEGIN
            sum2 := sum2 + adjust * val1   ;
            prod2 := prod2 * val1   ;
            sumsqr1 := sumsqr2 + SQR(val1)
        END  ;
    IF
        val2 < cutoff
    THEN
        BEGIN
            sum1 := sum1 + val2  ;
            prod1 := prod1 * val2  ;
            sumsqr1 := sumsqr1 + SQR(val2)
        END
```

Figure 4.6———————————————————————————————

Program for Example 4.2

```
ELSE
   BEGIN
      sum2 := sum2 + adjust * val2  ;
      prod2 := prod2 * val2  ;
      sumsqr2 := sumsqr2 + SQR(val2)
   END  ;
IF
   prod1 = 1
THEN
   prod1 := 0 ;
IF
   prod2 = 1
THEN
   prod2 := 0  ;
WRITELN ('SUM1:   ',sum1,'  SUM2:   ',sum2)  ;
WRITELN ('PROD1:   ',prod1,'  PROD2:   ',prod2)  ;
WRITELN ('SUMSQR1:   ',sumsqr1,'  SUMSQR2:   ',sumsqr2)  ;
WRITELN ('END OF RUN.')
END.
```

Figure 4.6

Program for Example 4.2 (Continued)

will serve two purposes: First of all, it will keep track of the number of times we go around the loop. At the same time, we can use it to determine the next number to add to sum24. (If count has some value n, the nth odd number is $2*n-1$. Thus, each time we go through the loop, we shall add 1 to count and $2*$count-1 to sum24.) To get things started, we initialize count to 1 and sum24 to 0. The resulting program fragment (Figure 4.8) conveys the intent clearly. Its structure is emphasized by indenting the compound statement relative to the WHILE part. (The same would have been done even if the activity in the loop were just a simple statement.) Note that the return to the test is automatic; there is nothing in the loop (or in the syntactic rule of Figure 4.7) that says explicitly, "Go back to the WHILE part and perform the test again." The WRITELN procedure is executed once, only when the test fails (i.e., count exceeds 24).

4.2.5 Example 4.3

The loop in Figure 4.8's program segment was set up to repeat a certain number of times (i.e., 24). This is just one way to control the operation of a loop. There are many circumstances in which the number of cycles is unimportant or irrelevant. One such situation is seen here: We shall expand Example 4.2 by requiring that the program handle a succession of input sets. (As before, an input set consists of a value for each of the variables

Figure 4.7

Syntax for the WHILE Statement

cutoff, val1, val2, and adjust.) The program is to leave two blank lines between each set of displayed results, and the message END OF RUN is to follow the last set. There is no advance information regarding the number of input sets in a run.

The pseudocode (Figure 4.9) is not terribly different from the previous version (Figure 4.6). Basically, all that needed to be done was to enclose the processing section (except for the terminating message) inside a WHILE-DO component. (Addition of two blank lines is a minor detail.)

Now that we have decided what to do, we need to determine how to do it. The pseudocode rather blithely says that the loop is to continue going around as long as there is a set of input values to process, no matter how many input sets we have processed already. How can we tell when the input has run out? There are all kinds of ways. For instance, the requirements in Example 4.2 stated that val1 and val2 never were less then 0.005. We can use that restriction to provide a special signal: An input set, placed after the last one we wish to process, in which val1 is some value conspicuously less than 0.005 (say, −1.0). Then, the program can include a test based on that signal. "Data" used in this way are known as *dummy data*. This is illustrated by the fragment shown below:

```
READLN (cutoff)  ;
READLN (val1, val2, adjust)     ;
        +
        +
        +
WHILE  val1 >= 0.005  DO
    BEGIN
        +
        +
        +
    END
 + + +
```

Although this approach is straightforward, it requires the user to remember to include the special dummy input set at the end of each run. Another way is provided by the standard function EOF. Pascal sets up an EOF value for each source of input. This value is either TRUE or FALSE. (Data with such characteristics are called *boolean* data.) Right now, we are using only the standard input source, in which case the specification EOF

```
    • • •
sum24 := 0              ;
count := 1              ;
WHILE  count <= 24 DO
    BEGIN
        sum24 := sum24 + 2*count-1      ;
        count := count +1
    END
WRITELN ('SUM24:   ',sum24)
    • • •
```

Figure 4.8

Construction of a Loop with the WHILE Statement

by itself is sufficient. At the start of program execution, EOF is initialized (by UCSD Pascal) to FALSE, and it stays that way as long as any attempt to read data from INPUT is successful. (INPUT is Pascal's name for the standard input source. Thus, EOF(INPUT) and EOF are equivalent.) When such an attempt fails (There is no more input to read), EOF automatically changes to TRUE. This mechanism, then, gives us the basis for a simple test: As long as EOF is FALSE, we know that the most recent attempt to read was successful, and we can continue processing. This can be expressed as follows:

```
WHILE  NOT EOF   DO
    BEGIN
        Processing statements
    END
```

(The reserved word NOT is a *boolean operation* that changes a value of TRUE to FALSE, and vice versa. In, effect, we are saying, "While EOF has a value of FALSE, we want to perform the processing described by the attached statement.") The resulting program is shown in Figure 4.10, and input and output for a sample run are given in Figure 4.11.

Note that the WRITELN statements without any specified output produce blank lines. A closer look at Figure 4.10 provides further insight into the EOF mechanism: The test for end of file is performed at the beginning of each cycle through the WHILE-DO loop. If there is input, the entire loop is processed; if not, the entire loop is bypassed. Thus, the last set of input shown in Figure 4.11 consists of values for cutoff, val1, val2, and adjust followed *immediately* by <cntrl>C, the end-of-file signal. As a result, there are input values for the loop to process, and it goes through one more time. When it gets to the end of the loop and automatically comes back to test for end of file, the signal is there, EOF is set to TRUE, and the terminating message is produced in response. (Why is the blank line missing just before the first output line for the last set of data?)

Declare real variables `val1`, `val2`, `adjust`, `sum1`, `sum2`, `prod1`, `prod2`, `sumsqr1`, `sumsqr2`.
Set `sum1`, `sum2`, `sumsqr1` and `sumsqr2` to 0.
Set `prod1` and `prod2` to 1.
Read the first set of input data.
WHILE   there are input values to process   DO:
    Display the input values just read.
    IF
        `val1` is less than `cutoff`
    THEN
        Add `val1` to `sum1`.
        Multiply `prod1` by `val1`.
        Square `val1` and add the result to `sumsqr1`.
    ELSE
        Multiply `val1` by `adjust` and add the result to `sum2`.
        Multiply `prod2` by `val1`.
        Square `val1` and add the result to `sumsqr2`.
    ENDIF
    IF
        `val2` is less than `cutoff`
    THEN
        Add `val2` to `sum1`.
        Multiply `prod1` by `val2`.
        Square `val2` and add the result to `sumsqr1`.
    ELSE
        Multiply `val2` by `adjust` and add the result to `sumsqr2`.
        Multiply `prod2` by `val2`.
        Square `val2` and add the result to `sumsqr2`.
    ENDIF
    IF
        `prod1` or `prod2` has a value of 1
    THEN
        Assign it a value of 0.
    ELSE
    ENDIF
    Display `sum1` and `sum2`.
    Display `prod1` and `prod2`.
    Display `sumsqr1` and `sumsqr2`.
    Display two blank lines.
    Read the next input set.
ENDWHILE
Display a terminating message.
Stop.

Figure 4.9
Pseudocode for Example 4.3

Numerical values are shown here in *floating point form*. In this notation, each value is accompanied by an exponent (the En or E-n) that indicates the power of 10 by which the number is to be multiplied to obtain the proper magnitude. For instance, the first value of `cutoff` (which we know to be 20 from the input) is displayed as 2.00000E1. This means that

```
(**********************************************************)
(*                      EXAMPLE 4.3                       *)
(**********************************************************)
(*  THIS PROGRAM DOES THE SAME PROCESSING AS IN           *)
(*  EXAMPLE 4.2. HOWEVER, THE PROCESSING IS REPEATED      *)
(*  FOR AN ARBITRARY NUMBER OF SUCCESSIVE INPUT SETS.     *)
(*  THE END OF FILE INDICATOR IS USED TO STOP THE RUN.    *)
(**********************************************************)


(*$L CONSOLE:*)
PROGRAM ex403  ;
VAR
   val1, val2, cutoff, adjust, sum1, sum2,
   prod1, prod2, sumsqr1, sumsqr2  ;  REAL  ;
BEGIN
   WHILE  NOT EOF  DO
      BEGIN
         WRITELN ('      ')  ;    WRITELN ('      ')  ;
         WRITELN ('ENTER A VALUE FOR CUTOFF.')  ;
         READLN (CUTOFF)  ;
         WRITELN ('ENTER VALUES FOR VAL1, VAL2, AND ADJUST.')  ;
         READLN (VAL1, VAL2, ADJUST)  ;
         WRITELN ('      ')  ;
         prod1 := 1 ;  prod2 := 1 ;
         sum1 := 0 ;  sum2 := 0 ;  sumsqr1 := 0 ;  sumsqr2 := 0 ;
         WRITELN ('CUTOFF:   ',cutoff)   ;


         WRITELN ('VAL1:  ',val1,'  VAL2:  ',val2);
         WRITELN ('  ADJUST:  ',adjust)  ;
                 '  ADJUST:  ',adjust)    ;

         IF
            val1 < cutoff
         THEN
            BEGIN
               sum1 := sum1 + val1  ;
               prod1 := prod1 * val1  ;
               sumsqr1 := sumsqr1 + SQR(val1)
            END
         ELSE
            BEGIN
               sum2 := sum2 + val1 * adjust ;
               prod2 := prod2 * val1 ;
               sumsqr2 := sumsqr2 + SQR(val1)
            END  ;
```

Figure 4.10

Program for Example 4.3

```
IF
    val2 < cutoff
THEN
    BEGIN
        sum1 := sum1 + val2  ;
        prod1 := prod1 * val2  ;
        sumsqr1 := sumsqr1 + SQR(val2)
    END
ELSE
    BEGIN
        sum2 := sum2 + val2*adjust  ;
        prod2 := prod2 * val2  ;
        sumsqr2 := sumsqr2 + SQR(val2)
    END ;
    IF
        prod1 = 1
    THEN
        prod1 := 0 ;
    IF
        prod2 = 1
    THEN
        prod2 = 0 ;
    WRITELN ('SUM1:  ',sum1,'  SUM2:  ',sum2) ;
    WRITELN ('PROD1:  ',prod1,'  PROD2:  ',prod2) ;
    WRITELN ('SUMSQR1:  ',sumsqr1,'  SUMSQR2:  ',sumsqr2) ;
END ;
    WRITELN ('END OF RUN.')
END .
```

Figure 4.10

Program for Example 4.3 (Continued)

the value being represented is 2.00000 times 10 to the first power. The system uses this notation automatically for real output unless we instruct it explicitly to do otherwise. We shall see how to do that a little later on. Since a boolean data item is defined as one with a possible value either of TRUE or FALSE, the test in the WHILE statement does not show any comparison. In essence, it says, "If the value of EOF is true (i.e., if the most recent attempt to read input data was successful), go ahead and work your way through the loop again. If not, skip the loop and continue beyond it."

4.3 PROGRAM STRUCTURE AND APPEARANCE

As seen in the previous examples, the use of indentation is helpful in highlighting individual program statements and their contribution to the structures in which they appear. This section offers additional ideas that tend to improve the clarity of the program as a whole. There is considerable payoff in taking the small amount of extra effort to prepare a legible program listing.

```
ENTER A VALUE FOR CUTOFF.
20 <enter>
ENTER VALUES FOR VAL1, VAL2, AND ADJUST.
12        30          0.5 <enter>

CUTOFF: 2.4000000000000000E1
VAL1: 1.1999999999999996E1  VAL2: 3.0000000000000000E1
  ADJUST: 5.0000000000000000E-1
SUM1: 1.2000000000000000E1  SUM2: 1.5000000000000000E1
PROD1: 1.1999999999999996E1  PROD2: 3.0000000000000000E1
SUMSQR1: 1.4399999999999994E2  SUMSQR2: 9.0000000000000000E2

ENTER A VALUE FOR CUTOFF.
24 <enter>
ENTER VALUES FOR VAL1, VAL2, AND ADJUST.
40        .25         0.4 <cntrl>C
CUTOFF: 2.3999999999999991E1
VAL1: 4.0000000000000000E1  VAL2: 2.5000000000000000E-1
  ADJUST: 4.0000000000000000E-1
SUM1: 2.5000000000000000E-1  SUM2: 1.6000000000000000E1
PROD1: 2.5000000000000000E-1  PROD2: 4.0000000000000000E1
SUMSQR1: 6.2499999999999994E-2  SUMSQR2: 1.6000000000000000E3

END OF RUN.
```

Figure 4.11

A Sample Run for Example 4.3

4.3.1 Program Layout

An important factor in a program's clarity is its relation to the pseudocode from which it is developed. Since the pseudocode emphasizes the structural components used to express an algorithm, similar emphasis in the code helps strengthen the correspondence between the two. For this reason is it a good idea to separate each component from its neighbors by one or more blank lines. If the component is a subprogram, it may be helpful to arrange the listing so that each function or procedure appears on a separate page. Similarly, if a program listing shows that a structural component crosses a page boundary, a {$P} pseudocomment can be inserted at the beginning of that component so that it will start on a new page in the next version of the listing.

4.3.2 Program Documentation

An important aspect of systematic program design is the keeping of careful records of each stage of the process. The pseudocode documents the algorithm and the program listing documents the implementation of that algorithm. In a sense, the listing is the ultimate record of the programming project. The use of comments, in addition to the layout techniques discussed in the previous section, can make the listing even more helpful.

Comments, when carefully constructed, can be helpful additions to the listing. A good practice is to include a comment at the beginning of a program that explains what the program does. The amount of detail, of course, will depend on the individual situation. In general, this comment would explain the algorithm (if it needs explaining) and define the important variables used in the program. Sometimes it helps to include some information about the program's structure. For example, if a program includes one or more user-defined subprograms (i.e., those other than Pascal's built-in functions and procedures), it is useful to indicate briefly what their names are and what they do.

This introductory comment usually is the most extensive one in the program. In many instances, it may be the only one. When additional comments are included inside a program, they generally are minimal (one or two lines), their main purpose often being to explain the processing specified by a particular structural component. If the processing is easy to discern from the statements, the comment is unnecessary, unless it helps to explain why the processing is done in that way and/or why it is done at that point. If the processing is intricate or complicated, the comment should be an explanation of the process and not a paraphrase of the individual statements. What not to do is illustrated best by the classic paraphrase; although the original occurrence is enshrined in the Computer Monument in Bilgewater, New Mexico, new ones keep showing up daily:

```
(*   Add 3 to chrvalue and store the result in tt1value   *)
     tt1value := chrvalue + 3
```

It is not necessary for you to contribute to this list of useless comments. The industry has more than enough already.

Pascal allows a comment to appear on the same line as a program statement. However, it usually is better to keep the comments on separate lines. They are more conspicuous that way.

Problems

1. Write the appropriate Pascal statement(s) for each of the following descriptions. Assume that v1, v2, v3, v4, v5, v6, etc., are real variables and j1, j2, j3, j4, j5, j6, etc., are integer variables. Assume further that all of the variables have known values.

(a)   IF
        ʋ1 is greater than ʋ2 + ʋ3
   THEN
        Compute ʋ4 as 6ʋ1.
   ELSE
        Compute ʋ4 as 8(ʋ2+ʋ3).
   ENDIF

(b)   Compute ʋ4 as the sum of the largest and smallest of the values ʋ1, ʋ2, and ʋ3.

(c)   IF
        ј1 is no greater than 90
   THEN
        do nothing.
   ELSE
        Assign twice ј2's value to ј3.
        Compute ј4 as 18 more than ј3.
        Display ј1, ј2, ј3, and ј4 on four separate lines.
   ENDIF

(d)   IF
        ј1 is at least as large as ј2
   THEN
        Compute ј3 as ј1 times the smaller of ј2 and ј4.
   ELSE
        Compute ј3 as ј1 times the larger of ј2 and ј4.
   ENDIF
   Display ј1 and ј2 on one line, followed by ј4 and ј3 on another.

(e)   Compute ʋ3 as the ratio of the smaller of ʋ1 and ʋ2 to the larger of ʋ1 and ʋ2. (Division of real numbers is specified as / in Pascal.) Compute ʋ4 as ʋ3's reciprocal. Then, display ʋ3 and ʋ4 on the same line.

(f)   ʋ5 = ʋ1 + ʋ3 – ʋ4

(g)   ʋ5 = (ʋ1 + ʋ3)

(h)   ј1 = i

(i)   ј2 = 8!

(j)   ј3 = ј4!

(k)   Compute ј3 as the sum of the first 7 multiples of 6.

(l)   Compute ʋ5 as the average of ʋ1, ʋ2, ʋ3, and ʋ4. Display ʋ5.

(m)   Compute ј5 as the sum of all integers larger than 100 and smaller than 10000 that are multiples of 12. (Note: Here is a case where a little thought could produce a better algorithm than one that might come to mind right away.)

(n)   ј4 = ј1

(o)   ј1 = ј4

2. Write a complete Pascal program from the following pseudocode description:

> Declare real variables h r s w o r k e d, p a y r a t e, s t r t p a y,
> o v t m p a y,
> g r o s s p a y, n e t p a y, d u e s, f e d t a x,
> s t t a x,
> s o c l s e c, t t l d e c.
> Declare integer variable i d n u m.
> Read i d n u m, h r s w o r k e d, p a y r a t e.
> Compute s t r t p a y (s t r t p a y = p a y r a t e*h r s w o r k e d for first 40 hours).
> Compute o v t m p a y (o v t m p a y = 1.5*p a y r a t e for h r s w o r k e d over 40).
> Compute g r o s s p a y = s t r t p a y + o v t m p a y.
> t t l d e c = sum of f e d t a x (23% of g r o s s p a y),
> s t t a x (5.5% of g r o s s p a y),
> s o c l s e c (6.9% of g r o s s p a y), and d u e s (3% of g r o s s p a y).
> Compute n e t p a y = g r o s s p a y − t t l d e c.
> Display i d n u m, h r s w o r k e d, p a y r a t e.
> Display s t r t p a y, o v t m p a y and g r o s s p a y.
> Display each deduction.
> Display n e t p a y.
> Stop.

Note: h r s w o r k e d may be less than 40. Run your program with the following values: i d n u m = 674, h r s w o r k e d = 48, p a y r a t e = 8.85.

3. Revise the program of Problem 2 so that it processes any number of input sets. Add the following input sets to your test run:

   i d n u m = 240, h r s w o r k e d = 24, p a y r a t e = 10.00
   i d n u m = 912, h r s w o r k e d = 56.5, p a y r a t e = 7.72

4. Take another look at Figure 4.7. Now explain why it is legal to have a WHILE statement inside another WHILE statement.

5. Clavicle Industries, Ltd. bought a DOLDRUM-7 computer system for $266,550 which they would like to write off in six years. Using the straight line method, this would mean that in each of the six years, the system would decrease in value by a fixed amount such that its value would be zero at the end of the sixth year. Write a pseudocode description and a Pascal program that displays the initial value of the system followed by a line for each year of the write-off period showing the value of the system at the end of that year. (If you look ahead to the next

problem, you will see that it is advisable to treat the initial value and the write-off period as input values.)

6. Revise the program in Problem 5 so that it produces the same kind of information for any number of initial values and write-off periods. In addition to the values from Problem 5, test your program with the following data:

Initial Value: $76000	Write-off Period: 12 years
Initial Value: $644225	Write-off Period: 3 years
Initial Value: $44000	Write-off Period: 7 years

7. Dirk Del Mannikin and his crack team of archaeologists are investigating his theory that an advanced civilization flourished on Earth tens of thousands of years ago. Not only was this civilization supposed to have had computers, but there were whispered hints that there may even have been a version of Pascal. Oh my. Now, word has come from far-off SmoozleKarpp that some peculiar writing was found by a peasant while she was digging for kvoobs (a fungoid delicacy that grows nowhere else). In the process of showing it to various people, the kvoob lady accidentally let it be seen by the mayor's son, known affectionately to all SmoozleKarppers as Hey Stupid. Hey had attended the entire third morning of a two-week Intensive Computer Workshop and therefore was able to recognize the writing as an ancient computer program. (That is why his excited father contacted Del Mannikin.) The helpful son also pointed out that time had rubbed away many of the semicolons in the program. (During that morning he had learned about semicolons.) Accordingly, he copied the program and began putting in semicolons with his usual enthusiasm. In the general hubbub, nobody noticed a local goat sneak over and grab the writing. By the time the alarm was raised, the precious morsel had been eaten, down to the last fragment. Hoo boy. Consequently, when Del Mannikin showed up the next day, all that was there for him was Hey's copy. Here is what it said:

```
PROGRAM quecosa);VAR;v1,v2,upv1,upv2,dnv1,dnv2;:INTEGER
BEGIN;READLN(v1,v2);upv1:=v1;dnv1:=v1;upv2:=v2;dnv2:=v2;WHILE NOT EOF
(INPUT)DO;BEGIN;IF v1>upv1 THEN upv1:=v1;IF v2>upv2 THEN upv2:=v2;
IF v1<dnv1 THEN dnv1:=v1;IF v2<dnv2 THEN dnv2:=v2;READLN(v1,v2);END;
WRITELN('UPV1:   ',upv1,'   UPV2;   ',upv2);WRITELN('DNV1:   ',dnv1,
'   DNV2:   ',dnv2);END.
```

(You might blame Hey for going wild with semicolons, but he had nothing to do with the rest of it; he copied it just the way it was recorded.)

(a) Rewrite the program in a form that makes it easier to read and analyze.

    (b)   Remove the extra semicolons.

    (c)   Write a brief description (2–3 sentences) of the processing done by this ancient program.

    (d)   Insert appropriate comments in your revised (reformatted) programming. "Appropriate comments" are those meant to help document the program, not those expressing your opinion of the program or the problem.

8.   Although the requirements for Example 4.3 specify that no value for val1 or val2 will fall below 0.005, a look at the program's statements raises a question as to what would happen if we do submit input that does not meet this requirement.

    (a)   Run the program in Example 4.3 (Figure 4.10) using a cutoff value of 5.5, val1 of 2.37, val2 of 0.00076, and adjust of 3.3 and see what happens.

    (b)   Modify the program so that attempts to violate the requirements for val1 and val2 are intercepted. The program's response should prevent computations for that input set, but it should not terminate the run if more input sets are available.

    (c)   Provide additional modifications to handle a similar violation with respect to the value(s) of adjust. Try a run with the following input sets:

20.5		(cutoff)
12.2	43.6	0.5
10.0		(cutoff)
0.002	21.4	0.77
2.6		(cutoff)
6.6	0.0017	0.164
12.0		(cutoff)
3.5	4.6	2.2 <cntrl>C

Chapter 5

Data

A program's effectiveness is tied to the way its data are organized and managed. UCSD Pascal emphasizes this by providing a powerful set of features for describing the types of data and the properties that a programmer wants them to have in a program. Moreover, these features are enforced by rules that make it impossible for the programmer to omit data definitions. As a result, every Pascal program includes a complete record of its data requirements. This chapter introduces the mechanisms for data description and examines their use.

5.1 DATA TYPES AND THEIR REPRESENTATION

No one can hope to list all the data types that might be useful. Certain fundamental forms, however, are applicable to a wide range of problems, and computers are designed to recognize and deal with them. For instance, all digital computers can handle integers, and many can process numbers with fractional portions. These are part of Pascal's standard data facilities. In addition to these and other *predeclared* data types, Pascal offers an extensive bookkeeping mechanism that enables the programmer to define his or her own data types for a particular program.

5.1.1 Numerical Data

Pascal recognizes two kinds of numerical data: INTEGER and REAL. The former type is extended in UCSD Pascal to include *long integers.*

Integers   Although the computer is built to work with binary integers (i.e., integers expressed in base 2), Pascal provides the necessary insulation that allows the programmer to use positive and negative integers in the familiar decimal form. Thus, the numbers 3, −101, 0, 3857, and −29 all are legitimate integer values and are referred to as *integer constants.* Numbers such as 38.6, −4.0, or 179, are *not* acceptable as integer constants because they have fractional portions. (The decimal point, even without anything after it, is enough to imply a fractional portion.) A value such as 3,407 is unacceptable (it will be rejected by Pascal even though it is an integer) because of the embedded comma.

The largest acceptable positive or negative integer usually depends on the type of computer being used rather than Pascal itself. For many small computers, the range is –32767 to +32767. However UCSD Pascal's facility for long integers permits this range to be extended to numbers up to 35 decimal digits long. (For some systems, this limit is 36 decimal digits.)

Storage for an integer variable is reserved by means of a VAR declaration as described in Chapter 3. Thus,

```
VAR
    incount, outcount  :  INTEGER
```

provides storage for two variables incount and outcount, each of which can accommodate a value in the range –MAXINT through MAXINT. A long integer variable is declared by specifying the maximum number of decimal digits that the particular variable can hold. For instance,

```
VAR
    bigsum  :  INTEGER[9]
```

reserves storage for a variable named bigsum capable of storing values like –30417528 or 106258144, but not 2417583906. Note that the maximum length specification in the long integer declaration is enclosed in square brackets.

Real Numbers   Numbers with fractional portions are called *real numbers* in Pascal's terminology. Here again, the programmer can use familiar decimal notation. Thus, values such as 18.8, 0.0061, 0.0, –5493., and –.072 all are acceptable REAL values (*real constants*).

Pascal also accepts REAL constants written in *floating-point notation*. This form (which was encountered briefly in Figure 4.11) provides a convenient way to write large or small values whose expression in conventional form would require many zeroes at the beginning or end of the values. For example, a number like 0.000000826 is awkward to read and susceptible to error. The situation can be improved by rewriting the value as 8.26×10^{-7}. This *scientific notation* provides the basis for floating-point notation which is just a more concise way of writing the same thing. For instance, the REAL constant 0.000000826 can be specified in Pascal as 8.26E–7 or 0.826E–6. The 0.826E–6 tells us (and Pascal) that if we multiply 0.826 by 10 to the –6th power, the result (0.000000826) is the value being expressed.

There is no "official" form for floating-point notation. For example, 3.7E5, 0.37E+6, 0.37E+06, 370E3, 370.0E+03, and 370000E0 all represent the same value (370000), and all are acceptable to Pascal. Despite this flexibility, it is best to select a particular form as a standard and use it consistently. A popular standard (and the one we shall use) is to adjust the exponent (the number following the E) so that the value to the left of the E is expressed as a single nonzero integer digit and a fraction. Applying this practice to the example values used above, 0.000000826 would be written 8.26E–7, and 370000 would be expressed as 3.7E5.

As is the case with integers, there are limitations on the expressible real values. There are two aspects to this: The *magnitude range* refers to the sizes of the largest and smallest expressible REAL numbers. The IBM Personal Computer's UCSD Pascal facility, for instance, is equipped to deal with real numbers as large as roughly plus or minus 10^{308} and as small as approximately 10^{-308}. Computer systems built around 8-bit micro-processors are likely to accommodate values from plus or minus 10^{35} to plus or minus 10^{-35}. Make sure you know the range for your particular system by checking with your instructor or consulting your system's refer-ence manual. A real value of zero (0.0 or 0.0E0), of course, also is express-ible. However, any attempt to specify a real value larger than zero but smaller than the minimum will not be accepted simply because the machine cannot recognize it.

The second type of restriction relates to the *precision* of a real value, i.e., the maximum number of significant digits that can be used. Many UCSD Pascal implementations on microcomputers can handle about 6 decimal digits, and some can accommodate as many as 16+ decimal digits. (For those UCSD Pascal implementations in the latter category, it is possi-ble to save space by restricting this upper limit to about 6 decimal digits. The technique for doing this is among the compiler options summarized in Appendix C.)

In a system supporting extended precision, this means that values like 2.736004 or 6.348907211538064E3 are acceptable, but values like 147.086217994523178 or 4.1079255386501228753E–1 are not. Note that a number like 0.00000000000000002038 is fine because there are only four significant digits. We can see this more clearly by rewriting the value as 2.038E–18. On the other hand, 4.000000000000000002038 is unaccept-able. (Why is that?)

As outlined previously in Chapter 3, real variables are defined within the VAR declaration:

```
VAR
   variablename  :  REAL
```

5.1.2 Character Data

Besides storing numerical values and performing arithmetic on them, computers can store and manipulate nonnumeric values as well. This capability is provided by representing such data as individual *characters*.

Computers are designed to recognize a standardized collection of characters called a *character set*. This set consists of letters, numerical digits, and special symbols like punctuation marks and basic mathematical signs such as +, –, etc. Many computers use a character set called ASCII (American Standard Code for Information Interchange). The ASCII codes are tabulated in Appendix B. (There may be UCSD Pascal implementations on computer systems that do not use the ASCII coding system, but the author is not aware of them.)

Individual characters can be combined in any desired way to form *character strings* of any length. The meaning of a particular character or string of characters is determined by the programmer, not by the machine. As far as the machine (or Pascal) is concerned, a string consisting of the six characters W3J.$E is just as legitimate as one consisting of the five characters BLOOM or the six characters 570329. When a character string consists solely of numerical digits (as does 570329 in the previous sentence), it still is a character string, not a number. It is up to us to determine what kinds of character strings we want to produce, what they mean, and how to use them.

When we want to specify a particular character or character string in UCSD Pascal, we write it as a *character constant* or *string constant*. This is done by placing an apostrophe at the beginning and end of the string. Thus, the character value B would be specified in Pascal as the character constant 'B'. Similarly, the character string 570329 would be written as the character constant '570329'. This enables Pascal to distinguish it from the integer constant 570329. The apostrophes, when used to bracket a character constant, serve as *delimiters*. To specify a character constant in which an apostrophe is one of the characters (or the only one, for that matter), we show two apostrophes for each one to be included. Pascal "knows" this rule, so that only one apostrophe is stored. Thus, the character string constant 'CAN''T' specifies the five character C, A, N, apostrophe, T. A character constant consisting of a single apostrophe, then, is specified as ''''.

A character variable, whose capacity is fixed at a single character, is declared as follows:

```
VAR
    variablename  :  CHAR
```

5.1.3 Boolean Data

A computer's decision-making capabilities generally are supported by simple mechanisms that operate like simple light switches: They are either "on" or "off." The usefulness of such a mechanism stems from our ability to test its state at a given instant and select a particular action based on the outcome. These decision aids, called *logical switches, binary switches,* or *boolean switches,* are represented in Pascal by *boolean data.* There can be only two boolean constants and, in Pascal, these are TRUE and FALSE. We shall see that numerous decision processes, including the IF-THEN-ELSE activity, are based on a test that checks whether a boolean value is TRUE or FALSE.

Declaration of boolean variables follows the same form used for other types:

```
VAR
    variablename  :  BOOLEAN
```

Recall [Figure 3.5(d)] that we established the standard data types as being part of a larger category (simple data types). Now we can restate that definition more completely within the larger context of simple data types. These definitions appear in Figure 5.1. (The concurrent data types are beyond the scope of this book.)

5.1.4 Names for Constants

The ease with which we can use constants is emphasized by the fact that we have included them in various computations without any fuss. Hidden behind an innocent statement such as:

```
result := 3.2*aval - 6.17*bval
```

is a collection of activities whereby Pascal recognizes the need for two REAL constants (3.2 and 6.17), produces them, and finds places to store them so that they are available when the program is run. All of this takes place without any explicit declarations by the programmer. The appearance of the constants in the statement is enough for Pascal. There are occasions, however, when the programmer wants to call attention to a constant by declaring it. Pascal has a specific feature for this purpose. Its use enables the programmer to give names to constants, after which those names may be used in other parts of the program as references to those values. In many instances, named constants can help greatly in clarifying the meaning of a particular computation. For instance, instead of specifying the value 3.14159 for pi in the statement

```
circum := 3.14159 * diam
```

we can declare pi as a named constant (named pi) in which case we can write

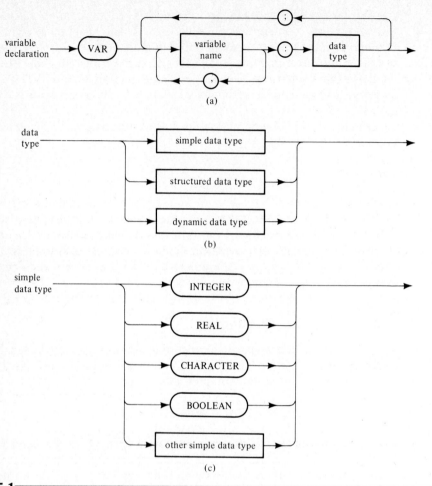

Figure 5.1

Declaration of Pascal Variables

```
circum := pi * diam
```

and Pascal will "know" enough to use 3.14159.

Declaration of Named Constants   Pascal's syntax for naming constants is shown in Figure 5.2. Applying this to the example of pi, the declaration

```
CONST
  pi = 3.14159
```

establishes pi as being synonymous with 3.14159. Similarly, the declaration

```
CONST
   blank = ' '
```

associates the name blank with a single blank character.

As Figure 5.2 indicates, several named constants may be defined together. Thus,

```
CONST
   bignum = 3872046898044  ;
   pi = 3.14159   ;
   blank = ' '
```

names a long integer constant as well as the two constants mentioned before. The CONST declaration always goes ahead of the variable declaration. This is seen in Figure 5.3, where the declaration section's syntax is developed in more detail than the basic form given originally in Figure 3.9(a). The additional components in the declaration section will be introduced later. As Figure 5.3 shows, all of these ingredients have certain positions in the declaration section. Regardless of the presence or absence of other declarations, CONST precedes VAR.)

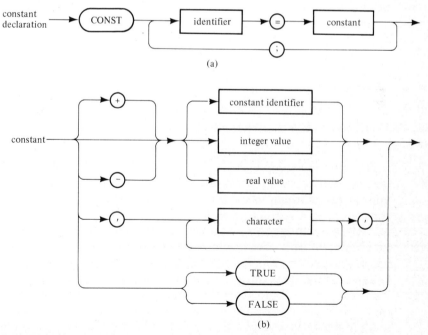

(a)

(b)

Semantics: A constant identifier is a name already associated with a constant earlier in the CONST declaration.

Figure 5.2

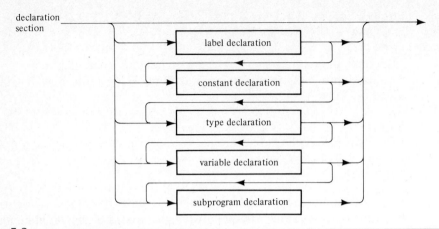

Figure 5.3

Construction of a Declaration Section

Standardized Named Constants In addition to the CONST facility described before, Pascal includes several permanently named constants. Besides the boolean constants TRUE and FALSE, Pascal provides the following standard names:

> MAXINT: The largest possible integer value that can be recognized by the particular computer being used. For UCSD Pascal, MAXINT is fixed at a value of 32767.
>
> NIL: A special value indicating a location of "nowhere." This will be useful later.

5.2 PROGRAMMER-DEFINED DATA

The data types described thus far relate directly to a computer's physical facilities for recognizing and processing such data. Any other type of data, regardless of how we express them or what they may mean to us, ultimately must be transformed into numbers, characters, or boolean values before a computer can do anything with them.

Pascal includes bookkeeping structures that handle these transformations automatically. For instance, let us suppose that a particular program becomes easier to prepare if it can make use of a data type called citrus. When a data item is a citrus, it may have one of the values grapefruit, lemon, lime, orange, or tangerine. Any other value (like tangelo, or cucumber, or 7) is illegal because we say it is. We can include the definition of a citrus as part of the program's declarations. As a result, Pascal sets up mechanisms for recognizing the allowable values and spotting the illegal ones. The new data type then is available for use throughout the program. It is as if the machine had been designed to recognize a `citrus` just as it recognizes an `INTEGER` or a `BOOLEAN` value.

5.2.1 Definition of Nonstandard Data Types

Any and all programmer-defined data types are described in a `TYPE` declaration whose syntax is shown in Figure 5.4(a). To establish the basic form, we shall define the `citrus` data type mentioned before:

```
TYPE
    citrus = (grapefruit, lemon, lime, orange, tangerine)
```

The information given to the right of the = sign specifies (in this instance) all the possible values for the `citrus` data type. When we specify a list of

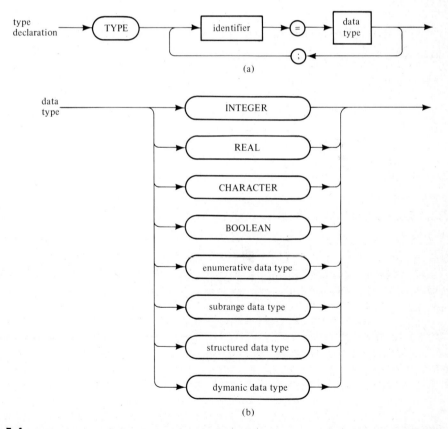

(a)

(b)

Figure 5.4 Construction of a `TYPE` Declaration

acceptable values for a citrus, we tell Pascal that a citrus is an *enumerative* data type. This is one of several kinds of simple data types. Recall (Figure 5.1) that this class includes the four standard types i.e., INTEGER, REAL, CHAR, BOOLEAN, along with a category we initially called "other simple types." The enumerative data type is one of them (Figure 5.4(b)). Classes other than simple types will be introduced a little later in the chapter.

The TYPE declaration (if there is one) is placed immediately prior to the VAR part of the declaration section. If a CONST declaration also happens to be included, it goes before the TYPE declaration. These three declarations (CONST, TYPE, and VAR, in that order) form the basic declaration section in simple programs (Figure 5.3). A LABEL declaration (introduced later but not used extensively) may appear before the CONST declaration. Subprogram declarations are included after the VAR declaration. These have been introduced in Chapter 3 and they, too, will be brought in as the plot develops.

5.2.2 Enumerative Data Types

We often deal with information that falls (or is pushed) into discrete categories. Thus, an undergraduate college student is (officially) either a freshman, sophomore, junior, or senior. Similarly, a current American coin is either a penny, nickel, dime, quarter, half dollar, or dollar. Data that can be categorized this way may be organized as an enumerative data type (Figure 5.5). Using studentyr and coin as the respective data type names for the two examples just mentioned, the declaration for these types would look like this:

```
TYPE
    studentyr = (freshman, sophomore, junior, senior)  ;
    coin = (penny, nickel, dime, quarter, halfdollar, dollar)
```

Declaration of Enumerative Data   Definition of a nonstandard data type merely establishes its existence. It gives us the opportunity to treat the new

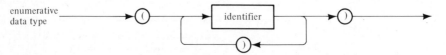

Semantics: The list of identifiers specifies the acceptable values for the data type.

Figure 5.5

Enumerative TYPE Declaration

type as if it were one of Pascal's predefined types. Accordingly, we can declare one or more variables of that type. For example, assuming the TYPE declaration for studentyr and coin given in the previous section, we can write something like this:

```
VAR
   studentstatus    :    studentyr    ;
   money, change    :    coin  ;
   count            :    INTEGER
```

As a result, we have a variable named studentstatus whose type is studentyr, meaning that it can have one of the four legal values defined for that type. In addition, we have two variables (money and change) both of type coin. Each of these may assume one of the six values defined for the type coin. Declaration of count as an ordinary integer variable was included for good measure just to show that variables of all data types are intermixed in one declaration. Real values cannot serve as a basis for an enumerative data type.

Assignment of Values for Enumerative Data Types   An enumerative variable can be given a value by means of an ordinary assignment statement. For example, assuming the TYPE and VAR declarations of coin and studentyr specified earlier, we can write a sequence such as

```
money := dime  ;
studentstatus := sophomore   ;
change := money
```

in which case the variables money and change each will have a value of dime, and studentstatus will have a value of sophomore.

Comparative Values of Enumerative Data   Even though the values associated with the data type coin in the previous example are words, they are not character strings. That is why the value on the right side of the assignment operator (:=) in each of the previous three statements was written without the apostrophes required for character string constants. For example, the statement

```
money := dime
```

was not written as

```
money := 'DIME'
```

because the value dime is conceptually different from the character string 'DIME'.

It is convenient (and not farfetched) to think of an enumerative data type as being supported by a table (invisible to the programmer) in which each value is represented by a code. For the type coin defined earlier, this table can be imagined as shown in Table 5.1.

Similarly, freshman, sophomore, junior, and senior would be associated, respectively, with codes of 0, 1, 2, and 3. The codes are not arbitrary. They correspond to the order in which the values are listed in the TYPE declaration. Since penny was listed first, its internal code is 0, nickel's internal code is 1 because it was listed second, and so on. These codes are not numbers. No arithmetic can be done with them nor are they directly accessible to the programmer. They indicate the *ordinal positions* of the values, thereby ranking them relative to each other. Thus, because dime appears earlier in the list than quarter, Pascal treats the value dime as being "less than" quarter. As a result, it is possible to compare such values in an IF-THEN-ELSE construction. For instance, assume that coin has been defined in a TYPE declaration as before, a variable named money has been declared as being of type coin, and money has been assigned some value. Now, we can say something like this:

```
IF
    money <= quarter
THEN
    action1
ELSE
    action2
```

The test in the IF statement is as simple as it looks. If the value in money is no greater than quarter (i.e., if it is penny, nickel, dime, or quarter), the outcome is TRUE and action1 is taken. In other words, the programmer exercises control over the relative values for new data types by selecting the order in which he or she lists those values in the TYPE declaration.

Table 5.1   Internal Coding for the Data Type coin

Value	Internal Coding
penny	0
nickel	1
dime	2
quarter	3
halfdollar	4
dollar	5

We shall explore additional mechanisms for enumerative data later on. The purpose at this point was merely to introduce them as part of the language's data declaration facilities.

5.2.3 Subrange Data Types

A subrange data type is one whose values are taken from a wider range of possibilities, with the restrictions being imposed by the meaning of the data. For instance, suppose we wanted to report an automobile's weight to the nearest pound. It certainly is possible to represent such a value with an ordinary integer, in which case we could declare a variable named mycarwt as follows:

```
VAR
    mycarwt  :  INTEGER
```

That means we can store any integer value in mycarwt as an "acceptable" automobile weight. If the value does not make sense (a car weight of −32 pounds, for example, does not make sense), it is up to the programmer to make sure that the program is safe from such situations.

Pascal provides the opportunity for a more automatic safeguard that allows the programmer to define a new data type in which the range of permissible values is specified. To illustrate, let us suppose that we are willing to agree that 1200 pounds is the lightest possible automobile weight, and 12000 pounds is the heaviest weight. We can use these limits to define a new data type:

```
TYPE
    autowt = 1200..12000
```

This says that autowt is being defined as a subrange data type whose values may be integers ranging anywhere from 1200 to 12000. Pascal recognizes the two extreme values as integers, and the two periods indicate the acceptability of everything (every integer value, in this case) in between. The general syntax is shown in Figure 5.6. Subranges of real values are illegal.

Now, we can define mycarwt as

```
VAR
    mycarwt  :  autowt
```

thereby setting up a variable for which the program will accept any integer in the range specified in the TYPE declaration. Any attempt to violate that range (for that variable) anywhere in the program will be rejected automati-

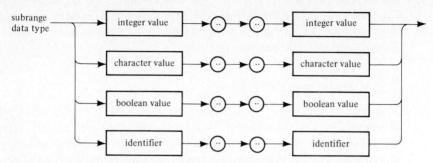

Semantics: The item on the left of .. must be "less than" the one on the right. ('A' < 'B',FALSE < TRUE). "identifier" refers to a value declared for an enumerative data type.

Figure 5.6

Subrange TYPE Declaration

cally by the Pascal compiler or by the P-System. If we wanted to do the same kind of thing for municipal spending, let us say, we could define a subrange type named budgetfigure:

```
TYPE
    budgetfigure = INTEGER[9]
```

A variable declared with the type budgetfigure could accommodate a value as high as 999999999 or a whopping deficit (−999999999), impressive for any city.

Subrange data types also can be defined using character values. For instance,

```
TYPE
    letter = 'A'..'Z'
```

defines a data type whose values are single characters taken from the 26 uppercase letters of the alphabet. Now we can write

```
VAR
    initial : letter
```

in which case a variable named initial can only have one of 26 possible values. It is illegal to define a subrange for REAL values. (Why is that a sensible restriction?)

Subranges of standard data types can be specified for individual variables without the need for separately defined data types. For example, the declarations

```
VAR
   initial   :   'A'..'Z' ;
   mycarwt   :   1200..12000
```

produce the same results as shown before. Since the acceptable values for both variables are subranges of standard types, Pascal recognizes them and no corresponding TYPE declarations are required. Thus, instead of being a variable of the autowt type, mycarwt now has been declared as an INTEGER variable with a limited range of legitimate values. Similarly, initial now is a CHARACTER subrange variable.

5.2.4 Subranges for Nonstandard Data Types

It also is possible to define a subrange for an enumerative data type because of the relation between the relative values and their positions in the declared list. To illustrate, consider the following sequence:

```
TYPE
   day = (mon, tue, wed, thu, fri, sat, sun) ;
   grade = (a, b, c, d, f)  ;
VAR
   weekday   :   mon..fri ;
   passgrade :   a..d
```

As a result of these declarations, the variable named weekday may have one the five values mon, tue, wed, thu, or fri. Similarly, the variable passgrade may have one of the four values a, b, c, or d. Of course, the VAR declarations would be meaningless if the full ranges had not been defined in appropriate TYPE declarations.

Our purpose, for now, has been to introduce the concept of enumerative and subrange data types as reasonable extensions of the standard data facilities. Once we have acquired additional fluency with other language features, we shall put these types to work.

5.3 ORGANIZATION OF DATA

The simple declaration of a variable or a named constant does more than signal our requirement for a place to store something. It also defines the type of data to be stored, and it can even impose restrictions on the range of acceptable values.

There is another aspect of data definition not yet considered. Thus far, each item has been declared as a separate unit with no inherent relation to other data items. When we specify a computation, we connect some of these items with each other to help fulfill the purpose of the particular algorithm. Outside of that computation, these connections no longer exist and the data, once again, are individual, independent items. Such values are called *simple values* or *single values,* and the variables we have been declaring and using all along are *simple variables* or *single-valued variables.*

There are many useful problem solutions that require their data to be organized into various kinds of collections. These collections, called *data structures,* are characterized by certain relationships among their individual members. Each type of data structure has its own set of relationships, and these define the kinds of data that can belong to a particular structure. In addition, rules associated with each data structure prescribe the kinds of operations available for it. Thus, each data item in a collection must be viewed as a member of that group, subject to the restrictions that may be imposed by the operating rules.

We can devise a limitless variety of data structures, each with its own organizational properties and operating rules. The need for such inventions depends on the kind of problems we are trying to solve. Certain data structures have been found to be useful in such a wide variety of applications that they have become standardized; accepted terminologies have grown up around their characteristics, and their use is taught as a distinct subject. In recognition of their general usefulness, several of these data structures are supported in Pascal by *structured data types* (Figure 5.7). Pascal is equipped with bookkeeping mechanisms that make it convenient for the programmer to set up and work with these structures. When such support is not available (as would be the case when a programmer needs a new kind of data structure), it is up to the programmer to bridge the gap between the way he or she wants to view the data and the way the data actually are organized in the machine. Methods and techniques for doing this are beyond the scope of this text. However, familiarity with some of the standard data structures will make it easier to deal with these issues in later work. Accordingly, this section takes a first look at some of the major data organizations and their representation in Pascal.

5.3.1 Strings

For those applications requiring multiple characters to be manipulated, UCSD Pascal supplements the simple CHAR type with the structured STRING type. A string is a sequence of characters whose length may vary during a program's progress.

Declaration of Strings   Section 5.1.2 established the use of named and unnamed string constants. UCSD Pascal supports facilities for string variables as well. Their declaration is handled within the regular VAR form. For instance,

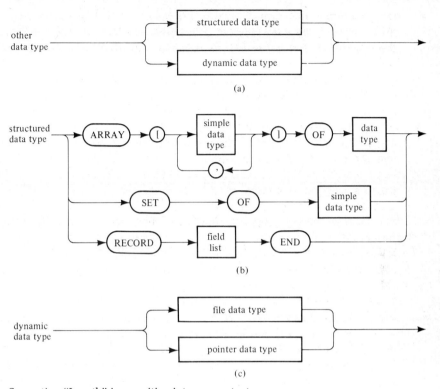

(a)

(b)

(c)

Semantics: "Length" is a positive integer constant.

Figure 5.7

Structured Data Types

```
VAR
    pageheading, footnote    :    STRING       ;
    partid                   :    STRING[6]    ;
    message                  :    STRING[120]
```

defines four string variables: The first two, pageheading and foot-note, each may contain as many as 80 characters. (When a STRING variable is declared with no explicit length, UCSD Pascal's default mechanism automatically assigns a maximum length of 80 characters.) The third variable, partid, will hold as many as 6 characters, and the fourth one, message, has a maximum capacity of 120. UCSD Pascal limits the length of a string to 255 characters. It is possible to have an empty character string, in which case its length (at that time) is zero. This is not the same as a string with blanks in it; a string with the value '   ' in it, for instance, has a length of 3.

Manipulation of Strings   String constants can be assigned to string variables, as long as the constant's length does not exceed the maximum declared for that variable. For instance, assuming the declaration of `message` as a string of up to 120 characters, the statement

```
message := 'GO HOME NOW.'
```

is a valid assignment. As a result, the variable `message` now contains the string constant 'GO HOME NOW.', and its associated length is 12. On the other hand,

```
partid := '327JE516'
```

will be rejected by Pascal because the constant's length (8) exceeds the maximum value declared for `partid`. Assuming `message` contains the value just assigned to it above, the subsequent assignment

```
message := ''
```

wipes out these contents and reduces the length of `message` to zero. Of course, other strings can be assigned to `message` as often as desired.

UCSD Pascal includes additional facilities for manipulating strings. These are presented as built-in functions which will be discussed later.

Decisions with String Data   String values may be compared with each other by taking advantage of the fact that each type of character is associated with a unique internal numerical value. This ordinal relationship among characters is called a *collating sequence* and is shown for the ASCII characters in Appendix B. For instance, a number (i.e., '0', '1', '2', ..., '9') is "less than" an uppercase letter, and an uppercase letter is "less than" a lowercase letter. Thus, the following test

```
IF  'ACTION' < 'OPTION'  THEN.......
```

has an outcome of TRUE because the (internal) numerical value for 'AC-TION' is less than (alphabetically precedes) 'OPTION'. Such comparisons are called *lexicographic* comparisons. Similarly, 'aa' is "greater than" 'Aa' or 'aA', but it is "less than" 'bA'. Check the table in Appendix B to make sure you understand why.

5.3.2 Arrays

An array is a collection of items with the following organizational characteristics:

1. All of the members (*elements*) have to be of the same data type.
2. The number of elements in an array is fixed for a given usage. That is, once the size of an array is defined, it stays that way. There are no computational operations whose results expand or contract the array. (We can pretend that an array changes its size by defining a big array and then using only part of it.)
3. All of the elements have to be located next to each other, in a certain order. Whether this is actually the case inside the computer is of secondary importance. The point is that this is the way an array is viewed by a person using it, and all array operations are based on that view. Consequently, Pascal (or any other programming language) must make any arrangements that may be needed to validate that view.
4. Any and all elements of an array are accessible at any time.
5. An array has a specific first element whose location serves as a reference. That is, any element in an array is identified in terms of its location relative to the first element.

To illustrate these fundamental properties, we shall declare a simple array and work with some of its elements:

```
VAR
    lengths   :   ARRAY [1..8] OF INTEGER   ;
      .
      .
      .
BEGIN
      .
      .
      .
    lengths[1] := 26   ;
    lengths[3] := 14   ;
    lengths[2] := lengths [3] - lengths [1]
      . . .
```

The declaration instructs Pascal to reserve enough storage for eight integer values under the collective name lengths. Hence, whenever the name lengths is mentioned, it refers to all eight elements, not to any one in particular. All of the values will be of the same type (INTEGER in this case). There are no values yet; as is true with any other declaration, we have only bookkeeping. The information inside the square brackets defines the way to identify each of lengths' elements. (Such an identifier is called an *index*.) In this case, the index is an integer ranging from 1 through 8. This is how Pascal "knows" that lengths is to have eight elements. Furthermore, the index specification informs Pascal that the first element (the reference element) is to be named lengths[1], the next (second) element is to have the name lengths[2], and so on, up through lengths[8]. Thus, the declaration produces the data organization shown in Figure 5.8, thereby satisfying the structural requirements for an array.

Now we can turn our attention to the assignment statements in the sequence given above. Since each array element has its own identifier, we can isolate it from the other elements and treat it just like an ordinary scalar variable. When the array index is applied to a particular element, the resulting index value is called a *subscript*. Thus, the first element has the subscript [1], and so on. Once this notation is clear, we can see that there is nothing special about the three assignment statements in the little example. As a result of these statements, three of lengths' eight elements now have values. This result is shown in Figure 5.9.

Automatic Loops for Arrays   An activity often applied to arrays is the systematic processing of its elements in succession. Pascal's FOR statement makes this easy to do. To illustrate, suppose we have the following declaration:

```
VAR
    lengths   :   ARRAY [1..8] OF INTEGER ;
    i         :   INTEGER ;
    .
    .
    .
  FOR i :=1 TO 8 DO
     READLN (lengths[i])
     ...
```

As a result, eight input values will be read and stored, respectively, in lengths[1] through lengths[8]. Control mechanisms associated with the FOR statement regulate the loop so that its single READLN statement is executed exactly eight times. The variable i (the *index variable*) is set to an initial value of 1 (in response to the FOR statement's directions) and is increased by 1 automatically for each repetition. A *limiting value* (8 in this case) stops the cycling. Since the FOR statement's index variable

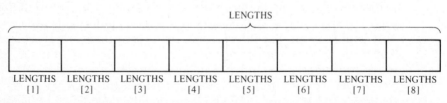

Figure 5.8

Array Organization

26	–12	14	?	?	?	?	?

Figure 5.9

Manipulation of Individual Array Elements

also is used to designate the subscript in the READLN statement, the element specified by the READLN changes with each repetition.

The activity in such a loop can be extended as desired by using a compound statement to specify it. Suppose that we wanted to compute the sum of lengths' elements. Using sumlengths for this purpose, we can write the following fragment:

```
VAR
    lengths  :  ARRAY [1..8] OF INTEGER  ;
    i, sumlengths : INTEGER ;
    .
    .
    .
sumlengths := 0 ;
FOR i:=1 TO 8 DO
    BEGIN
        READLN ( lengths[i] ) ;
        sumlengths := sumlengths + lengths[i]
    END
    ...
```

Now, each time an element's value is read, it is added to sumlengths as part of that cycle through the loop. Since nothing was changed in the FOR statement, it still allows exactly eight cycles. UCSD Pascal has additional capabilities that enable the programmer to specify operations on entire arrays with single statements that do not have to be part of a loop. These facilities will be examined later on.

Other Data Types as Array Indices   Integers are not the only legitimate subscript values for Pascal arrays. Characters, as well as any enumerative or subrange data types, can be used to identify individual array numbers. Of course, the data type to be used as the index has to be specified in the array declaration. For instance, consider the following declarations:

```
TYPE
    letter = 'A'..'Z' ;
VAR
    whichletter  :  letter ;
    codes        :  ARRAY [letter] OF INTEGER
        ...
```

First, we defined a data type named letter whose values can be taken from the 26 characters 'A' through 'Z'. Once declared, this subrange type can be used as an index for an array, and that is just what is done in the declaration for codes: We set up an array of integers that is indexed by the letter's data type. This means that codes has 26 elements, the first of which is codes['A'], the second is codes['B'], and so on. Thus, the statement

```
codes['L'] := 37
```

assigns a value of 37 to the twelfth element in array codes.

An enumerative or subrange index identifies individual elements just as an integer index does. Consequently, its use to regulate a loop requires no special considerations. To illustrate, we shall assign a value of 180 to each of codes' first 16 elements and a value of –61 to each of the last 10. Assuming the declarations given above, the following two statements do the job:

```
FOR whichletter := 'A' TO 'P' DO
   codes[whichletter] := 180 ;
FOR whichletter := 'Q' TO 'Z' DO
   codes[whichletter] := -61
```

5.3.3 Other Structured Data Types

Pascal recognizes other structured data types (Figure 5.7) whose usefulness will become more apparent when we gain additional experience with the language. We shall just mention them briefly here to acquaint you with their fundamental properties.

Sets A set (in Pascal) is a collection of data items with the following characteristics:

1. Members (elements) of a set all must belong to the same data type. The type from which a set's members are drawn is called the *base type*.
2. The REAL type cannot be used as a base type.
3. The number of elements in a set is not fixed. Sets may grow or shrink to fit the particular occasion at any instant. A set may be *empty* (i.e., it may have no values at all.)
4. Each eligible value may appear in a set only once.
5. Sets are manipulated in their entirety. Consequently, there is no explicit relationship between individual elements and respective locations.

A reference to a set is a reference to all the elements (if there are any) in that set at that time.

The definition of a set [Figure 5.7(b)] must show the values that are eligible for membership in that set. For example, the declaration

```
VAR
    winners  :  SET OF 10974, 20063, 41798, 62875
```

defines a set named winners with a base type of INTEGER. Thus, elements of winners must be INTEGER values, but not just any integers. Membership is restricted to the four values shown in the definition. winners could consist of any one of these values, any two of them, any three, all four, or none at all (the empty set). Similarly,

```
VAR
    lastsix  :  SET OF 'U'..'Z'
```

declares lastsix to be a set variable whose values could be any or all of the characters U, V, W, X, Y, Z, or empty.

Programmer-defined data types also may be used as elements in sets. Consider the following caloric example:

```
TYPE
    topping = (hotfudge, marshmallow, pineapple,
              butterscotch, nuts) ;
VAR
    goo  :  SET OF topping
```

This says that the variable goo is a set whose members may consist of any, all, or none of the five values listed for the enumerative type topping.

Set variables can be given values via simple assignments. Assuming the previous declarations of lastsix, the statement

```
lastsix := ['Z','W','X']
```

assigns the three characters 'Z', 'W', and 'X' to lastsix, replacing whatever may have been there before. The statement

```
lastsix := []
```

assigns the empty set to lastsix.

Records When it is convenient to organize a collection of data in which the individual items may be of different types, we do so by constructing a *record*. Each type of record to be used in a program is defined by a TYPE declaration whose syntax is shown in Figure 5.7(b). We shall defer the formal definition of a field list. The simple example in the next paragraph illustrates the most common type of field list construction.

For example, somebody's address could be constructed as a record. Let us say that the address consists of a street number (an integer up to five digits long), a street name (up to 20 characters long), a city (up to 20 characters long), a state (two characters long), and a zip code (for which we shall use five characters). The following declaration

```
address = RECORD
    streetnum   :   1..99999  ;
    streetname  :   STRING[20]  ;
    city        :   STRING[20]  ;
    state       :   STRING[2]  ;
    zipcode     :   '10000'..'99999'
END
```

defines a data type named address as consisting of the component shown. Each component in a record is called a *field*. Then, the declaration

```
VAR
    homeaddr, businessaddr  :   address
```

defines two record variables, each consisting of the five components listed in the TYPE declaration.

Each component of a record may be treated as if it were a single-valued variable of the particular data type. The WITH statement is used to avoid ambiguities that could arise because of the use of the same component name in different records. (For instance, homeaddr and businessaddr both have components named city.) If we write the following statement

```
WITH businessaddr DO
    BEGIN
        streetnum := 12  ;
        streetname := 'IMPORTANT AVE.'  ;
        city := 'UPWARD'  ;
        state := 'IL'  ;
        zipcode := '60094'
    END
```

there is no doubt that we are dealing with the components of businessaddr and not homeaddr. Another way to provide an unambiguous reference is to *qualify* a component's name by using the record's name as a prefix. Thus, the individual assignments

```
homeaddr,streetname := 'MAWKISH LANE' ;
businessaddr,streetname := 'IMPORTANT AVE,'
```

speak for themselves.

5.3.5 Dynamic Data Types

Pascal handles two other data types named *files* and *pointers* whose properties differ from those of types discussed so far. These are called *dynamic data types* to indicate that their *structures* (as well as their size) may change during the course of a program's execution. We already have an intuitive idea of what files are. Pointers are used to refer to variables for which storage is not allocated until the program runs and a particular instruction requests the creation of a variable. Uses of dynamic data types (and techniques for dealing with them) will be discussed later.

Problems

1. The values shown below may or may not be legal Pascal integer constants. Point out the illegal ones and indicate what is wrong with them:

    (a)   26.5   (d)   3,627
    (b)   −0   (e)   −48.0
    (c)   128   (f)   414−

2. The values shown below may or may not be legal Pascal real constants. Point out the illegal ones and indicate what is wrong with them:

    (a)   312.4   (k)   .2E3
    (b)   −7,08.8   (l)   −.2E3
    (c)   226.48426   (m)   −417.42E−4
    (d)   −5   (n)   27E−27
    (e)   680,449.320,447   (o)   8.0E.6
    (f)   −.8   (p)   E3
    (g)   .008   (q)   −3.16E−3.16
    (h)   0.0089   (r)   2.E+0
    (i)   1000.03−   (s)   2.0E+00
    (j)   2E3   (t)   17.17E−17
                            (u)   6E−.06

3. Specify the number of significant digits in each of the following values:

   (a) 36   (g) 81.264
   (b) −20   (h) 810.0264
   (c) 8000.0   (i) −0.00005712
   (d) 5.7   (j) 3.2E6
   (e) 57   (k) 871.8E−3
   (f) 0.000005700   (l) 2.1E+04

4. Express each of the following as a real constant in floating point using the text's standard form defined in Section 5.1.1, under *Real Numbers*.

   (a) −808   (g) 21573283.6
   (b) 41.4   (h) 3.1E−7
   (c) 21.8673   (i) 668 × 10
   (d) −.007414   (j) 0.000746E8
   (e) 365407.88   (k) 0.0004872E−02
   (f) −86E−2   (l) −41.04 × 10

5. Which of the following are illegal Pascal string constants? Why?
   (a) BRAN   (e) 'ALES"
   (b) '7..E'   (f) ST'B4'
   (c) 'A7..W'   (g) '. . . .'
   (d) 'E25W6J   (h) 'T"A"'
                           (i) '$@'E'+07'

6. Set up each of the following declarations:
   (a) Declare a real constant named gravity with a value of 32.164.
   (b) Declare an integer constant named upperlimit with a value of 208.
   (c) Declare three character constants named spaces, dashes, and dots with respective values of six blanks, four hyphens, and seven periods.
   (d) Declare two boolean constants named yessir and youbet, each with a value of TRUE.
   (e) Declare a real constant named duckbill with a value of 318000000, an integer constant named goornisht with a value of zero, and a character constant named empty with a value of the five characters 'EMPTY'.

7. Write declarations for each of the following:
   (a) A data type named tones consisting of the 12 notes in our musical system. (bflat is such a note.)

(b) A data type named homestyle consisting of the standard kinds of single-family dwellings. (ranch and capecod are examples.)

(c) A data type named mmmmm consisting of the flavors at your favorite ice cream parlor.

(d) A data type named melon consisting of the various kinds of melons commonly available.

(e) A data type named allplus consisting of all nonzero positive integers.

(f) A data type named starter consisting of the first eight letters of the alphabet.

(g) A data type named ranks consisting of the ranks (in order) in the United States Army, and a variable named brass (of type ranks) whose values are limited to second lieutenant and higher.

8. Write a declaration for each of the following:

(a) A 12-element array named act of real numbers indexed by integers from 1 through 12. Name the fifth element in the array.

(b) A 5-element array named wd of characters indexed by integers from 1 through 5. Name the second element in the array.

(c) A 26-element array named listwd of integers indexed by the characters 'A' through 'Z'. Assign a value of −8 to the ninth element.

(d) Declare an array of REAL values named freq indexed by the data type tones defined in Problem 7(a). How many elements are there in freq?

(e) Declare an array of characters named codes indexed by the starter data type defined for Problem 7(f). Write two assignment statements, the first of which places the character constant 'K' in the fourth element of codes, and the second of which copies the value from the fourth element into the sixth one.

(f) Declare an array of REAL numbers named bonus indexed by the data type ranks defined for Problem 7(g). Now write the statements necessary to assign a value of 540.75 to each element of the array. Declare any additional variables you may need.

(g) Using the array declaration prepared for the previous problem [8(f)], write the statements necessary to assign a value of 898.50 to those elements of bonus corresponding to second lieutenant and higher. Declare any additional variables you may need.

9. Write the necessary declaration(s) defining each of the following data types:

(a) evens, a set consisting of the first 12 positive even integers.

(b) psquares, a set consisting of the first 10 perfect squares.

(c) baseball, a set consisting of the nine fielding positions (e.g.,

b1 is first base, 1f is left field, etc.). The base type is named
positionb.

(d) football, a set consisting of the 11 traditional football positions (e.g., le is left end, rh is right halfback, etc.). The base
type is named positionf.

10. Write a sequence of statements to produce each of the following:

(a) Define a data type named cardvalue with values consisting of
the 13 types of playing cards (e.g., 2, 3, 4, . . ., 10, jack,
queen, king, ace). Then, using cardvalue as a base type,
construct three variables: allcards, a set consisting of all 13
cards; facecards, a set consisting of the high cards (10 and
up), and lowcards, a set consisting of cards 2 through 9.

(b) Using positionb and baseball from Problem 9(c), define
outf as a set consisting of the outfield positions, inf as a set
consisting of the infield positions, and btry as a set consisting
of the battery positions.

11. The East Poopik Symphony Society has launched its annual campaign and the contributions are pouring in. There are six categories
for such donations: groupie ($5), member ($25), fan ($50), pat-
ron ($100), pussycat ($500), and oboy ($1000). Each contribution
is recorded on a separate line consisting of the identification number
(an integer), and the amount (one of those given above). Write a
program that computes and prints the number of donors in each
category. Use an identification number of zero to terminate the run,
and print each category on a separate line. For example,

```
GROUPIES:      41
MEMBERS:      189
FANS:         212
```

After the final category, print a final line showing the total number of
donors and the total amount contributed.

12. Modify the program in Problem 11 to meet the following additional
requirement: The Society's ruling board has found out that they are
losing many contributions because people object to the predefined
amounts. To correct the situation, a new donor category has been
added: The freespirit category covers those contributors who
wish to give an amount other than those specified on the Society's
tasteful Donor Card Future Pledge Form and Raffle. Now, in addition
to the output specified before, the revised program is to produce a line
(after the oboy category) showing the number of donors in the
freespirit category, the total amount of their donations, and the
average donation size in this category. The last line still shows the
total number of donors (including freespirits) and the total

amount donated. The input does not change. (Remember that freespirits may donate amounts that are not whole dollars.)

13. I Scungili di Bensonhurst is a community basketball league consisting of six teams. The coaches, players, and fans are interested in statistics showing the performance at each position during each game. Accordingly, every time a game is played, the league prepares two cards (lines), one for each team. Each card (line) contains a collection of input data consisting of the game number (each game of the season is given a unique integer identification), the team number (the teams are numbered 1 through 6), and the number of points scored for each of the five positions. The points are listed in the following order: left guard, left forward, center, right forward, right guard. For example, the following input line

54   3   15   12   23   11   18

shows that during game number 54, Team 3's left guard(s) scored 15 points, 12 points were scored by the people playig left forward, the center position scored 23 points, the right forward position accounted for 11 points, and the right guard position added 18. Your program is to compute and print a line for each position showing the total number of points scored, and the average number scored (per game) for that position. Then, after those five lines of output, the program is to leave a blank line and print the overall statistics (the total number of points scored for all positions, along with the overall average points per game for an individual position). Use a team number of zero to terminate the run.

14. Define a record type for each of the following everyday data collections:
    (a) Your driver's license.
    (b) Your library card.
    (c) Your oil company credit card.
    (d) Your bank or American Express/Diner's Club credit card.
    (e) Your telephone bill.
    (f) The information on a postage stamp.
    (g) Your medical insurance card.
    (h) Your school registration card.
    (i) Your personal property tax form.
    (j) (Colossal challenge): The IRS Form 1040.

Chapter 6

Arithmetic in Pascal

Pascal does an excellent job of insulating the programmer from the machine's relatively limited scope of arithmetic capabilities. Extensive computations can be specified as expressions that resemble conventional algebraic formulas. As a result, we have been able to treat the construction and use of these arithmetic capabilities naturally. This chapter builds on our previous experience to present a more detailed picture of these features.

6.1 THE ASSIGNMENT STATEMENT

The power and flexibility of Pascal's assignment statement are hidden behind a deceptively innocent syntax. Before delving into the statement's marvelous properties, we shall make sure that the fundamental rules are clear.

6.1.1 Basic Syntax

As Figure 6.1 indicates, the assignment statement establishes a relationship between an expression that produces a value and a variable (called the *destination variable*) that receives the value. The operation, *assignment*, denoted by :=, transfers the value to its destination, replacing what was there before. Thus, in the statement

```
timer := 0
```

the value currently in the variable named timer is replaced by zero, the value of the expression on the right-hand side of the assignment operator. The zero, representing the simplest kind of expression (but an expression nevertheless), is just one instance of a pattern that enables us to build an endless variety of expressions (including rather complicated ones) while working within the same structural rules.

Replacement (or assignment) is a key concept here. Recall that we can make sense out of a statement like

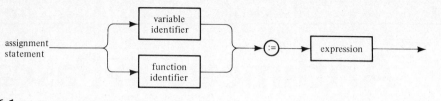

Figure 6.1

Assignment Statement Syntax

```
timer := timer + 1
```

by emphasizing the separation between replacement and computation. The expression describes a particular arithmetic task: Take the value in the variable named timer and add 1 to it, thereby producing a new value. Period. There is nothing in the *expression* to tell Pascal what happens next. That information is supplied by the replacement operator and the destination named to the left of the := operator. Thus, we can imagine that there is an instant, just before the replacement occurs, when timer still has its original value and the new value is suspended somewhere (in a temporary storage place) poised and ready, eager to be sent speeding homeward. This idea will make it easier to understand and use the concepts that follow.

6.1.2 Semantics of the Assignment Statement

The specifications at the bottom of Figure 6.1 tell us several things about the assignment statement that cannot be conveyed by the syntax:

1. When Pascal completes the computations specified by an expression, it produces a value of a particular data type. Selection of the result's data type is no accident; rather, it is determined by a set of internal rules applied to the ingredients of a particular expression. If that expression is constructed in violation of these rules, the computations cannot be performed.

2. The destination variable, too, has a specific data type, assigned as part of its declaration. Consequently, it has nothing to do with the data type of the value of an expression until the two are brought together in an assignment statement. The way an expression is evaluated and the nature of its result are not influenced by the destination variable.

3. When an expression is evaluated, there is no reason to expect that the data type of the resulting value will be the same as that of the destination variable. Consequently, the assignment operation requires more than a transfer of the expression's value to the destination. There must be an associated mechanism that examines the respective data types of the result and destination. If they are the same, the transfer proceeds

without further processing. If the data types differ, the appropriate data conversion takes place *if it can*, so that the data type of the value finally transferred matches that of the destination variable. Even if the expression itself is constructed in accordance with Pascal's rules, and the computations take place as specified, final assignment still may not occur because the result's data type cannot be converted to that of the destination. For example, the expression may produce a real numerical value and the destination variable may have been declared as a programmer-defined enumerative type. UCSD Pascal's compatibility rules for arithmetic assignment are summarized in Table 6.1

4. Compatibility of the two items on either side of the := operator also includes concern about whether the involved variables are scalar or not. For instance, the assignment will not work if the destination variable is a scalar variable and a variable in the expression refers to an array.

The next few sections will explore the rules governing the use of Pascal's arithmetic facilities and the construction of assignment statements specifying arithmetic computations.

6.2 BASIC ARITHMETIC OPERATIONS

Pascal deals with two sets of arithmetic operations: those performed on integers (producing integer results) and those performed on real numbers (producing real results). After examining these separately, we shall be ready to look at them in combination.

Table 6.1   Arithmetic Assignment Rules for UCSD Pascal

Data Type of Result	Data Type of Destination			
	Real	**Integer**	**Long Integer**	**Integer Subrange**
Real	no conversion necessary	illegal; compiler will reject	illegal; compiler will reject	illegal; compiler will reject
Integer	conversion will take place	no conversion necessary	acceptable if the expression is an integer constant; otherwise, result is uncertain	acceptable if the expression is a constant; otherwise, result is uncertain
Long integer	illegal; compiler will reject	illegal; compiler will reject	no conversion necessary	illegal; compiler will reject
Integer subrange	illegal; compiler will reject	illegal; compiler will reject	acceptable	no conversion necessary

6.2.1 Addition, Subtraction, and Multiplication

Addition, subtraction, and multiplication, denoted by +, –, and *, respectively, for both types of arithmetic are straightforward. Unlike conventional algebra, however, in Pascal multiplication always must be shown explicitly. Thus, if ʋ1, con, and pr are INTEGER variables, Pascal will reject

```
pr := conv1
```

or

```
pr := con v1
```

or

```
pr := con (v1)
```

The multiplication operator must be shown:

```
pr := con * v1
```

The same is true for multiplication of real numbers.

6.2.2 Division

Division receives special handling in Pascal.

Division of Real Values   The symbol / denotes real division. That means that both divisor and dividend have to be real values, and Pascal will produce a real result. Thus, if bflag and total are declared as REAL, the assignment

```
bflag := total/4
```

will not be accepted, whereas

```
bflag := total/4.0
```

will be all right.

Division of Integer Values   The symbol DIV specifies division of one integer by another, thereby producing an integer quotient. There is no remainder because there are no provisions for keeping one. Thus, the expression

```
18 DIV 20
```

causes a computation in which the integer 18 is divided by the integer 20, producing a quotient of zero. The remainder (0.9) is trekked off to a desolate tundra in the Yukon where it is unceremoniously dumped on a growing pile of remainders to be frozen and forgotten. A separate symbol is used for integer division to emphasize the different type of arithmetic. DIV works for long integers, but real values cannot be used with the DIV operator.

In many applications the remainder is not needed and integer division is used specifically to produce an integer quotient. (The process of removing the fractional part is called *truncation*.) However, Pascal provides an integer operation that makes the remainder available. No, it does not bring it back from the frozen wastes; the remainder is produced by a separate process using the MOD operation. For example, the expression

```
18 MOD 20
```

divides the integer 18 by the integer 20, producing a *remainder* expressed as an integer (18 in this case). With this operation, the quotient is discarded (scientists still have not figured out where it goes). Similarly, the expression

```
18 MOD 3
```

produces a remainder of zero, the amount left over when 18 is divided by 3. If we want to divide an integer value by another one and obtain both the quotient and remainder, it requires two operations. For example, if ttl, quot, and remain all are declared with type INTEGER, the sequence

```
quot := ttl DIV 9 ;
remain := ttl MOD 9
```

places the quotient in quot and the remainder in remain. Assuming a value of 34 for ttl, quot will receive a value of 3 and remain will be assigned a value of 7. The MOD function cannot be used with long integers.

6.2.3 Other Arithmetic Operations

The basic operations discussed in the previous sections are supplemented by a collection of standard *built-in functions*. Each of these permanently installed subprograms provides a mathematical process made to appear (to the programmer) as a single arithmetic operation. Examples of such functions, i.e., SQR and SQRT, were seen earlier, and others will be discussed in the next chapter.

6.3 CONSTRUCTION OF ARITHMETIC EXPRESSIONS

The arithmetic expressions we have used thus far have been rather simple, so that we have been able to write them intuitively. When it comes to more ambitious computations, it will be necessary to become familiar with Pascal's rules of construction.

Starting with a general syntactic definition [Figure 6.2(a)], we classify an expression as being either a simple expression or a comparison expression. A simple expression, in turn, is categorized as being either an arithmetic expression or a simple boolean expression [Figure 6.2(b)]. We shall be concerned in this chapter with arithmetic expressions. Accordingly, we define the arithmetic expression as shown in Figure 6.2(c).

Recall the simple assignment statement in Section 6.1.1:

```
timer := 0
```

Comparison of the expression (0) with Figure 6.2(c) identifies the zero as a single arithmetic term. The second assignment statement in that section, namely,

```
timer := timer + 1
```

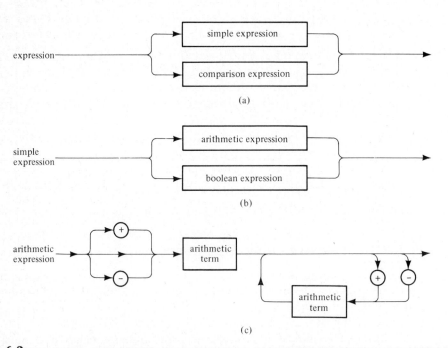

(a)

(b)

(c)

Figure 6.2

General Characterization of Pascal Expressions

has an expression (timer +1) that follows the alternative loop in Figure 6.2(c): There are two arithmetic terms (timer and 1) connected by the + operator.

6.3.1 Arithmetic Terms

Figure 6.3 shows the construction of an arithmetic term. We see that, in its most elementary form, an arithmetic term can consist of a single arithmetic factor. This is exactly the case with each of the terms in the two expressions just examined. The zero in the first assignment statement, for instance, is an arithmetic expression consisting of a single arithmetic term, and that term consists of a single arithmetic factor. In other words, the zero, in this particular appearance, is a factor, a term, and a complete expression. On the other hand, timer and 1 in the second statement each are terms consisting of a single factor. That is, timer is both a term and a factor, and the same is true for the 1. The two of them, brought together by the +, form a complete arithmetic expression. Now, we can take a look at an expression such as

```
18 DIV 20
```

in light of what Figure 6.3 shows. We see that the 18 and the 20 are *not* individual arithmetic terms. Instead, each is an arithmetic factor and the two of them, when connected by the DIV operator, form a single arithmetic term. Note (from Figures 6.2 and 6.3) that the + and − operators connect terms while the *, /, and DIV operators connect factors.

6.3.2 Arithmetic Factors

For convenience, arithmetic factors are classified in Figure 6.4(a) as simple arithmetic factors and extended arithmetic factors. We shall limit our present discussion to the simple arithmetic factors. The extended possibilities will be introduced at appropriate points later on. The first two possibilities in Figure 6.4(b) are already familiar. Now, when we see a statement

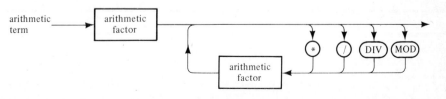

Figure 6.3

Construction of an Arithmetic Term

such as

```
adj := x - y + 6*wrth
```

we can recognize that the expression consists of three terms: x, y, and 6*wrth. x and y are factors, and the 6*wrth consists of the two factors 6 and wrth.

The third possibility will be explored in more detail in the next chapter, but some initial discussion is appropriate here. An example of this kind of factor is

```
SQRT (225)
```

We know from Chapter 3 that the activity triggered by this reference causes the built-in function SQRT to work on the value 225 and to deliver its square root to the expression in which it is used. The value thus delivered is just another factor in that expression. (Of course, it may be the only factor in the expression, but it is a factor in any case.) The component inside the

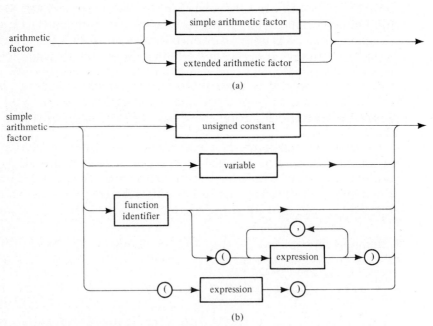

(a)

(b)

Semantics: The data type of the destination (variable or function identifier) must be compatible with that of the value of the expression.

Figure 6.4

Syntax for a Factor

parentheses is designated as an expression, thereby allowing such usage as

`SQRT (x + 3 * y)`

or even

`SQRT (x + 3 * SQRT (y))`

This usage is clear enough. However, the designation of an expression as a possible component of a factor raises a peculiar issue: If we work our way back through the series of syntactic definitions in Figures 6.4, 6.3, and 6.2, we remind ourselves that this whole discussion started with the decomposition of an arithmetic expression into terms and, ultimately, into factors. This leaves us with the seemingly awkward situation in which an expression is defined (ultimately) as being part of itself. This is another instance of a recursive definition. By the time we find that a factor can be built by attaching a parenthesized expression to a function name, we already know enough ways of building complete expressions so that the definition makes sense.

The fourth possibility in Figure 6.4 simply indicates that an expression can be enclosed in parentheses to form a factor for potential use in a more complicated expression. When we discuss Pascal's arithmetic rules in the next section, we shall see that the characterization of a parenthesized expression as a factor fits nicely with those rules.

6.4 PASCAL'S RULES FOR DOING ARITHMETIC

There is virtually no practical limit to the length or complexity of arithmetic expressions in Pascal. Yet, the Pascal compiler must be prepared to handle any and all such expressions properly. The only way this can be assured is to define a set of carefully constructed rules that govern Pascal's behavior and to design the compiler so that these rules are followed to the last detail. This section examines the rules and applies them to a variety of situations.

6.4.1 Use of Real and Integer Values in Arithmetic Expressions

Arithmetic expressions can be built from a mixture of REAL and INTEGER values. When a computation is to be performed with two different types of numbers, Pascal will convert the INTEGER value to REAL. For example, if `pwr` is declared as REAL, the expression

`2 * pwr`

will cause Pascal to convert the 2 into an equivalent REAL factor (2.0) for use in the multiplication. The result of the multiplication will be a REAL value that is available for further arithmetic or assignment, depending on the contents of the rest of the statement. In general, Pascal is designed to take a safe approach. Consequently, arithmetic operations with mixed values cause conversion from INTEGER to REAL rather than the other way around. Thus, the expression

```
2 * pwr - 8
```

forces Pascal to convert the 2 to a REAL value. The multiplication then produces a REAL result. Before the subtraction takes place, the 8 is converted to REAL. Thus, the final value of the expression is REAL even though two of the three original values were INTEGER.

As Section 6.2.2 pointed out under *Division of Integer Values*, there are two exceptions to the use of mixed arithmetic values: The DIV and MOD operations require INTEGER values. However, an INTEGER term still can be part of a legitimate arithmetic expression containing REAL terms. For instance, the expression

```
3.6 * pwr + 28 DIV 17 - 5.5
```

consists of three terms: the REAL term obtained by multiplying the two REAL factors 3.6 and pwr; the INTEGER term obtained when 28 is divided by 17; and the REAL term consisting of the single factor 5.5. In order to complete the computations, Pascal will convert the INTEGER quotient (1) to REAL (1.0), so that the final result will be REAL.

6.4.2 Precedence of Arithmetic Operations

In order to process arithmetic expressions consistently, Pascal follows a set of rules that define the relative priorities of the various arithmetic operations. These rules, called *precedence rules*, force Pascal to perform certain operations before others. The scheme is as follows:

1. Computations are performed from left to right. It is possible for Pascal to get to the end of an expression without having completed the computations. When this happens, the left-to-right tour is repeated as many times as necessary.
2. Multiplication and division (*, /, DIV, and MOD) are processed before addition (+) and subtraction (−).
3. Addition and subtraction are performed last.

Thus, in the expression

```
pwr - res/ind * ext + plc
```

the evaluation proceeds as follows (assume all variables are REAL):

1. res is divided by ind, producing a REAL result. For convenience, let us call that intermediate result result1.
2. result1 is multiplied by ext, producing another partial result. Let us call that result result2.
3. Pascal, reaching the end of the expression and finding no more multiplication or division to perform, goes back and starts again. The work left to be done is

    ```
    pwr - result2 + plc
    ```

    Accordingly the next operation is pwr − result2, producing a REAL value which we shall call result3. (Temporary storage for this value is handled automatically, as it is for all intermediate results.)
4. Finally, result3 and plc are added together to produce the final value.

These rules make it awkward to write certain kinds of expressions. For instance, the simple algebraic expression

$$\frac{a - b}{c + d}$$

would cause some inconvenience if additional tools were not available. This shortcoming is remedied through the use of parentheses, as the next section shows.

6.4.3 Parentheses in Arithmetic Expressions

Pascal is designed so that the programmer can use parentheses "naturally." That is, parentheses can help divide an expression into easily recognizable components that establish the overall meaning simply and clearly. As Figure 6.4 indicates, an expression enclosed in parentheses becomes a factor in a larger expression. This means that by putting parentheses around a group of terms or factors, we can force Pascal to pay attention to the parenthesized material and perform the computations described there ahead of others. Stated another way, *expressions in parentheses receive highest priority, ahead of multiplication and division.* To illustrate, suppose a, b, c, and d all were declared as REAL. The expression

```
a - b/c + d
```

is processed according to Pascal's arithmetic rules:

1. Pascal does a left-to-right tour looking for parentheses. Finding none, it goes back and starts again.

2. The division b/c is performed. Let us call the temporary result r1.

3. Finding no more multiplications or divisions, Pascal starts a new tour.

4. Pascal does a − r1, and a new result (call it r2) is produced.

5. Finally, r2 and d are added to develop the final expression value.

Now, let us see the effect of parentheses. If we modify the expression so that it says

```
(a - b) / (c + d)
```

the evaluation will proceed differently, even though the same rules are followed:

1. Pascal, finding a parenthesized expression, will produce a value for *that* expression, following the same rules it always does. In this case, the expression consists only of two terms. Thus, the subtraction a − b will be performed, producing a temporary result we shall call d1.

2. Continuing on its tour, Pascal finds another parenthesized expression. Accordingly, it applies its rules to that expression until its computations are completed. Here again, there are only two terms, so that a single tour takes care of it. The addition c + d is performed, leaving a temporary result we shall call d2.

3. Working with the modified expression

```
d1 / d2
```

Pascal starts a new tour. The remaining division is performed, producing the final result.

Note that the parentheses enabled Pascal to perform addition and subtraction before it did the multiplication.

Pascal will accept parentheses even when they are not needed. For instance, the expressions

```
a - b/c + d     and     a - (b/c) + d
```

produce exactly the same results. Consequently, if there is even the slightest doubt about how Pascal will handle a particular expression, it is a good idea to remove that doubt by using parentheses.

Parenthesized expressions may be placed inside other parenthesized expressions. (This is implied by Figure 6.4, but you have to stare at it a little while to see why: Since an entire expression can be placed inside parentheses, one of the factors in *that* expression can itself be a parenthesized expression.) This type of construction is called *nesting*, and it may be used to any extent desired. Thus, an expression such as

```
4.11 * (a + b * (c - 6)) / (SQRT (8.7 * (a + c)) - b)
```

is acceptable. (If you look back in Section 6.3.2, you will note that nested parentheses were used in an expression in which SQRT was used twice. No emphasis was necessary since such usage is "natural" and easy to follow.)

6.4.4 Example 6.1

We shall illustrate some simple arithmetic by writing a program that reads a sequence of four-digit positive integer values. Each value is to be displayed on a separate line. If at least one of the digits in a particular value is a 7, the message SPECIAL VALUE is to be displayed alongside the value. After all the values have been processed, the program is to a leave a blank line and display the number of values read and the number of special values. 7028, 1720, and 2177 are examples of special values. The EOF function (see Example 4.2) will be used to terminate the run.

The program's structure is straightforward (Figure 6.5). We need call attention only to the use of the DIV and MOD operations to isolate a value's individual digits: If tvalue is such a value, then

```
tvalue  MOD  10
```

gives us its rightmost digit. By assigning that to some other variable, we can make it available for subsequent processing. On the other hand,

> Define value, tvalue, numvalues, numspecials, digit.
> Initialize numvalues, numspecials.
> Read the first input value.
> *While* there still are input data to process, *Do:*
>   Add 1 to numvalues.
>   *If*
>   any of value's digits is 7
>   *Then*
>   Add 1 to numspecials.
>   Display value and message: SPECIAL VALUE.
>   *Else*
>   Display value.
>   *Endif*
>   Read the next value.
> *Endwhile*
> Display numvalues and numspecials.
> Stop.

Figure 6.5

Pseudocode Description for Example 6.1

```
tvalue := tvalue  DIV  10
```

removes the rightmost digit and places what is left back in t v a l u e. Thus, by applying these two operations, we have the basis for a mechanism for extracting and examining an integer's individual digits. The Pascal statements for this program are given in Figure 6.6.

```
(************************************************************)
(**                   EXAMPLE 6.1                        **)
(************************************************************)
(** VALUE IS A 4-DIGIT POSITIVE INPUT VALUE;             **)
(** TVALUE IS A TEMPORARY WORK AREA FOR VALUE;           **)
(** NUMVALUES AND NUMSPECIALS ARE COUNTERS FOR INPUT VALUES **)
(** DIGIT IS AN INDIVIDUAL DIGIT EXTRACTED FROM VALUE.   **)
(** SIGNAL IS FALSE IF VALUE IS NOT SPECIAL, TRUE IF IT IS. **)
(** NOTE THAT SIGNAL IS INITIALIZED TO FALSE FOR EACH VALUE. **)
(************************************************************)
PROGRAM ex601  ;
CONST
   zero = 0 ;      seven = 7 ;      ten = 10 ;
VAR
   value, tvalue, numvalues, numspecials, digit  :  INTEGER    ;
   signal  :  BOOLEAN  ;
BEGIN
   numvalues := zero ;    numspecials := zero ;
   WRITELN ('ENTER FIRST VALUE.') ;
   READLN (value) ;
   WHILE  NOT EOF(INPUT)  DO
      BEGIN
         tvalue  := value ;
         numvalues := numvalues + 1   ;
         signal := FALSE  ;
         WHILE tvalue <> zero DO
            BEGIN
               digit := tvalue  MOD  ten  ;
               tvalue := tvalue  DIV  ten  ;
               IF
                  digit = seven
               THEN
                  BEGIN
                     signal := TRUE  ;
                     numspecials := numspecials + 1 ;
                     tvalue := zero
                  END
               ELSE
            END  ;
```

Figure 6.6

Program for Example 6.1

```
        IF
            signal = TRUE
        THEN
            WRITELN (value,'  SPECIAL VALUE')
        ELSE
            WRITELN ('VALUE: ',value)  ;
        WRITELN ('ENTER NEXT VALUE.')  ;
        READLN (value)
    END  ;
  WRITELN ('          ')  ;
  WRITELN ('NO. OF ITEMS PROCESSED:  ',numvalues)  ;
  WRITELN ('NO. OF SPECIAL VALUES:  ',numspecials)
END .
```

Figure 6.6

Program for Example 6.6 (Continued)

Problems

1. Assume the following declarations:

```
CONST
  maxdev = 20   ;
  refr = 8.5 ;
TYPE
  indic = 1..maxdev  ;
VAR
  cl1, cl2, cl3      :    ARRAY [indic] OF REAL  ;
  txr, swb, yval     :    REAL  ;
  num, nval, amt     :    INTEGER  ;
  d11                :    INTEGER [10]  ;
  u, v, g            :    indic
      ...
```

Assuming further that each of the variables has a value, indicate which of the following statements are illegal and show why:

(a) `txr := txr + swb`
(b) `refr := refr - 0.2`
(c) `num := num + indic + maxdev * v`
(d) `u := v - g DIV u`
(e) `v := maxdev * g DIV v`
(f) `swb := maxdev * g DIV v`
(g) `yval := refr * maxdev DIV txr`
(h) `v+g := yval - txr`
(i) `txr := maxdev * txr`
(j) `u,g := maxdev`

```
(k)  yval := num/amt + refr
(l)  dl2 := refr
(m)  dl3 := dl2/cl1[v]
(n)  cl2[maxdev] := yval - refr
(o)  u := num + cl1
(p)  num := num + amt(nval + maxdev)
(q)  amt := cl1[v] + cl2[u]
(r)  txr := swb * (num + nval)/yval
(s)  swb := (cl1[txr] + refr)/yval
(t)  cl1[v] := maxdev * (yval+/swb)
(u)  cl2[yval] := refr * (cl1[u] -
     refr * (cl3[u] + swb))/(g*txr)
(v)  swb := (maxdev + 4)*(refr-
     (nval DIV num)*(cl2[u] + v*cl3[v])))
```

2. Using the declarations given in Problem 1, write a Pascal expression for each of the following algebraic expressions:

(a) $\dfrac{amt}{nval} - r$

(b) $\dfrac{num}{amt + 4}$

(c) $txr(yval) - refr$

(d) $uvg(txr + amt)$

(e) $nval\left(\dfrac{u}{v} - \dfrac{num + tant}{txr}\right)$

(f) $\dfrac{refr}{10.2}\left(\dfrac{u + txr + v}{g(num + 2)} + maxdev\right)$

(g) $\dfrac{txr + refr}{v}\left(\dfrac{num\left(amt - g\left(v + \dfrac{u - 6}{nval + 3}\right)\right)}{(swb - refr)\left(\dfrac{g + v}{yval(u + 5)}\right)}\right)$

3. List the factors and terms for each of the expressions developed for Problem 2. (Note: Some of the terms may also be factors.)
4. Indicate the data type for the result in each of the expressions in Problem 2.

5. Using the declarations from Problem 1, assume the following values:

    0.1, 0.5, and 0.8 for txr, swb and yval, respectively;
    2, 6, and 17 for num, nval and amt, respectively;
    3, 5, and 12 for u, v and g, respectively.

    Indicate the value produced for each of the following:

    (a) txr * swb
    (b) txr * (swb + u)
    (c) u * (maxdev + v DIV g)
    (d) (swb + yval) / (refr * txr)
    (e) (u + v) DIV (maxdev - g) * txr
    (f) g - (maxdev * txr) / (num + nval * g DIV v)
    (g) (amt DIV (num + nval - maxdev) + txr
          * amt) / yval * nval
    (h) num * ((txr - u) - (refr *
          (nval + g DIV u)) * (swb + num))

6. Expand the program in Example 6.1 so that it computes and displays the sum of the digits for each input value in addition to the information already being produced. (For instance, if the input value is 4365, the sum of its digits is 18.)

7. Revise the program in Example 6.1 or in Problem 6 so that it displays the message SPECIAL VALUE next to the value if it has exactly one 7 in it, and it displays the message EXTRA SPECIAL VALUE next to the value if it has two or more 7s in it. Thus, 4070 is a special value, but 7074 and 7877 are extra special values. Indeed they are.

8. Input for this problem consists of an unknown number of 3-digit positive integer values. Write a program that counts the number of values in which the middle digit is numerically equivalent to the sum of the outer two. For example, the numbers 264 and 880 are such values while 212 and 074 are not. Display each input value on a separate line. If a particular value meets the criterion described above, display the message SPECIAL VALUE on the same line. After the last value has been processed (use a value of zero to terminate the run), display the number of special values.

9. Expand the program in Problem 8 so that, in addition to displaying the number of special values, the program displays the largest special value encountered during the run, the smallest special value, and the average special value.

10. Suppose startval is the original dollar value of a product (to the nearest cent), and salvageval is the salvage value. When the

straight line depreciation method is applied over nyrs years, the yearly decrease in value is

$$\frac{startval - salvageval}{nyrs}$$

Write a program that reads a sequence of input groups, each group consisting of startval, nyrs, and salvageval. For each group, the program is to display a line showing the input data. This is followed by a line for each year showing the year number and the (depreciated) value of the product at the end of that year. Use a startval of zero to terminate the run.

11. Another way to compute depreciation is based on the assumption that a product, starting with a value of startval, loses a constant percentage of its current value each year until it reaches salvageval. For instance, if startval is 5000.00 and the fractional loss per year is 0.1 (i.e., 10%), then the loss over the first year is 10% of 5000.00 or 500.00. Thus, the value at the end of the first year is 4500.00. The loss over the second year is 10% of 4500.00 or 450.00, so that the product has a value of 4050.00 going into the third year, and so on. Write a program that reads and processes a series of input groups where each input group consists of startval, lossrate (expressed as a fraction), nyrs, and salvageval. For each input group, the program is to display a line repeating the input data. After that, it is to display a line for each of the nyrs years showing the year number and the (depreciated) value of the product at the end of that year. You may assume that nyrs always will be small enough so that the depreciated value will not fall below lossrate*startval. Terminate your run as in Problem 10.

12. Modify the program in Problem 10 so that it does not make any assumptions about nyrs. Specifically, this version must regulate the computations so that, if necessary, it cuts them off when the current (depreciated) value falls below lossrate*startval. For instance, if startval is 100.00 and lossrate is .2, the computations should be stopped as soon as the current value falls below .2*100.00 or 20.00.

13. Modify the program from either Problem 10 or Problem 11 so that it will produce one of two types of output for each input group: Depending on the contents of that input group, the program will display a year-by-year report as before, or it will display only one line (after the input values are repeated) showing the depreciated value after nyrs have gone by. Include comments in your program specifying the input requirements for each option.

14. A popularly held (though unproven) belief is that every positive even number can be expressed as a sum of two prime numbers. (For instance, 28 = 23 + 5, or 62 = 59 + 3). Write a program that reads in successive integer values (one per line). For each integer read, the program is to produce a line of output consisting of the input value followed by two prime numbers whose sum equals that of the input value. If a particular value is not a positive even number, the program is to display a line showing the value followed by the message THIS VALUE IS INAPPROPRIATE. After the last value has been processed, the program is to leave a blank line and then display the total number of input values, the number of values processed, and the number of values rejected as being inappropriate.

15. If we plot two points on rectangular coordinates (Figure 5.7), we can describe their positions in terms of their coordinates $(x1, y1)$ and $(x2, y2)$. Then, if we draw a straight line through those points, that line can be described in terms of its slope $a1$ and intercept $a0$ as defined by the equations in Figure 6.7. Write a program that reads a succession of input values. Each group consists of four coordinate values: $(x1, y1)$ and $(x2, y2)$ in that order, with all four values appearing on a single line. For each group read, the program is to display two lines of output. The first repeats the input values, and the second gives the slope and intercept of the resulting straight line. You may assume that the points in each input pair will have different Y-coordinates. Run your program with the following input:

```
1.00    1.00    2.00    2.00
    1.00    2.00    2.00    4.00
       -8.5   2.5    1.5    -3.5
          3.8   6.75   8.5   3.25
```

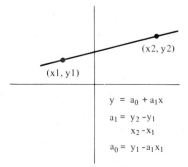

$(x2, y2)$

$(x1, y1)$

$$y = a_0 + a_1 x$$

$$a_1 = \frac{y_2 - y_1}{x_2 - x_1}$$

$$a_0 = y_1 - a_1 x_1$$

Figure 6.7

Straight-line Equation from Two Points

16. Revise the program in Problem 15 so that it no longer makes the assumption specified there. Include the following test data in your run:

```
1.00      3.00      1.00      7.85
   -5.00      2.00      5.00      2.00
```

17. Expand the program from Problem 15 or 16 as follows: Each input group now consists of six values describing three points. The order is (x1,y1), (x2,y2), and (x3,y3). For each group processed, display two lines: The first line shows the input values. The second line shows the slope and intercept for the straight line through (x1,y1) and (x2,y2) as before. In addition, the program is to display one of two messages on that second line: If the third point lies on the line drawn through the first two, the message is to say POINT 3 LIES ON THE LINE. If not, the message is to say POINT 3 DOES NOT LIE ON THE LINE.

18. *Special Challenge:* Revise the program for Program 17 so that each input group consists of a line giving (x1,y1) and (x2,y2), followed by an unknown number of lines, each one containing a third point (x3,y3). For each group, the first line of output shows (x1,y1) and (x2,y2). Then, for each additional point processed, the program is to display a line showing that point's coordinates and one of the two messages specified in Problem 17, depending on whether that point fell on the line described by (x1,y1) and (x2,y2). Thus, there will be a sequence of third points to test against a particular line. After that sequence has been processed (it will be up to you to determine how to detect the end of such a sequence), the program is to read in the next set of (x1,y1) and (x2,y2) values and go through the process again with a new collection of third points.

Chapter 7

Extended Arithmetic with Built-In Functions

UCSD Pascal's basic arithmetic operations are supplemented by a collection of built-in functions, each of which allows the programmer to treat a relatively complicated arithmetic process as if it were a single operation. This facility makes it easier to express extensive computations in terms that are close to conventional mathematical notation, so that the resulting programs convey their intent directly and clearly. Since no collection of built-in functions can be complete, these are designed to serve as manageable building blocks for more complex computations in addition to providing commonly used facilities on their own. This chapter examines Pascal's arithmetic functions and some of the computational opportunities that they present.

7.1 "EQUAL" VALUES ARE NOT ALWAYS EQUAL

Before discussing the various computational aids provided by UCSD's Pascal's arithmetic functions, we shall introduce an important hazard of computer arithmetic so that it can be recognized and avoided.

There are times when a simple computation will produce a result that is not exactly right. An answer that is supposed to come out 8.7 may be 8.6999998 instead. "Big deal," you say. In human terms, the difference may be nothing to get excited about, and we can decide that 8.6999998 is "the same as" 8.7. However, when this small discrepancy occurs as part of an automatic computation, there is no one there to make such a judgment. As far as the computer is concerned, 8.6999998 definitely is *not* the same as 8.7. Consequently, if `result` is a computed REAL value, a simple test such as

```
IF result = 8.7 THEN ...
```

will fail more often than we think it will because of small differences that *we* would be willing to overlook. Similarly, two variables (one of them read and the other computed, let us say) may be "equal" for our purposes, but they will fail a test for equality because of a difference in the last place.

   We cannot do anything about the machine's arithmetic. However, we can adjust the way we specify arithmetic to force actions that will avoid these effects. Some programming languages are designed to do this for us automatically; Pascal is not. The next section describes built-in functions that help support computational adjustments.

7.2 COMPUTATIONAL FUNCTIONS

7.2.1 The ABS Function

This function simply delivers the absolute value of its single REAL or INTEGER argument. Thus, ABS(−87.4) is 87.4 and ABS(518) is 518. One way to overcome the effects of the uninvited small differences discussed in the previous section is to define a range within which such differences can be ignored. For example, suppose we have a program in which a REAL value htloss is computed. A certain action is to be taken when htloss is equal to some value critval. We are willing to accept a value as high as critval+.0002 or as low as critval−.0002 as being "equal to" critval. The ABS function gives us a convenient way of specifying this range as part of a test:

```
IF ABS(htloss-critval) <= 0.0002 THEN
    action1
ELSE
    action2
```

Of course, the acceptable range would be defined to suit each situation.

7.2.2 The ROUND Function

The ROUND function brings a real value to the nearest integer. Thus, ROUND(83.7) produces 84, and ROUND(83.4) produces 83. By combining this function with some simple computations, we can provide a powerful facility for controlling computational results.

   For example, suppose we were performing the following computation. (Assume all the variables are REAL):

```
newbal := oldbal + oldbal*rate*time
```

newbal represents an amount of money to be displayed to the nearest cent. One effective way to do this is to round newbal to two places after it has been computed. However, since the ROUND function produces only an integer, it cannot be used directly. Instead, we multiply by one hundred, apply the ROUND function, and then divide by one hundred to obtain the proper value. To illustrate, suppose the value in newbal is 4207.8096247. If we apply ROUND directly, i.e.,

```
newbal := ROUND(newbal)
```

the function produces a value of 4208. Since the rounded value is to be assigned to newbal (which is REAL), the program converts the 4208 to 4208.0000000 and stores *that* value in newbal. This is not what we want. Instead, we can write

```
newbal := ROUND(newbal * 100.0)/100.0
```

First, newbal is multiplied by 100.0 to produce an intermediate value of 420780.9624700. Next, that value is rounded, resulting in 420781, the nearest integer. Then, division by 100.0 forces reconversion (to 420781.0000000) and this value, when divided by 100.0, produces 4207.8100000.

The same general technique can be used to round to some other desired number of places. For example, if we wanted to round newbal to the nearest dime, we would multiply and divide by 10.

7.2.3 The TRUNC Function

Another mechanism for computational control is the TRUNC function. As its name implies, it truncates to the nearest integer. Thus,

```
TRUNC(4207.8096247)
```

produces 4207 (recall that ROUND(4207.8096247) produces 4208) whereas TRUNC(396.4721408) and ROUND (396.4721408) both produce 396. TRUNC (–4207.8096247) produces –4207. (This function also can be used with a long integer argument to convert the value to regular integer form as long as the argument's value is between -MAXINT and MAXINT.

7.2.4 The ODD Function

This function provides a convenient way of determining whether an integer value is odd. ODD *(value)* produces a value of TRUE if *value* is odd; a value of FALSE is produced when *value* is even. Thus, the expression ODD (717) produces a value of TRUE.

7.3 ALGEBRAIC FUNCTIONS

Six of USCD Pascal's functions provide convenient mechanisms for specifying common algebraic operations.

7.3.1 The EXP, LN, and LOG Functions

Each of these functions uses a REAL or INTEGER value (submitted as a constant, variable, or expression) to produce a REAL value. The value given to the EXP function is used as an exponent to produce the value of e (the base of natural logarithms) raised to that exponent. Thus, EXP(2) = e^2 = 7.3890560, and EXP(−1.92) = $e^{-1.92}$ = 0.1466069.

LN (*value*) and LOG (*value*), respectively, produce the natural and common logarithms of *value*. The programmer must make sure that the argument to the log functions is greater than zero. If it is not, the program will stop and an error message will be displayed.

7.3.2 The PWROFTEN Function

This function takes an INTEGER argument and raises 10 to that power. The result is returned as a REAL value. Thus, PWROFTEN (4) returns the value 1.00000E4.

7.3.3 The SQRT and SQR Functions

SQRT is familiar and needs no further discussion except for one thing: It is up to the programmer to make sure that the argument given to SQRT is (or works out to be) a positive value or zero. A negative value causes an error message to be displayed, and processing terminates. As seen earlier, SQR computes the square of the REAL or INTEGER value given to it.

7.3.4 Exponentiation

We can use USCD Pascal's algebraic functions to raise a numerical value other than 10 to a specified power. For instance, suppose we wanted to raise 3.54 to the 1.76th power and store the result in REAL variable mpr. A convenient way to do this would be by combining the EXP and LN functions:

```
mpr := EXP(1.76 * LN(3.54))
```

Similarly, if we want to raise the term bxt−1 to the (n+4)th power and assign the result to xpn, we would say

```
xpn := EXP((n+4) * LN(bxt-1))
```

In certain special situations, it is more desirable to compute exponents another way. One frequently occurring circumstance involves the computation of the polynomial P where

$$P = A_0 + A_1X + A_2X^2 + A_3X^3 + \ldots + A_nX^n$$

This formula can be rewritten as follows:

$$P = A_0 + X(A_1 + X(A_2 + X(A_3 + \ldots)) \ldots)$$

If we were to complete the process of factorization for a fourth-order polynomial (N=4), we would get

$$P = A0 + X(A1 + X(A2 + X(A3 + X(A4))))$$

This formulation, called *Horner's method*, provides us with a computational approach for polynomials that is less complicated than the more general method using EXP and LN. To use it, we create a data structure in which the coefficients A0, A1, etc. are represented as an array. IF eqdegree is the degree of the polynomial (let us say that eqdegree is 6), Horner's method can be specified as shown in Figure 7.1:

```
CONST
    eqdegree = 6  ;
VAR
    i         :  INTEGER  ;
    poly, x   :  REAL  ;
    a         :  ARRAY [0..eqdegree] OF REAL  ;
            . . . . . . . . . . . . . . . . .
            . . . . . . . . . . . . . . . . .
(***   IN CHAPTER 5 WE INTRODUCED THE FOR STATEMENT AS ***)
(***   A WAY TO REPEAT A LOOP A CONTROLLED NUMBER OF    ***)
(***   TIMES. THE STATEMENT ENABLES US TO INITIALIZE    ***)
(***   AN INDEX VARIABLE, AFTER WHICH PASCAL AUTOMA-    ***)
(***   TICALLY ADDS 1 TO IT EACH TIME THROUGH THE LOOP.***)
(***   WE CAN INITIALIZE AN INDEX VARIABLE AND FORCE    ***)
(***   PASCAL TO SUBTRACT 1 FROM IT EACH TIME BY USING ***)
(***   THE PASCAL WORD DOWNTO. THUS, THE FOLLOWING LOOP***)
(***   STARTS WITH 1 SET TO NUMCOEFF. THEN, AFTER EACH ***)
(***   TRIP THROUGH THE LOOP, I IS REDUCED BY 1.        ***)
    poly := 0  ;
    FOR i := eqdegree DOWNTO 1 DO
        poly := x * (poly + a[i])  ;
    poly := poly + a[0]
            . . . . . . . . . . . . . . . . . . . . .
            . . . . . . . . . . . . . . . . . . . . .
```

Figure 7.1 ─────────────────────────────────

Horner's Method for a Polynomial with Seven Coefficients

7.3.5 Trigonometric Functions

UCSD Pascal includes three built-in functions for fundamental trigonometric computations: SIN *(value)* computes the sine of *value*, and COS *(value)* produces the cosine of *value*. The argument for either function may be REAL or INTEGER, and both functions expect their respective arguments to be in radians. Thus, if we wanted the sine of 31 degrees, we could request it by specifying

```
CONST
  Pi = 3.14159
    .
    .
    .
  sinofx := SIN(31*Pi/180.0)
```

Similarly, if xdeg is an angle in degrees and we want its tangent, we might convert to radians and store the result in a separate variable xrad and then compute the tangent:

```
xrad := xdeg*Pi/180.0  ;
tanofx := SIN(xrad)/COS(xrad)
```

Other basic trigonometric functions are readily computed from SIN and COS.

A single function, ARCTAN (also known in UCSD Pascal as ATAN), provides access to the inverse trigonometric computations. ARCTAN uses the REAL or INTEGER argument submitted to it to compute a REAL value representing an angle in radians. Computation of the inverse tangent in degrees, then, could proceed as shown below, assuming the earlier declaration for Pi:

```
xrad := ARCTAN (x) ;
xdeg := xrad*180.0/Pi
```

Since xdeg is a REAL value, the angle thus represented is expressed in degrees and fractions of a degree. Consequently, transformation of the fractional part to minutes (if that is desired) involves a separate step but a simple one:

```
xminutes := ROUND((xdeg - TRUNC(xdeg))*60.0)
```

Other inverse trigonometric functions are computed easily enough starting with ARCTAN. For instance, if sinval contains a REAL value and we want its inverse sine in a variable named myangle, we can obtain it by specifying

```
myangle := ARCTAN(sinval/SQRT(1.0-SQR(sinval)))
```

Similarly, if `cosval` is a `REAL` variable whose inverse cosine is to be assigned to `yourangle`, the computation is

```
yourangle := ARCTAN(SQRT(1.0-SQR(cosval))/cosval)
```

7.3.6 Hyperbolic Functions

UCSD Pascal provides no built-in facilities for the direct computation of hyperbolic functions. However, their computation from available functions is straightforward enough. For instance, if `x` is a `REAL` variable whose hyperbolic sine we want in `hypsin`, the appropriate computation would be

```
hypsin := 0.5 * (EXP(x)-EXP(-x))
```

The hyperbolic cosine, assigned to a variable named `hypcos`, would be handled like this:

```
hypcos := 0.5 * (EXP(x)+EXP(-x))
```

The hyperbolic tangent is simply the hyperbolic sine divided by the hyperbolic cosine.

Inverse hyperbolic functions are no more difficult. If `x` is a `REAL` variable whose inverse hyperbolic sine, cosine, and tangent are to be assigned to `invsinhx`, `invcoshx`, and `invtanhx`, respectively, the following statements will fulfill these requirements:

```
invsinhx := LN (x+SQRT(SQR(x)+1.0))  ;
invcoshx := LN (x+SQRT(SQR(x)-1.0))  ;
invtanhx := 0.5*LN ((1.0+x)/(1.0-x))
```

7.4 ARITHMETIC WITH PROGRAMMER-DEFINED DATA

Except for `TRUNC`, the built-in functions described thus far cannot be used with long integers. However, they can be used with subrange data based on the `INTEGER` data type. This capability is just a natural extension of ordinary numeric processing and needs no elaboration. When it comes to enumerative types, however, the arithmetic capabilities are limited, and the relationship between these capabilities and Pascal's ordinary arithmetic facilities is rather specialized. Consequently, this topic will be considered in a separate chapter.

Problems

1. Write Pascal expressions for each of the following:

    (a) $\sqrt{X^2 + Y^2}$

    (b) $\dfrac{X^2 + A}{Y^2 - B}$

    (c) $\sqrt{X^2 + |Z|Y^2}$

    (d) $\dfrac{X^2 + (A/B)^{-1}}{\ln (X^2 + A/B)}$

    (e) $\sqrt{\sin X \cos X}$

    (f) $\ln \left(e^{2x} + \dfrac{1}{2e^x} \right)$

    (g) $\sqrt{\dfrac{xy^2}{1 + \cot(x + 2)}}$

    (h) $\ln^2 \left(\left(\dfrac{x + y}{x - y} \right)^2 \dfrac{X \tan Y}{+ Y \tan^2 X} \right)$

    (i) $\dfrac{X(Y^3 + \ln|Y|)}{1 + Y}$

    (j) $\dfrac{\ln X \sinh (Y + X^2)}{\exp(2x^2 + \sqrt{\tan 2Y})}$

2. Among the algebraic equations given below, there may be some that require more than one pascal statement to represent an equivalent set of computations. For each expression, write the necessary statement or statements to produce the required result. If you need to specify additional variables (for temporary storage, perhaps), you may assume that t1, t2, t3, etc., have been declared as REAL. Assume further that each variable name (except for the temporary ones) is one letter long.

    (a) $z = \sqrt{x^2 + 2y^4}$

    (b) $w = (\sqrt{x^2 + 2y^4})^3$

(c) $\quad y = \left(\dfrac{x + \ln|w|}{x + \ln w^2} \right)^{z/2}$

(d) $\quad z = \dfrac{3.5(y + \sqrt{y^3}}{e^{x+\sqrt{y}}}$

(e) $\quad p = \dfrac{ax^{b+2}e^{x+2}}{c^2(x + a)^3}$

(f) $\quad r = \left(\dfrac{dvh}{m} \right)^8 \left(\dfrac{mc}{k} \right)^4$

3. If variable x is declared as REAL and y is declared as INTEGER, fill in the expression in the statement

```
y := expression involving x
```

so that x and y follow the relationship implied by these sample values:

x	y
0.0	0
0.5	0
1.0	0
2.8	0
3.0	1
3.6	1
4.75	1
5.88	1
6.0	2
6.7	2
8.95	2
9.00	3

4. Write a Pascal program that reads a succession of input values arranged so that each line consists of four different integer values r, s, t, and u. Display each input line (on a separate line) right after it is read. After all the lines have been read and displayed (use EOF to determine this), display a line showing smallsum, the sum of the smallest values from each input line, and a final line showing bigsum, the sum of the largest values from each input line.

5. Rewrite the program specified in Problem 4 so that it can process several (an arbitrary number) of collections of input lines. After each collection the program is to display smallsum and bigsum for that collection and then leave two blank lines before starting the output for the next collection. It is up to you to determine how to separate the collections.

6. Write a program that reads a positive integer into a variable named limit (limit < 50). Starting with INTEGER variable i set at 1 and proceeding up to and including limit, the program is to display i, i^2, LN(i) and $\sqrt{i}$ i on a line for each value of i. Include appropriate column labels at the top of the output page.

7. Write a program that reads a positive integer into a variable named limit (limit < 20) and displays a table showing the logarithms to the base 2 of all integers starting with 1 up to and including limit. Each line of the table is to show an integer value and its logarithm to the base 2. The values of the logarithms should be rounded to five places.

8. Modify the program described in Problem 7 so that the ouput table starts with the highest value (limit) and its base 2 logarithm and displays the entries in decreasing order. The final line of output, then, will be the value 1 and its logarithm.

9. Generalize the program in Problem 7 or 8 as follows: Input consists of two positive integers, both greater than 1. The first value, to be stored in a variable named base, indicates the base to which the required set of logarithms is to be computed. The second input value, limit, serves the same purpose as in Problem 7 or 8.

10. Write the appropriate Pascal statement(s) for each of the following computations. In each case, store the final result in a variable named rslt:
    (a) Round the value 8.7 to the nearest integer.
    (b) Round the value 172.99 to the nearest tenth.
    (c) Adjust the value 346.81 to the largest integer that does not exceed the original value.
    (d) Round the value 8612.84 to the nearest thousand.
    (e) Round the value in REAL variable visc to the nearest hundredth.
    (f) Bring the square root of the value in variable smax to the nearest integer.
    (g) Round the largest of the variables st, br, and wh to four decimal places.
    (h) Round the sum of the largest and smallest of the values in REAL variables p1, f2, p3, f4, and p5 to the nearest thousandth.

11. The English Channel Tunnel Project, Europe's dream for centuries, is

going badly. Morale is low, the employee turnover is intolerably high, and the next shipment of wine has been delayed another week. To keep things going, the Tunnel Authority decided to implement a bold payment plan: On a given day (to be known as the Given Day), all employees' pay will be set to 0.1 franc per day, and it will increase by 50% on each successive day from that day on. New employees will start at the 0.1 franc rate (regardless of the day on which they start), with the same rate of increase applying to them. Tres bien!

When an employee has had enough of the Channel Tunnel and resigns, a line of input is prepared showing his or her employee number (1–9999) and the number of days worked under the bold new plan. Write a program that displays a line of output for each employee read in, showing his or her number, number of days worked, and total pay.

12. Expand the program in Problem 11 so that, after all input has been processed, the program leaves a blank line and displays the number of employees processed, the average number of days worked, and the average daily pay rate at the time of resignation. Round the averages to three places.

13. A number of workers have approached the Tunnel Authority with the following proposition: Each of them has in mind a particular amount of money he or she is interested in making, and is willing to be hired (under the bold new plan) for the number of days required to reach or exceed that amount. Each such employee is given a number (as in Problem 11), and a line of input is prepared containing that number and the desired total earnings for that employee. Write a program that reads these data and, for each employee, displays a line containing the employee number, desired earnings, minimum number of whole days required to reach or exceed those earnings, and the actual earnings for that period. After all of the input has been processed, leave a blank line in the output and display the number of employees hired under these conditions, the average amount they wish to earn, and the average number of days that each employee will work. Round your averages to three places.

14. The Natural Herbal Food Works manufactures wholesome-looking confections to be sold under local brand names. The basic mixture, to which desired flavoring and coloring is added, consists of two ingredients whose relative proportions are determined strictly by price. Ingredient A (you do *not* want to know what it is) costs 51 cents a pound and B (the good stuff) costs $1.17 a pound. Write a program that computes mixtures for a succession of requirements. Each input set consists of a batch number (six-digit integer), total number of pounds in the mixture, and the final price per pound. The final price

is the amount charged. To cover its costs and to make a reasonable profit, the Natural Herbal Food Works sets its price at double its costs for ingredients A and B in a given blend.

Output for each input set is to show the batch number, weight of the order, price per pound, and the weights of A and B used to fill the order. If a set of specifications present an impossible situations (for example, the required price is too low), display a line with that batch number, along with the message REQUIREMENTS CANNOT BE MET. On the other hand, if a price is too high (that is, the required price is greater than what the Works regularly charges), the Natural Herbal Food Works (who, after all, are not pigs) wants the program to display the batch number, the message REQUIRED PRICE IS EXCESSIVE, and an additional line showing the batch number (again) and the total amount of excess (required total price – actual total price).

15. Prices change. To reflect this, write the program for Problem 14 so that each set of input consists of a batch number, total pounds, and final price as before. However, the first input set is to be preceded by a single line showing the current prices (per pound) for A and B, in that order.

16. Good news. The Natural Herbal Food Works has decided to expand by opening an international sales division. What this means is that orders will be coming in from customers who will specify their requirements in kilograms and dollars per kilogram. The Works will note this by changing the form of their input data so that an odd batch number will indicate that weights are in pounds (and prices are on a per pound basis) while an even-numbered batch will specify everything in terms of kilograms. Modify the program in Problem 14 or 15 accordingly.

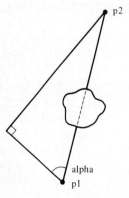

Figure 7.2

Diagram for Problem 17

17. The Pancreas County Highway Authority has to define the path of a road through an expanse of mountainous terrain. Each mountain presents a problem as to whether to tunnel through or go around it. Figure 7.2 summarizes the problem for a portion of the distance. In this figure, ᴘ1 and ᴘ2 define the points under consideration. If the direct route is used, a tunnel must be built at a cost tunnelcost. If the mountain is to be circumvented, the road must detour from point ᴘ1 at an angle alpha and then make a right angle (well, we can consider it a right angle) and continue to point ᴘ2. In any event, there is a construction cost kmcost associated with each kilometer of roadway (exclusive of tunnel costs) that may change for each section. Data for this project are prepared so that each line contains the following information for a given section:

section number (section), a three-digit integer;
number of mountains in section (mtns), either one or zero;
tunnelcost, in dollars;
kilometers from ᴘ1 to ᴘ2 (ᴘ1ᴘ2) to the nearest .1 km;
kmcost in dollars per kilometer, to the nearest dime;
the integer portion of alpha, in degrees;
the fractional portion of alpha, in minutes
(to the nearest minute).

Write a program that decides whether to tunnel or detour for each section of road that is read in. The output should contain the following information: section number and total distance for each section, for direct as well as detour route; cost for each section using the alternative approaches, minimum cost for the total road project, along with the corresponding highway length; and total cost with no detours, along with *that* highway length.

18. A wide variety of mathematical functions can be computed as series in which the accuracy of the function value depends on the number of terms used in the computation. For example, we can get a value of e, the base of natural logarithms, from Pascal by using the EXP function with an argument of 1.0. This value, which turns out to be 0.2718281E+01, can be computed from the series

$$e = 1 + \frac{1}{1!} + \frac{1}{2!} + \frac{1}{3!} + \frac{1}{4!} + \ldots$$

We can examine the effect of each additional term by evaluating the series with one term, two terms, etc., and comparing each of the results with the reference value. Thus, for e, the comparison would look like this:

No. of Terms	Series Value	Ser.Val. - Ref.Val.
1	0.1000000E+01	−0.1718281E+01
2	0.2000000E+01	−0.7182810E+00
3	0.2500000E+01	−0.21828190E+00
4	0.2666667E+01	−0.5161400E−01
5	0.2708334E+01	−0.9947400E−02
6	0.2716667E+01	−0.1613700E−02
7	0.2718056E+01	−0.2252000E−03
8	0.2718230E+01	−0.5140000E−04
	etc.	

We can see that by the eighth term, the computed value agrees with the reference value to four decimal places. Prepare such a table for each of the following functions. Obtain the reference value by nvoking the appropriate Pascal function or constructing an appropriate computation if Pascal does not have a function for direct computation.

$$\sin x = x - \frac{x^3}{3!} + \frac{x^5}{5!} - \frac{x^7}{7!} + \frac{x^9}{9!} - \ldots \quad \text{(use x=0.5)}$$

$$\cos x = 1 - \frac{x^2}{2!} + \frac{x^4}{4!} - \frac{x^6}{6!} + \frac{x^8}{8!} - \ldots \quad \text{(use x=0.5)}$$

$$\ln x = 2 \left[\frac{x-1}{x+1} + \frac{1}{3} \left(\frac{x+1}{x+1} \right)^3 + \frac{1}{5} \left(\frac{x-1}{x-1} \right)^5 + \ldots \right] \quad \text{(use x=2.0)}$$

$$\tan^{-1} x = x - \frac{x^3}{3} + \frac{x^5}{5} - \frac{x^7}{7} + \ldots \quad \text{(use x =0.5)}$$

$$e^x = 1 + x + \frac{x^2}{2!} + \frac{x^3}{3!} + \frac{x^4}{4!} + \ldots \quad \text{(use x=2.5)}$$

19. The distance between two points $(x1,y1)$ and $(x2,y2)$, when plotted on rectangular coordinates, can be computed by the formula

$$\sqrt{(x2 - x1)^2 + (y2 - y1)^2}$$

Write a program that reads and processes sets of four points $(x1,y1)$, $(x2,y2)$, $(x3,y3)$ and $(x4,y4)$. For each set, the program is to compute and display the distances between all pairs of points. Each set is to produce a line for each distance showing the coordinates of the points and the distance between them. Leave a blank line between input sets.

20. Modify the program in Problem 19 so that it produces three additional lines of output for each input set processed: The first additional line is to show the largest of the distances computed for that set of points, followed by a line showing the smallest distance, and a final line showing the average distance. Each of these additional lines is to be labeled clearly.

21. When an airplane sets out to fly in a certain direction, that direction may be affected by a prevailing wind. For example, an airplane traveling due west at 585 miles per hour may encounter a wind blowing due south at 45 miles per hour (Figure 7.3). This means that after, say, an hour of flying under these conditions (without correcting for them), the plane would have traveled 585 miles west and 45 miles south.

   In order to correct for this effect, it is necessary to determine the ground speed of the aircraft (groundspeed) and the drift angle (driftangle). Using variable names airspeed and windspeed for air speed and wind speed, respectively, and using airwind to refer to the angle between the aircraft heading and the wind direction (90 degrees in the example of Figure 7.3), we can use the law of cosines to solve for groundspeed:

$$\text{groundspeed} = \sqrt{\text{airspeed}^2 + \text{windspeed}^2 - 2\ \text{airspeed}(\text{windspeed})\cos(\text{airwind})}$$

   and the law of sines then can help us solve for driftangle:

$$\frac{\text{groundspeed}}{\sin(\text{airwind})} = \frac{\text{windspeed}}{\sin(\text{driftangle})}$$

   Write a program in which an input set consists of airspeed, windspeed, and airwind (the latter in degrees). For each set, the program is to reproduce (echo) the input, using one line for each value accompanied by its name. Then, the program is to display groundspeed and driftangle on one line. driftangle is to be shown

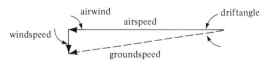

Figure 7.3

Diagram for Problem 21

in degrees. Leave a blank line between sets of output. Run your program with the following input sets:

airspeed	windspeed	airwind
325.0	0.0	0.0
280.0	10.0	0.0
300.0	20.0	180.0
300.0	55.0	90.0
400.0	50.0	120.0

Chapter 8

Arrays

Organization of data into arrays (introduced in Chapter 5) provides certain advantages for a variety of information-handling processes. This chapter looks at some of these processes and discusses UCSD Pascal's facilities for supporting them.

8.1 DECLARATION OF ARRAYS

The description of an array includes a considerable amount of information:

1. The array's name;
2. The number of elements in the array;
3. The type of data to be stored in the array;
4. The way the elements are organized;
5. The method for referring to an individual element (i.e., the way an element is indexed).

All these specifications are contained within the concise declaration whose form is defined in Figure 8.1. (Figure 5.7 places this syntax in context with the other variable declarations.)

For example,

```
VAR
    total : ARRAY[1..24] OF INTEGER
```

allocates storage under the collective name `total` for an array of 24 `INTEGER` values indexed by the subrange of integers from 1 through 24. That is, the first of `total`'s 24 elements is designated as `total[1]`, the second as `total[2]`, and so on.

8.1.1 Dimensionality of Arrays

Implied in these declarations is the fact that `numsold` and `total` are *one-dimensional* arrays. This means that only one distinguishing charac-

145

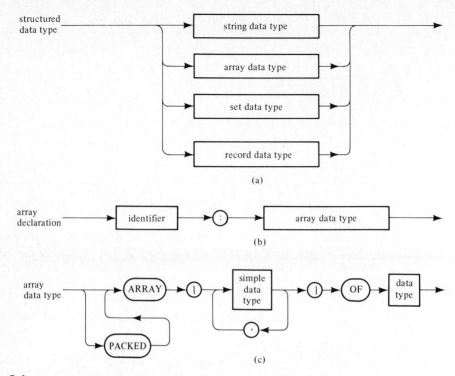

Figure 8.1

Syntax for an Array Declaration

teristic (i.e., one *subscript*) is needed to isolate any element in the array. In the case of t o t a l, that subscript is an integer not less than one and not greater than 24.

The *dimensionality* of an array reflects the number of subscripts required to isolate an element. For example,

```
VAR
    word : ARRAY[1..3,1..4] OF STRING[4]
```

defines an array of character strings in which each element may be up to four characters long. There are 12 elements organized into three *rows* and four *columns* as shown in Figure 8.2. Thus, the statement

```
word[2,3] := 'BIZE'
```

places the string BIZE in the element occupying the second row and third column of w o r d. The fact that this is the seventh of w o r d's elements does not mean that we could refer to it by the alternative designation w o r d[7].

Column 1	**Column 2**	**Column 3**	**Column 4**	
word[1,1]	word[1,2]	word[1,3]	word[1,4]	**Row 1**
word[2,1]	word[2,2]	word[2,3]	word[2,4]	**Row 2**
word[3,1]	word[3,2]	word[3,3]	word[3,4]	**Row 3**

Figure 8.2

Structure of the 3 × 4 Array word

Conditions defined by our declaration compel us to use two subscripts, each within the respective range defined for it.

Note that each of the following arrays

```
VAR
    vocabule : ARRAY[1..12] OF STRING[4] ;
       utter : ARRAY[1..4,1..3] OF STRING[4] ;
        noun : ARRAY[0..2,7..10] OF STRING[4] ;
       scrab : ARRAY[1..2,1..3,1..2] OF STRING[4]
```

occupies the same amount of storage for the same number of elements of the same type as does word. The differences, therefore, are organizational, and the implications are worth noting:

1. vocabule is a one-dimensional array. Consequently, a reference to vocabule[2,6] would be illegal, just as a reference to word[5] would be.
2. utter, like word, is a two-dimensional array, but its organization into four rows and three columns makes it structurally different from word. A reference to word[2,4] would be legal, but the compiler would reject a reference to utter[2,4]. On the other hand, utter[4,1] identifies one of its elements while a reference to word[4,1] falls on unsympathetic ears.
3. noun is disturbingly similar to word. Both are two-dimensional STRING[4] arrays, and each is organized with three rows and four columns. The difference lies in the way the subscripts are defined: noun's rows are designated 0, 1, and 2, and its four columns are identified as 7, 8, 9, and 10. Thus, noun[2,8] isolates the second element in noun's third row. The element in word with the same *organizational* position is word[3,2].

Who wants such a thing? Different people. Sometimes the use of a desired subscript range improves clarity. For example, suppose the Achilles Shoe Company makes runners' shoes in three models (Galumpho, Callousthenics, and Supercorn). Although each model is changed slightly every year, there is enough demand for earlier models to enable Achilles to keep producing previous years' models. If we wanted to build an array for the prices of each model over the years 1976 through 1983, we could set up the following declarations:

```
TYPE
    shoemodel = (galumpho, callousthenics, supercorn) ;
VAR
    shoeprice : ARRAY[shoemodel,1976..1983] OF REAL
```

Now, if we were to refer to the element shoeprice [galumpho,1978], for instance, we know immediately that its value represents the price for a pair of 1978 Galumphos. (Beautiful shoes; wings on the feet.)

4. scrab gives us an array with twelve string elements (like word) but with a more intricate structure: Now, we have a three-dimensional array organized into two *rows*, three *columns*, and two *blocks* (Figure 8.3). The first element is designated scrab[1,1,1], the second one is scrab[1,1,2], the third is scrab[1,2,1], and the last one is scrab[2,3,2]. (The form scrab[2],[3],[2] also is accepted, but we shall use a single set of brackets to enclose all the subscripts.)

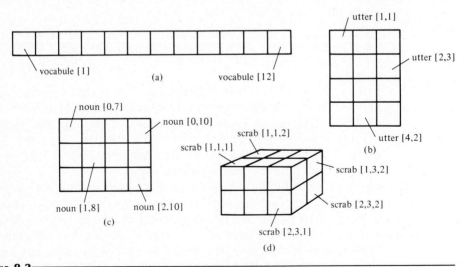

Figure 8.3

Alternative Organization for 12-element Arrays

UCSD Pascal places no limit on the number of dimensions an array may have. Such limitations must be imposed by the programmer in line with the array's usefulness and the programmer's ability to keep track of its elements. However, there is a limit of 16383 words (*not elements*) on the size of an array, regardless of its dimensions.

8.1.2 Packed Arrays

You will notice that Figure 8.1(c) shows the Pascal word PACKED as an optional part of an array declaration. This relates primarily to character arrays, in which case it gives the programmer the opportunity to conserve storage. (Strings are already packed.) Ordinarily, UCSD Pascal places each element of a character array in the rightmost byte of a word of storage. (For many personal computers, the word length is two bytes, so that one byte is wasted for each character stored this way.) When PACKED is specified, the characters are stored more compactly (e.g., two per byte in computers based on 16-bit processors). Assuming such a processor, then, based on the following declarations:

```
VAR
    banner : ARRAY [1..20] OF CHAR ;
    squeeze : PACKED ARRAY [1..20] OF CHAR ;
    acronym : ARRAY [1..9] OF CHAR ;
    acrnm : PACKED ARRAY [1..9] OF CHAR
```

UCSD Pascal will allocate 20 words, 10 words, 9 words, and 5 words, respectively, for banner, squeeze, acronym, and acrnm.

Analogous savings also may be realized by packing arrays of subrange and enumerative data types. For instance, we know (from Chapter 5) that Pascal associates an internal integer value with each value defined for an enumerative data type. Thus, when we declare

```
TYPE
    shoemodel = (Galumpho, Callousthenics, Supercorn) ;
VAR
    shoes : ARRAY [1..8] OF shoemodel
```

Pascal associates internal values of 0, 1, and 2 with the three respective values for the showmodel data type. Consequently, it allocates a word of storage for each of the eight elements of shoes. If we make shoes a packed array, i.e.,

```
VAR
    shoes : PACKED ARRAY [1..8] OF shoemodel
```

Pascal allocates only one word for the whole thing; each element, which can have an internal value of only 0, 1, or 2, needs no more than two bits for its representation. Consequently, a 16-bit word accommodates all eight elements. (If we had declared shoes as a packed array of nine elements, Pascal would allocate two words. Those same two words still would be sufficient for 10, 11, 12, or even 16 elements. Do you know why?)

Now that we see what the packing mechanism does with enumerative variables, we can apply it easily to subrange data. The declaration

```
VAR
    lengths : ARRAY [1..24] OF INTEGER
```

reserves 24 words. Alternatively,

```
VAR
    lengths : PACKED ARRAY [1..24] OF 0..3
```

obtains the same capacity with three words. (Two bits per element, eight elements per word). Since Pascal (sensibly) will not split a value across words, the declaration

```
VAR
    lengths : PACKED ARRAY [1..24] OF 0..6
```

reserves five words. Pascal stores five elements in each of the first four words, and the last four elements in the fifth word.

Pascal, like many other things in life, is devoid of free lunches. Consequently, there is a price for using packed arrays:

1. Packed arrays cannot be compared with regular (unpacked) values, even if they are the same data type.
2. Character arrays are the only kind of packed arrays that can be read or written.

Just how steep this price is depends on the individual situation.

8.1.3 Arrays as Data Types

The syntax of Pascal's TYPE declaration is flexible enough to allow definition of programmer-defined types consisting of arrays. To illustrate, let us use the little 3 × 4 array we examined in the first section. This time we shall describe that data structure in a data type named wordtable:

```
TYPE
    wordtable = ARRAY [1..3,1..4] OF STRING[4]
```

Now, we can say

```
VAR
    noun, verb, adjective : wordtable
```

in which case we have allocated three two-dimensional arrays of string elements.

We shall carry the idea one step further so that you see what the possibilities are. By expanding our TYPE definition as follows

```
TYPE
    wordstrength = (weak, neutral, intense) ;
    wordtable = ARRAY [wordstrength,1..4] OF STRING[4]
```

and declaring noun, verb, and adjective as before, we define data structures for which we can write statements such as

```
adjective[neutral,2] := 'FAIR'
```

or

```
noun[intense,3] := 'SLOB'
```

8.2 ARRAY PROCESSING

A basic reason for setting up an array is that there are certain processes we wish to apply in common to all or some of its elements. UCSD Pascal, being acutely aware of this, makes it convenient to describe such processes. Much of what we shall do requires no special features. Rather, we shall make good use of simple techniques based on familiar language components.

8.2.1 Assignment of Values to Array Elements

There is only one operation that applies to an entire array: UCSD Pascal allows assignment of an array's values to another array of the same data type and organization. For example, if we say

```
VAR
    oldtotal, newtotal : ARRAY [1..18] OF INTEGER
```

and oldtotal has values in its elements, the statement

```
newtotal := oldtotal
```

will copy `oldtotal[1]` into `newtotal[1]`, and so on. Any other operations on arrays must be specified for each of the elements, one at a time. Once an array element is identified by an appropriate subscript, it can be treated like any single-valued variable. For example, it is perfectly legitimate to specify the following type of computation:

```
newtotal[6] := 3.8*newtotal[5] + oldtotal[12]
```

8.2.2 Loops for Processing Groups of Elements

When a computing activity is to be applied to a series of array elements, the process is described most conveniently as a loop controlled by a `FOR` statement. To illustrate, let us assume the following situation:

```
VAR
    limit, which_one, leftover : INTEGER ;
    newtotal : ARRAY [1..18] OF INTEGER
      .
      .
      .
    READLN (limit, leftover)
```

The `INTEGER` variable `which_one` will be used as an index whose changing value will enable the loop to process a different element of `newtotal` each time around. `leftover` and `limit` are additional `IN-TEGER` variables whose values are available to us.

First let us review the processing of an entire array by setting all of `newtotal`'s elements to a common value (we shall use `leftover`):

```
FOR  which_one := 1 TO 18  DO
    newtotal[which_one] := leftover
```

Now, going back to the declarations and `READLN`, and assuming no prior value assignments to `newtotal`, we shall assign zero to `newtotal`'s first 11 elements and `leftover`'s values to the other seven elements:

```
FOR  which_one := 1 TO 18  DO
  IF  which_one <= 11
      THEN
         newtotal[which_one] := 0
      ELSE
         newtotal[which_one] := leftover
```

As a third example (again assuming no prior processing for `newtotal`), we shall set the first `limit` elements (i.e., `newtotal[1]` through newtotal[limit]) to leftover and the rest to zero. To add a little suspense, we shall recognize (and account for) the possibility that limit, which must have a value between 1 and 18 to make any sense, may not meet that requirement. If that happens, we shall set all of newtotal's elements to –1. Here is a reasonably simple way to specify the processing:

```
IF   (limit <  1) OR (limit >  18)
   THEN
     FOR   which_one := 1 TO 18   DO
       newtotal[which_one] := -1
   ELSE
     FOR   which_one := 1 TO 18   DO
       IF   which_one <= limit
         THEN
           newtotal[which_one] := leftover
         ELSE
           newtotal[which_one] := 0
```

Just to complete the picture, we shall rewrite the activity using two separate loops to fill newtotal's elements as we did before:

```
IF   (limit <  1) OR (limit >  18)
   THEN
     FOR   which_one := 1 TO 18   DO
       newtotal[which_one] := -1
   ELSE
     BEGIN
       FOR   which_one := 1 TO limit   DO
         newtotal[which_one] := leftover ;
       FOR   which_one := limit+1 TO 18   DO
         newtotal[which_one] := 0
     END
```

This version looks innocent enough. In fact, it will perform properly, even when limit is 18. (Try it.) However, this approach is the less desirable one because its behavior is not apparent from the code itself.

Incidentally, we could have made Pascal responsible for testing limit's value by declaring limit as a subrange variable, i.e.,

```
VAR
   limit : 1..18
```

However, if we did that, the program would intercept an attempt to read an out-of-range value for limit, and we would have had a more difficult time setting newtotal's elements to their proper values and continuing with whatever processing might follow.

Series of elements in two-dimensional arrays are handled with nested loops. Since it takes two subscripts to identify an individual element in a two-dimensional array, we need a separate index for each subscript. To illustrate, we shall go back to the 3 × 4 array of 4-character strings named word and make the following declarations:

```
CONST
    blanks = '    ' ;   stars = '****' ;
VAR
    word : ARRAY[1..3,1..4] OF STRING[4] ;
    rownum : 1..3 ;  colnum : 1..4
```

Now, if we want to set all 12 elements to blanks, we can say

```
FOR  rownum := 1 TO 3  DO
    FOR  colnum := 1 TO 4  DO
        word[rownum,colnum] := blanks
```

To set the second row to asterisks while setting the others to blanks, we can construct the following loops:

```
FOR  rownum := 1 TO 3  DO
    FOR  colnum := 1 TO 4  DO
        IF  rownum = 2
            THEN  word[rownum,colnum] := stars
            ELSE  word[rownum,colnum] := blanks
```

Problems

1. Each part of this problem refers to the array in Figure 8.4. Assuming the array is declared as follows:

   ```
   VAR
   level : ARRAY[1..4,1..5] OF INTEGER
   ```

   (a) Give the respective subscripts of the largest and smallest elements.
   (b) Which column has the greatest number of negative values?
   (c) What is the value of level[2,4] + level[4,3]?
   (d) Show what is displayed by the following:

   ```
   IF  level[2,4] <= level[4,2]-level[3,4]
       THEN  WRITE('CHOICE IS: ',level[2,3])
       ELSE  WRITE('CHOICE IS: ',level[3,2])
   ```

16	−3	212	72	−81
26	27	704	36	7
41	−28	8	801	84
−5	73	−7	50	61

Figure 8.4

Array for Problems 1, 2, and 3

(e)   What is the value of the ninth element in level?

(f)   Assuming partsum to be declared as an INTEGER variable, write the necessary statement(s) to compute (and assign to partsum) the sum of the first three rows of level.

(g)   Given partsum as in part (f), write the necessary statement(s) to compute (and store in partsum) the sum of the last three columns of level.

(h)   Using partsum as before, write the statement(s) to compute (and store in partsum) the sum of level's elements having odd values.

(i)   Using partsum again, write the statement(s) to compute (and store in partsum) the sum of all of level's elements having odd row numbers and even column numbers.

(j)   Using partsum one more time, write the statement(s) to compute (and store in partsum) the sum of each of the largest value in each of level's columns.

2.   Using the same array as in Figure 8.4, repeat Problem 1 based on the declaration

```
VAR
shift : ARRAY[0..3,-2..2] OF INTEGER
```

3.   Using Figure 8.4 again, assume the following declarations:

```
TYPE
    season = (fall, winter, spring, summer) ;
    model = (standard, special, custom, deluxe, hooboy) ;
VAR
    adjust : ARRAY[season,model] OF INTEGER ;
    partsum : INTEGER ;
    result : REAL ;
    when : season ;
    status : model
```

(a) Repeat Problem 1(a).

(b) Repeat Problem 1(b).

(c) Write the statement(s) to compute and store in partsum the sum of all winter values in adjust.

(d) Write the statement(s) to compute and store in result the average deluxe value rounded to two decimal places.

(e) Repeat Problem 1(f).

(f) Repeat Problem 1(g).

(g) Repeat Problem 1(h).

(h) Repeat Problem 1(i).

(i) Repeat Problem 1(j).

(j) Write the statement(s) to compute and store in result the average ratio of winter values to summer values.

4. Each part of this problem applies to a 12-element one-dimensional INTEGER array named numbers and an INTEGER variable named j:

(a) Write the statement(s) to store the first 12 positive integers in numbers.

(b) Write the statement(s) to store the first 12 multiples of 14 in numbers.

(c) Write the statement(s) to store the first six multiples of 17 in numbers[1], numbers[3], numbers[5], etc. and the squares of those values in numbers[2], numbers[4], numbers[6], etc.

(d) Write the statement(s) to store −5 in numbers[1], −7 in numbers[2], −9 in numbers[3], etc.

(e) Write the statement(s) to store the same values as in (d), but in reverse order.

(f) Write the statement(s) to store 17, 19,...,27 in numbers[1] through numbers[6], respectively, and 27, 25,...,17 in numbers[7] through numbers[12], respectively.

(g) Given the following statements:

```
numbers[1] := 8;
FOR  j := 2 To 12  DO
   numbers(j) := (j-1)*numbers[j-1] DIV j-1
```

show the resulting contents of numbers.

5. Write a program that operates on a 50-element one-dimensional array of integers to find the maximum value and its position in the array, the minimum value and its position, and the difference between the two extreme values. Test your program with the data given below:

```
32 31 54 67 –8 96 43 –20 9 10 21 19 6 44 57 78 11 –9 46 101
–77 42 59 33 65 76 87 98 109 –109 28 41 52 63 74 85 7 18 12 20
4 51 62 73 84 15 100 71 –4 101
```

6. Write a program that operates on a 50-element one-dimensional array of integers to find the second largest value and its position in the array. Test your program with the data given in the previous problem.

7. Write a program that examines a 50-element one-dimensional array of integer values. If there are more odd values than even values, produce a second array with the original values sorted in descending order. If there are more even values than odd values, the second array's elements should be sorted in ascending order. If the original array contains the same number of odd and even values, the second array's elements should be in reverse order from those in the original array. Here are three arrays with which to test your program:

```
11 99 13 97 15 95 17 93 19 91 21 89 23 87 25 85 27 83 29 81
31 79 33 77 35 75 37 73 39 71 41 69 43 67 45 65 66 68 70 72
–74 76 –78 80 82 84 86 88 90 92
2 98 4 96 6 94 8 92 10 90 12 88 14 86 16 84 18 82 20 80
3 5 7 9 11 23 25 27 29 31 33 35 37 39 41 –43 –45 –47 49 –51
–8 42 44 46 48 –50 52 54 56 58
11 13 15 17 19 21 23 25 27 29 99 97 95 93 91 89 87 85 83 81
66 64 62 60 58 56 54 52 50 48 46 44 42 40 38 36 28 30 32 34
101 102 103 104 105 208 207 206 205 204
```

8. Modify the program in Problem 5 so that it treats the 50 elements as a 5 × 10 array. Use the same data.

9. Modify the program in Problem 6 so that it treats the 50 elements as a 5 × 2 × 5 array. Use Problem 5's data to test your program.

10. Data smoothing, a process frequently used in data analysis, seeks to reduce the effect of incidental local disturbances in data values by replacing those values with numbers that emphasize the trend rather than the individual reading. A common type of data smoothing involves the computation of *moving averages*. When we take a series of readings at fixed time intervals over an extended period, we report the results by replacing each reading with the average value of that reading and some number of subsequent readings. For instance, suppose we were interested in stock market trends as measured by the Dow Jones Industrial Average. On the basis that daily fluctuations are less important than the overall direction, we could compute, say, a 10-day moving average. As a result, each day's (adjusted) value would be reported as an average of the values for 10 consecutive days

beginning with that day. Thus, for day 1, the reported figure would be the average of days 1 through 10, for day 2 it would be the average of days 2 through 11, and so on. The same could be done for an individual stock, the day's high temperature reading, or anything else that is believed to be subject to local fluctuations. Now that all of that has been said, write a program that processes a series of real values and reports the 10-day moving averages rounded to two decimal places. There is no information as to how many individual values are to be processed for a given input set, but the program must be ready to process any number. For a given run, there also is a possibility that there may not be enough input values to prepare even one 10-day moving average. Here are three sets of input on which to test your program:

```
5.5 5.6 5.5 5.4 5.6 5.5 5.7 5.9 5.9 5.9 5.9 6.0 5.6 5.4 5.5 5.8
5.8 5.9 5.9 6.0 6.3 6.2 6.1 6.0 6.0 6.4 6.3 6.3 6.2 6.6 6.3 6.1
6.2 6.7 6.4 6.5 6.4 6.5 6.4 6.5 6.8 6.9 6.8 6.7 6.7 6.8 6.5 6.6
6.4 6.8 6.8 6.8 6.7 6.9 6.9 7.0 6.8 6.9 6.8 6.9 7.0 7.1 6.9 6.8
-9.9
3.8 3.9 4.1 4.4 4.5 4.6 3.9 4.2 4.4 4.5 4.5 4.5 5.3 4.9 4.8 4.9
5.2 5.4 5.4 5.5 5.7 5.8 5.8 5.3 5.4 5.6 5.9 6.3 6.3 6.2 6.1 6.4
6.3 6.6 6.6 6.5 6.4 6.5 6.7 6.7 6.5 6.8 6.9 6.8 6.4 7.2 7.0 7.1
7.3 7.4 7.4 7.3 7.7 7.6 7.8 7.6 7.8 7.6 7.4 7.6 7.8 7.8 7.9 7.9
8.1 8.1 8.2 8.0 8.1 7.8 7.6 7.7 7.7 7.4 7.1 7.2 7.0 7.1 6.9 7.0
-9.9
4.5 6.6 4.4 6.7 4.4 6.5 4.6 6.6 4.8 6.6 4.9 6.5 4.8 6.7 4.9 6.6
4.9 6.6 5.1 6.8 5.3 6.6 5.2 6.7 5.2 7.0 6.3 7.0 7.0 6.1 7.3 6.1
7.2 5.8 7.2 5.7 7.1 5.8 7.1 5.7 6.6 5.7 6.7 5.6 6.6 5.6 6.6 5.5
6.4 5.5 6.4 5.3 6.1 5.3 6.1 5.4 6.0 5.3 5.3 5.8 5.4 5.7 5.3 5.3
-9.9
```

(The -9.9 is used to separate the individual collections of input values. You may want to use the same technique in preparing your own input, or you may prefer another approach.)

11. Generalize the program in the previous problem so that it prepares and displays moving averages as before. However, the number of readings included in the averages now will be a variable that the user submits interactively for each input set in response to the program's request. Thus, for example, the user might request 10-day moving averages for the first input set, 12-day moving averages for the second set, 5-day moving averages for the third set, and so on. Use the test data from the previous problem.

12. Here is a slightly more intricate version of the previous problem: Before each collection of input data is read, the program asks for the

period over which the averages are to be computed (as before). The difference is that there is a built-in default of 10 days (readings). Thus, if the user specifies some value other than 10, the program will use it. If not, the program will use the 10-reading default. Of course, if the user specifies 10 readings anyway, no harm is done. Test your program with the data from Problem 10.

13. Now we shall complicate the previous problem just a bit more: The program asks for a time period, and it has a built-in default of 10 as in the previous problem. The user now has a third option in addition to specifying a new time period or directing the program to use the default. As a third possibility, the user can direct the program to use the time period it used for the previous collection of input values. If the user specifies the "use what you used the last time" option, and there was no last time (i.e., the first set of input values is about to be read and processed), the program is to display a message to that effect and give the user another chance. As before, use Problem 10's test data.

14. *Small fanfare for the Special Challenge:* In this deluxe version of the moving averages problem, we want to work with only a single collection of input values (we can use the first collection from Problem 10). This time, using that single collection, we are interested in seeing the effect of the time period on the computed results. Accordingly, design a moving averages program that asks the user for a time period (there is no default value) and produces the moving averages with that time period. Then it asks the user for another time period, rereads the data, and produces the averages with *that* time period. This goes on until the user (by some signal) stops the run.

15. One more wrinkle and we shall drop the issue. Design and prepare the program described in the previous problem with one difference: Instead of allowing the user to specify as many time periods as he or she wants, the program will limit the number of examinations to 10. If the user specifies an impossible time period (for instance, the user wants a time period of 70 and there are only 54 readings), the program, of course, must reject the request, but it counts as an examination. Anyway, the program keeps track of which periods have been requested so that it can prevent the user from requesting the same period more than once. As before, use the first set of input values from Problem 10.

16	−3	212	72	−81
26	27	704	36	7
41	−28	8	801	84
−3	73	−7	50	62

Chapter 9

Nonnumeric Data Handling

The rapid growth of word processing, electronic mail, and other text-based computer applications has focused renewed attention on the importance of nonnumeric data processing. UCSD Pascal acknowledges this importance by supporting a variety of useful operations on character strings and enumerative data. This chapter examines these operations and illustrates their use.

9.1 STRING PROCESSING

UCSD Pascal's approach to string processing is to support a collection of simple operations. With these as a basis, the programmer can construct more extensive processes in accordance with the application's requirements. A significant convenience in this regard is the STRING data type itself. Its inclusion in UCSD Pascal (it is not part of standard Pascal) lessens our dependence on the more restrictive CHAR data type as a vehicle for string processing. As a result, much of the emphasis here will be on the STRING type.

9.1.1 Declaration of String Variables

There is little to add to the introductory discussion in Chapter 5. Recall that a string is declared with a specified length enclosed in square brackets. For example,

```
VAR
    heading : STRING[30]
```

defines a string variable named heading that may be anywhere from 0–30 characters long. UCSD Pascal accepts a maximum declared length of 255

161

characters, and the default length (if no length is specified) is 80. As was seen in the previous chapter, arrays of strings may be declared and processed like any other arrays. Elements in such arrays all will have the same maximum length, but it is not necessary for all elements to have the same (apparent) length at any given time.

9.1.2 Basic String Operations

UCSD Pascal's only direct string operation is that of simple assignment. For example, in the following sequence

```
VAR
   id_name : STRING[10] ;
   abbrev : STRING[3]
   + + + + + + + + + + + + + + +
   abbrev := 'ZNV' ;
   id_name := abbrev
```

the string id_name receives the value 'ZNV', and its current length (after the assignment) is 3. A string variable can be emptied (reduced to the null string) simply by assigning the null string ''. Thus,

```
id_name := ''
```

reduces id_name to the null string (thereby making its current length zero) regardless of the length of the variable's previous contents. Other types of string manipulations are handled by built-in subprograms as described in the rest of this section.

Current String Length   UCSD Pascal does not actually vary the length of a string variable; there is sufficient bookkeeping so that the program "knows" how many of the string's declared positions are occupied at any time. This information is available via the LENGTH function. For instance, assuming id_name is declared as STRING[10] and howlong is declared as INTEGER, the sequence

```
id_name := 'TALLY' ;
howlong := LENGTH(id_name)
```

will place a value of 5 in howlong.

Concatenation   The process of building larger strings from smaller ones is called *concatenation*. (Catenation would have been enough, but a con artist was at work.) UCSD Pascal's CONCAT function performs the appropriate synthesis. For instance, the expression

```
CONCAT('First Class',' is ','but a nickel more.')
```

produces the string 'First Class is but a nickel more.' This is a single string constant and as such may be assigned to any string variable with sufficient declared length. CONCAT takes any number of arguments, each of which may or may not be a string expression. To clarify the idea of concatenation in your mind, make sure you understand how it is that the following sequence

```
VAR
    phrase : STRING[20] ;
    pwd1, suffix : STRING[4]
    .
    .
    .
    pwd1 := 'coil' ;
    suffix := 'able' ;
    phrase := CONCAT('un',pwd1,suffix,CONCAT(' c',suffix))
```

stores the string 'uncoilable cable' in phrase and marks phrase's current length at 16.

Substrings   A *substring* is part of a larger string. The smallest substring, of course, is a single character, and we can refer to any character in a string by specifying its position in the string. (The leftmost character always is at position 1.) Thus, in the following sequence

```
VAR
    term, name, handle : STRING [6]
    .
    .
    .
    name := 'BAGELS' ;
    handle := 'PRAWN' ;
    term := name ;
    term[1] := handle[1] ;
    term[5] := handle[2]
```

handle ends up with the string 'PAGERS'. This is a convenient way to replace single characters in strings. However, it is not a universally effective way to manipulate one-character substrings. For instance, UCSD Pascal will not accept something like name[3] as an argument for the CONCAT procedure. Because of this and other restrictions, we shall avoid the use of this form and emphasize the more flexible COPY function for extracting substrings of any length.

UCSD Pascal's COPY function provides a general facility that allows us to extract any designated portion of a string and make it available for subsequent use. The general form for invoking COPY is

COPY(*sourcestring,startingposition,length*)

When COPY is invoked, it goes to the string specified by the first argument and, starting at the position indicated by the second argument, copies the number of consecutive characters indicated by the third argument. For instance,

```
COPY('partridge',2,3)
```

produces the substring 'art' and

```
COPY('partridge',5,5)
```

produces 'ridge'. Note that the source string does not change. The substring merely is found and copied. Going back for a minute to the previously declared name and handle, the following assignment

```
term := CONCAT (COPY(handle,1,1), COPY(name,2,3),
                COPY(handle,2,1), COPY(name,6,1))
```

produces the same value for handle as before. If you can work through the following sequence

```
CONST
   blank = ' ' ;
VAR
   name : STRING[20] ;
   birdie : STRING[10] ;
   where : INTEGER
   .
   .
   .
   where := 2 ;
   birdie := 'PARTRIDGE'  ;
   name := CONCAT(COPY(birdie,where,3),blank,COPY(birdie,2,1),
               COPY(birdie,where+6,2))
```

and convince yourself that the string finally stored in name is 'ART AGE' you will not have any trouble with CONCAT or COPY.

Example 9.1 In the kingdom of Funfeh (where everyone speaks through the nose) there is great intrigue. Coded messages travel hither and yon in great profusion. The Royal Palace has become such a giant hatchery for plots and counterplots that playwrights lurk in every dark corner (and a few that are well lit) hoping to steal ideas. Especially active in these goings on is the Princess Adenoida, third-from-youngest daughter of King Znehvn by his second-favorite concubine Unnhnye. Noida (as she is known to her many friends and acquaintances) sends secret notes to her lover Vnm (the Gorgeous Goatherd) by hiding the messages in innocent-looking news reports. The way she does it is to construct the message from individual characters in the news story. Directions for finding the appropriate characters consist of a series of integers, each specifying the position to be used next. For instance, suppose there was the following news report:

`'SOURCES CLAIM A VINTAGE YEAR FOR FUNFEH''S GRAPES!'`

and Noida wanted to tell her friend

`'I LOVE MY VNM!'`

She would send the news release as is and, hidden in the ear of Vnm's pet goat Mehmeh would be the sequence

```
12   8   10   2   17   6   24   13   25   14   17   19   13   49   -1
```

(The −1 is Noida's special end-of-message indicator.) News stories never exceed 240 characters, and Noida's secret messages never exceed 80 characters. Vnm has won a BOOVIZ Personal Computer in the Annual Goatherds Drawing, but he has no program to find the hidden messages. In the interest of good causes we shall write Vnm's program. To focus attention on the string-handling aspects, we shall simplify matters by saying that the input consists of the position numbers, concluded by a −1. The −1, in turn, is followed by the text containing the news story.

The program (Figure 9.1) is organized so that the decoding directions and the news report are read by separate procedures. By the time the main program is ready to extract the message, its length (`howlong`) is already known. (The length of the news story can be determined easily, but it is not needed.)

`message`, the string from which the final message will be displayed, is initialized to the empty string, and the characters are added to it, one by one.

Expansion of Strings In addition to `CONCAT`, which enables us to expand a string by appending characters to it, UCSD Pascal provides the `INSERT` procedure, a subprogram for expanding strings by incorporating other strings in them. The general form is

`INSERT(newaddition,oldstring,position)`

```
{*********************************************************************}
{                            EXAMPLE 9.1                             }
{*********************************************************************}
{   THIS PROGRAM USES A SERIES OF INTEGER VALUES TO FIND AND EXTRACT  }
{   CHARACTERS FROM A STRING TO FORM A MESSAGE. THE SOURCE STRING MAY }
{   BE UP TO 240 CHARACTERS LONG, AND THE MESSAGE EXTRACTED FROM IT MAY }
{   BE UP TO 80 CHARACTERS LONG.                                      }
{*********************************************************************}
{   news: the source string;                                         }
{   inline: a temporary place for the next line of news;             }
{   message: the message extracted from news;                        }
{   howlong: the length of the message;                              }
{   key: the series of position indicators for the message's characters }
{*********************************************************************}
PROGRAM  ex901 ;
VAR
  news : STRING[240] ;
  inline, message : STRING ;
  key : ARRAY[1..80] OF INTEGER ;
  sw : BOOLEAN ;
  i, howlong, next : INTEGER ;
BEGIN
  howlong := 0 ;      sw := TRUE ;
  WRITELN ('TYPE IN THE CLUES; END WITH -1,') ;
  WHILE  sw  DO
    BEGIN
      READ (key[howlong+1]) ;
      howlong := howlong + 1 ;
      IF  key[howlong] = -1
        THEN
          BEGIN
            howlong := howlong-1 ;
            READLN ;
            sw := FALSE
          END
    END ;
  news := '' ;   {'' IS THE NULL (EMPTY) STRING.}
  sw := TRUE ;
  WRITELN ('GIVE ME NEWS.') ;
  READLN (inline) ;
  WHILE  sw  DO
    BEGIN
      news := CONCAT (news,inline,' ') ;
      WRITELN ('GIVE ME MORE NEWS OR HIT <CNTRL>C TO QUIT.') ;
      READLN (inline) ;
      IF  EOF
        THEN
          sw := FALSE
    END ;
```

Figure 9.1————————————————————————

Program for Example 9.1

```
  message := '';
  FOR  i := 1 TO howlong  DO
    BEGIN
      next := Key[i] ;
      message := CONCAT(message,COPY(news,next,1))
    END ;
  WRITELN ('HERE IS THE MESSAGE:') ;
  WRITELN (message) ;
  WRITELN ('THANK YOU, CALL AGAIN,')
END ,
```

Figure 9.1

Program for Example 9.1 (Continued)

When INSERT is invoked, the string specified by the first argument is inserted into the string variable named in the second argument starting at the position indicated by the integer value in the third argument. For example,

```
VAR
  report : STRING[30]
  ,
  ,
  ,
  report := 'This is outrageous,' ;
  INSERT(' not so',report,7)
```

expands report to 'This is not so outrageous,' and adjusts its length indicator accordingly. It is up to the programmer to make sure that the newly-expanded string will not exceed the maximum length declared for it.

Contraction of Strings   Substrings may be removed from string variables with UCSD Pascal's DELETE procedure:

```
DELETE(oldstring,position,length)
```

shortens the value in the variable named in the first argument by removing the number of characters specified in the third argument starting from the position stated in the second argument. (What?) For example,

```
DELETE(report,3,8)
```

requests that the string variable report be shortened by removing 8 consecutive characters starting with the one in position 3. As a result, the characters in positions 3–10 will be removed, the resulting hole will be "closed up" and the length indicator's value will be decreased by eight. Thus, the following sequence

```
VAR
  report : STRING[30] ;
  filler : STRING[8]
  .
  .
  .
  report := 'This is not so outrageous,' ;
  filler := CONCAT (COPY(report,21,1), COPY(report,10,1),
                    COPY(report,19,1)) ;
  DELETE(report,9,12) ;
  INSERT(filler,report,9)
```

will leave the string variable report with 'This is gorgeous,' (That was what the Pascal programmer said about the Grand Canyon just before they threw him over.) The programmer must make sure that he or she does not seek to delete more characters than there are in the string. (When this happens, the program ignores the request.)

9.1.3 String Comparisons

String expressions may be compared with each other using Pascal's regular relational operators. The basis for comparison is the internal collating sequence of the computer's character set (Appendix B). Such comparisons are called *lexicographic comparisons*. Recall (Section 5.3.1, *Substrings*) that, in the ASCII sequence, 'A' is earlier (i.e., "less than") 'B', 'Z' is "less than" 'a', and so on. The numerical characters ('0' through '9') are less than the uppercase letters, and the blank is less than '0'. Consequently, when a letter is "less than" another letter, it is the same as saying (in a program) that the first letter would be ahead of the second letter in an alphabetized list. The same rule applies to strings containing several characters. Thus, the comparison

```
'BASH' < 'BATH'
```

would produce an outcome of TRUE. (The S in 'BASH' puts it alphabetically (i.e., lexicographically) ahead of 'BATH'.) For the same reason, the comparison

```
'BASH' < 'bash'
```

produces an outcome of TRUE because uppercase letters are lexicographically less than lowercase letters. To push this further, note that 'WASH' also is less then 'bash'.

UCSD Pascal does not require strings of equal length for comparison. The easiest way to deal with Pascal's rule for comparing strings of unequal lengths is to think of the strings being lined up at their left ends, after which corresponding characters are compared one at a time. As soon as there is a mismatch, Pascal makes a decision on that basis, regardless of the strings' lengths or the rest of their contents. For example, suppose we were comparing 'barn' and 'Barnyard'. As soon as Pascal sees that the first character of 'barn' is lexicographically greater than the first character of 'Barnyard' the show is over. In an alphabetized list (as far as Pascal is concerned), 'Barnyard' precedes 'barn'.

When two strings of different sizes are compared and Pascal keeps finding the corresponding characters equal until it runs out of characters in the shorter string, the longer string is lexicographically greater. Thus, 'barn' is less than 'barnyard', 'barn' is less than 'barnYARD', and 'BARN' is less than 'BARNyard'.

9.1.4 Searching Character Strings

We can examine a string to see if it contains another, smaller string by using UCSD Pascal's POS function. For instance, the following sequence

```
VAR
    where : INTEGER ;
    message : STRING[40]
    message := 'What makes Murray so stubborn?' ;
    where := POS('ray',message) ;
    DELETE(message,where,3)
```

will locate the beginning of the string 'ray' in the variable message and store that position (15, as it turns out) in the INTEGER variable where. The subsequent statement, then, can remove the three letters from message, so that it ends up with the string 'What makes Mur so stubborn?'. An unsuccessful search returns a value of zero.

If a string contains more than one occurrence of a specified substring, POS finds only the first occurrence. It is up to the programmer to set up the necessary processing loop for finding multiple occurrences. A straightforward way to do this is to start by searching the entire string. This will locate the first occurrence (if there is one). Then, before another search is undertaken, it is necessary to "fence off" that part of the string already searched so that POS does not find the same substring twice. Thus, each time another occurrence is found, the next search takes place over a shorter substring.

This process continues until the search is unsuccessful or there is no more string to search. Simple, yes? No. The problem is that when POS finds what it is looking for while searching a *substring*, the position it reports is the position relative to the beginning of the substring and not the beginning of the entire string. That means it is up to the programmer to translate the returned value of POS to an actual position in the complete source string. An easy way to do this is shown in Example 9.2.

9.1.5 Example 9.2

Dr. Nasal B. Flatte, the famous paleosocioanthropsychomusicologist, feels she is close to an important breakthrough. Her theory is that, hidden in the titles of ancient hunting and gathering songs (and perhaps in some more recent ones, too) are characteristic syllables and fragments that can reveal hitherto hidden insights about the people who sang (sing) those songs. To facilitate her data analyses, she would like an interactive program that reads a song title and a string for which that title should be searched. In response, the program is to display the position(s) in which the specified substring appears.

The heart of the program (Figure 9.2) is a loop that sets a new starting position for the substring to be searched based on the position of the last successful match. Note that the starting point is one position removed from the previous successful match, even though the program is designed to look for strings that are more than one character long. This takes care of situations like the one where we might be looking for the string 'eee' and the source string contains 'teeeeef'. There are three occurrences of 'eee' there, and the only way to find all of them is to advance through the string one position at a time.

9.1.6 Characters and Integers

There are several functions which, when applied to character data, give the programmer convenient access to the ASCII collating sequence. We shall just describe their characteristics briefly, leaving it to you to find a use for them.

CHR and ORD   The ORD function relates each ASCII character to the numerical equivalent of its internal representation. (These are tabulated in Appendix B.) For instance, if whatnum is declared as an INTEGER variable, the assignment

```
whatnum := ORD('W')
```

stores a value of 87 in whatnum because the bit pattern used to represent a W, when interpreted as a binary integer, is equivalent to an integer value of 87.

```
PROGRAM    ex902 ;
VAR
  song : STRING ;
  clue : STRING[3] ;
  current_1, total_1, start, where, mark : INTEGER ;
BEGIN
  WRITELN ('TYPE IN THE SONG TITLE AND <ENTER>.') ;
  READLN (song) ;
  REPEAT
    WRITELN ('WHAT CLUE ARE YOU LOOKING FOR?') ;
    READLN (clue) ;
    mark := 0 ;
    start := 1 ;
    total_1 := LENGTH(song) ;
    current_1 := total _1-start+1 ;
    where := -1 ;
    WHILE  where <> 0   DO
      BEGIN
        where := POS(clue,COPY(song,start,current_1)) ;
        IF  where <> 0
          THEN
             BEGIN
               mark := mark+where ;
               WRITELN ('MARK: ',mark) ;
               start := mark + 1 ;
               IF  start > total_1-2  THEN  where := 0
                                      ELSE  current_1 := total_1-start+1
           END
         ELSE  WRITELN ('I CANNOT FIND ',clue,' IN YOUR SONG.')
      END ;
    WRITELN ('ENTER ANOTHER SONG OR <CNTRL>-C TO QUIT.') ;
    READLN (song)
  UNTIL  EOF ;
  WRITELN ('END OF RUN.')
END .
```

Figure 9.2———————————————————————————————————

Program for Example 9.2

The function CHR works in the opposite direction. If quan is declared as INTEGER and is given a value of 116, and syll is declared as STRING[4], the assignment

syll := CHR(quan)

will place the character 'm' in syll. To cement things down once and for all, the assignment

```
quan := ORD(CHR(110))
```

will place the integer value 110 in quan, and

```
word := CHR(ORD('S'))
```

will place the character 'S' in word. There are other ways to get nowhere but they are beyond the scope of this book.

The ORD function does not translate a character into an integer. ORD('7') is not 7. (It happens to be 55 in the ASCII collating sequence.) If we want to translate a numerical character string into an integer, we have to write a sequence of statements to do it. Here is one way that is simple, but it is specifically oriented to the ASCII character set. The technique is based on the fact that the 10 numeric character strings occupy consecutive positions in the collating sequence. (They do in other collating sequences as well.) That being the case, the integer value for any numeric character is the difference between its internal representation and that of '0'. For instance, ORD('7') - ORD('0') will produce a 7.

We shall use this idea as the nucleus of a loop for converting a string consisting of four numerical characters to a four-digit integer. Remember that the leftmost digit of a four-digit integer has to be multiplied by 1000 to obtain its actual magnitude, the next one has to be multiplied by 100, and so on:

```
CONST
    reference = ORD('0') ;
VAR
    digit, i, convert : INTEGER ;
    numstring : STRING[4]
    .
    .
    .
    READ (numstring)
    .
    .
    .
    convert := ORD(COPY(numstring,4,1)) - reference ;
    {WE HANDLED THE RIGHTMOST DIGIT SEPARATELY BECAUSE}
    {IT DOES NOT NEED ANY MULTIPLICATION TO ADJUST IT.}
    {MORE PRECISELY, IT NEEDS MULTIPLICATION BY 1.     }
    FOR  i := 3 DOWNTO 1 DO
       BEGIN
         digit := ORD(COPY(numstring,i,1)) - reference ;
         convert := convert + PWROFTEN(4-i)*digit
       END
```

ᴘ ʀ ᴇ ᴅ **and** ꜱ ᴜ ᴄ ᴄ   The ability to find a character's position in the collating sequence is complemented by two functions that identify the characters on either side. PRED('W') returns W's predecessor (i.e.,'V'), PRED('3') returns '2', and so on. Similarly, SUCC('W') return's W's successor (i.e.,'X'), and SUCC('3') returns '4'. For those with a continuing interest in going nowhere at computer speed, SUCC(PRED('3')) returns '3', but with a flourish and a cloud of smoke.

Incidentally, PRED and SUCC can be applied to any simple data type except REAL. Thus, PRED(3297) is 3296, and SUCC(-81) is −80.

9.2 PROCESSING OF CHARACTER DATA

Inclusion of the STRING data type in UCSD Pascal reduces the utility of CHAR data. However, there still may be situations where it is advantageous to deal with one character at a time.

9.2.1 Declaration of Character Variables

The declaration

```
VAR
     letter : CHAR
```

sets up a variable with a capacity of one character. If we want to use the CHAR type for a string of several characters, we must set up an array. Thus,

```
VAR
     ltrstring : ARRAY[1..20] OF CHAR
```

gives us the equivalent of a 20-character string in which each character can be isolated by attaching an appropriate subscript. However, it should be understood that none of the string-handling subprograms can be used on CHAR data, arrays or otherwise.

There are two convenient ways to initialize character arrays: One technique, i.e., a loop controlled by a FOR statement, is well worked in by now, so we shall not belabor it. As an alternative, UCSD Pascal provides the FILLCHAR procedure for packed character arrays. The general form is

```
FILLCHAR(destination,length,character)
```

in which the first argument specifies the starting element in the array to be initialized, the second argument specifies the number of elements to be initialized, and the third argument indicates the single character to be placed in the designated elements. Thus, if `ltrstring` is the 20-element array declared before, the statement

```
FILLCHAR(ltrstring,20,'*')
```

fills the entire array with asterisks (another all-star cast).

9.2.2 Character Manipulation

There are no special operations for `CHAR` data. Assignment is really the only available activity. Moreover, certain restrictions drastically limit the interchange between `CHAR` and `STRING` data. For instance, if `sym` and `hdr` are declared as `CHAR` and `STRING[6]`, respectively, and both have values in them, the assignment

```
sym := hdr[3]
```

is legal, but

```
hdr[4] := sym
```

is not.

9.2.3 Processing of Character Arrays

`FILLCHAR` is just one of UCSD Pascal's special subprograms for handling packed `CHAR` arrays. (It turns out that these subprograms [including `FILLCHAR`] can be used with arrays containing other types of data, but such usage is tricky, and being tricky is not our major intent here.)

`MOVELEFT` **and** `MOVERIGHT`   A group of consecutive character array elements can be transferred to another array (or another part of the same array) by using UCSD Pascal's `MOVELEFT` or `MOVERIGHT` procedures. Each of these subprograms is invoked as follows:

```
MOVELEFT     (source,destination,numberofcharacters)
MOVERIGHT
```

The first argument specifies the location (in a character array) of the first character to be copied (for `MOVELEFT`) or the last character to be copied (for `MOVERIGHT`); the second argument specifies the location to receive that character, and the third argument gives the number of characters to be copied. As implied by the respective meanings of the first arguments, `MOVELEFT` moves from left to right, and `MOVERIGHT` moves from right to left. To see how this works, consider the following situation:

```
VAR
   here, there : PACKED ARRAY [1..10] OF CHAR ;
   ltr : CHAR ;
   i : INTEGER
   .
   .
   .
   FILLCHAR (there,10,'*') ;   {there has '**********'}
   ltr := PRED('A') ;
   FOR  i := 1 TO 10 DO
      BEGIN
         ltr := SUCC(ltr) ;
         here[i] := ltr
      END                      {here has 'ABCDEFGHIJ'}
```

Given this situation, the statement

```
MOVELEFT (here,there,5)
```

copies the first five characters of here into the first five elements of
there, so that there's contents become 'ABCDE****'. This is the same
as saying

```
FOR  i := 1 TO 5 DO
   there[i] := here[i]
```

The same results are obtained with

```
MOVERIGHT (here,there,5)
```

which, in turn, is equivalent to

```
FOR  i := 5 DOWNTO 1  DO
   there[i] := here[i]
```

Starting with the same situation, the statement

```
MOVERIGHT (here[2],there[3],4)
```

produces '**BCDE****' in there. So does

```
MOVELEFT (here[2],there[3],4)
```

The situation gets a little more complicated when the same array serves as
both source and destination. For one thing, MOVELEFT and MOVERIGHT

have different effects. For example, starting with the situation defined before,

```
MOVELEFT (here[2],here[5],5)
```

produces 'ABCDBCDBCJ' in here while

```
MOVERIGHT (here[2],here[5],5,)
```

produces 'ABCDBCDEFJ'. (The exact details are left for you to deduce.)

Searching Character Arrays UCSD Pascal's SCAN function performs essentially the same kind of operation on a character array as POS does on a string. The basic difference (understandably) is that SCAN looks for a single character. Suppose there is a PACKED ARRAY[1..10] OF CHAR containing the characters 'A' through 'J' in here[1] through here[10], respectively, and where is an INTEGER variable. The statement

```
where := SCAN(10,='E',here)
```

triggers the following activity: The array here is scanned from left to right, starting with element here[1], in an enthusiastic search for the character 'E'. All 10 elements will be examined (if necessary) as directed by the first argument. The search stops when an 'E' is found or, failing that, when the specified number of elements has been examined. In this particular case, the search is successful and the position is reported as an integer value relative to the search's starting point. As far as SCAN is concerned, the position of the starting point always is zero, regardless of that starting point's location. For our example, this means that a value of 4 (not 5) will be stored in where. An unsuccessful search returns a value equal to that in the first argument. Thus,

```
where := SCAN(10,='R',here)
```

stores a value of 10 in where. The statement

```
where := SCAN(8,='E',here[3])
```

defines a new starting point (here[3] instead of here[1]). Consequently, here[3] is now position 0, and the value stored in where will be 2. An unsuccessful search, given the same length and starting position, yields a value of 8.

It also is possible to search for a mismatch. If we have an array containing a sequence of the same character and we want to find out where that sequence ends, we can use SCAN with $<>$ instead of $=$. Assuming elements there[1] through there[10] contain the sequence '******S***', the statement

```
where := SCAN(10,<>'*',there)
```

stores the value 6 in where. $<>$ and $=$ are the only acceptable operators.

If SCAN's first argument is negative, the search proceeds from right to left, and SCAN uses the third argument as the *rightmost* position. When this happens, the returned value is either zero or negative. For instance, using here and where as before, the statement

```
where := SCAN(-10,='E',here[10])
```

gets the search started at here[10] (i.e., here[10] is position 0). Under these conditions, the match occurs at position −5, and it is that value that is stored in where. Similarly,

```
where := SCAN(-7='J',here[8])
```

produces a value of −7 in where.

9.2.4 Input/Output of Character Data

Character data can be transmitted using READ, READLN, WRITE, and WRITELN. Unlike string data, character data may appear anywhere in an input line. Since each character variable holds exactly one character, a READ or READLN reads exactly one character, and it is the next one available. Consequently, the programmer must be careful about which character is being read. One of the most common difficulties occurs when the programmer forgets about this and prepares an input line in which a numerical value is followed by a separating blank which, in turn, is followed by the character to be read. Instead of picking up the character, the READ brings in and stores the blank instead. One way to overcome this difficulty is to place the input character value immediately after the previous input value.

9.3 PROCESSING BOOLEAN DATA

Boolean data (with values of TRUE or FALSE) may be stored as single-valued variables or BOOLEAN arrays declared via the usual VAR mechanism. The declarations

```
VAR
    switch : BOOLEAN ;
    selector : ARRAY[1..8] OF BOOLEAN
```

are typical examples.

Pascal recognizes three fundamental BOOLEAN operations: AND, OR, and NOT, from which boolean expressions may be constructed. We have used these in setting up IF-THEN-ELSE decisions, so that their properties are familiar to us.

9.3.1 Evaluation of Boolean Expressions

A boolean expression can be built by combining boolean terms and factors just as we would construct an arithmetic expression. For instance, assuming sw1, sw2, sw3, and sw4 to be declared as single-valued BOOLEAN variables, we can write assignment statements such as

```
sw4 := sw1  AND  sw2  OR  NOT sw3
```

These expressions may be as complex as necessary, but the final result inevitably must be TRUE or FALSE. Further insight into the behavior of boolean expressions can be gained by knowing that Pascal uses the following priority ranking for performing boolean computations:

1. NOT
2. AND
3. OR

Thus, using sw1, sw2, and sw3, the expression

```
NOT sw1 AND sw2
```

is equivalent to

```
(NOT sw1) AND sw2
```

and

```
sw2 OR sw1 AND sw3
```

is equivalent to

```
sw2 OR (sw1 AND sw3)
```

Here, as in arithmetic expressions, the programmer is well-advised to use parentheses to be sure that the boolean processing conveys his or her exact intent.

9.3.2 Relational Operators in Boolean Expressions

We already know that Pascal's relational operators can be used to construct comparisons between expressions so that the outcome is either TRUE or FALSE. In addition, these same relational operators (=, <>, <=, >=, <, >) are accepted as boolean operators. This is based on Pascal's internal use of 0 for FALSE and 1 for TRUE. The obvious consequences (by definition) are that

1. FALSE is "less than" TRUE ;
2. SUCC(FALSE) is TRUE ;
3. PRED(TRUE) is FALSE .

This means that we can apply any type of comparison to boolean expressions and expect the resulting processing to follow a set of rules consistent with the foregoing relationships. These rules can be summarized conveniently by constructing a *truth table* in which the outcome of each comparison is shown for all possible combinations of boolean values. (Since two boolean values are being compared, the truth table needs to show only four combinations.) This information is given in Table 9.1 (with AND, OR, and NOT thrown in for good measure).

Table 9.1 Boolean operations (SW1, SW2, and SW3 are declared as BOOLEAN)

					<>	<=	>=	>	<
SW1	SW2	AND	OR	=	(Exclusive OR)	(Implies)	(Is implied by)	(Does not imply)	(Is not implied by)
T	T	T	T	T	F	T	T	F	F
T	F	F	T	F	T	F	T	T	F
F	T	F	T	F	T	T	F	F	T
F	F	F	F	T	F	T	T	F	F

SW3 resulting from SWe := SW1 operation SW2

SW1	SW2 := Not SW1
T	F
F	T

9.3.3 Other Considerations

There is not much more to say in this context about the processing of boolean values, but it is helpful to know what *cannot* be done. Although boolean values may be used as arguments for subprograms (and they may be returned by functions), UCSD Pascal prohibits their use for input or output.

9.4 PROCESSING ENUMERATIVE DATA

Although programmer-defined enumerative data types cannot be read or written, Pascal provides limited facilities for their internal manipulation.

9.4.1 Assignment of Enumerative Values

Given the nature of programmer-defined enumerative data types, it would not make sense to support such data with extensive arithmetic or character-handling capabilities. Accordingly, the manipulative facilities are limited to simple assignment, examples of which we have already seen in previous chapters. We shall complete the story here by defining a couple of data types, declaring appropriate variables, and exercising Pascal's facilities on them:

```
TYPE
    eyecolor = (blue, brown, gray, green, hazel) ;
    ocean = (Atlantic, Pacific, Indian, Arctic, Antarctic)
VAR
    peepers, orbs : eyecolor ;
    waterbody, vastness : ocean
```

Given these declarations, assignments such as

```
waterbody := Pacific ;
vastness := waterbody
```

and

```
peepers := blue ;
orbs := SUCC(peepers)
```

are legitimate. In the latter case, the variable orbs will receive a value of brown. Similarly, PRED(Indian) is Pacific, and SUCCSUCC (brown)) is green.

9.4.2 Enumerative Data and Integers

Since enumerative values are represented internally as integers (see Table 5.1), it is consistent for Pascal to provide a pathway from an enumerative value to the corresponding (internal) integer representation. This is done with the ORD function. The integer value returned by the function can be used like any other integer. Thus, ORD(Pacific) returns a value of 1, and the expression

```
ORD(peepers) + ORD(orbs)
```

is legal. Whether it makes any sense or not depends on the particular situation. Since these enumerative values are *not* character strings, the CHR function is irrelevant here and cannot be used.

$\mathcal{P}$roblems

1. Assume we have the following declarations and assignments:

    ```
    VAR
          dsc1 : STRING[12] ;
          dsc2 : STRING[7] ;
          loc1, loc2 : INTEGER
          .
          .
          .
          dsc1 := 'THOROUGHFARE' ;
          dsc2 := 'SUMMARY' ;
          loc1 := 1 ;
          loc2 := 4
    ```

    Indicate the value for each of the following:
    (a) COPY(dsc1,1,10)
    (b) The character in position 4 of dsc1
    (c) The positions of the letters in dsc2 that also appear in dsc1
    (d) COPY(dsc2,3,4)
    (e) COPY(dsc1,6,6)
    (f) COPY(dsc2,4,3)
    (g) COPY(dsc1,loc1,loc2)
    (h) COPY(dsc2,loc1,loc2-1)
    (i) CONCAT(dsc1,'S')
    (j) CONCAT('CAR',COPY(dsc1,9,loc2))
    (k) CONCAT('C',COPY(dsc2,5,6),
             COPY(dsc2,2*loc2+loc1,SUCC(3*loc1)))
    (l) COPY(dsc1,7,loc2)
    (m) CONCAT(COPY(dsc1,2+SUCC(loc2),PRED(loc2)),
             CHR(SUCC(ORD(COPY(dsc1,2,1)))))

2. Assume the following declaration:

```
VAR
     prep : ARRAY [1..4,1..3] OF STRING[8]
```

and some type of processing that fills the array with the values shown below:

AT	TO	BY
WITH	UNTIL	IN
FROM	WITHIN	WITHOUT
BEYOND	BELOW	OVER

Specify the value or write the Pascal description for each of the following:
(a) The value in `prep[3,2]`
(b) The value in `COPY(prep[3,2],2,3)`
(c) The value in `COPY(prep[2,2],3,3)`
(d) The value in `prep`'s ninth element
(e) The location of the element containing the most vowels
(f) The string 'WITH' occurs in three places; describe each one
(g) The value formed by the expression
     `CONCAT(prep[1,1],prep[1,2])`
(h) The value formed by `CONCAT(prep[2,3],`
     `COPY(prep[1,3],1,2))`
(i) An expression that forms the string 'ROVER' using only the characters in a single element of `prep`
(j) An expression that forms the string 'FORMAT' using only those elements in `prep`'s first column
(k) Declare a 4-character string name `first` and write the statement(s) to fill `first` with the string 'BIWO'

3. Write a program that will place a string's characters in reverse order. The program is to handle strings up to 80 characters long.

4. Write a function named `squeeze` that operates on strings of 80 characters or less and removes excess blanks between words. Test your program using the following data. (Each line starts a new string):

Seers   Find a Ready   Market   For   Predictions   in   Users
But   few corporations in   any   field   are more   close-mouthed
Tourists   Hail Their Courtesy; Foreigners Residing There Disagree.

5. Write a program that is to read a succession of data sets where each data set consists of three strings named `which-string`, `oldstring`, and `newstring`. The program is to look through `whichstring` for an occurrence of `oldstring`. If it finds

oldstring, it is to replace it by newstring. The strings in old-string and newstring are not necessarily the same size, nor is it guaranteed that oldstring actually appears in whichstring. It is up to you to figure out what the program should report for each input set, and how the program should report it.

6. Generalize the program from the previous problem so that it does the replacement for all occurrences of oldstring in whichstring.

7. Write an interactive program that will read and process a succession of strings having a length of 15 characters or less. For each string read, the program is to display the string with all vowels replaced by dollar signs.

8. Write a program that processes strings as in the previous problem. This time, the program is to produce an output string consisting of all the vowels in the input string.

9. Write a program similar to the one for Problem 8. This time, the output string is to be the same length as the input string, and it is to consist of the vowels from the input string, placed in the rightmost positions of the output string and padded on the left with asterisks.

10. The H. P. Middleman Company is a wholesale distributor dealing in a wide variety of manufactured parts and components. For years they managed their business in a haphazard way, but now the competition is killing them with computers: Everything is systematized and Middleman must mend their ways. One of the areas that needs tightening is the scheme for identifying the various parts, invented decades ago by the founder's brother-in-law, William E. Nilley, Jr. Some parts were identified by numbers, some by names containing only letters, others by combinations of letters and numbers—all in all a mess. This is to be straightened out by a simple system that assigns an all-numerical identifier to each part:

1. Identifiers containing only numbers are left alone.
2. Identifiers containing only letters are converted with each letter being replaced by a number corresponding to that letter's position in the alphabet. For instance, A is replaced by 1, E by 5, X by 24, and so on.
3. Identifiers containing letters and numbers are handled by leaving the numbers alone and converting the letters as described for all-letter identifiers. In addition, a 0 (zero) is placed at the beginning of the converted identifier. (It was found that there are no part identifiers beginning with zero in the current system.)

A few examples will clarify this: A part identifier of 62505 remains 62505; an identifier of GUZZLR would be converted to 72126261218; an identifier of 21GJ7B would convert to 02171072. Careful examination of the inventory assured one and all that this conversion would guarantee against producing the same identifier for more than one type of item.

Write a program that reads a succession of old identifiers (one to a line) interactively and displays that identifier, along with its new version. An old identifier is never more than six characters long, no matter what type it is. (Of course, some new ones will have to be longer.) Stop the run with end-of-file. Each line of output is to look like this:

PART NAME   GUZZLR   CHANGES TO   72126261218

After all the input has been processed, the program is to display four additional lines showing how many all-digit part identifiers were processed, how many all-letter identifiers were processed, how many mixed identifiers were processed, and the total number of identifiers processed. One more thing: Old identifiers consist only of litters and/or numbers.

11. Write a batch version of the program specified for the previous problem and use the following input values when you run the program:

FOOZIK
304665
G569J
PLEVVL
P6K45H
(*HC77   (it is up to you to decide how to handle this)
400400
400400
−20476
BENDL

12. Sir Sedgewick Thruncklestrop left a peculiar will: He was sure that the hamlet of Threckfordshirehamburghville-on-the-Grobe was the cradle of his family, and that many of his distant relatives still lived there. The villagers didn't know they were descended from the famous Duke of Thrunklestrop, but Sir Sedgewick had a theory. He believed that his family could be traced through their names. If the last name had a TH in it, followed anywhere by a CK, that family (or so Sir Sedgewick believed) was related. Accordingly, the will set up a fund that would pay for a crack team of genealogists to travel to Threckfordshirehamburghville-on-the-Grobe and check the population. Every family with the appropriate type of last name would then receive a handsome simulated vinyl wall sculpture of the Thrunklestrop coat of arms (at no charge) and a fine certificate attesting to the

fact that the family had indeed received a handsome simulated vinyl wall sculpture, etc. The sleepy village of (oh no, we are not going to go through that again) will never be the same after that.

Luckily, the village is considerably more modernized than was first thought. For each household, the genealogists were amazed to find that there existed a line of computer-compatible data showing a six-digit identification number and a last name (up to 25 letters). Now, they need a program to process the data and display the name and i.d. number for each family eligible to receive a handsome, simulated, etc. After the last household has been processed, the program is to print a line indicating the total number of households processed and the total number of eligible households. (Note that a name like THROCKLEY is eligible while a name like BRACKTHIS-TLE is not; reread the problem if you are not sure why this should be so.) Run the program interactively using the following data:

```
334068THROCKMORTON
109877SNAPTHICKET
207654BILGEWEATHER
886002CROCKTHRESHER
797634TRICKLETHORPER
453231THIMBLEDERRICK
795112HIPTHWACKER
603114THWEBWYTHE
842331CRAZZWOCKER
785409BICKTHWICKMORESHAM
```

13. Write a batch version of the program described in the previous problem, and test the program with the same data.

14. Just as the genealogical program was being written, somebody discovered that the team had been misinformed. The household data are available, sure enough, but the order actually is reversed: The i.d. number follows the name. Rewrite the program so that it will handle these values.

15. Prepare a version of the program described in Example 9.2. Instead of reading a song title and a string for which that title is to be searched, arrange for the program to read the string to be matched first. Then this may be followed by any number of song titles to be searched for that same string. After all the titles have been processed, the program is to display the number of titles searched and the maximum number of matches in any one title.

16. Write a truth table for each of the following expressions or statements. Assume that all of the variables have been declared as BOOLEAN, but do not assume that all of the expressions or statements are written correctly.

```
(a)   m1 OR TRUE
(b)   m2 OR NOT TRUE
(c)   m3 := m1 OR NOT m2
(d)   m3 := m1 AND (NOT m2 AND NOT m3)
(e)   m1 <> (m2 AND m3)
(f)   m4 := m4 <= (m3 > m2)
(g)   m3 := m1 = m2
(h)   m3 := NOT m1 AND NOT (m2 <= NOT m4)
```

17. Indicate what the final value will be for each of the following independent statements. Assume that all variables are declared as BOOLEAN, and that they have the following values just before the statement is executed:

```
m1, m3, and m5 are TRUE; the rest are FALSE.
```

```
(a)   m3 := m3 AND TRUE
(b)   m5 := m1 AND m2 AND m3 AND m4
(c)   m4 := (m4 <= m1) >= (m3 AND m2) OR m1
(d)   m5 := (m1 < m2) OR NOT (m2 <> m3) AND (m3 AND m4)
```

18. Write a program that processes a succession of 20-element one-dimensional INTEGER arrays consisting only of 1s and 0s. For each one, the program is to produce an integer indicating the number of elements that have values of TRUE. For purposes of the problem, a 1 represents TRUE and a 0 represents FALSE.

19. Write a program that processes a succession of 20-element one-dimensional INTEGER arrays consisting only of 1s and 0s. For each one, the program is to produce an integer indicating the number of elements that have values representing FALSE. (As in the previous problem, 1 represents TRUE and 0 represents FALSE.)

20. Combine the processing for the previous two problems by developing a program that, for each input array, allows the user to specify whether he or she wants the number of TRUEs or FALSEs reported. The program computes the number, along with some kind of signal that indicates what is being reported.

21. Write a program that processes a succession of input sets in which each input set consists of a 24-element INTEGER array consisting only of 1s and 0s, two integers defining which part of the array is of interest, and another integer indicating how many TRUE values we are seeking. (As before, use 1 to represent TRUE and 0 for FALSE.) For example, the input set

```
1 0 0 1 0 0 1 1 1 0 1 1 1 0 0 1 0 1 0 1 1 0 0 1 12 22 8)
```

asks the program to examine elements 12 through 22. If it finds at least 8 values of TRUE, it is to report success; if not, it is to report failure.

Chapter 10

Introduction to Input/Output Operations

Our use of the READLN and WRITELN procedures with the standard INPUT, OUTPUT, and KEYBOARD files exploits only part of Pascal's facilities for transmitting individual data items between the central processor and the outside world. This chapter looks more closely at these input/output processes and the mechanisms behind them.

10.1 TEXT FILES AND INTERACTIVE FILES

Pascal's READ, READLN, WRITE, and WRITELN procedures are based on a view of a file as a series of characters followed by an end-of-file mark, (<cntrl>c serves as this mark in UCSD Pascal.) Such a file is called a *textfile*. Our use of WRITELN, for instance, causes the program to form a sequence of characters from the parenthesized output list and send that sequence to a standard (predeclared) textfile named OUTPUT. The system automatically associates OUTPUT with the video screen, just as it associates the text file INPUT with the keyboard. (These associations can be changed, but that subject is beyond the scope of this book.) Since the output list for a WRITELN may include numerical values, Pascal automatically converts them to characters so that their form is consistent with the textfile's requirements. The characters in a textfile are punctuated further by additional markers called *end-of-line-indicators* or *line separators*. (We shall refer to the end-of-line indicator as <eol>. Whenever we type <return> in a textfile, the system generates an <eol>.) These are invisible to the programmer, but they can be detected by Pascal. Consequently, they can be used to influence the appearance of output text and to help control certain input processes. The length of a line in a textfile is not fixed.

Instead, it is simply the number of characters (including blanks) between the line separators.

In UCSD Pascal, INPUT and OUTPUT are special kinds of textfiles called *interactive files*. These are constructed and organized like ordinary textfiles, but they cause certain differences in the way input/output operations are performed. Every time one of our programs issues a prompt message and waits for input values, we are taking advantage of an interactive file's special properties. We have not had to include any specific commands that tell the program to stop and wait for input. Yet it "knows" to do that.

The automatic mechanism providing this information is part of UCSD Pascal's internal treatment of an interactive file. If INPUT, OUTPUT, and KEYBOARD were ordinary textfiles, the program would expect input data to be prepared and available for the processor (typically from an online diskette) before execution started. Thus, once the program was running, it could complete its work without stopping. The data items would not be typed at the keyboard during execution. We shall use such textfiles later on.

10.2 READLN AND WRITELN OPERATIONS

When we use READLN, we are telling Pascal to interpret the characters in a textfile in accordance with certain rules. By the same token, a call to WRITELN implies a directive that controls the way the resulting textfile is prepared.

10.2.1 The READLN Procedure

When we use READLN in the form employed thus far, we tell Pascal to assume that each value in the interactive file has a certain appearance:

1. An integer value consists of a string of numerical characters (the digits 0 through 9) that may or may not be preceded by a sign. Pascal recognizes the end of an integer value by the appearance of the first nonnumeric character. (This usually is a blank.) For example, suppose nv is an INTEGER variable, the program says

   READLN (nv)

   and we type this:

   −47 ⟨return⟩

   UCSD Pascal would find the first eligible character (the minus sign in this instance) and continue reading until it found the first blank to the right of the last digit. The resulting string of three characters (minus sign, 4, and 7) would be converted automatically to the internal form used by the computer to represent integers, and the value thus produced would be stored in `nv`. The program then would skip over the blanks (or anything else that might be there) and stop at the `<eol>`. The same rules apply to long integer and integer subrange data values.

2. A real value consists of a string of non-blank numerical characters preceded by an optional sign and punctuated by those symbols acceptable in a real constant. The "end" of a real input value is reached when Pascal finds a character that does not belong in a real constant (e.g., a blank). Thus, if `rate` and `cwt` are `REAL` variables, and our input request looks like this,

```
READLN (rate, cwt)
```

the input line

```
3.274   −8.871E−4<return>
```

results in the storage of 3.274E0 and −8.871E−4 in `rate` and `cwt`, respectively.

3. Since a `CHAR` value always consists of a single character, Pascal finds such a value (when requested to do so) simply by using the next character in the file. For example, if `initial` is a `CHAR` variable (and `nv`, `rate`, and `cwt` are defined as they were earlier), then

```
READLN (nv, rate, initial, cwt)
```

applied to the following input line

```
361   3.274 −8.871E−4<return>
```

will produce values of 361, 3.274E0, and −8.871E−4 in `nv`, `rate`, and `cwt`, respectively, and a blank in `initial`. After finding and converting the 361 to integer form, Pascal finds the five characters 3.274, converts them to a real number and stores it in `rate`. The next character (the one after the 4), which is a blank, is stored (without conversion, of course) in `initial`. Finally, Pascal looks for (and finds) a character string (−8.871E−4) representing a real value, converts it to real form, and stores the result in `cwt`. In doing so, Pascal skips over the W since it already has found a character value for `initial` and, at that point, is looking for a real value. If we wanted a W in `initial`, our input line (assuming the same `READLN` request) would have to say

```
361   3.274W   −8.871E−4<return>
```

4. A string may appear as input, but it must be followed by ⟨eol⟩. Consequently, there can be only one string in a line, and it must be the last input item on that line. For example, assuming the following declaration:

```
VAR
  nv       :  INTEGER ;
  cwt      :  REAL ;
  message  :  STRING[30]
```

the statement

```
READLN (nv, cwt, message)
```

when presented with the typed entry

361bbb−8.871E−4bbbWHAT HO GOOD CHARLES⟨return⟩

will store 361 in nv, -8.871E-4 in cwt, and bbbWHAT HO GOOD CHARLES in message. (We showed the blanks to make it clear that the characters stored in the string variable message included the three blanks immediately following the 4.

READLN is designed to look for the ⟨eol⟩ indicator and use it as a signal to conclude its activity. For example, assuming variables nv, rate, and cwt as before, suppose we prepare the following line of input:

24   −311.56   6500.7   487   608.727   FMNEH⟨return⟩

to be read by

```
READLN (nv, rate, cwt)
```

the program reads the first three values, converts them, and stores them in nv, rate, and cwt, respectively. Then, it moves across the rest of the line until it finds the ⟨eol⟩. As a result, the next item ready to be read is the first item on the next line. The values after the third value (i.e., the 487, 608.727, and FMNEH) are skipped over and lost.

It is possible to use READLN without specifying any list of variables. The form

```
READLN
```

causes the program to move across the INPUT file till it finds and reads the next ⟨eol⟩.

Example 10.1 The Sostenuto Piano Company keeps the following line of data for each piano sold:

Name	Description	Form
serial	serial number	integer
piano	type of piano (U=upright; S=spinet; C=console; B=baby grand; G=grand; L=largegrand)	character
yrofsale	year in which piano was sold	integer
pianowt	piano weight to the nearest pound	integer
price	selling price, dollars	integer
custloc	customer location (two-character state code; e.g., NY=New York; FS=foreign sale).	string

We shall write a program that determines, for a specified time span (e.g., from 1974 through 1977) how many of each type of piano were sold. The algorithm is straightforward: An initial prompt will ask for a starting year startyr and an ending year endyr. After these values are read and stored, the data for each piano will be read in succession (in response to a prompt) and used (if the year of sale is in the specified range) to update the counter for the appropriate piano type. As the pseudocode in Figure 10.1 indicates, this process will be repeated as long as the end of the input file has not been reached. Once the last data line has been brought in and examined, the results will be displayed and the program will conclude.

The first line of input (startyr and endyr) is handled easily enough by typing the two values on a line in response to the prompt:

```
1947  1960<return>
```

The program picks them up with the statement

```
READLN (startyr, endyr)
```

Subsequent input data are processed by a loop, each cycle of which brings in another line containing values for INTEGER variable serial, CHAR variable piano, INTEGER variables yrofsale, pianowt, and price, and the two-character string custloc. We must make sure that numerical values are separated by nonnumeric characters. At the same time, the character data must be positioned in such a way that we do not (mistakenly) force the program to take one of the separating blanks and use it as an input value; in our example, this means that the character value for

Define serial, pianowt, yrofsale, startyr, endyr, numsold for each type
of piano, price, custloc, and piano.
Initialize numsold for each piano type.
Read startyr and endyr.
WHILE
there is input to be processed
    Read a set of input values for a piano that was sold.
    IF
        the piano was sold between years startyr and endyr
    THEN
        increment the number sold for that piano type.
    ENDIF
ENDWHILE
Display headings.
Display piano type and number sold for each type.
Display terminating message.
Stop.

Figure 10.1

Pseudocode for Example 10.1

piano must be placed immediately after the integer value for serial; a
separating blank between the two would be picked up and used. Blanks
may appear between piano and yrofsale, yrofsale and
pianowt, and pianowt and price. The final value for a given piano,
i.e., custloc, must appear immediately after price for the same reason
given in the case of piano, and it must be followed immediately by
⟨return⟩. Thus, a typical line of input would look like this:

31006G   1971   655   8755TX⟨return⟩

To help enhance the program's clarity, we shall define an enumerative
data type named pianotype, and we shall convert the character value for
piano to the corresponding name for the appropriate pianotype. The
resulting program is shown in Figure 10.2 and a sample run is given in
Figure 10.3.

Take special note of the loop that initializes the elements of numsold
to zero. The *index* that controls and monitors the number of cycles through
the loop (pianosize) is not an ordinary integer. Instead, it is a programmer-defined variable which takes on values that do not appear to be
integers. However, we know (from Section 5.2.2, Subrange Data Types) that
Pascal associates the sequence of values defined for an enumerative data
type with corresponding internal numerical values. Consequently, given
the TYPE definition for pianotype, the statement

```
FOR pianosize := upright TO mislabel  DO
                etc.
```

sets up a loop that will go through exactly seven cycles.

```
(***************************************************************)
(**                    EXAMPLE 10.1                        **)
(***************************************************************)
(** THIS PROGRAM READS A SUCCESSION OF DATA VALUES, EACH LINE **)
(** DESCRIBING THE SALE OF A PIANO BY THE SOSTENUTO PIANO CO. **)
(** THESE VALUES ARE PRECEDED BY A STARTING YEAR AND ENDING   **)
(** YEAR WHICH BRACKET A TIME SPAN TO BE CONSIDERED DURING THIS**)
(** RUN. FOR EACH TYPE OF PIANO, THE PROGRAM PRINTS THE NUMBER **)
(** SOLD DURING THE SPECIFIED TIME SPAN.                     **)
(** VARIABLES:                                               **)
(**    SERIAL: A PIANO'S IDENTIFICATION NUMBER               **)
(**    PIANO: TYPE OF PIANO (U=UPRIGHT, S=SPINET, C=CONSOLE,  **)
(**                    B=BABYGRAND, G=GRAND, L=SUPERGRAND)   **)
(**    PIANOSIZE: AN INTERNAL (ENUMERATIVE) VARIABLE DERIVED  **)
(**               FROM PIANO                                 **)
(**    PIANOWT: A PIANO'S WEIGHT                             **)
(**    YROFSALE: THE YEAR A PARTICULAR PIANO WAS SOLD        **)
(**    PRICE: A PARTICULAR PIANO'S SELLING PRICE            **)
(**    CUSTLOC: TWO-LETTER CODE INDICATING CUSTOMER'S LOCATION **)
(**    NUMSOLD: THE NUMBER OF PIANOS (OF A PARTICULAR TYPE) SOLD**)
(**               DURING THE SPECIFIED TIME SPAN            **)
(**    STARTYR, ENDYR: STARTING AND ENDING YEARS            **)
(***************************************************************)
PROGRAM ex1001 ;
TYPE
   pianotype = (upright, spinet, console, babygrand,
                grand, largegrand, mislabel)  ;
VAR
   serial, pianowt, yrofsale, price, startyr, endyr  :   INTEGER    ;
   numsold  :   ARRAY[pianotype] OF INTEGER  ;
   custloc  :   STRING[2]  ;
   piano  :  CHAR  ;
   pianosize  :    pianotype  ;
BEGIN
   FOR  pianosize := upright TO mislabel   DO
      numsold[pianosize] := 0  ;
   WRITELN ('ENTER startyr, endyr.')  ;
   READLN (startyr, endyr)  ;
   WRITELN ('SOSTENUTO PIANO COMPANY')  ;
   WRITELN ('SALES FROM YEAR ',startyr, ' THROUGH ',endyr')  ;
   WRITELN ;    WRITELN ;
```

Figure 10.2

Program for Example 10.1.

```
WHILE  NOT EOF(INPUT)  DO
    BEGIN
        WRITELN ('ENTER serial,piano,yrofsale,pianowt,price,
                 custloc') ;
        READLN (serial, piano, yrofsale, pianowt, price, custloc) ;
        (*** CHECK WHETHER YEAR SOLD IS IN RANGE ***)
        IF  (yrofsale >= startyr) AND (yrofsale <= endyr)  THEN
            BEGIN
                (*** FIND THE PIANO TYPE ***)
                IF  piano = 'U'  THEN  pianosize := upright
                ELSE IF  piano = 'S'
                     THEN  pianosize  := spinet
                     ELSE IF  piano = 'C'
                          THEN  pianosize := console
                          ELSE IF  piano = 'B'
                               THEN pianosize := babygrand
                               ELSE IF  piano = 'G'
                                    THEN  pianosize := grand
                                    ELSE IF  piano = 'L'
                                         THEN pianosize := largegrand
                                         ELSE  pianosize := mislabel ;
                (*** NOW THE APPROPRIATE COUNTER IS        ***)
                (*** EXPRESSED SIMPLY AS NUMSOLD[PIANOSIZE] ***)
                numsold[pianosize] := numsold[pianosize] + 1
            END
    END  ;
    (*** ALL DATA HAVE BEEN PROCESSED. TIME TO WRITE THE OUTPUT. ***)
    WRITELN  ;    WRITELN  ;
    WRITELN ('UPRIGHTS: ',numsold[upright])      ;
    WRITELN ('SPINETS: ',numsold[spinet])  ;
    WRITELN ('CONSOLES: ',numsold[console]) ;
    WRITELN ('BABY GRANDS: ',numsold[babygrand])   ;
    WRITELN ('GRANDS: ',numsold[grand])  ;
    WRITELN ('LARGEGRANDS: ',numsold[largegrand]) ;
    WRITELN ('MISLABELED: 'numsold[mislabel]) ;
    WRITELN  ;
    WRITELN ('END OF RUN.')
END.
```

Figure 10.2——

Program for Example 10.1 (Continued)

10.2.2 The WRITELN Procedure

Each call to the WRITELN procedure produces output with a concluding
< eol >. Note that WRITELN does not *start* a new line. The < eol > placed
by WRITELN at the end of the list of output means that the first value
written by the *next* output statement will start a new line. (Look at Figure

```
ENTER startyr, endyr,
1960 1970<return>
SOSTENUTO PIANO COMPANY
SALES FROM YEAR 1960 THROUGH 1970

ENTER serial, piano, yrofsale, pianowt, price, custloc
1121U 1967 505 986NY<return>
ENTER serial, piano, yrofsale, pianowt, price, custloc
667G 1964 899 2100CA<return>
ENTER serial, piano, yrofsale, pianowt, price, custloc
1017S 1966 287 1144CT<return>
ENTER serial, piano, yrofsale, pianowt, price, custloc
3141L 1970 1093 21665TX<return>
ENTER serial, piano, yrofsale, pianowt, price, custloc
1207U 1969 587 1204IL<return>
ENTER serial, piano, yrofsale, pianowt, price, custloc
884W 1963 665 1355MO<return>
ENTER serial piano, yrofsale, pianowt, price, custloc
3286B 1968 994 4320PA<cntrl>c

UPRIGHTS: 2
SPINETS: 1
CÓNSOLES: 0
BABY GRANDS: 1
GRANDS: 1
LARGEGRANDS: 1
MISLABELED: 1

END OF RUN,
```

Figure 10.3———————————————————————————

Sample Run for Example 10.1

10.3 and see if you can explain why there is only one blank line before Example 10.1's output. Recall (Figure 10.2) that there are two blank WRITELN calls before the value of numsold[upright] is displayed. Thus, if INTEGER variable nv has a value of −31 and rate and cwt have respective values of 3.274 and −0.0008871, the procedure call

```
WRITELN (nv, rate, cwt)
```

produces a line like this:

```
−313.27400E0−8.87100E−4<eol>
```

(Of course, we cannot see the <eol>.) If we had written

```
WRITELN (nv, cwt) ;
WRITELN (rate)
```

instead, the result would have been two shorter lines, i.e.,

```
-313.27400E0 <eol>
-8.87100E-4 <eol>
```

It is up to the programmer to provide separation between the displayed values. Thus, if we say

```
WRITELN (nv,' ',rate,' ',cwt)
```

UCSD Pascal will obey, producing

```
-31bb3.27400E0bb-8.87100E-4 <eol>
```

(Recall that each b represents a blank. We shall use this representation to indicate the beginning of an output line, or to make sure that the exact separation between output items is clear.) A more effective alternative is to label the output (as has been our practice in the example programs) and build the blanks into the labels:

```
WRITELN ('nv = ',nv,'  cwt = ',cwt,'  rate = ',rate)
```

Of course, such labeled output is appropriate only when the amount of output is limited.

WRITELN, like READLN, can be used without an output list. The result is that the program writes an <eol>, after which it is ready to write on the next line. For instance, assuming the previous values for nv, rate, and cwt, the sequence

```
WRITELN ('NV: ',nv)  ;
WRITELN
WRITELN ('CWT: ',cwt,'  RATE: ',rate)
```

produces two lines of written output with a blank line between them:

```
NV: -31
CWT:b3.27400E0bbRATE:b-8.87100E-4
```

(Now that the appearance of <eol> is familiar to us, we shall show it only where specific clarification is needed.)

10.3 THE READ AND WRITE PROCEDURES

Individual input/output items in textfiles can be controlled by means of the READ and WRITE procedures. Each time one of these procedures is called, it reads (or writes) one data item and stops, with no consideration being given to ⟨eol⟩s.

10.3.1 Properties of READ

To see how the READ procedure operates, let us assume that nv is an INTEGER variable and that the statement

```
READ (nv)
```

is greeted by the typed input line

```
24   311   6500   7⟨return⟩
```

The program will read the first value and store it as an integer (24) in nv. It does not need an ⟨eol⟩ to bring in the value. UCSD Pascal's mechanism for interactive files uses the blank after the 24 for that purpose. Once that activity is complete, the program is ready to read the next value (i.e., the 311). Of course, it is up to the programmer to ask for it and to specify an appropriate destination. On the other hand, if we had read the data with

```
READLN (nv)
```

the variable nv still would have received a value of 24. However, the program would have skipped over the 311 and 6500. Additional comparisons between READ and READLN are shown in Table 10.1.

10.3.2 The EOLN Function

The READ procedure reads as many items as its list specifies. This is true regardless of the number of lines on which the items are typed. For instance, if nv, total, maxnum, and zsum are declared as INTEGER variables, and we say

```
READ (nv, total, maxnum, zsum)
```

we shall get the same results whether we type

```
24   311   6500   7⟨return⟩
```

or

```
24   311<return>
6500   7<return>
```

or even

```
24<return>
31<return>
6500<return>
7<return>
```

To implement this, UCSD Pascal makes READ insensitive to <eol> signals. <eol> is treated like a blank or any other symbol used to separate data items.

However, that does not mean that <eol> has no effect at all when READ is used. A special function, EOLN, is provided to sense <eol> signals and make their presence known to the program. EOLN produces a boolean value depending on the presence or absence of an end-of-line indicator. Whenever the program begins reading from a new input line, EOLN automatically is set to FALSE. As soon as the end of that line is reached, EOLN automatically changes to TRUE. The programmer can test for the end of a line in the standard INPUT file simply by testing EOLN. Suppose we had to know how many data items there were on a particular input line, and there was no guarantee as to the exact quantity. We could set up a little loop using READ to bring the items in one at a time (into a variable we shall call invalue) and a counter (which we shall call num_ of_values) to keep track of the number. Our loop could look like this:

```
num_of_values := 0 ;
WHILE  NOT(EOLN)  DO
   BEGIN
      READ (invalue) ;
      num_of_values := num_of_values + 1
         . . . . . . . . . .
      process invalue
         . . . . . . . . . .
   END ;
WRITELN ('THIS LINE HAS ',num_of_values,'VALUES.')
      . . . . . . . . . . .
```

10.3.3 Properties of WRITE

The WRITE procedure is related to WRITELN in the same way as READ is to READLN: After WRITE has completed its activity, the program is ready to write in the next position of the current output line. If the WRITE proce-

Table 10.1 Comparison of READ and READLN Procedures

nv, total, maxnum, zsum are declared as INTEGER variables; input for each example consists of the following four lines:

24	311	6500
7	631	7200
0	79	400
−6	32	511

Input operation(s)	nv	total	maxsum	zsum	next value
READLN (nv, total, maxnum)	24	311	6500	?	7
READ (nv) ; READ (total); READ (maxnum)	24	311	6500	?	7
READ (total) ; READ (nv) ; READ (zsum)	311	24	?	6500	7
READLN (nv) ; READLN (total); READLN (maxnum)	24	7	0	?	−6
READ (nv total) ; READ (maznum, zsum)	24	311	6500	7	631
READLN (nv, total) ; READLN (maxnum, zsum)	24	311	7	631	0
READLN (nv, total) ; READ (maxnum, zsum)	24	311	7	631	7200
READ (nv, total) ; READLN (maxnum, zxum)	24	311	6500	7	0

dure's list of data items overflows the line, the program simply fills the line and (after adding an ⟨eol⟩) continues writing on the next one.

The role of the ⟨eol⟩ can be seen more clearly by looking at a direct comparison between WRITE and WRITELN with the same output list. Using INTEGER variables nv and num_of_values with respective values of 31 and 416, and REAL variable xarea with a value of 5028.96, the specification

```
WRITELN ('NV: ',nv,' XAREA: ',xarea,'  NO, OF VALUES: ',
                          num_of_values)
```

produces the line

    NV:b31bbXREA:b5.02896E5bbNO. OF VALUES:b416 ⟨eol⟩

If we wanted to produce the same result using WRITE procedure, we would have to say

```
WRITE ('NV: ',nv) ;
WRITE ('  XAREA: ',xarea) ;
WRITE ('  NO, OF VALUES: ',num_of_values) ;
WRITELN \
```

or

```
WRITE ('NV: ',nv,'  XAREA: ',xarea,'  NO, OF VALUES: ',
                          num_of_val) ;
WRITELN
```

Without the concluding WRITELN, there would be no ⟨eol⟩ after the third value, and the next WRITE or WRITELN would place output on the same line.

10.4 FORMAT CONTROL OF DATA VALUES

The use of READ, READLN, WRITE, or WRITELN discussed so far depends on Pascal's automatic internal mechanisms to deal with individual data items. Although this reliance on Pascal simplifies input/output processes, it forces the programmer to give up some control over data transmission. As an alternative, we can exercise full control over output data formats. This is done by means of a simple extension to the information specified in WRITE and WRITELN.

10.4.1 Control of Output Formats

The presentation of output in convenient (easily readable) form is an important part of any successful computer program. Consequently, UCSD Pascal enables the programmer to describe each position of an output textfile. Format control is provided by specifying each variable in an output list together with a field length that indicates the number of positions the variable will occupy on the line. We shall look at how this works for each of UCSD Pascal's standard data types.

Control of Pages   Unless otherwise directed by the programmer, UCSD Pascal uses its own internal mechanisms to determine when to start a new output page. We need not resign ourselves to this tyranny if we do not want to. The PAGE procedure forces the start of a new page. For the standard OUTPUT file, the call is

```
PAGE (OUTPUT)  or simply  PAGE
```

For instance, the sequence

```
WRITELN ('NV: ',nv) ;
PAGE (OUTPUT) ;
WRITE ('NO, OF VALUES: ',num_of_values) ;
WRITELN
```

writes the first line and then starts a new page before writing the next one. Note that this is part of the executing program and, therefore, is quite different from the compiler directive (*$P*) that starts a new page when the Pascal statements are listed.

Format Control for Integer Values   When we specify a length for an integer output value, UCSD Pascal uses a position for each digit and an additional position for the sign. For instance, if reltime is an INTEGER variable whose range is known to be between −880 and +400, we need at least four positions to display its value. Thus, the specification

```
WRITELN ('      RELTIME=',reltime:4)
```

applied to a reltime value of −423 will produce

```
bbbbbRELTIME=−423 <eol>
```

For a reltime value of 317 the display would be

```
bbbbbRELTIME=b317 <eol>
```

(The positive sign is not shown; its place is occupied by a blank.) If the specified field length is greater than that required for the value, Pascal places the value in the rightmost positions and fills the extra ones with blanks. If reltime had a value of 27, for instance, the WRITELN specification given above would produce the display

```
bbbbbRELTIME=bb27 <eol>
```

We can separate integer output values with a specific number of blanks by using an intentionally longer field for each value. For instance, knowing that `reltime` never will need more than four positions for its display, a specification of `reltime:9` guarantees a string of (at least) five blanks before the value.

If we do not provide adequate length for an integer value, UCSD Pascal ignores our specification and uses the number of positions required to display the entire value. For positive values, the sign is not shown and there is no blank in its place. Thus, if `reltime` is −726, the specification

```
WRITELN ('bbbbbRELTIME=',reltime:2)
```

produces

bbbbbRELTIME=−726 ⟨eol⟩

but the same `WRITELN` applied to a `reltime` value of +387 produces

bbbbbRELTIME=387 ⟨eol⟩

It is nice of UCSD Pascal to take care of us this way, but it is not always a good idea to rely on this assistance. There are times when we want to arrange our output so that certain variables appear in certain positions. The only way to guarantee that is to specify enough room.

Formatted Display of Real Values   Real values can be displayed in floating-point form (the form used thus far) or conventional form. When we want a conventional display, we must tell Pascal how many positions to allocate for the overall value and how many of those to use for decimal places. This information is specified by the form

name:overall length:decimal places

For instance, if `REAL` variable `velocity` has a current value of −327.064, the specification

```
WRITELN ('VELOCITY=',velocity:8:3)
```

would produce

VELOCITY=−327.064 ⟨eol⟩

Note that the overall length has to include a space for the decimal point and one for the sign. (As is the case with integer values, a blank replaces the sign

Table 10.2 Formatted Output of Real Values in Conventional Form

Results of WRITELN (' VELOCITY=',velocity:lgth:dec)
and WRITELN (' VELOCITY=',velocity:lgth)

velocity	lgth	dec	result
-327.064	9	3	bbbbbVELOCITY=b–327.064
-327.064	8	3	bbbbbVELOCITY=–327.064
-327.064	11	3	bbbbbVELOCITY=bbb–327.064
-327.064	11	4	bbbbbVELOCITY=bb–327.064b
-327.064	8	4	bbbbbVELOCITY=–327.064b
-327.064	7	2	bbbbbVELOCITY=–327.06
-327.064	7	3	bbbbbVELOCITY=–327.064
81.27	8	3	bbbbbVELOCITY=bb81.27
81.27	3	2	bbbbbVELOCITY=81.27
-327.064	12	—	bbbbbVELOCITY=bb–3.27064E2
-327.064	10	—	bbbbbVELOCITY=–3.27064E2
-327.064	9	—	bbbbbVELOCITY=3.27064E2
-327.064	6	—	bbbbbVELOCITY=–3.27064E2

for positive values.) Differences between specified lengths and required lengths are handled in the same way as they are for integers. That is, the displayed value is right justified and the extra positions at the left are filled with blanks. Examples are shown in Table 10.2.

When a real value is to be displayed in floating-point form with a length controlled by the programmer, the length is described by a single specification:

variable name:length

Enough length must be provided to accommodate an exponent value, an exponent sign, the letter E, the fraction (typically 5 digits), a decimal point, a single digit to the left of the decimal point, and a sign (or a blank if the sign is positive). For example, if we expect the values for a particular variable to range from −4500.00 to 8000.00 and to include small values like 0.09 or −0.17, we would have to provide enough positions to display −4.50000000000000E3 or 8.00000000000000E3 or 9.00000000000000E−2 or −1.70000000000000E−1. It is clear, then, that at least 20 positions are required for such a variable. Using our velocity value of −327.064 as another example, the specification

WRITELN ('bbbbbVELOCITY=',velocity:21)

produces

bbbbbVELOCITY=bb−3.27064000000000E2 〈eol〉

Our specified length of 21 provides the positions for the standard material as described before, including 14 positions for the fraction. After all of that is taken care of, there are two extra positions, and those are filled with blanks and placed to the left of the minus sign.

An insufficient length specification forces UCSD Pascal to add enough positions to accommodate the value anyway. Some examples are given in Table 10.2. Here again, the best thing to do is to make sure that enough length is specified to assure the placement of the values exactly where you want them each time.

Formatted Display of Character Data   A character value, normally occupying a single position in an output textfile, can be included as part of a larger field. To illustrate, suppose the character value 'T' in variable dtype is displayed by saying

```
WRITELN ('bbbbbbbDTYPE=',dtype:4)
```

The result is

bbbbbbbDTYPE=bbbT 〈eol〉

Formatted String Data   Output lengths for string data are specified the same way as they are for integers. If the specified length exceeds that of the current value of the string, UCSD Pascal will pad the string with blanks at the left. An insufficient length causes the rightmost characters to be lost. For instance, if string variables word and header have respective values of 'SPECKLE' and 'CAMBER', the statement

```
WRITE ('WORD=',word:10,'bbHEADER=',header:4)
```

produces WORD=bbbSPECKLEbbHEADER=CAMB

10.4.2 Example 10.2

We shall expand the processing in Example 10.1 to include more elaborate output. In addition to showing the number of pianos sold for each type, the output is to show the total weight of pianos sold, the total price, and the average price, all for each type. Results are to be displayed in tabular form, accompanied by appropriate headings. The required format is given in Figure 10.4.

Since the processing is not appreciably more complicated than it was for the previous version, we shall concentrate on the design of the output format. Our first heading is 23 characters long. Using a page width of 80

SOSTENUTO PIANO COMPANY
SUMMARY OF PURCHASES FOR YEARS 1969 THROUGH 1977

PIANO TYPE	NO. SOLD	TOTAL WT.	TOTAL PRICE	AVG. PRICE
UPRIGHT	2	1356	$ 9133.00	$ 4566.50
SPINET	3	2776	$ 44178.48	$ 14726.16
CONSOLE	1	997	$ 9750.99	$ 9750.99
BABYGRAND	1	1105	$ 12300.00	$ 12300.00
GRAND	1	1550	$ 20000.99	$ 20000.99
SUPERGRAND	1	2112	$ 23456.88	$ 23456.88
MISLABEL	1	776	$ 10000.00	$ 10000.00

END OF RUN.

Figure 10.4

Sample Output for Example 10.2

positions, this means that we have 80 − 23 or 57 unused positions to be split into (more or less) equal lengths on either side of the heading. Accordingly, the heading will be preceded by 29 blanks to provide the appropriate centering, and the WRITELN call would look like this:

```
WRITELN ('bbbbbbbbbbbbbbbbbbbbbbbbbbbbb',
         'SOSTENUTO PIANO COMPANY')
```

The second heading includes the input values for the starting year and concluding year. A total of 48 positions are involved (from the S in SUM-MARY through the rightmost digit of the concluding year), so that a left margin of 16 positions centers the text on an 80-position line. Our output call, then, says

```
WRITELN ('bbbbbbbbbbbbbbbbbSUMMARY OF PURCHASES FOR ',
         startyr:4,' THROUGH   ',endy:4)
```

We shall start the column headings in the positions shown in Figure 10.4. When we include the appropriate number of blank characters, the output descriptions look like this:

```
WRITELN ('bbbbbbbbbbPIANObTYPE','bbbbbNO.bSOLDbb',
         'TOTALbWT.bb','TOTALbPRICEbbbbb',
         'AVG.bPRICE')
```

Each line of output starts with a string constant that names the type of piano. (Remember, we cannot use an enumerative variable's values for input or output.) We shall use a common length of 10 so that the format is consistent for all seven types. The length specifiers for numsold and totalwt include the blanks that precede the respective values. A separate string constant ('bbbbb$') supplies the string of blanks and the dollar sign required in front of totalprice and avgprice. To illustrate, the output specification for grand piano results will say the following:

```
WRITELN ('bbbbbbbbbb','GRANDbbbbb',numsoldCgrandJ:10,
         totalwtCgrandJ:10,'bbbbb$',totalpriceCgrandJ:10:2,
         'bbbbb$',avgpriceCgrandJ:10:2)
```

The revised program is shown in Figure 10.5.

```
(**********************************************************************)
(**                          EXAMPLE 10.2                          **)
(**********************************************************************)
(** THIS PROGRAM IS SIMILAR TO THE ONE FOR THE PREVIOUS            **)
(** EXAMPLE. IN ADDITION TO THE SALES FIGURES, IT PRINTS THE       **)
(** TOTAL WEIGHT SOLD FOR EACH TYPE, AS WELL AS THE AVERAGE        **)
(** PRICE FOR EACH TYPE.                                           **)
(** TWO ADDITIONAL VARIABLES ARE USED:                            **)
(**    TOTALPRICE: TOTAL SALES AMOUNT FOR A GIVEN PIANO TYPE       **)
(**    AVGPRICE: AVERAGE PRICE PAID FOR A PIANO OF A GIVEN TYPE    **)
(**********************************************************************)
PROGRAM ex1002 ;
TYPE
    pianotype = (upright, spinet, console, babygrand,
                 grand, largegrand, mislabel) ;
VAR
    serial, pianowt, yrofsale, startyr, endyr  :  INTEGER  ;
    numsold, totalwt  :  ARRAYCpianotypeJ OF INTEGER   ;
    price, realnum  :  REAL ;
    totalprice, avgprice  :  ARRAYCpianotypeJ OF REAL  ;
    custloc  :  STRING [2] ;
    piano  :  CHAR ;
    pianosize  :  pianotype  ;
BEGIN
  FOR  pianosize := upright TO mislabel  DO
    BEGIN
        numsoldCpianosizeJ := 0  ;
        totalwtCpianosizeJ := 0  ;
        totalpriceCpianosizeJ := 0.0
    END  ;
  READLN (startyr, endyr)  ;
  WHILE  NOT EOF(INPUT)  DO
    BEGIN
        WRITELN ('ENTER serial,piano,yrofsale,pianowt,price,
                  custloc.')  ;
        READLN (serial, piano, yrofsale, pianowt, price, custloc)  ;
```

Figure 10.5——————————————————————————————

Program for Example 10.2

```
    (*** CHECK WHETHER YEAR SOLD IS IN RANGE ***)
    IF  (yrofsale >= startyr) AND (yrofsale <= endyr)  THEN
        BEGIN
            (*** FIND THE PIANO TYPE ***)
            IF  piano = 'U'  THEN  pianosize := upright
            ELSE IF  piano = 'S'
                  THEN  pianosize := spinet
                    ELSE IF  piano = 'C'
                          THEN  pianosize := console
                            ELSE IF  piano = 'B'
                                  THEN  pianosize := babygrand
                                    ELSE IF  piano = 'G'
                                          THEN  pianosize := grand
                                            ELSE IF  piano = 'L'
                                                  THEN  pianosize := largegrand
                                                    ELSE  pianosize := mislabel ;

            (*** NOW THE APPROPRIATE INDEX IS ***)
            (*** EXPRESSED SIMPLY AS PIANOSIZE ***)
            numsold[pianosize] := numsold[pianosize] + 1 ;
            totalwt[pianosize] := totalwt[pianosize] + pianowt ;
            totalprice[pianosize] := totalprice[pianosize] + price
        END
    END ;

(*** ALL DATA HAVE BEEN PROCESSED. TIME TO WRITE THE OUTPUT. ***)
FOR  pianosize := upright TO  mislabel  DO
    BEGIN
        realnum := numsold[pianosize]) ;
        avgprice[pianosize] := totalprice[pianosize]/realnum
    END ;
PAGE ;
WRITELN ('                                   ',
        'SOSTENUTO PIANO COMPANY') ;
WRITELN ;
WRITELN ('                    SUMMARY OF PURCHASES FOR YEARS ',
        startyr:4,' THROUGH ',endyr:4)   ;
WRITELN ;
WRITELN ;
WRITELN ('          ','PIANO TYPE','        ','NO. SOLD  ',
        'TOTAL WT.  ','  ','TOTAL PRICE',
        '      ','AVG. PRICE')  ;
WRITELN ;
WRITELN ('              ','UPRIGHT    ',numsold[upright]:10,
        totalwt[upright]:11,'     $',
        totalprice[upright]:10:2,'      $',
        avgprice[upright]:10:2)   ;
```

Figure 10.5

Program for Example 10.2 (Continued)

```
    WRITELN ('              ','SPINET    ',numsold[spinet]:10,
           totalwt[spinet]:11,'      $',
           totalprice[spinet]:10:2,'       $',
           avgprice[spinet]:10:2)  ;
    WRITELN ('            ','CONSOLE   ',numsold[console]:10,
           totalwt[console]:11,'      $',
           totalprice[console]:10:2,'       $',
           avgprice[console]:10:2)   ;
    WRITELN ('            ','BABYGRAND ',numsold[babygrand]:10,
           totalwt[babygrand]:11,'       $',
           totalprice[babygrand]:10:2,'        $',
           avgprice[babygrand]:10:2)      ;
    WRITELN ('              ','GRAND       ',numsold[grand]:10,
           totalwt[grand]:11,'      $',
           totalprice[grand]:10:2,'       $',
           avgprice[grand]:10:2) ;
    WRITELN ('             ','LARGEGRAND',numsold[largegrand]:10,
           totalwt[largegrand]:11,'       $',
           totalprice[largegrand]:10:2,'       $',
           avgprice[largegrand]:10:2) ;
    WRITELN ('             ','MISLABEL   ',numsold[mislabel]:10,
           totalwt[mislabel]:11,'      $',
           totalprice[mislabel]:10:2,'       $',
           avgprice[mislabel]:10:2)  ;
    WRITELN  ;
    WRITELN ('            END OF RUN,')
END,
```

Figure 10.5 ————————————————————

Program for Example 10.2 (Continued)

Problems

Assume the following declarations for Problems 1, 2, and 3:

```
VAR
    trwt, pvol, roof  :  REAL  ;
    xct, obs, nmax, side  :  INTEGER  ;
    ltr, sym, vwl  :  CHAR ;
    phrase, slogan  :  STRING[20]
```

1. Show what will be stored in the indicated variables as a result of applying each of the following sequences to the appropriate amount of the following input data. Treat each problem independently.

31bbbb47.08bb6bb−9bbb85.1 ⟨ r e t u r n ⟩
−2806.9bbb77bbbRWB ⟨ r e t u r n ⟩
3Jb−42bKbAbbC61 ⟨ r e t u r n ⟩
5b508b4M7 ⟨ r e t u r n ⟩

```
(a)  READ   (xct, pvol, obs)
(b)  READLN (xct, pvol, obs)
(c)  READ (pvol)  ;
     READ (trwt)  ;
     READ (xct)
(d)  READLN (nmax, pvol, roof, nmax)
(e)  READLN (side, roof, xct, sym, ltr, phrase)
(f)  READLN (obs, roof, nmax, xct) ;
     READLN (sym)
(g)  READ (obs) ;
     READLN (pvol, trwt) ;
     READLN (roof, slogan);
     READLN (sym, xct)
(h)  READ (obs, pvol) ;
     READLN ;
     READLN (vwl, ltr) ;
     READ (trwt, xct)
```

2. Show the output produced by each of the indicated sequences applied to as much of the input data in Problem 1 as appropriate. Treat each sequence independently:

```
(a)  READ (obs, pval)          ;
     WRITELN (pval, obs, pval)
(b)  READLN (xct, roof, side, nmax)  ;
     READLN (phrase)  ;
     READ (obs)   ;
     READ (sym)   ;
     WRITELN (obs, sym, '     ', side)  ;
     WRITE ('ROOF =',roof)  ;
     WRITE ('NMAX IS ',nmax, xct) ;
     WRITE ('PHRASE IS ',phrase)
(c)  READLN  ;
     READ (pvol, xct) ;
     READ (vwl, sym) ;
     WRITELN (xct, pvol) ;
     WRITE (sym) ;
     WRITELN (xct, vwl, sym, xct) ;
     WRITE (ltr)
(d)  READLN (side, trwt, nmax)      ;
     READLN  ;
     READ (obs, sym)   ;
     READLN  ;
     READ (side)  ;
     WRITELN ('sym = ', sym:1, side:6, obs)   ;
```

```
            WRITELN  ;
            WRITE ('OBS = ',obs:12, trwt:15, trwt:14:3) ;
            WRITE (nmax,'bbSLOGAN:b',slogan,'bbPHRASE:b',
                                           phrase:4)
     (e)    READ (obs, roof)  ;
            WRITELN (roof:15, roof:15:5) ;
            WRITE (obs,obs:6)   ;
            READ (xct, side)  ;
            READLN  ;
            READ (trwt)  ;
            READLN (nmax) ;
            WRITE (trwt:12:3)   ;
            WRITELN  ;
            WRITELN (side:7, xct:8, nmax)
```

3. Write a program that reads in sets of four 3-digit integers (call them wval, xval, yval and zval) and displays them in ascending order, one set to a line. Each input set is on a separate line. If all four input values in a given set are equal to each other, display only their sum. The numbers may be positive, negative, or zero. Use end of file to stop the run.

4. Eastern Incendia's great political enemy is Northwestern Euphoria. (So much so, in fact, that when the High Command wants to call a meeting of Incendian intelligence agents, it is necessary to charter six buses to bring back the contingent from Euphoria.) Anyway, nothing warms the Incendian bureaucratic heart as much as news of the capture of secret Euphorian documents. Accordingly, each time such a feat is executed, an input line is created showing the agent's initials (all Incendians have four names), the number of documents captured (sometimes in the thousands), the documents' total weight to the nearest gram, and a score from 1 to 9, depending on the relative importance of the booty. When a group of such input sets has been accumulated, it is run through a program that computes and displays a Mathematical Heartwarming Score for each set. The MWS (as the High Command affectionately refers to it) is computed as

$$MWS = 0.28 ndoc(wt)^{1.75/score}$$

where ndoc is the number of documents captured, wt is their weight, and score is the scored value. The three highest scores are singled out for commendation.

Write a program that finds the top three document collectors. (It is possible in this scheme for all three prizes to be won by the same agent.) For each winner, the program is to display a line showing the initials, the number of documents captured, and the MWS. Label your output clearly.

5. Modify the previous program based on the recognition that there may be ties in MWS values. Being quite generous, Eastern Incendia wants to award duplicate commendations. That is, it wants to give commendations for the top three scores, even though one or more of them may have been achieved by several agents. With the assurance that there will never be more than two duplicate scores at any level, arrange to display the output previously described for each of the agents having one of the top three scores.

6. Haig Bareboodjian, powerful rug merchant, is the world's leading specialist in four highly popular rug designs. His agents comb the major weaving centers (and some minor ones too) making sure that Big HB is kept up to date on who is weaving what where. This information is sent to him in code, and it eventually is typed into a terminal. For each rug, the following data are acquired:

> Representative's initials (3 letters)
> Rug's identification number (4-digit integer)
> Design Code (1, 2, 3, or 4)
> Country of manufacture (1=Pilvoonia; 2=Halvahstan; 3=Smenfh,
>   4=Qamranq; 5=Tfimfim)
> Rug length, to the nearest inch (nnnn)
> Rug width, to the nearest inch (nnnn)

Write a program that produces a one-page report summarizing the data about the rugs in production. For each design, display the number of rugs, total rug area (in square yards), and the number of countries in which that design is being produced. Include appropriate headings.

7. Haig Bareboodjian (the same Haig Bareboodjian from Problem 6) operates in a hectic world where prices fluctuate rapidly. Accordingly, he finds it useful to know the potential value of the rugs currently in production. Toward this end, modify the program in the previous problem so that prior to the input described before, it reads the current month and year, and four values giving the respective prices, in dollars per square yard, for each of the four designs. Then, for each rug, the revised program is to produce a line of output giving the rug's i.d., the representative's initials, the numerical code for the country in which the rug is being woven, the length and width (in feet, to the nearest foot), the area in square yards (to the nearest square yard), and the price. After data for all the rugs have been processed, the program is to display a line showing the number of rugs processed, the total square yardage, and their total value. Prepare your output so that it follows the format shown in Figure 10.6.

HAIG BAREBOODJIAN
RUG SUMMARY FOR 10/82

DESIGN 1: $42.50 PER SQ. YD.   DESIGN 2: $61.70 PER SQ. YD.
DESIGN 3: $88.15 PER SQ. YD.   DESIGN 4: $53.35 PER SQ. YD.

I.D.	REP	WHERE WOVEN	LENGTH	WIDTH	AREA, SQ. YD.	COST
3276	MHP	2	14	10	16	$nnnnn.nn
1008	CYD	1	22	12	29	$nnnnn.nn

Figure 10.6

Output Format for Problem 7 of Chapter 10

8. The El Warpo Company sells 3/4″ thick plywood in three grades: finished, semi-finished, and pwg (please wear gloves). Finished plywood sells for $1.78 per square foot, semi-finished for $1.45 per square foot, and pwg for $1.19 per square foot. These plywood sheets come in various standard rectangular sizes.

    Sales summaries are to be produced on a daily basis. Each line of input describes the sale of a quantity of sheets of a given grade and size to a specified customer on that day:

Item	Format
date of sale	mmddyy (e.g., 03 28 82)
customer number	six-digit (unsigned) integer
grade	1, 2, or 3 (1 = finished)
number of sheets purchased	nnn
length (in feet and inches)	nn nn (e.g., 7 6 = 7 ft., 6 in.)
width (in feet and inches)	same as length

All orders for a given customer are grouped together, and these data are preceded by a separate line showing today's date. Write a program that processes a day's sales and produces the following output:

A line for each input line showing the input data (except for the date), the total area in square feet (with fractional square feet truncated), and the price for that material.

A line for each customer showing the total number of square feet purchased and the total price.

A set of lines after the last customer line (starting on a new page) showing the number of customers processed, average order size (in square feet), and the average sales amount for the orders.

A suggested arrangement is shown in Figure 10.7.

9. After a number of embarrassing episodes, El Warpo found that it cannot be certain that all of the input lines for a given run will show the same date. Consequently, modify the program for Problem 8 so that it finds and rejects all input lines with the wrong date. After displaying the summary for the run, the revised program is to show an additional line indicating the number of lines thus rejected.

10. *An American Tradition:* In a recent landmark decision, the Supreme Court let stand a historic ruling by a lower court: It is a misdemeanor to publish and distribute a text, booklet, film, or videodisc on programming (in any language) in which the Indian Problem does not appear at least once. Your author, above all, is law-abiding. Consequently, in the interest of Good Government, here is the Indian Problem: In 1624, there was disquiet among the normally tranquil Canarsie Indians. The problem was Manhattan Island. Long an unkempt, noisy eyesore on the otherwise orderly Indian landscape, things on the island were going from bad to worse. The bars were getting rowdier by the day, the rivers and inlets were literally filling with garbage, and there were places where innocent citizens actually were in physical danger. Numerous council meetings were held to determine What to Do about That Stinking Rock. At the height of this

EL WARPO PLYWOOD CO.
SALES SUMMARY FOR mm/dd/yy

CUST NO.	GRADE	NO. OF SHEETS	LENGTH	WIDTH	TOTAL AREA	TOTAL PRICE
nnnnnn	2	44	10' 6"	3' 2"	nnnnn.nn	$nnnnn.nn
nnnnnn	1	16	9' 0"	6' 0"	nnnnn.nn	$nnnnn.nn

*** SUMMARY FOR CUSTOMER nnnnnn ***
TOTAL AREA: nnnnnn.nn SQ. FT.   TOTAL PRICE: $nnnnnn.nn

(a) Output for an individual customer (Problem 8 of Chapter 10)

EL WARPO PLYWOOD CO.
OVERALL SUMMARY FOR mm/dd/yy

```
NUMBER OF CUSTOMERS PROCESSED:    nnn
AVERAGE ORDER:    nnnnnn.nn SQ. FT.
AVERAGE ORDER AMOUNT:    $nnnnnn.nn
```
(b) Overall summary

Figure 10.7

perplexity, who should appear but Peter Minuit and a group of settlers interested (no, eager) to persuade the Canarsies to part with this
real estate. The settlers offered about $24 worth of trendy costume
jewelry and reasonably good theatrical accessories, and the Indians
discussed the matter among themselves. A short time later, they told
the settlers that it was a deal, and the land changed hands. (It is a
matter of historical record that no single Canarsie giggled until the
settlers were miles away.) Within hours of the exchange, the smiling
Canarsies sold the merchandise to a troupe of Bohemian gypsies for
$28.75. They bought $4.75 worth of nifty fishing lures (from those
selfsame gypsies) and put the remaining $24 into the Succotash Fund,
a conservative investment vehicle paying 6%, and There The Money
Has Sat.

Since then, the Canarsies have turned their attention to other
matters, and nobody has paid much attention to the money in the
Succotash Fund. What is needed is a program to let the people know
what has been happening. Write a program that reads in the current
year (thisyear) and produces a year-by-year display showing the
value of the $24 plus accrued interest from the year 1624 through
thisyr.

11. In this version of the program, the output is to be limited to 50 years
on each page. Every time a new page is started, the program is to
display the column headings.

12. As a more challenging version of the previous problem, write a
program that reads two integer values startyr and endyr. In
response to these values, the program is to display the value of the
Canarsies' investment for each year in the specified range.

13. Here is another, more involved version of the Manhattan Problem:
Read in five values for five different interest rates. (For instance, an
input value of 6.5 represents an interest rate of 6.5 percent, i.e., 0.065.)
The program is to produce an expanded version of the table in problem 10: Each line is to show a particular year and the value of the $24
and accrued interest for each of the five interest rates.

14. The Deluxe Version of the Manhattan Problem is similar to Problem
13 with one specific exception: Input consists of anywhere from one
to five interest rates. Accordingly, the number of columns in the
output table will depend on the number of input values. (A single
input value will produce a two-column table like the one in Problem
10, and five input values will duplicate Problem 13.)

15. When somebody borrows money to buy something like a house, an
automobile, a personal computer, or other major appliance, the conditions of the loan are arranged so that the interest is a fixed fraction of
the amount owed at that time. For instance, suppose somebody borrows $10,000 and the interest rate is 1.5% per month on the unpaid

balance. That means that the initial payment must include interest amounting to 0.015*10000 or $150. Then, suppose that, in addition to the interest, the borrower pays off $200 of the loan. As a result, the next monthly payment will require interest amounting to 0.015*(10000 − 200) or $147.

As a convenience to the lender as well as the borrower, such loans usually are arranged so that the monthly payments are set at a fixed amount. The distribution of that fixed amount between interest and loan repayment will vary with each payment, the first payment having the highest fraction tied up in interest, and the last payment contributing little or nothing to interest. Given an initial loan amount loanamt, the annual interest rate annrate and the number of payments numpay, the monthly payment can be computed as

$$
\text{mnthrate(loan amt)} \left[\frac{(1 + \text{mnthrate})^{\text{numpay}}}{(1 + \text{mnthrate})^{\text{numpay}} - 1} \right]
$$

where mnthrate is annrate/12. The program is to produce an initial line of output showing the loan number, amount of the loan, and number of monthly payments. A second line is to show the amount of the (fixed) monthly payment. Then, after two blank lines, the program is to produce a table in which each line shows the payment number, balance owed prior to that payment, amount of the payment credited toward the loan, amount of payment used for interest, and the new balance owed. These five columns are to have appropriate headings, and the headings are to be repeated at the top of each new page. The program is to be designed so that it processes any number of loans.

Chapter 11

Decision and Control Structures

The capabilities we have used thus far represent only part of Pascal's resources for specifying decision-making processes. In this chapter, we look at some more ambitious decision mechanisms and some additional ways of constructing them conveniently.

11.1 SIMPLE SELECTION—THE IF STATEMENT

Extensive use has enabled us to characterize the IF statement's service: It lets us set up a comparison between two values such that there are two possible outcomes: TRUE or FALSE. Each outcome is associated with a corresponding action expressible as a Pascal statement. This is reflected in the syntax diagram shown in Figure 3.12 and repeated for convenience in Figure 11.1(a).

The opportunities presented even by this basic selection process go beyond those explored earlier. Consequently, we shall spend a little time in this section on extending these possibilities.

11.1.1 Construction of Comparisons

Figure 11.1(a) does not say much about what a comparison is or how to build one. We have not missed this information because the comparisons used so far were constructed "naturally," without the need for detailed attention to their exact syntax. Now, the structural rules become important if we are to take advantage of the IF statement's flexibility.

The structure of a comparison is developed in Figure 11.1(b). We see that the relational operator, defined earlier in Table 4.1, is used to combine two expressions to produce a test whose outcome is TRUE or FALSE. For example, if vel and maxvel are REAL variables, the construction

```
2.3 * SQRT (vel) < 0.8*maxvel
```

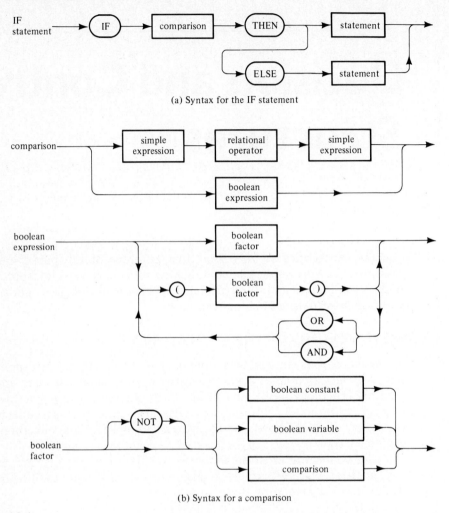

(a) Syntax for the IF statement

(b) Syntax for a comparison

Figure 11.1

(a) Syntax for the IF Statement (b) Syntax for a Comparison

describes a comparison whose outcome is TRUE if 2.3 times the square root of the current value in vel is less than 0.8 times the current value in maxvel. The semantic considerations require us to make sure that the two expressions brought together by the relational operator are reasonable partners in the comparison. For example, comparison of two integer values would be reasonable, but comparison of a character with an integer value probably would not be.

We can expand a comparison's possibilities by noting that the outcome of a comparison, being either TRUE or FALSE, is nothing more than a boolean value. Since the IF statement is concerned specifically with testing such a value, it does not "know" where the value came from or how it was developed. This means that the boolean expression, which also produces a value of TRUE or FALSE, can serve as a comparison to be processed by an IF statement. Accordingly, Figure 11.1(b) shows the boolean expression as being one type of comparison. The next few sections discuss the uses of this added flexibility.

11.1.2 Comparisons between Nonnumeric Values

It is not necessary to base decisions solely on numerical comparisons. Besides enabling the programmer to set up comparisons between characters and boolean values, Pascal also accepts comparisons between programmer-defined data values.

Comparisons between Characters   Suppose we have the following sequence:

```
VAR
    letter, symbol  :  CHAR
      .
      .
      .
    symbol := 'Z'  ;
    WRITELN ('TYPE IN A LETTER.')  ;
    READLN (letter)
```

It is clear that we can set up a decision rule like this:

```
IF  letter = symbol  THEN
    action1
ELSE
    action2
```

The program will perform *action1* if letter has the same character as symbol, and it will perform *action2* if the two characters are different. However, such comparisons need not be limited to equality or nonequality. It is legal to write, say,

```
IF  letter < symbol  THEN
    action1
ELSE
    action2
```

What happens is this: Since each type of character has its own internal numerical representation, a comparison between two characters translates eventually to a comparison between two numerical quantities. Thus, the example given above will produce a value of TRUE if the internal numerical representation of the character in letter is less than the number used to represent the uppercase letter Z, i.e., the value previously stored in symbol.

Internal representations for the various types of characters are assigned as part of a code built into the computer's design. This code, called a *collating sequence,* is one of two types in general use. The one of concern to us is the American Standard Code for Information Interchange (ASCII). Incidentally, the other type of code in wide use is called the Extended Binary Coded Decimal Interchange Code (EBCDIC). (The available characters, together with their respective numerical representations, are tabulated in Appendix B.) The numerical sequence is in alphabetical order, so that 'A' is "less than" 'B', 'B' is "less than" 'C', and so on. Moreover, the lowercase letters have higher numerical representations than the capital letters so that 'z' is "greater than" 'a', and 'a' is "greater than" 'Z'. Numbers have lower internal representations than letters. For example, '0' is less than '9', and '9' is less than 'A'.

Comparisons between Programmer-defined Data Values   The scope of expressible decision rules is broadened further by the ability to compare enumerative data values. This is done by taking advantage of the sequencing implied by the declaration of an enumerative data type. For instance, in Example 10.1 we defined a data type named pianotype and a variable of that type named pianosize:

```
TYPE
    pianotype = (upright, spinet, console, babygrand, grand,
                 largegrand, mislabel)
      .
      .
      .
VAR
    pianosize :   pianotype
```

Given these declarations, the following decision rule,

```
IF  pianosize >= console   THEN
    action1
ELSE
    action2
```

triggers *action1* if pianosize is anything equal to or greater than console (namely, console, babygrand, grand, largegrand, or mislabel).

11.1.3 Extended Comparisons

Decisions often require tests in which several conditions have to be considered. Construction of such tests is handled conveniently by using boolean operations to combine comparisons.

Tests Based on Multiple Comparisons   When we want to set up a test in which several conditions have to be met, we can use Pascal's AND operation for that purpose. For example, suppose we are conducting a medical investigation calling for the selection of certain patients' records from a large collection. Each patient's information includes:

> an identifying number (ptntid);
> year of birth (birthyr);
> sex (sex): 0 = female, 1 = male;
> height (ht) in inches;
> weight (wt) in pounds;
> result of the Foop test (foop), a REAL number.
> result of the Poznik color test (poznik): 0 = no color, 1 = trace, 2 = light, 3 = medium, 4 = heavy color.

Let us say that we are interested in reading the data for each patient and displaying the patient identification numbers for those individuals between the ages of 30 and 40. To do this, we can define a variable thisyr and read into it the value for the current year. An additional variable named age will be used to store the computed age (thisyr - birthyr) for the patient whose record is currently being processed. The corresponding part of the declaration section might look like this:

```
VAR
    ptntid, birthyr, sex, ht, wt, poznik,
    thisyr, age  :  INTEGER   ;
    foop  :   REAL
```

After reading the data for a particular patient and computing age, we can determine whether that patient falls in the required age range by testing age against each of the limits:

```
READLN (thisyr)
   .
   .
   .
READLN (ptntid, birthyr, sex, ht, wt, foop, poznik)   ;
age := thisyr - birthyr ;
IF  (age >= 30)  AND  (age <= 40)  THEN
    WRITELN (ptntid)
```

Now the value of ptntid will be shown only if both outcomes are TRUE. Note that if we were to write

```
IF   (age >= 30  AND   <= 40)   THEN
    WRITELN (ptntid)
```

the Pascal compiler would reject it because the structure is improper. The AND operator must connect two complete comparisons.

Suppose we wanted to be even more selective and display identification numbers only for male patients between the ages of 30 and 40. This requires three comparisons, all of whose outcomes must be TRUE before the patient is selected:

```
IF        (age >= 30)
    AND   (age <= 40)
    AND   (sex = 1)    THEN
  WRITELN (ptntid)
```

Tests based on more extensive combinations of criteria can be built in the same way. The only limit is that imposed by the programmer to keep such structures from becoming too involved.

Tests Based on Choices   Sometimes a decision is based on one of several tests, any of which is sufficient to trigger the associated action. Referring to the data in the previous section, suppose we wanted to select the following patients and display their identification numbers:

>   male patients with Foop readings above 32.7;
>   female patients with Foop readings above 40.4.

Two comparisons are required to identify eligible male patients. These are combined, as before, with the AND operation. Thus,

```
... (sex = 1)   AND   (foop > 32.7) ...
```

selects the male patients. Similarly, female patients are selected by the combination

```
... (sex = 0)   AND   (foop > 40.4) ...
```

The choice between these two possibilities is specified by using Pascal's OR operation:

```
IF        (sex = 1)   AND   (foop > 32.7)
    OR    (sex = 0)   AND   (foop > 40.4)   THEN
    WRITELN (ptntid)
```

Negative Tests   Another type of circumstance requires a decision based on a negative outcome. For instance, suppose our medical study required the selection of all patients *except* males over 52. We can describe such a decision rule by saying

```
IF      (sex = 1)   AND   (age <= 52)
    OR  (sex = 0)
THEN
    WRITELN (ptntid)
```

Even though we achieve the desired result, the decision rule is not described in the way we intended. It is sufficiently complicated to require us to stop a moment and figure out what it says. Pascal's NOT operation enables the programmer to specify such decision rules more naturally. To illustrate, we shall rewrite the previous test using this operation:

```
IF  NOT( (sex = 1)   AND (age > 52) )   THEN
    WRITELN (ptntid)
```

The same general construction applies to more intricate decision rules. For instance, let us select all patients except men over 60 and women over 55:

```
IF  NOT  (        (sex = 1)   AND   (age > 60)
             OR   (sex = 0)   AND   (age > 55) )   THEN
    WRITELN (ptntid)
```

11.2 DECISION NETWORKS WITH MULTIPLE TESTS

A course of action cannot always be determined by a single test, no matter how complex that test may be. Often, it is necessary to set up a procedure that must work its way through a series of tests before a final decision can be made. To illustrate this type of situation, suppose the patients in our previous example are to receive a specific amount of a therapeutic drug based on their sex and the Foop test result:

> Males with a Foop result less than 35.5 receive 500 units of the drug;
> Males with a Foop result of at least 35.5 receive 630 units;
> Females with a Foop result less than 27.6 receive 420 units;
> Females with a Foop result of at least 27.6 receive 520 units.

The appropriate dose is to be reported in an INTEGER variable named dose. Then, instead of displaying information only for certain patients, we would like to display the i.d. and dose for each patient in the population.

Until now we have worked with tests that varied in their complexity but produced a single outcome whose value immediately determined what action to take. In the situation just described, a single test is not enough. We have to go through a series of tests before we learn everything we need to know to select the correct response. In other words, we need a decision structure in which the outcome of the first test tells us which test to perform next.

Such test series are easily built by using an IF statement whose THEN or ELSE portion consists of another IF statement. (A quick check of Figure 11.1 shows that this structure is consistent with Pascal's rules.) The result is called a *nested IF construction*. To represent the test series for our example, we simply can follow the rules stated before:

```
READLN (ptntid, birthyr, sex, ht, wt, foop, poznik)   ;
IF  (sex = 1)  THEN
    IF  foop < 35.5  THEN
        dose := 500
    ELSE
        dose := 630
ELSE
    IF  foop < 27.6  THEN
        dose := 420
    ELSE
        dose := 520  ;
WRITELN (ptntid, dose)
```

Here, as is true in many other types of nested constructions, indentation is of considerable help in keeping track of which ELSE goes with which IF. Nested IF constructions can be extended as far as desired; however, the programmer is well advised to place his or her own limits on the maximum degree of nesting to use. When it appears necessary to exceed that limit, this often can be taken as a good sign that the underlying decision structure is too complicated and needs further study. Sometimes nesting may be so extensive that the resulting indentation forces the statement off the end of the line to be gobbled up by one of the four giant tortoises that hold up the Earth. Beware.

There is no guarantee that every decision structure will be symmetrical. There will be countless situations in which the first test will produce two possible outcomes, one of which produces a final decision without further testing while the other leads to a long series of additional tests. As long as we have a clear idea of the decision rules, their systematic representation in Pascal will give us no trouble. For instance, let us define a new decision structure for our patients and their dosages. We have an improved drug whose dosage for females can be fixed at one standard level, but the amount given to males depends on age as well as Foop result:

Females
The standard dose is 465 units.
Males

Age	Foop result	Dose
less than 34	less than 35.5	440 units
less than 34	at least 35.5	520 units
at least 34	less than 41.4	580 units
at least 34	at least 41.4	665 units

The pseudocode is shown in Figure 11.2, and the corresponding Pascal statements appear in Figure 11.3.

11.3 MULTIPLE SELECTION—THE CASE STATEMENT

Another type of realistic test situation is one in which there are more than two possible outcomes. Each outcome is associated with a particular action that is to be taken when that outcome occurs. For instance, suppose that the

```
Read thisyr.
    :
Read a patient's record.
Compute the patient's age (thisyr - birthyr).
IF
      the patient is male
THEN
    IF
            the patient's age is less than 34
    THEN
        IF
              the patient's Foop result is less than 35.5
        THEN
            set dose to 440.
        ELSE
            set dose to 520.
        ENDIF
      ELSE
        IF
              the patient's Foop result is less than 41.4
        THEN
            set dose to 580.
        ELSE
            set dose to 665.
        ENDIF
    ENDIF
ELSE
    set dose to 465.
ENDIF
```

Figure 11.2

Pseudocode Description of a Nested Decision Structure

```
READLN (thisyr)
    .

    .

    .
READLN (ptntid, birthyr, sex, ht, wt, foop, poznik)   ;
age := thisyr - birthyr ;
IF  sex = 1   THEN
    IF  age < 34   THEN
        IF  foop < 35.5   THEN
            dose := 440
        ELSE
            dose := 520
    ELSE
        IF  foop < 41.4   THEN
            dose := 580
        ELSE
            dose := 665
ELSE
    dose := 564   ;
WRITELN (ptntid, dose)
```

Figure 11.3

A Multilevel Decision Rule Expressed as a Nested `IF` Statement

situation with our patients becomes more complicated because of the introduction of yet another medicine. The only way to make full use of its improved effectiveness is to tie the dosage to a more extensive set of criteria involving the Poznik test result as well as some other factors. This is shown in Table 11.1.

11.3.1 Basic Structure of the `CASE` Statement

In the example of Table 9.1, the decision rule pivots on a test that can have five different outcomes, and there is a specific activity associated with each outcome. The programming structure that describes that kind of situation (one in which a decision rule is based on a test that has more than two possible outcomes) is called a *CASE component*. It occurs often enough so that Pascal has a separate `CASE` statement with which such rules can be specified easily. The syntax, shown in Figure 11.4, allows the programmer to represent the multiple selection directly, regardless of the number of choices required. For our example, the variable motivating the selection is `poznik`, and the five alternatives follow immediately. This is shown in Figure 11.5. In this example, `poznik` acts like a multiway switch that guides the program toward one of the five alternative actions. Each action is associated with a particular value, so that when `poznik` has a value of 2, for instance, the program will proceed directly to the statement tagged with that value. Once that action is completed, the other actions are ignored and

Table 11.1   An Example of a Situation Motivating a CASE Construction

Poznik Test Outcome	Dosage
Category 0 (no color)	0.82 units for each pound of weight
Category 1	0.74 units for each pound of weight and 0.11 units for each year in the person's age.
Category 2	140 units for males, 166 units for females.
Category 3	0.90 units for each pound of weight. Subtract 0.10 units for each year for males or 0.12 units for each year for females.
Category 4	For males: 0.93 units per pound of weight less 0.05 units per year. Subtract 18.5 units if Foop test exceeds 50.6. For females: 0.86 units per pound of weight plus 0.027 units per year. Subtract 10.6 units for females over 55 with Foop test results below 35.6.

the program continues at a point immediately after the concluding END. The programmer should make sure that the CASE statement has an action for every possible outcome. If there is no match during a particular use, the program ignores the entire CASE statement.

11.3.2 Identical Actions for Different Outcomes

All of the actions associated with a CASE statement do not have to be different from each other. For instance, suppose it were to turn out that dosages for category 3 (from Table 11.1) could be computed the same as for category 2. This can be specified by attaching both outcome values to the appropriate action. For our example, the revised statements would appear as shown in Figure 11.6.

11.3.3 Multiway Switches with Programmer-defined Values

The selection capabilities of the CASE statement can be applied to situations where the choices are values other than integers. Decision rules can be set up to select from any group of alternatives as long as the choices are clearly defined. For instance, if we defined a data type named season and declared a variable of that type as follows:

```
TYPE
   season = (winter, spring, summer, fall)
   .
   .
   .
VAR
   timeofyear  :  season
```

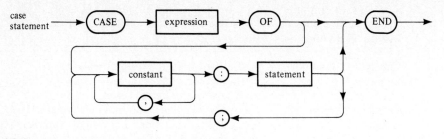

Figure 11.4

Syntax for the CASE Statement

Then, assuming t i m e o f y e a r had a value assigned to it, we could use it as a switch to select one of four actions:

```
CASE  timeofyear  OF
   winter :    action for winter  ;
   spring :    action for spring  ;
   summer :    action for summer  ;
   fall   :    action for fall
END
```

11.4 EXPLICIT TRANSFER OF CONTROL

Although Pascal provides specific statement types for the major control structures, there may be occasions where an explicit transfer to some other part of the program is useful. A situation where this might be applied is one in which a loop is to be provided with an opportunity for a sudden exit in mid-cycle.

Such transfers are specified by Pascal's GOTO statement whose general form is

```
GOTO label
```

where *label* is a numerical tag (i.e., an unsigned integer in the range 0..9999) attached to the destination statement. For example,

```
GOTO  24
```

indicates that the next statement to be executed is the one labeled 24. That statement, then, would have the label 24 attached to it, i.e.,

```
24: statement
```

```
READLN (thisyr)
  .
  .
  .
READLN (ptntid, birthyr, sex, wt, ht, foop, poznik)  ;
age := thisyr - birthyr ;
CASE  poznik  OF
  0:    dose := 0.82 * wt  ;
  1:    dose := 0.74 * wt + 0.11 * age  ;
  2:    IF  sex = 1  THEN
            dose := 140
        ELSE
            dose := 166 ;
  3:    IF  sex = 1   THEN
            dose := 90 * wt - 0.10 * age
        ELSE
            dose := 90 * wt - 0.12 * age  ;
  4:    IF  sex = 1   THEN
            BEGIN
              dose := 0.93 * wt - 0.05 * age  ;
              IF  foop > 50.6  THEN
                  dose := dose - 18.5
            END
        ELSE
            BEGIN
              dose := 0.86 * wt + 0.027 * age  ;
              IF      (age > 55)
                AND (foop < 35.6)  THEN
                  dose := dose - 10.6
            END
END ;
WRITELN (ptntid, dose)
```

Figure 11.5————————————————————————

Implementation of Decision Structure for Section 11.3.1

This statement may appear anywhere in the program, but it must be the only one labeled 24. Moreover, every label must be declared like the other identifiers. This is done at the beginning of the declaration section (i.e., immediately after the identification section, and immediately prior to the TYPE declarations (if there are any). Thus, the declaration

```
LABEL
  10, 18, 26, 334, 71
```

informs Pascal that there will be five labeled statements somewhere in the program, and that their label numbers will be as shown.

```
CASE  Poznik  OF
  0    :    dose := 0.82 * wt ;
  1    :    dose := 0.74 * wt + 0.11 * age ;
  2, 3  :   IF  sex = 1  THEN
                 dose := 140
            ELSE
                 dose := 166
      4 :   IF  sex = 1  THEN
               BEGIN
                 dose := 0.93 * wt - 0.05 * age  ;
                 IF  foop > 50.6  THEN
                     dose := dose - 18.5
               END
            ELSE
               BEGIN
                 dose := 0.86 * wt + 0.027 * age  ;
                 IF      (age > 55)
                    AND  (foop < 35.6)  THEN
                     dose := dose - 10.6
               END
END  ;
WRITELN (Ptntid, dose)
```

Figure 11.6—————————————————————————————

CASE Construction with Identical Actions for Multiple Outcomes

Problems

1. Indicate the output produced by each of the independent sequences
    given below. (*Note:* some of these sequences may contain errors that
    prevent any output from being produced.) Assume the following
    declarations and assignments:

```
CONST
  yes = TRUE  ;
  no = FALSE  ;
TYPE
  doublereed = (englhorn, oboe, bassoon, contrabassoon) ;
  cartype = (coupe, sedan, stawag, convert, sports) ;
VAR
  r1, r2, r3, r4  :  REAL  ;
  num1, num2, num3  :  INTEGER  ;
  ltrs, bell  :  STRING [4]  ;
  wdi, sym, utm  :  CHAR  ;
  test1, test2,  :  BOOLEAN  ;
```

```
blaser  :   doublereed  ;
flivver, liz  :  cartype  ;
r1 := 4  ;
r2 := 5  ;
num2 := 2 ;
num3 := 6  ;
ltrs := 'MY'  ;
bell := 'WHAT'  ;
wdi := '*'  ;
sym := ' '  ;
utm := '='  ;
test1 := yes  ;
blaser := oboe
```

```
(a)  IF  no  THEN
        WRITELN (r1, r2, num2, num3)
(b)  IF  test1 = yes  THEN
        ltrs := wdi  ;
        ltrs := sym
     ELSE
        ltrs := sym ;
        ltrs := utm  ;
        WRITELN (ltrs:4)
(c)  r4 := 0  ;
     IF  r1*r2 < SQR(num2*num3 DIV 3)  THEN
        BEGIN
           r4 := r1*(r2 + num2)        ;
           ltrs := sym  ;
           WRITELN (ltrs, r4)
        END
     ELSE
        BEGIN
           r3 := num2 * (r1+r2) ;
           r4 := r4 + 0.5*r3  ;
           ltrs := wdi  ;
           WRITELN (r4, r3, wdi, ltrs)
        END
(d)  IF  blaser <= bassoon  THEN
        flivver := convert
     ELSE
        flivver :- sedan                ;
     IF  flivver >= staway  THEN
        BEGIN
           num3 := num3 * SQR(num2)    ;
           r3 := r1 * (r1+r2)          ;
           WRITELN (num3, r3)
        END
     ELSE
        WRITELN (r2:12, num2:10, r1:12, num1:10)
```

```
(e)  IF  NOT(yes  AND  test1)  THEN
         r4 := r1*r2/(r1+r2)
     ELSE
         ltrs := 'FMEH'  ;
     WRITELN (r4:12, ltrs:6)
(f)  IF  (num2 <= SQR(num1)) OR (sym <= wdi)   THEN
         ltrs := sym
     ELSE
        BEGIN
            ltrs := wdi  ;
            r4 := (r1+r2)/(r1*r2)
        END ;
     WRITELN (r4)  ;
     WRITELN  ;
        WRITE (ltrs:3)
(g)  IF  (TRUNC(r1*r2)  DIV  num3 <  num2-
     num3) OR (blaser >= englhorn) THEN
         num1 := ROUND(r1*r2) DIV (num2+num3)
     ELSE
        IF  wdi < ltrs  THEN
           BEGIN
               num1 := ROUND ((num2+num3)/r2) + num2   ;
               ltrs := 'N'
           END
        ELSE
            num1 := TRUNC ((num2+num3)/r2) - num2
     WRITELN (ltrs:8, num1:8, ltrs:6)
```

2. Write a sequence of statements to represent each of the specifications given below. Use the same declarations and initial assignments shown for the previous problem.

(a) After reading in values for r1 and r2, set num1 to 3 if r1 is greater than r2; otherwise set num1 to 4.

(b) Read a value for ltrs.
```
     IF
         ltrs is not the same as bell
     THEN
         set sym to '@'
     ELSE
         set sym to '*'.
     ENDIF
```

(c) Read a value for wdi.
```
     IF
         wdi's value is 'A' through 'R'
     THEN
         double the value in num2.
```

ELSE

subtract 1 from the value in num2.

ENDIF

(d) Read a value for sym.

IF

sym is between 'a' and 'm' and 'N' and 'Z'

THEN

set wdi's value to '&'.

ELSE

set wdi's value to '%'.

ENDIF

(e) Read values for r2, r3, and r4. Assign to r1 a value equal to the sum of the two largest input values.

(f) Read values for num1, num2, and num3. Store the square of the largest odd number in r1, the sum of the odd values in r2, the overall sum in r3, and the square of the largest even number in r4. Whenever a value cannot be produced (e.g., there are no odd values among those read in), store a zero for that result.

3. Variables dval, bval, aval, and cval are declared INTEGER. For the following sequence:

```
IF   bval = 2*aval   THEN
IF   cval = 4*dval   THEN
IF   bval = cval-4   THEN
zval :=12
ELSE
IF   aval = dval+6   THEN
IF   cval = aval+14  THEN
zval := 22
ELSE
zval := 11
ELSE
zval := 31
ELSE
zval := 41
```

state the value of zval when

(a) aval is 10, bval is 20, cval is 24, and dval is 6.
(b) aval is 9, bval is 20, cval is 24, and dval is 6.
(c) aval is 10, bval is 20, cval is 24, dval is 7.
(d) aval is 3, bval is 6, cval is 4, and dval is 5.
(e) aval is 2, bval is 4, cval is 8, and dval is 16.

4. A series of five-digit decimal integers are available, one per input line. Write a program that counts and displays the number of values read in and the number of values ending with a 6 and evenly divisible by 4.

5. Values for integer variables val1 and val2, respectively, are recorded on an input line. There is an arbitrary number of input lines. Write a program that performs the following processing:

   (a) Count and display the number of pairs of values in which the product is not more than 10 times the ratio of the first value to the second.

   (b) Compute the sum of the products of all pairs meeting the criteria in (a).

   (c) Compute the product of the sums of all pairs in which both values are even.

   (d) Count the number of times the digit 2 appears in the data.

   Zero is a legitimate value, but no two members of a pair will have identical values. Provide appropriate labels for all output.

6. Write a program to perform the following processing: Each input line contains a three-digit positive integer value posintgr. If the rightmost (third) digit is equal to the sum of the other two digits, that number is to be shown on a separate line along with the message. "THIS IS A SPECIAL NUMBER." If not, there is to be no output for that number. Thus, 246 and 729 are special numbers while 264 and 381 are not. A run may consist of any number of input values. After the last value is processed, the program is to show the number of values that met the requirement described before (specials) and the number of values that did not (regulars). Here are some suggested input values:

   303
   627
   718
   339
   336
   347
   112

7. Generalize the program in the previous problem so that it processes any number of runs. Insert three blank lines to separate consecutive runs and keep track of the number of runs. Before the first line of output for each run, show a line that says "RUN NUMBER nn." After the last run, start a new page and show the number of runs, total number of values read, total number of special values, and total number of regular values.

8. Here is a more challenging version of the previous problem: We still are reading positive integer values. However, the number of digits is not fixed. If a particular number reads the same way in either direction, the program is to show the value, along with the message "THIS IS A SYMMETRICAL NUMBER," If not, there is to be no output for that input value. Thus, 8228, 757, 4004, 47574, and 88 are symmetrical numbers while 6161, 20, 32732, and 9 are not. As in the previous problem, there may be any number of runs, each consisting of any number of input values. For each run, the program is to show the number of symmetrical values (numsym), their sum (sumsym), the total number of values (numval), *their* sum (sumval), and the ratio of sumsym to sumval, rounded to three places. After the last run, on a separate page, the program is to show the number of runs (numruns), the total number of symmetrical values (ttlsym), and the total number of values (ttlnumval).

9. Write a program that reads three integer values lower, middle, and upper. These values are different from each other, with lower being the smallest, and upper being the largest. These values are followed by a succession of integers (which may be positive, negative, or zero), one to a line. After the last integer has been read and processed, the program is to produce the following output:

First line: The number of values read (not counting lower, middle, or upper).
Second line: The number of values less than lower.
Third line: The number of values greater than lower but less than middle.
Fourth line: The number of values greater than middle but less than upper.
Fifth line: The number of values greater than upper.
Sixth line: The number of values equal to lower, middle, or upper.

10. This is a more intricate version of the previous problem: Input still consists of three integers followed by an arbitrary number of additional integer values. The difference is that the three initial input values are not guaranteed to be in any numerical order. Moreover, they are not guaranteed to be all different. Consequently, the program must determine whether they are. If they are, the program is to proceed as in the previous problem, producing the results indicated there. If they are not all different, the program is to produce one of the following messages, depending on the situation:

ALL THREE TEST VALUES ARE EQUAL.
THE TWO HIGHER TEST VALUES ARE EQUAL.
THE TWO LOWER TEST VALUES ARE EQUAL.

11. The Pampered Pancreas (known affectionately as P-squared) is a limited-menu restaurant specializing in mediocre food, a fact hidden only with partial success by a bewildering collection of prefab cutesy decorations and a folk guitarist with severe vocal problems. One of the P-squared's popular specialties is a prepackaged Dinner for Eight (reservations three days in advance, please) whose basic cost is $62.00. For that amount, each Pampered Pancreas Patron (known as a P-cube to the Innermost Crowd) gets a salad, an entree, a beverage, and a dessert. Fantastic. This sounds simple enough, but it gets a little involved because of the conditions under which the items are selected:

(a) Everybody gets the same salad.

(b) There are three entrees (beefarama, ultrachicken, and super-cod). The fixed price entitles the group to eight entrees, but at least three of them must be beefarama, at least two of them must be ultrachicken, and at least one must be supercod. Beyond that, the other choices may be any of the three types.

(c) Everybody gets any of the three beverages on the menu. (Well, limited is limited.)

(d) P-squared offers two desserts: Sunset and Paradiso. (I don't know what they are either.) Four of the desserts must be from each type.

Of course, the diners have the right to deviate from these rules, but it will cost them:

(e) If less than three beefaramas are ordered, there is a $2.00 penalty for each one less. If less than two ultrachickens are ordered, there is a $1.75 penalty for each one less.

(f) If more than eight beverages are ordered, there is an additional charge of $1.50 each for the first five and $1.25 each beyond that.

(g) Sunsets are $1.80 each and Paradisos are $1.95 each. If diners order less than four desserts of either type, there is no credit for the unordered dessert. For instance, if a party of eight gets six Sunsets and only two Paradisos, they are charged $3.60 extra for the two additional Sunsets.

The P-squared would like a program that computes and displays a total amount to be billed for each party of eight. Input (for each party) consists of eight lines. Each contains the party number (an integer), the number of beefaramas, the number of ultrachickens, the number of supercods, the number of beverages, the number of Sunsets, and the number of Paradisos. This series of input sets is preceded by a single line showing today's month, day, and year. For each party, the program is to produce five output lines: The party number, total surcharge for entrees, total surcharge for beverages, total surcharge for desserts, and the total amount billed. Leave a blank line between output sets and include appropriate labels for the various items shown. Precede the first output set with a line showing today's date, and follow the last output set with three blank lines and an additional output line showing the number of parties and the total amount billed.

12. In this version of Problem 11, use the same decision rules and produce the same output. However, the results for each party are to appear on a single line of a five-column table equipped with appropriate column headings. The date still goes at the top as before. After all the sets have been processed, the program is to leave two blank lines and then show an additional line containing the string "TOTAL" in the first column (where the party number was shown for the individual sets) and the various total figures in the other four columns.

13. Write a program that computes a date (month/day/year) given a starting date and an elapsed time period in years, months, and days. That is, each input line consists of six integer values: starting month (startmo), starting day (startday), starting year (startyr), number of elapsed years (years), number of elapsed months (months), and number of elapsed days (days). These are used to compute a final date (finalmo, finalday, finalyr). Each input set produces three lines of output. For instance, the input line

```
7   7   1982   3   4   16
```

will give the following output:

```
STARTING DATE:      7/ 7/1982
ELAPSED TIME:       3   YEARS,   4   MONTHS,   16   DAYS
FINAL DATE:         11/23/1985
```

Leave a blank line between output sets. The following assumptions apply here:

(a) All data will be in the twentieth century.
(b) months will never exceed 12, days will never exceed 31, and years will always be sized so as not to violate (a).
(c) All starting dates will be valid.
(d) All time lapses will be forward. That is, the final date will always be later in time than the starting date.

14. Here is a slight variation on the previous problem. Instead of specifying the elapsed time in years, months, and days, an input set in this instance consists of the first three values as before and the elapsed

time *in days*. The first and third lines of output remain as they were, and the second line changes in accordance with the modified input.

15. In this problem, produce a version of the program in either of the previous two problems where the output is arranged as a table in which the output produced for each set appears as a single line. If you select Problem 13 as a basis, your table will have five columns (starting date, elapsed years, elapsed months, elapsed days, and final date). The requirements from Problem 14, on the other hand, suggest a three-column table (starting date, elapsed days, and final date). In either version, include appropriate column headings.

16. To complicate things a bit further, write a program that meets the requirements given in Problem 13, 14, or 15 with one exception: Assumption (c) no longer holds. The only thing we can say about the first three input values is that they will be integers. This means that not only will you have to check for ridiculous dates (e.g., 14/42/1978), but it will also be necessary to check dates that are legal to make sure that assumption (a) is not violated. If you find a starting date that will not meet these conditions, produce a line of output showing the date and the message "IMPROPER STARTING DATE," and go on to the next input set.

17. Now we shall complicate the elapsed time problem further by removing assumption (b) (see Problem 13). Thus, an elapsed time period of 0 years, 14 months, and 47 days, for example, is acceptable under these relaxed rules. Write the program requested in Problem 13 or 14 with assumptions (b) and (c) removed.

18. As a final complication, write the program specified for Problem 17 with the additional stipulation that assumption (a) is removed. This leaves only assumption (d), and the more adventurous may remove that one as well.

19. Here is a research question: Pick your favorite (or least favorite) airline and find out how many different ways there are to determine what it costs to fly between two particular cities. Then, having defined the information you need to make the computations, write a program that reads this information and computes the appropriate cost. Some suggested journeys are listed below. A few are easier than others, but remember that all of them are subject to such considerations as class of flight, family plans, group plans, length of stay, advance reservations, and so on. Have a good trip:

(a) St. Louis to Kansas City
(b) Philadelphia to Pittsburgh
(c) New York to Chicago
(d) New York to Miami
(e) New York to Los Angeles

(f)   New York to London
(g)   New York to Las Vegas
(h)   New York to Washington, D.C.
(i)   New York to Honolulu
(j)   Washington, D.C., to Chicago
(k)   Washington, D.C., to Los Angeles
(l)   Chicago to Honolulu
(m)   Chicago to London
(n)   Los Angeles to London
(o)   Tyler, Texas to Syracuse, New York

Chapter 12

Loops

Chapter 3 discussed the loop's fundamental importance as a structural component, and we have made frequent use of Pascal's facilities for building and controlling such loops. In this chapter we elaborate on these features and take a more detailed look at the kinds of repetitive processes that they support.

12.1 LOOPS FOR COUNTING—THE FOR STATEMENT

A commonly used type of computational process is one consisting of a specified number of trips through a loop. It is not necessarily true that the number of trips is the same every time the process is used, but that number, whatever it is, always is known at the start. Pascal's FOR statement (Figure 12.1) makes the construction of such loops convenient because it maintains a counter that keeps track of the cycles and automatically cuts off the repetitions when the required number has been completed.

Example 12.1 A simple illustration will remind us how easily such loops are built: In this example we shall compute the sum sumval and the sum of the square roots sumroots of eight real input values, each one of which

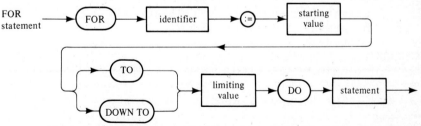

Semantics: starting value and limiting value are expressions whose values must be such that starting value must not be greater than limiting value when TO is specified; alternatively, starting value must not be less than limiting value if DOWNTO is used.

Figure 12.1

Syntax and Semantics for the FOR Statement

will be read, in turn, into a variable newval. In addition, we shall find the largest of these eight values (largestval). An integer named counter will be used to keep track of the number of cycles through the loop.

The heart of the program (Figure 12.2) is the FOR loop in which each of the eight cycles brings in an input value, uses it to update sumval and sumroots, and to replace the current value for largest if appropriate.

```
(**********************************************************************)
(**                         EXAMPLE 12.1                            **)
(**********************************************************************)
(** THIS PROGRAM ILLUSTRATES THE CONSTRUCTION OF A SIMPLE COUNTING **)
(** LOOP, A LOOP IS SET UP IN WHICH EACH OF ITS EIGHT CYCLES READS **)
(**  A REAL VALUE FOR newvalue, ADDS IT TO sumval, ADDS ITS SQUARE **)
(** ROOT TO sumroots, AND COMPARES ITS VALUE TO largest, REPLACING **)
(** largest IF THE NEW VALUE EXCEEDS IT.                           **)
(**********************************************************************)
PROGRAM ex1201 ;
VAR
    counter : INTEGER ;
    newval, sumval, sumroots, largest : REAL ;
(**********************************************************************)
(** largest WILL BE INITIALIZED TO A SMALL VALUE SO THAT THE FIRST **)
(** INPUT VALUE WILL BE SURE TO REPLACE IT UPON COMPARISON.        **)
(**********************************************************************)
BEGIN
    WRITELN ('ENTER NEWVAL,') ;
    sumval := 0,0 ;
    sumroots := 0,0 ;
    largest := -1.0E40 ;
    FOR counter := 1 TO 8 DO
        BEGIN
            READLN (newval) ;
            sumval := sumval + newval ;
            sumroots := sumroots + SQRT(newval) ;
            IF newval > largest THEN
                largest := newval
        END ;
    WRITELN ('LARGEST OF EIGHT INPUT VALUES:  ',largest) ;
    WRITELN ('SUM OF EIGHT INPUT VALUES:  ',sumval) ;
    WRITELN ('SUM OF SQUARE ROOTS: ',sumroots)  ;
    WRITELN ;
    WRITELN ('END OF RUN,')
END,
```

Figure 12.2

Pascal Statements for Example 12.1

12.1.1 Loops with Varying Numbers of Cycles

Since the number of cycles in a FOR loop need not be specified as a constant (it may be an expression, as Figure 12.1 indicates), we have an opportunity to vary the number of cycles each time the looping process is used. This is illustrated by revising the requirements in Example 12.1 so that, instead of reading and processing exactly eight values each time the program is run, the modified version (Figure 12.3) reads an input value that tells the program how many subsequent values to read and process. Note

```
(*******************************************************************)
(**                      EXAMPLE 12.2                           **)
(*******************************************************************)
(**   THE LOOP IN THIS PROGRAM STILL GOES THROUGH A PREDEFINED   **)
(**   NUMBER numnew OF CYCLES, BUT THAT NUMBER IS AN INPUT VALUE  **)
(**   THAT CAN CHANGE FROM RUN TO RUN.                           **)
(*******************************************************************)
PROGRAM  ex1202  ;
VAR
    numnew, counter  :  INTEGER  ;
    newval, sumval, numroots, largest  :  REAL  ;
BEGIN
    sumval := 0.0  ;
    sumroots := 0.0  ;
    largest := -1.0E40  ;
    WRITE ('ENTER NUMNEW: ')  ;
    READLN (numnew)  ;
    WRITELN ('NUMBER OF VALUES TO BE READ:   ',numnew)  ;
    FOR   counter := 1 TO numnew   DO
       BEGIN
          WRITE ('TYPE A NEW VALUE: ')  ;
          READLN (newval)   ;
          sumval := sumval + newval ;
          sumroots := sumroots + SQRT(newval)   ;
          IF   newval > largest    THEN
             largest := newval
       END   ;
    WRITELN ('LARGEST OF ',numnew, ' VALUES:   ',largest) ;
    WRITELN ('SUM OF ',numnew ,' VALUES:    ',sumval) ;
    WRITELN ('SUM OF ',numnew,' SQUARE ROOTS:    ',sumroots)  ;
    WRITELN ;
    WRITELN ('END OF RUN.')
END.
```

Figure 12.3

Pascal Statements for Example 12.2

that the index that monitors the number of cycles (counter in this example) is changed automatically as part of the control mechanism built into the FOR statement. *The programmer does not and should not change the index by anything he or she specifies in the loop.*

12.1.2 Automatic Decrementation in FOR Loops

Another form of the FOR statement enables the programmer to set up a loop in which an index is initialized and then decreased (*decremented*) by 1 before each cycle. In this form, the reserved word TO is replaced by the reserved word DOWNTO to indicate explicitly that the index will be decreased by 1 automatically. The initial and final index values, which may be specified as constants or more extensive expressions, must be consistent in that the initial value must be greater than the final value when DOWNTO is used. It is up to the programmer (and not Pascal) to make sure that the program specifies the proper direction in which the index value is to change (i.e., TO for automatic increase by 1, DOWNTO for automatic decrease by 1). If there is any inconsistency (for instance, if the FOR statement says TO and the starting value for the index is greater than the final value, the program skips the entire FOR statement.

We saw this feature used to compute a polynomial value (Figure 7.1). To illustrate another use of this form, we shall declare an array letters of 18 characters and store them in reverse order. That is, the first input character will be stored in letters[18], the second in letters[17], and so on:

```
VAR
   which    :   INTEGER ;
   letters  :     ARRAY [1..18] OF CHAR
   •
   •
   •
   FOR  which := 18 DOWNTO 1  DO
      READ (letters[which])
```

12.1.3 Use of the Loop Index in Computations

Although the index in a FOR loop is to be changed only by the automatic mechanism built into the FOR statement, it can participate in any computations specified within the loop. For example, suppose we wanted to compute the quantity hfact, where

$$\text{hfact} = \sum_{\text{lower}}^{\text{upper}} \text{tracker LOG (tracker)}$$

In this formulation, lower and upper are integer values that define the limits of the computation and may vary from one instance to the next. Accordingly, we shall show them as input values:

```
VAR
   lower, upper, tracker   :    INTEGER   ;
   hfact   :    REAL ;
   .
   .
   .
   READLN (lower, upper)  ;
   hfact := 0.0  ;
   FOR   tracker := lower TO upper  DO
      hfact := hfact + tracker*LOG(tracker)
```

Although the index (counter in this example) plays a dominant role in the computations, its value is not affected by those computations.

12.1.4 Loops with Programmer-defined Indexes

Examples 10.1 and 10.2 (Figures 10.2 and 10.5) included a FOR loop with an index variable of type pianotype—an enumerative type defined in the programs themselves. As Section 10.2.2 explained, Pascal can manage such counters by using the internal sequencing associated with the list of values in a TYPE declaration. For example, suppose we make the following declarations and assignments:

```
TYPE
   luggage = (makeupcase, overnight, airplane, weekend,
              pullman, trunk, omigod) ;
VAR
  grip, littlecarrier, bigcarrier   :   luggage
   .
   .
   .
  littlecarrier := overnight ;
  bigcarrier := pullman
```

Then the loop

```
FOR   grip := littlecarrier TO bigcarrier   DO
         action
```

will execute four times. So would the loop

```
FOR   grip := pullman DOWNTO overnight   DO
         action
```

12.2 MORE GENERAL EVENT-CONTROLLED LOOPS

Completion of a predetermined number of cycles is just one kind of event that can be used to control the behavior of a loop. There are more general situations where the number of cycles is not crucial in determining whether a loop should continue or not. Instead, some other circumstance serves as the basis for such a decision. For example, it often makes sense to build a loop whose activity continues to repeat as long as input values are available, a practice we have used frequently throughout the book. This section looks at additional considerations in the construction and use of such loops.

12.2.1 The WHILE Statement Revisited

Our extensive use of the WHILE-DO construction (and the corresponding WHILE statement) makes it unnecessary to dwell on its properties here. One point worth re-emphasizing is that the placement of the test at the entrance to the loop makes it possible to include situations in which the loop is not entered at all.

For example, suppose we were to add each successive real input value testvalue to a sum sumoftests as long as testvalue exceeds some minimum value minvalue. Assuming all the necessary declarations, our code might look like this:

```
READLN (minvalue)  ;
sumoftests := 0.0  ;
READLN (testvalue)  ;
WHILE  testvalue > minvalue  DO
    BEGIN
        sumoftests := sumoftests + testvalue  ;
        READLN (testvalue)
    END
next statement
```

The loop pays no attention to the number of input values used. Consequently, if the first value of testvalue turns out to be too small (i.e., not greater than minvalue), the test in the WHILE statement fails even before the first cycle, and the entire loop structure is bypassed.

12.2.2 The REPEAT-UNTIL Structure

A special case of the WHILE-DO loop occurs when the programmer wishes to guarantee at least one trip through the loop regardless of the number of additional trips that may be completed. This type of situation occurs often enough so that it has been identified as a distinct structural component, i.e.,

REPEAT
    activity
UNTIL this condition is true.

Figure 12.4

Pseudocode Representation for the REPEAT-UNTIL Construction

the REPEAT-UNTIL construction. The basic property of this type of loop is that the test which controls continued cycling is at the end of the loop (rather than at the beginning, as is the case in the WHILE-DO construction). Moreover, the test is expressed in such a way that an outcome of TRUE breaks the loop and forces the process to move to the next activity. An outcome of FALSE sends the program back through the loop for another trip. The pseudocode representation of this loop is shown in Figure 12.4. Pascal's REPEAT statement (Figure 12.5) is a direct expression of this structure: The activity specified after the reserved word REPEAT is performed once before the program checks to see whether to repeat the process or move on. To emphasize the difference between the WHILE-DO and REPEAT-UNTIL components, we shall compare two similar programs. The basic intent is to read a succession of values for real variable pval and compute the sum of their logarithms sumlogpvals. Figure 12.6 shows a common set of declarations followed by alternative procedural sections. The version on the right is designed to expect at least one input value. If that actually is the case, the two versions will produce the same results. In the extreme case where there are no input values (such things can and do happen), the more general version on the left will operate as usual, but the alternate construction will terminate with an error message.

12.3 NESTED LOOPS

Many situations call for loops which themselves contain other loops. For instance, the second hand of a clock must go through a complete set of (60) movements for the minute hand to move one notch. Similarly, the minute hand must go through a complete set of (60) movements for the hour hand to move one notch. Loops contained in other loops are said to be *nested*. Pascal's facilities for building such processes are easy to use because they are direct extensions of the fundamental FOR, WHILE, or REPEAT statements. Since the cyclic activity for any of these forms can be expressed as a

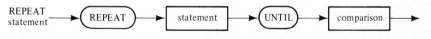

REPEAT statement → (REPEAT) → statement → (UNTIL) → comparison →

Figure 12.5

Syntax for the REPEAT Statement

```
(*******************************************************************)
(** THIS PROGRAM COMPUTES smlog, THE SUM OF THE LOGS OF    **)
(** AN ARBITRARY NUMBER OF INPUT VALUES FOR pval, THE      **)
(** PROCESSING LOOP IS SHOWN IN TWO VERSIONS.              **)
(*******************************************************************)
      PROGRAM  whileuntil  ;
      VAR
          pval, smlog    :    REAL  ;

BEGIN                                  BEGIN
   smlog := 0.0  ;                        smlog := 0.0  ;
   WRITELN ('TYPE IN PVAL.')  ;           WRITELN ('TYPE IN PVAL.')   ;
   READLN (pval)  ;                       READLN (pval)  ;
   WHILE  NOT EOF  DO                     REPEAT
      BEGIN                                  BEGIN
         smmlog := smlog+pval  ;               smlog := smlog+pval   ;
         WRITELN ('NEXT PVAL.')  ;              WRITELN ('NEXT PVAL.')   ;
         READLN (pval)                          READLN (pval)
      END  ;                                 END
   WRITELN ('SMLOG: ',smlog)             UNTIL  EOF  ;
END.                                     WRITELN ('SMLOG: ',smlog)
                                       END.
```

Figure 12.6

Comparison between WHILE-DO and REPEAT-UNTIL Constructions

compound statement, that statement may consist of a sequence that includes another loop. *That* loop, in turn, may itself incorporate a complete loop, and so on. These relationships, examples of which are depicted in Figure 12.7, make it possible to extend nested loop systems to any desired level without changing the overall structure. Note that the nesting possibilities are completely general in that a FOR loop may be nested in a WHILE loop or a REPEAT loop, and so on. When a FOR loop is nested in another FOR loop, the programmer must make sure he or she uses different index variables for each loop.

Example 12.3   A good way to summarize these fundamental processes (as it has been since Neanderthal Man stumbled on the first loop uncharted eons ago) is to set up a program that reads in elements for a one-dimensional array and displays the array with its elements arranged in descending order (i.e., the largest value in the first element, etc.). To keep our attention focused on the processing itself, we shall use a small (6-element) integer array named ht.

The algorithm selected for this example is called a *bubble sort* because larger values are systematically "bubbled" toward one end of the array

```
loop specification 1
   BEGIN
      statement ;
      statement
      ..........
      loop specificaton 2
         BEGIN
            statement ;
            statement
            ..........
            loop specification 3
               BEGIN
                  statement
                  ..........
                  statement
               END ;
            statement
            ..........
         END ;
         statement ;
         statement
         ..........
         loop specification 4
            BEGIN
               statement
               ..........
               statement
            END
   END
loop specification is either FOR index := start TO finish DO
                          or    FOR index := start DOWNTO finish DO
                          or    WHILE test outcome is true DO
                          or    REPEAT
                                   activity
                                UNTIL
                                   test outcome is true
```

Figure 12.7

Construction of Nested Loops

while the smaller elements percolate their way toward the other end. In addition, the algorithm includes a signal (the BOOLEAN variable noswap) that prevents unnecessary cycling if the elements are already in proper order. A pseudocode description is given in Figure 12.8.

A simple loop brings the array's elements into the processor, and a similar process displays them. (No, we cannot transmit an entire array with a single READ, READLN, WRITE, or WRITELN.) The program itself is

Define 6-element array HT, indexes I and K, switch NOSWAP.
Read HT.
DO for the first 5 elements of HT using index I:
    Initialize NOSWAP to TRUE.
    DO for HT[6} down to HT[I+1] using index K:
        IF
            HT[K] is greater than HT[K-1].
        THEN
            Exchange HT[K] and HT[K-1].
            Set NOSWAP to FALSE.
        ELSE
        ENDIF
    ENDDO
    IF
        NOSWAP is TRUE
    THEN
        Sort is complete; exit from the loop.
    ELSE
    ENDIF
ENDDO
Display the sorted array.
Display terminating message.
Stop.

Figure 12.8

Pseudocode for Example 12.3

shown in Figure 12.9(a). Of special interest is the appearance of a GOTO statement. This is one of a few special situations in which this dreaded statement simplifies the processing: When the value in noswap tells us that the program has worked its way through a cycle without having to rearrange any elements, we can conclude that the array is sorted and needs no further treatment. Consequently, we would like to stop the cyclic process abruptly, right at that point, even though the FOR statement "expects" more cycles. Under those circumstances, the GOTO statement gives us a clean, direct getaway.

We can rewrite the sorting process without the toxic GOTO statement by using noswap to control a WHILE...DO structure. This organization is shown in Figure 12.9(b). The "proper" version is a matter of judgment.

If the exact operation of an algorithm leaves some questions, a helpful technique is to "walk through" its operations as if we were the processor. We shall do that for the sorting loop of this example by starting with the array

7   2   4   9   6   3

```
{******************************************************************}
{                          EXAMPLE 12.3                        **}
{******************************************************************}
{  THIS PROGRAM SORTS A 6-ELEMENT INTEGER ARRAY IN DESCENDING ORDER  }
{  USING A BUBBLE SORT TECHNIQUE. THE NORMALLY INSIDIOUS GOTO IS    }
{  USED TO PROVIDE A QUICK EXIT FROM THE SORTING LOOP WHEN FURTHER  }
{  EXAMINATION OF THE ARRAY IS DETERMINED TO BE UNNECESSARY.        }
{  NOTE THE PLACEMENT OF THE LABEL DECLARATION.                     }
{******************************************************************}
PROGRAM  ex1203  ;
LABEL
   99  ;
CONST
   arraylimit = 6  ;
VAR
   ht  :  ARRAY[1..arraylimit] OF INTEGER  ;
   i, k, temp_ht  :  INTEGER  ;
   noswap  :  BOOLEAN  ;
BEGIN
   FOR  i := 1 TO arraylimit  DO
     BEGIN
       WRITELN ('SUBMIT ELEMENT ',i,' OF ARRAY HT.')  ;
       READ (ht[i])
     END  ;
   FOR  i := 1 TO arraylimit-1  DO
     BEGIN
         noswap := TRUE  ;
         FOR  k := arraylimit DOWNTO i+1  DO
           IF
             ht[k] > ht[k-1]
           THEN
             BEGIN
               temp_ht := ht[k] ;   ht[k] := ht[k-1] ;
                          ht[k-1] := temp_ht ;
               noswap := FALSE
             END  ;
         IF  noswap  THEN GOTO 99
     END  ;
99:    WRITELN ('SORTED ARRAY:')  ;
   FOR  i := 1 TO arraylimit  DO
     WRITE (ht[i]:8)  ;
   WRITELN  ;
   WRITELN ('END OF RUN.')
END.
```

Figure 12.9(a)————————————————————

Program For Example 12.3

```
      READ (ht[i])
   END ;
noswap := FALSE ;
i := 1 ;
WHILE ((i < arraylimit) AND (NOT noswap))  DO
   BEGIN
      noswap := TRUE ;
      FOR  k := arraylimit DOWNTO i+1  DO
        IF  ht[k] > ht[k-1]
           THEN
              BEGIN
                 temp_ht := ht[k] ;  ht[k] := ht[k-1] ;
                 ht[k-1] := temp_ht ;
                 noswap := FALSE
              END ;
      i := i + 1
   END ;
WRITELN ('SORTED ARRAY:') ;
```

Figure 12.9(b)

Sorting Process for Example 12.3 without the GOTO Statement

Original Array:		2	7	4	9	6	3	
i=1;	k=6:	7	2	4	9	6	3	
	k=5:	7	2	4	9	6	3	
	k=4:	7	2	9	4	6	3	(NOSWAP=FALSE)
	k=3:	7	9	2	4	6	3	
	k=2:	9	7	2	4	6	3	
								(NOSWAP=TRUE)
i=2;	k=6:	9	7	2	4	6	3	
	k=5:	9	7	2	6	4	3	(NOSWAP=FALSE)
	k=4:	9	7	6	2	4	3	
	k=3:	9	7	6	2	4	3	
								(NOSWAP=TRUE)
i=3;	k=6:	9	7	6	2	4	3	
	k=5:	9	7	6	4	2	3	(NOSWAP=FALSE)
	k=4:	9	7	6	4	2	3	
								(NOSWAP=TRUE)
i=4;	k=6:	9	7	6	4	3	2	(NOSWAP=FALSE)
	k=5:	9	7	6	4	3	2	
								(NOSWAP=TRUE)
i=5;	k=6:	9	7	6	4	3	2	
SORT COMPLETE.								

Figure 12.10

Step-by-Step Example of the Bubble Sort (Worst Case)

and seeing the effect of each individual cycle. Using the same index variables (i and k) defined in the program, the results of such a walk-through are given in Figure 12.10.

Problems

1. Write the Pascal statement(s) necessary to implement each of the following processes. Assume all necessary declarations:

   (a) Find the sum of 20 successive input values for integer numsold. Store the sum in totalsold.

   (b) Read an integer value breakval. Then, add each of the next 23 input integer values (each of which is stored in newval) either to lowsum if it is less than breakval or to highsum if it is not.

   (c) Read an integer value howmany and then compute the square root of the sum of the natural logarithms of the next howmany input values. Each of these values will be a real number to be stored in nextval.

   (d) Compute sumfirstm, the sum of the first m positive integers. The value for m is to be read as input.

   (e) Compute sumfirstoddm, the sum of the first m odd integers. The value for m is to be read as input.

   (f) Compute numberofprimes, the number of prime numbers in the first m positive integers. The value of m is read as input.

   (g) Expand the statements in (f) so that they also produce bigprime, the largest prime number in the first m positive integers.

   (h) Compute numberofsevens, the number of times the digit 7 appears in the positive integers ranging from input value low to 999. Assume low is always a positive integer less than 999.

2. Rewrite the program in Example 12.2 so that processing repeats automatically for an arbitrary number of sets of input values.

3. Write a program that reads sets of input consisting of two positive integers m and n. For each set, the program is to produce a table in which there is a line for each integer i between m and n. Each line shows i, its square, its cube, its square root, and its logarithm. There is no guarantee that m and n are different, nor is it assured that m is always the smaller of the two when they are different.

4. Write a program that produces the same kind of table as that specified for Problem 3. The difference is that, instead of restricting the input values to integers, each table is produced in response to three real input values: lowval, the lowest value, hival, the highest value, and increment, the amount to be added to the current value to

produce the basis for the next line of the table. For example, input values of

1.0   50.0   0.2

would produce a table whose first line shows the square, cube, etc. of 1.0, the second line shows similar information for 1.2, the third line for 1.4, and so on up to and including 50.0. Assume increment is always greater than zero and that hival is always greater than lowval.

5. Write the same kind of program described for the previous problem, but do not make either of the assumptions stipulated there.

6. Revise the program in Example 12.3 so that it processes any number of input sets.

7. Revise the program in Example 12.3 so that it processes arrays of 20 elements.

8. Revise the program in Problems 6 or 7 so that it sorts the elements in ascending order (lowest value in ht[1], etc.)

9. Write a program that counts the number of ways to make change for a dollar using pennies, nickels, dimes, quarters, and/or half dollars.

10. In the distant land of Poopikonia, the unit of currency is the Riegloch. There are three Zoopchiks to the Riegloch, seven Glepniks to the Zoopchik, eleven Fnivs to the Glepnik, and four Digidehs to the Fniv. Write a program that counts the number of ways to make change for a Riegloch.

11. Revise the program in Problem 9 or 10 so that it displays each combination producing change for a Riegloch as long as that combination does not involve any Fnivs.

12. Revise the program in Problem 8 so that it will process arrays of 20 elements or less. Each array is preceded by an integer value elements that specifies the number of elements in the array that follows.

Chapter 13

Subprograms

A major attribute of a well-constructed program is its clarity—its success in conveying succinctly and accurately the processing activities embodied in it. To enhance a program's clarity, we will focus on the procedural steps required by the *algorithm* and submerge our concern with the detailed expression of those steps in the *program*. This is exactly what we do when we use one of Pascal's standard (permanent) subprograms or write one ourselves: By expressing the action in the main program as a single statement or operation, we are able to pretend that the processing is really accomplished in one step; details of the activity, hidden away in a subprogram, can be as extensive and/or tedious as they need to be without upsetting this illusion.

13.1 EXAMPLE 13.1

We can see how to submerge the operating details of an activity by rewriting Example 12.3 from the previous chapter. In that program there is a pair of nested loops that sort the array. The size and complexity of these loops is dictated by the algorithms used and by Pascal's properties. However, our view of this activity is considerably simpler: "Sort the array's elements in descending order."

To bring the program in Example 12.3 closer to this view, we shall move the sorting process out of the main program and convert it into a separate subprogram whose description will appear in the declaration section. In its place (in the main program) will be a simple request for the rearrangement to be performed. This reorganization is shown in the overall structure of the revised program (Figure 13.1). The sorting process is recast as a *procedure*. The statement that uses *(invokes)* the procedure (Figure 13.1[b]) simply specifies the procedure's name (arraysort) and a value (ht) on which the procedure is to operate. The procedure, in response, produces results that are *returned* to the invoking program. This is no different from our use of READLN or any of Pascal's other standard procedures.

Details of the procedure's activities are described in its definition (Figure 13.1[c]), and the program is given in Figure 13.1(d). Since

```
PROCEDURE arraysort (VAR values : vector) ;
VAR
    i, k, temp_val : INTEGER ;
    noswap : BOOLEAN ;
BEGIN
    FOR i := 1 TO arraylimit-1 DO
        BEGIN
        noswap := TRUE ;
        FOR k := arraylimit DOWNTO i+1 DO
            IF
                values[k] > values[k-1]
            THEN
                BEGIN
                temp_value := values [k] ;
                values[k] := values [k-1] ;
                values[k-1] := temp_value ;
                noswap := FALSE ;
                END ;
            IF noswap THEN EXIT(arraysort)

        END
END ;
```

(c) Definition of the arraysort Procedure

ARRAYSORT(ht)

(b) Invocation of arraysort

(a) Overall organization

```
PROGRAM ex1301
```

declarations for constants,
data types, and variables

| description of the sorting process |

```
BEGIN
    FOR which := 1 TO arraylimit DO
        BEGIN
        WRITELN ('SUBMIT ELEMENT ', WHICH,' OF ARRAY HT,') ;
        READ (ht[which])
        END ;

        ARRAYSORT(ht)
```

| sort the array |
```
    FOR which := 1 TO arraylimit DO
        WRITE (ht[which]) ;
        WRITELN ;
        WRITELN ('END OF RUN,')

    END.
```

Figure 13.1 ——— Program Organization for Example 13.1

256

```
{*********************************************************************}
{                            EXAMPLE 13.1                            }
{*********************************************************************}
{  THIS PROGRAM SORTS A 6-ELEMENT INTEGER ARRAY IN DESCENDING ORDER }
{  USING A BUBBLE SORT TECHNIQUE. EXIT IS A UCSD PASCAL FUNCTION     }
{  THAT PROVIDES AN IMMEDIATE DEPARTURE FROM A SUBPROGRAM. THIS      }
{  REPLACES THE GOTO USED TO PROVIDE A SUDDEN EXIT FROM THE LOOP     }
{  IN EXAMPLE 10.3. FOR CONVENIENCE, THE 6-ELEMENT ARRAY IS SET UP   }
{  AS AN DATA TYPE.                                                  }
{*********************************************************************}
PROGRAM  ex1301  ;
CONST
   arraylimit = 6  ;
TYPE
   vector  :   ARRAY[1..arraylimit] OF INTEGER   ;
VAR
   ht  :   vector  ;
   which  :   INTEGER  ;
PROCEDURE  arraysort(VAR values : vector) ;
VAR
  i, k, temp_val  :   INTEGER  ;
  noswap  :  BOOLEAN  ;
BEGIN
   FOR  i := 1 TO arraylimit-1  DO
     BEGIN
       noswap := TRUE  ;
       FOR  k := arraylimit DOWNTO i+1  DO
         IF
           values[k] > values[k-1]
         THEN
           BEGIN
             temp_value := values[k] ;
             values[k] := values[k-1] ;
             values[k-1] := temp_value ;
             noswap := FALSE
           END  ;
       IF  noswap  THEN EXIT(arraysort)
     END
   END  ;
{  HERE IS THE MAIN PROGRAM.  }
BEGIN
  FOR  which := 1 TO arraylimit  DO
    BEGIN
      WRITELN ('SUBMIT ELEMENT ',WHICH,' OF ARRAY HT.')  ;
      READ (ht[which])
    END  ;
```

Figure 13.1(d)————————————————————————

Program for Example 13.1

```
  arraysort (ht)  ;
  WRITELN ('SORTED ARRAY:')  ;
  FOR  which := 1 TO arraylimit  DO
    WRITE ht[which]:8)  ;
  WRITELN  ;
  WRITELN ('END OF RUN.')
END.
```

Figure 13.1(d)

Program for Example 13.1 (Continued)

arraysort appears as part of the program's declaration section, its position in the program is totally unrelated to its usage. The only way any subprogram's activity gets performed is by invocation from some point in the main program's procedure section. Subprograms may be invoked any number of times from many different places in the procedure section, thereby emphasizing their versatility.

UCSD Pascal extends this versatility even further by providing a way to construct programs using subprograms whose descriptions are attached to the main program instead of being embedded in it. This additional alternative allows these *external units* to be compiled individually, with the resulting p-machine instructions being stored as p-System code files for later use. Although the pertinent techniques (and the situations for which they are particularly advantageous) will not be discussed until later, it is important to know that the p-System makes them available. The use of these external program components is an organizational alternative, but it exploits exactly the same principles that in general make subprograms useful: They promote clarity and ease of development by allowing us to break a large complex problem into several smaller, individually manageable problems. Once we understand how to make that idea work for us by using regular (internal) subprograms, its extension to external program units becomes straightforward.

Having introduced the basic relationship between subprograms and their use in a program, we can turn our attention to their properties and construction. These issues are the subject of this chapter.

13.2 STRUCTURE OF SUBPROGRAMS

Pascal recognizes two kinds of subprograms: the function and the procedure. The function enables the programmer to treat a process as if it were a single operation. This characterization is supported by the function's structural properties:

1. A function operates in a predefined way on an appropriate number of values (*arguments*) to produce a single result.

2. A function is invoked in an expression, and the result is returned to that expression for further processing within the same statement.

A procedure (traditionally called a *subroutine*) is a more general type of subprogram that enables the programmer to treat a process as if it were a single subprogram that enables the programmer to treat a process as if it were a single Pascal statement. This is reflected in the following properties:

1. A procedure operates in a predefined way on an appropriate number of arguments with no limit imposed on the number of values produced. (In Example 13.1, the procedure `arraysort` operates on six numbers, even though we referred to them collectively with a single argument.)

2. A procedure is invoked as a separate statement. Regardless of the complexity of the underlying process, the procedure's mechanism ensures that when the procedure is completed, the program continues right after the statement that invoked *(called)* the procedure.

Because of this relationship, it turns out that any function also can be expressed as a procedure, but the reverse is not true for all procedures.

The syntax diagrams for functions and procedures (Figures 13.2[a] and 13.2[b], respectively) describe similar constructions. Each subprogram has two major components:

1. The subprogram's *identification*. This group of specifications appears at the beginning of the description and defines exactly how the subprogram is used.

2. The *body* is a block containing the processing statements and the supporting data structures.

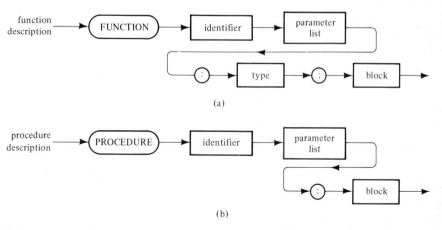

(a)

(b)

Figure 13.2

Organization of Pascal Subprograms

These components are identified in Figure 13.1(b) for the arraysort procedure.

The identification component for either type of subprogram includes a *parameter list* (Figure 13.3) that specifies the number of data items (and their respective types) to be supplied to the subprogram when it is invoked. (Note that the parameter list for a given subprogram may be empty.) Each of these specifications is expressed as a *formal parameter*. This is not an actual value or a reference to an actual value. Instead, it is a piece of bookkeeping that helps define the way the subprogram works. The role of each formal parameter is described in the body of the subprogram by that parameter's appearance(s) in the computational statements. As pointed out earlier, these computations do not take place until the subprogram is invoked. At that time, the arguments (or *actual parameters*) supplied by the invocation are used, guided by the association that the program establishes between these values and the corresponding formal parameters. In Example 13.1, values is a formal parameter. The VAR indicates that the parameter's values are likely to change as a result of the subprogram's activity. When the function is invoked (Figure 13.1[b]), the program uses the actual parameter (ht) wherever values appears in the computations. Since formal parameters do not represent variables in storage, they are not declared. Their appearance in the parameter list establishes their purpose. Note, however, that the arraysort procedure in Figure 13.1(b) does have declarations (i, K, temp_val and noswap) that do not appear in the parameter list. These variables have no purpose outside the subprogram. Consequently, they have been removed from the main program's declara-

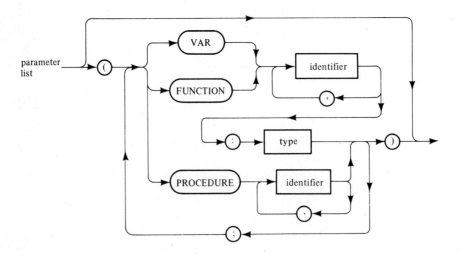

Figure 13.3

Syntax of a Parameter List

tion section, and their existence is limited to the activities within the procedure. Such variables are called *local variables*.

13.2.1 Construction of Functions

The requirements for a function's description (Figure 13.2[a]) underscore Pascal's intent with regard to a function's uses: The function performs some type of process that produces exactly one resulting value. This value is delivered in a variable carrying the function's name, and its data type is defined by the specification following the formal parameter list.

As seen in Figure 13.3, there are several kinds of formal parameters. The simplest merely specifies a name and a data type. During invocation, the value of the corresponding actual parameter will be used, but not changed during the processing. When the word VAR is placed in front of a parameter's name (as it was in Example 13.1), it identifies that parameter as one whose corresponding actual value can be expected to change as a result of the processing. Either form of parameter can be used in a function's parameter list. However, we shall impose an additional constraint by avoiding the use of VAR. This restriction brings a Pascal function closer in concept to a mathematical function. As a result, we shall characterize a function more specifically as a process that produces a single result without changing the values of any of its parameters.

Pascal places no restriction on the type(s) of data that a function may process or on the type produced as the single result. Consequently, a function can be built to operate on and/or produce programmer-defined data as long as such values are not subjected to input/output operations.

13.2.2 Construction of Procedures

As Figure 13.2 indicates, the procedure is structurally similar to the function: It has an identifying portion that defines its requirements and a body that describes its processing. The detailed differences reflect the procedure's complete generality, placing no limitations on the number of returned results. Because of this, there is no point in assigning a specific data type to the procedure's name. Instead, the parameter list includes formal parameters representing all the items returned by the procedure as well as those brought to the procedure.

13.3 INVOCATION OF SUBPROGRAMS

Inclusion of a subprogram's definition enables us to use that subprogram as often as we need it from any number of different places in our program with arbitrarily different lists of actual parameters. Invocation itself simply is patterned after the definition given in the subprogram's FUNCTION or PROCEDURE statement.

13.3.1 Invocation of Functions

When we invoke a function, we arrange to present it with the required number and types of values on which it is to operate. The function is not "aware" of how these values originally appear in the invocation. Consequently, (as Figure 13.2 indicates), an actual parameter can be presented in a variety of forms, as long as the resulting data type matches that specified by the corresponding formal parameter.

Example 13.2   As an example, consider the simple function integer-power defined in Figure 13.4(a). When invoked, this function computes the value of the first parameter raised to the positive integer power specified by the second parameter. Figure 13.4(b) shows a fragment of a main program in which integerpower is invoked from several different places:

In the first invocation, the function computes 3.56^3 and stores the result in the variable xcat. Both actual parameters are constant values requiring no further processing prior to their delivery to integerpower. In the second invocation, the values used by integerpower are taken from the two locations associated with in4 and uplim. The result thus produced, namely 2.61^6 represents only an intermediate step in the computations requested by the expression in which the invocation appears. Once integerpower completes its work, the main program resumes processing at the point it left off. Accordingly, the value delivered by integerpower is added to relwt's value, and that sum is then assigned to yval. (For reference, the result is 319.613.)

The last statement in Figure 13.4(b) contains three separate invocations of integerpower. First, the function is called upon to raise to a power a value (SQRT(relwt)) that itself must be computed before the integerpower can use it. That computation involves the invocation of another function, SQRT. Similarly, the power to which the first actual parameter is to be raised (i.e., uplim-lowlim-1) also has to be computed. Thus, when the main program turns control over to integerpower, all of this preparatory work will have been done, and what the function "sees" as its actual parameters are the values 1.87083 and 3. The result, 6.54688, is delivered back to the main program where it will be a term in the larger expression for zval. A second invocation asks integerpower to use as its first actual parameter a value (integerpower(in4,3)) whose computation involves another invocation of that same function. Pascal takes the request in stride by invoking integerpower again. The function, using the values 2.61 (i.e., in4) and 3 as its actual parameters, delivers a result of 17.7796 back to the point of the most recent invocation.

```
FUNCTION  integerpower (value : REAL ; power : INTEGER) : REAL  ;
VAR
   tracker : INTEGER  ;
BEGIN
   IF  power = 0  THEN
      integerpower := 1.0
   ELSE IF  power = 1  THEN
      integerpower := value
         ELSE
            BEGIN
               integerpower := value  ;
               FOR  tracker := 1 TO power-1  DO
                  integerpower := integerpower * value
            END
END
```

(a) Definition of the function integerpower

. . . .

```
VAR
   xcat, yval, zval, relwt, in4  :  REAL  ;
   uplim, lowlim, n1, acct       :  INTEGER
```
. . . .
```
   relwt := 3.5   ;
   in4 := 2.61    ;
   uplim := 6     ;
   lowlim := 2    ;
   n1 := 4        ;
   acct := 5
```
. . . .
```
   xcat := integerpower (3.56,3)
```
. . . .
```
   yval := relwt + integerpower (in4,uplim)
```
. . . .
```
   zval := integerpower (SQRT(relwt),uplim-lowlim-1)
        + 3.1*integerpower (integerpower(in4,3),acct-n1)
```
. . . .

(b) Invocation of the function integerpower

Figure 13.4

Multiple Uses of a Function in a Main Program

At that point, the 17.7796, together with a value of 1 (acct − n1), provide the actual parameters for integerpower's previous invocation. Consequently, the function now delivers a value of 17.7796 (more precisely, 17.7796 to the first power) to the expression, where this result is multiplied by 3.1, added to the first term (6.54688), and the final result (61.6636) is assigned to zval.

To summarize, the computation of $zval$ can be considered to take place as follows:

1. Compute $SQRT(relwt)$ (1.87083) and store in $t1$.
2. Compute $uplim-lowlim-1$ (3) and store in $t2$.
3. Compute $t1$ (6.54688) and store in $t3$.
4. Compute $in4$ (17.7796) and store in $t4$.
5. Compute $acct-n1$ (1) and store in $t5$.
6. Compute $t4$ (17.7796) and store in $t6$.
7. Multiply $t6$ by 3.1 (55.1168) and store in $t7$.
8. Add $t3$ and $t7$.
9. Store the result (61.6636) in $zval$.

13.3.2 Invocation of Procedures

As we have seen in Section 13.1 and Example 13.1, the invocation of a procedure forms a complete statement. To illustrate this further, we shall construct a procedure that produces several values: If we locate two points on a set of X-Y coordinates by defining their respective horizontal and vertical positions as X1, Y1 and X2, Y2, a straight line connecting these points will have a slope A of

$$\frac{Y2 - Y1}{X2 - X1}$$

and an intercept B of

$$Y1 - A(X1)$$

Our procedure, to be named $strline$, will operate on four real values (represented by formal parameters $x1$, $y1$, $x2$, and $y2$), submitted in that order, to produce the slope a, the intercept b, and the length $linelgth$ of the segment between the two points.

Figure 13.5(a) shows $strline$'s definition, and its use is illustrated by two invoking statements in the main program fragment of Figure 13.5(b). The first invocation provides $strline$ with four actual parameters expressed as constants. In response, the procedure will deliver the values

$$\frac{13.7 - 6.8}{5.4 - 3.7} \qquad 6.8 - \left(\frac{13.7 - 6.8}{5.4 - 3.7}\right)(3.7)$$

and

$$\sqrt{(13.7 - 6.8)^2 + (5.4 - 3.7)^2}$$

```
PROCEDURE  strline (x1, y1, x2, y2 : REAL ;
                    VAR a, VAR b, VAR linelgth : REAL)  ;
BEGIN
   a := (y2 - y1)/(x2 - x1)  ;
   b := y1 - a*x1  ;
   linelgth := SQRT (SQR(y2-y1) + SQR(x2-x1))
END
```

 (a) Description of the procedure strline

```
...................
VAR
   veloc, time1, time2, accel, slope, intercept, dist  :  REAL
   ....................
   description of the strline procedure
   ....................
   strline (3.7, 6.8, 5.4, 13.7, slope, intercept, dist)  ;
   WRITELN ('SLOPE:  ',slope,'  INTERCEPT:  ',intercept,'  DIST:  ',dist)
   ....................
   veloc := 2.1  ;
   time1 := 8.0  ;
   time2 := 12.0  ;
   accel := 11.0  ;
   strline (0.0, 3.6*time1, 1.2, veloc*time2 + 0.5*accel*SQR(time2),
            slope, intercept, dist)  ;
   WRITELN ('SLOPE:  ',slope,'  INTERCEPT:  ',intercept,'  DIST:  ',dist)
   ....................
```

 (b) Invocation of the procedure strline

Figure 13.5————————————————————————————————
  Multiple Uses of a Procedure in a Main Program

to slope, intercept, and dist, respectively. A second invocation
specifies the two vertical coordinates as expressions. These are evaluated
automatically by the program, and the resulting values are delivered to the
procedure. Thus, the second and fourth actual parameters for this invocation will be 3.6 * 8.0 and 2.1 * 12.5+11.0 * SQR(12.5), respectively.

13.4 NESTED CONSTRUCTION OF SUBPROGRAMS—EXAMPLE 13.3

Hidden within the innocent appearance of Figure 13.2 are opportunities to
construct intricate, multilayered subprograms. Since the body of a subprogram is (organizationally) a block, its declaration section may contain
any number of complete subprogram definitions. This type of *nested construction* is helpful when the processing in a subprogram can be classified

by representing some of its multistep activities as single operations or statements. Example 13.3, given below, illustrates this idea.

Triad County is a peculiar place in that it is dotted with dozens of triangular lakes. Geologists say this cannot happen, but there they are. The Water Authority would like to know the total area covered by these lakes. For this purpose they hired flying ace Louppe de Loupe to take a series of aerial photographs which were combined to form a county map. Onto this map the county surveyor superimposed a set of X-Y coordinates with the origin beyond the southwest corner of the county. This gave every point in the county a positive set of X- and Y-coordinates (Figure 13.6), allowing each lake to be described by specifying three points.

At its highest level, the program for computing the total area is straight-forward: A set of input consists of the six real values ($x1$, $y1$), ($x2$, $y2$), and ($x3$, $y3$) describing that lake's position, followed by the lake's name (20 characters). For each set read, the program computes the area, adds it to a running total, and displays a line showing the name, the three points, and the area. This processing is reflected in the pseudocode description of Figure 13.7(a), in which the computation of the area is represented as a single step.

To promote the single-step representation mentioned above, the area's computation will be organized as a separate procedure lakearea that

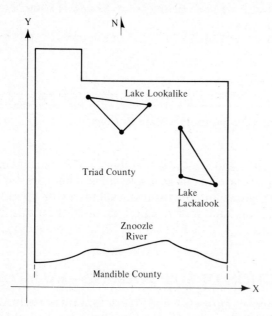

Figure 13.6

Triad County Set in X-Y Coordinates

Define lakename, point1, point2, point3, numoflakes, area, totalarea.
Initialize numoflakes, totalarea.
Read the first set of input.
WHILE there are data values to process, DO:
    compute the triangle's area from point1, point2, and point3.(*)
    Add the area to totalarea.
    Display the input data and the triangle's area.
    Read the next set of input data (if there are any).
ENDWHILE
Display summary information (numoflakes and totalarea).
Stop.

(a) Overall pseudocode description for Example 13.3

    (*)   Define base, side[1], side[2], and side[3].
          Compute each side's length from two points(**).
          Compute base = 0.5 * (side+side+side).
          Compute area = base*(base-side*(base-side*(base-
              side).

(b) Expanded pseudocode for triangular area computation

    (**)   Given points (X1,Y1) and (X2,Y2):
           length = (Y2–Y1)*(Y2–Y1)+(X2–X1)*(X2–X1)

(c) Expanded pseudocode for computation of a side's length

Figure 13.7

Pseudocode for Example 13.3

operates on the three points to produce the area. The pertinent formula for the area is

$$base = \tfrac{1}{2}\,(\text{side } 1 + \text{side } 2 + \text{side } 3)$$

$$area = \sqrt{base(base - \text{side } 1)(base - \text{side } 2)(base - \text{side } 3)}$$

$$\text{where} \quad \begin{aligned} \text{side } 1 &= \sqrt{(X2 - X1)^2 + (Y2 - Y1)^2} \\ \text{side } 2 &= \sqrt{(X3 - X1)^2 + (Y3 - Y1)^2} \\ \text{side } 3 &= \sqrt{(X3 - X2)^2 + (Y3 - Y2)^2} \end{aligned}$$

This closer look at the area computation is reflected in the expanded pseudocode description of Figure 13.7(b).

One of the activities listed in Figure 13.7(b) calls for the procedure to compute the lengths of the lake's three sides. More precisely, it requires the same computation to be applied three times, each time to a different pair of points. There is a clear opportunity here for another procedure (which we shall call sidelgth), this one designed to compute the length between two given points on an X-Y coordinate system. (We have already used this computation in the previous section.) Since this computational service is something needed specifically by the lakearea procedure, we shall place its definition inside lakearea so that the entire process appears as a single structural entity. As a result, we can bring the simplicity of the specifications in Figure 13.7(a) directly to the corresponding main program (Figure 13.8). The processing details are submerged within the lakearea procedure, and some of *its* details are submerged further within sidelgth.

```
(*****************************************************************************)
(**                              EXAMPLE 13.3                             **)
(*****************************************************************************)
(** THIS PROGRAM CONSISTS OF A MAIN PROGRAM AND TWO SUBPROGRAMS, ONE      **)
(** NESTED INSIDE THE OTHER. THE MAIN PROGRAM PRODUCES AND DISPLAYS       **)
(** A SERIES OF AREAS, EACH COMPUTED FROM A SET OF THREE INPUT POINTS.    **)
(** EACH TRIANGULAR AREA IS COMPUTED BY A SUBPROGRAM FROM THE THREE       **)
(** SIDES, EACH OF WHICH, IN TURN, IS COMPUTED FROM A PAIR OF POINTS      **)
(** BY A SECOND SUBPROGRAM INVOKED BY THE ONE THAT COMPUTES THE AREAS.    **)
(*****************************************************************************)
PROGRAM ex1303  ;
CONST
   blank5 = '     '  ;
   blank2 = '  '  ;
TYPE
   coordinate = (horizontal, vertical)  ;
   lakepoint = ARRAY [coordinate] OF REAL   ;
VAR
   point1, point2, point3 :  lakepoint   ;
   lakename  :  STRING[20]  ;
   area, totalarea  :  REAL  ;
   i, numoflakes  :  INTEGER   ;
   sw  :  BOOLEAN  ;

   PROCEDURE  lakearea (p1, p2, p3 : lakepoint ; VAR a : REAL)   ;
   VAR
      side : ARRAY [1..3] OF REAL   ;
      base : REAL   ;

      PROCEDURE  sidelgth (pta, ptb : lakepoint ; VAR dist : REAL)   ;
      BEGIN
         dist := SQRT(SQR(pta[horizontal] - ptb[horizontal])
                  + SQR(pta[vertical] - ptb[vertical]))
      END  ;
```

Figure 13.8 ──

Program for Example 13.3

```
BEGIN
   sidelgth (P1, P2, side[1])  ;
   sidelgth (P1, P3, side[2])  ;
   sidelgth (P2, P3, side[3])  ;
   base := 0.5 * (side[1] + side[2] + side[3])  ;
   a := SQRT(base * (base-side[1]*(base-side[2]*(base-side[3])))
END  ;
(*******************************************************************************)
(**                       THE MAIN PROGRAM                                  **)
(*******************************************************************************)
BEGIN
   WRITELN  ;  WRITELN  ;
   sw := TRUE  ;
   numoflakes := 0  ;
   totalarea := 0.0  ;
  WHILE  sw  DO
    BEGIN
        WRITELN ('ENTER DATA FOR 3 POINTS FOLLOWED BY LAKE NAME.') ;
        READ (point1[horizontal],point1[vertical]),
             (point2[horizontal],point2[vertical]),
             (point3[horizontal],point3[vertical])  ;
        READ (lakename)  ;
        numoflakes := numoflakes + 1  ;
        lakearea (point1, point2, point3, area)  ;
        totalarea := totalarea + area  ;
        WRITELN  ;
        WRITE (blank2,lakename:20,'(',point1[horizontal]:5:1,',',
                                    point1[vertical]:5:1,')',
                          blank2,'(',point2[horizontal]:5:1,',',
                                    point2[vertical]:5:1,')',
                          blank2,'(',point3[horizontal]:5:1,',',
                                    point3[vertical]:5:1,')',
                          blank5,area:8:2)  ;
        WRITELN  ;
        READLN  ;
        IF  EOF  THEN sw := FALSE
    END  ;
   WRITELN  ;   WRITELN  ;
   WRITELN ('NUMBER OF LAKES: ',numoflakes)  ;
   WRITELN ('TOTAL LAKE AREA:  ',totalarea:12:2)  ;
   WRITELN ('END OF RUN.')
END.
```

Figure 13.8

Program for Example 13.3 (Continued)

13.5 DEVELOPMENT OF SUBPROGRAMS

Besides the enhancements to program clarity mentioned earlier, the use of a subprogram offers an additional advantage: Since a subprogram is a distinct structural entity, it can be developed and tested by itself, outside the context of any main program into which it ultimately might be integrated. Once the developer is satisfied that the subprogram operates properly, it can be installed as a "prefabricated" component in any program that has a use for it.

A subprogram, by its nature, cannot operate by itself. Consequently, its independent development requires a main program that will invoke it. Such a program, called a *driver*, is constructed to provide just enough support so that the subprogram can be invoked in the same way as it would be in actual use. When the subprogram's development has been completed, the driver can be thrown away without remorse in the same way that scaffolding is torn down when a building is finished.

To illustrate the use of a driver, we shall write one for the strline procedure of Figure 13.5(a). Bear in mind that we want to focus our attention on the procedure and not on the main program. Consequently, the driver will have no unnecessary complications. For instance, the four values on which strline will operate simply will be assigned in the driver. The driver is shown in Figure 13.9.

Note also that the driver includes simple statements for displaying the results. Thus, the procedure's behavior is revealed in a convenient, straightforward fashion.

```
PROGRAM strdriv  ;
VAR
   h1, h2, v1, v2, slope, intercept, seglength  :  REAL  ;

                    strline procedure

BEGIN
   h1 := 1.0  ;
   v1 := 6.0  ;
   h2 := 2.0  ;
   v2 := 11.0  ;
   strline (h1, v1, h2, v2, slope, intercept, seglength)  ;
   WRITELN ('INPUT VALUES:')  ;
   WRITELN ('(H1,V1):   ', h1, v1)  ;
   WRITELN ('(H2,V2):   ', h2, v2)  ;
   WRITELN ('SLOPE:   ',slope,'INTERCEPT:   ',intercept)  ;
   WRITELN ('LINE LENGTH:   ',seglength)
END.
```

Figure 13.9

strline Procedure for Figure 13.5(a) with Its Driver

13.6 TRANSFER OF INFORMATION AMONG SUBPROGRAMS

The examples developed in the previous chapter showed subprogram definitions that included parameter lists. Then, when the subprograms were invoked, the calling expressions or statements contained corresponding lists of actual parameters. These were seen to consist of constants, variables, or expressions. In this section we shall examine these invoking mechanisms more closely and explore the ways in which a Pascal main program and its subprograms can communicate with each other.

13.6.1 Transfer by Value

When we specify an actual parameter, we activate a mechanism by which Pascal transfers that actual parameter's value to the invoked module. This mechanism is known as *passing by value* or *transfer by value*. To understand this type of data transfer, it is helpful to think of it as follows: Suppose we specify a variable name as an actual parameter. That name is associated with a location containing a value, and it is this value that is copied and sent to the invoked subprogram. The location from which the value was copied is not part of the information thus sent. As a result, the invoked subprogram cannot change the contents of that location because it does not "know" the address.

The same mechanism applies to the use of constant values for actual parameters. Since the transfer of actual values is completely detached from the production of those values, Pascal does not "care" where such a value comes from or how it was produced. Thus, when we specify a constant as an actual parameter, it makes no difference (to the program) that the value is produced "on the spot," so to speak. For instance, if we were to invoke the SQRT function by writing a statement such as

```
freeval := SQRT (325.87)
```

the value 325.87 would be generated and passed to SQRT for processing. As expected, the function would return a value equal to the square root of 325.87, and that value would be stored in freeval.

A more extensive expression is handled no differently. Thus, if we invoke the SQR function in the statement

```
magnif := SQR(x-2.2*y)
```

the values are copied from locations x and y and used to produce a single number, and *that* value, in turn, is delivered to SQR. The function, as before, has no access to the variables' locations. Consequently, if we write a subprogram in which we attempt to change an actual parameter passed by value, the Pascal compiler will reject the statement in which the attempt appears.

13.6.2 Transfer by Reference

When we attach the VAR specification to a formal parameter, Pascal associates that parameter with its *pass-by-reference* or *transfer-by-reference* mechanism. This means that when a corresponding actual parameter is named during a subprogram's invocation, Pascal supplies the *location* of that parameter to the invoked subprogram. Since the subprogram now "knows" where the value is stored, it can obtain the value from its source. More importantly, *it can change that value* simply by assigning a new one.

The conceptual difference between the pass-by-value and pass-by-reference mechanisms makes it easier to clarify the intended use of the parameters in our subprograms: Generally, input items are passed by value, and output destinations are passed by reference. (We have already seen that grouping the input items next to each other in the parameter list also helps clarify the subprogram's description.)

There may be exceptions to this distinction because the pass-by-value mechanism requires more storage than the pass-by-reference mechanism. Delivery of a variable's value (rather than its location) means that the value has to be copied and put someplace so that the subprogram can work with it. This is no big deal when a small number of values are involved. However, if a subprogram is designed to process a large input array or any other appreciable data collection, the additional storage may make the resulting program too large for the processor. Thus, there are times when the programmer might attach the VAR specification to an input parameter, even though there is no intent to change its value in the subprogram. This practice should be considered an emergency measure. If it is followed, the programmer must make sure that the input data are not in fact changed. Pascal gives up this responsibility when the pass-by-reference mechanism is used.

Example 13.4   First Class Science, Ltd. wants to conduct a series of tests on a new chemical. In each test, acidity readings are to be taken on 16 samples of liquid. For this initial investigation, they want a program that prepares the mean and standard deviation for each group of 16 readings. There may be any number of tests in a run. Input for a test consists of an integer representing the test number followed by the 16 readings. (A typical reading is 4.6). Output for each test is to consist of two lines, the first of which gives the test number while the second shows the mean and standard deviation. There will be two blank lines between adjacent test results. After the last test has been processed, the program will leave three blank lines and display a summary giving the number of tests processed, the highest mean value, the lowest mean value, and their respective test numbers. First Class Science assures us that each mean value will be unique.

If *acidity* is an individual reading $(i = 1, 2,...,16)$, the mean, *avgacidity*, is computed as

$$avgacidity = \frac{1}{16} \sum_{i=1}^{16} acidity_i$$

and *stdevacid*, the standard deviation, is computed as

$$stdevacid = \sqrt{\frac{1}{16-1} \sum_{i=1}^{16} (acidity_i - avgacidity)^2}$$

(The formula for standard deviation requires all 16 readings to be available. In one of the problems at the end of this chapter, an alternative computation is given in which only one reading at a time need be in storage.)

We shall organize the processing as shown in Figure 13.10. The overall activity is a loop that cycles once for each test. During that cycle:

1. The test number and the 16 readings are brought in.
2. Values for the mean and standard deviation are computed.
3. The output for that test is displayed.
4. The overall run is updated by adding 1 to the number of tests processed and replacing either the highest or lowest mean with a new value if appropriate.

Define variables for test number, test readings, mean, standard deviation,
    test counter, and maximum and minimum test numbers and mean values.
    Description of computations for mean and standard deviations.
    Description of computations for updating the maximum and/or
        minimum mean values.
WHILE there is input to process:
  Read the test number.
  Read the 16 test results.
  Compute the mean and standard deviations for the test results.
  Replace the minimum or maximum values if appropriate.
  Increment the test counter.
  Display the mean and standard deviations for this test.
ENDWHILE
Display the number of tests, maximum and minimum mean values, and
    corresponding test numbers.
Stop.

Figure 13.10

Organization of the Program for Example 13.4

The summary information is displayed after this loop has gone through the necessary cycles (controlled by the end-of-file condition).

Activities (2) and (3) will be implemented as separate subprograms to keep the main program simple. These are shown in Figure 13.11 as procedures mstdev and update. The transfer of the 16 readings is set up conveniently by defining a data type named testgroup and then specifying that type to be one of the formal parameters for mstdev, the procedure for computing the mean and standard deviation. Note (Figure 13.11) that the mean value and test numbers for the current test (named thismean and thistest, respectively) in update's formal parameter list, are passed by value because they are used by update as input. These same items are passed by reference in mstdev because that is where their values are computed and assigned. hi_mean, low_mean, hi_testnum, and low_testnum are set up for passing by reference because they are subject to change. (Of course no more than two of these values may change during any invocation, but we do not know which two, if any, will change.)

Since acidity is passed by value, all 16 readings are duplicated for mstdev's use. The same would be true if acidity were to consist of 14, 232, or 10000 readings. This duplication can be avoided by changing the formal parameter rdg in the procedure mstdev to a VAR parameter:

```
PROCEDURE   mstdev (VAR rdg : testgroup ; VAR thismean : REAL ;
                    VAR thisdev : REAL)
```

Now, invocation of mstdev will deliver acidity's location. There is no change in the output. (As far as the observer is concerned, there is no apparent change in the program's behavior either.)

13.7 RECOGNITION OF NAMES IN PROGRAMS

When we declare a variable in a Pascal program, we make that variable available to different parts of the program. Thus far, our movement of variable values (or their addresses) between blocks might leave the impression that once a variable is declared, we can refer to it anywhere in the program and it will be recognized. This is true only under certain organizational conditions. When these conditions are not met, Pascal restricts a variable's availability to carefully defined parts of the program. This section discusses these rules and their application.

13.7.1 Scope of Variables

Declaration of a variable establishes a range of statements over which that variable's name is recognized. This is known as the variable's *scope*. The general rule that defines the scope of a Pascal variable can be stated simply:

```
PROGRAM ex1304    ;
CONST
  numofreads = 16 ;
TYPE
  testgroup = ARRAY [1..numofreads] OF REAL  ;
VAR
  acidity : testgroup ;
  avgacidity, stdevacid, maxmean, minmean  :  REAL  ;
  testid, numoftests, maxtest, mintest, i  :  INTEGER  ;

PROCEDURE mstdev (rdg : testgroup ; VAR thismean : REAL ;
                                    VAR thisdev : REAL) ;

VAR
  index  :  INTEGER  ;
  sumrd, sumsqr  :  REAL  ;
BEGIN
  sumrd := 0.0  ;
  sumsqr := 0.0  ;
  FOR index := 1 TO numofreads  DO
    sumrd := sumrd + rdg[index]  ;
  thismean := sumrd/numofreads  ;
  FOR index := 1 TO numofreads  DO
    sumsqr := sumsqr + SQR(rdg[index]-thismean)  ;
  thisdev := SQRT(sumsqr/(numofreads-1))
END ;

PROCEDURE update (thismean : REAL ; thistest : INTEGER ;
                  VAR hi_mean : REAL ; VAR low_mean : REAL ;
                  VAR hi_testnum : INTEGER ; VAR low_testnum : INTEGER) ;
BEGIN
  IF  thismean > hi_mean  THEN
    BEGIN
      hi_mean := thismean ;
      hi_testnum := thistest
    END ;
```

Figure 13.11   Program for Example 13.4

275

```
    IF  thismean < low_mean  THEN
        BEGIN
            low_mean := thismean ;
            low_testnum := thistest
        END ;

{                    THE MAIN PROGRAM                    }

BEGIN
    numoftests := 0 ;  maxmean := -200.0 ;  minmean := 200.0 ;  sw := TRUE ;
    WHILE  sw  DO
        BEGIN
            WRITELN ('ENTER A VALUE FOR TESTID.') ;
            READLN (testid) ;
            WRITELN ('TYPE THE GROUP OF 16 TEST READINGS FOLLOWED BY <ENTER>.') ;
            FOR i := 1 TO numofreads  DO
                READ (acidity[i]) ;
            READLN ;
            mstdev (acidity, avgacidity, stdevacid) ;
            update (avgacidity, testid, maxmean, minmean, maxtest, mintest) ;
            numoftests := numoftests + 1 ;
            WRITELN ;
            WRITELN ('TEST NO.: ',testid) ;
            WRITELN ('MEAN ACIDITY: ',avgacidity:7:3,' STD DEV.: ',
                                        stdevacid:7:3) ;
            WRITELN ;
            WRITELN ('HIT <ENTER> TO CONTINUE OR <CNTRL>-C TO QUIT.') ;
            READLN ;
            IF  EOF  THEN  sw := FALSE
        END ;  WRITELN ;
    WRITELN ('SUMMARY:') ;
    WRITELN ('NO. OF TESTS THIS RUN: ',numoftests) ;
    WRITELN ('TEST NUMBER ',maxtest,' HAD A HIGH MEAN OF  ',maxmean:7:3) ;
    WRITELN ('TEST NUMBER ',mintest,' HAD A LOW MEAN OF  ',minmean:7:3) ;
    WRITELN ('END OF RUN.')
END.
```

Figure 13.11 ———— Program for Example 13.4 (Continued)

A variable is recognized throughout the entire block in which it is declared.
This is true regardless of the number of blocks that may be contained in the
block in which the variable is declared. To illustrate, consider the program
outline shown in Figure 13.12. Organizationally, the program consists of an
outer block (associated with the name P1) containing a block named P11.
Note that the REAL variable bfac declared in the outer block does not
appear as a formal parameter in P11's list, nor does it appear as an actual
parameter in P1's invocation statement. Yet, its appearance in assignment
statements in both blocks is legal. Since P11 is contained in P1, the
program has no trouble finding the location associated with the name
bfac and changing the value there. The same rule, when applied to the
variable stnd, makes that variable available throughout P11 but nowhere
else. stnd is said to be *local* to P11, and bfac is said to be *global*.

The same is true for the more complicated organization outlined in
Figure 13.13: The nesting is more extensive here, in that outer block P2
contains block P21 which, in turn, contains another block P211. By taking
a look at the declarations and applying the rule stated earlier, we can
determine each variable's scope:

1. Since qvar is declared in the outer block, its scope extends over the
   entire program. Thus, it is legal (as Figure 13.13 shows) to read qvar's

```
PROGRAM P1
    . . . . . . . . . . . . . . . . . .
VAR
    asx, trn, stc, frb, bfac : REAL
    . . . . . . . . . . . . . . . . . .
    PROCEDURE   P11 (v1, v2, : REAL ; VAR v3, VAR v4 : REAL) ;
    VAR
        stnd : REAL
        . . . . . . . . . . . . . . .
    BEGIN
        . . . . . . . . . . . . . . .
        bfac := bfac + 2.5
        . . . . . . . . . . . . . .
    END
    . . . . . . . . . . . . . . . . .
BEGIN
    . . . . . . . . . . . . . . . . .
    bfac := 17.0
    . . . . . . . . . . . . . . . . .
    P11 (asx, trn, stc, frb)
    . . . . . . . . . . . . . . . . .
END.
```

Figure 13.12

A Program with Global and Local Declarations

```
PROGRAM  P2
    ................
VAR
    qvar, ctr, mvb, cvac, pmtr, emuk   :   REAL
    ..................
    PROCEDURE  P21 (r1, r2 : REAL ; VAR r3, VAR r4 : REAL) ;
    VAR
       b1, b2 : REAL
       ................
       PROCEDURE  P211 (t1 : REAL ; VAR t2, VAR t3 : REAL)  ;
       VAR
          w1, w2, emuk : REAL
          .............
       BEGIN
          READLN (w1, w2)
          .............
          emuk := 0.0  ;
          t3 := w1 + b1 - qvar
          .............
       END
       .............
    BEGIN
       .................
       READLN (b1, b2)
       .................
       r3 := b1 + SQRT(qvar)   ;
       P211 (b2, r3, r4)
       .................
    END
    .................
BEGIN
    emuk := 24.0  ;
    READLN (qvar, ctr, mvb)
    ....................
    P21 (ctr, mvb, cvac, pmtr)
    ....................
    WRITELN (qvar, ctr, mvb, cvac, pmtr)
    ....................
END.
```

Figure 13.13————————————————————————

Program Organization with Nested Subprograms

value in the main program and then to use it as a term in blocks P21 and P211.

2. Variables b1 and b2 are declared in block P21, thereby defining their scope as that entire block, including the block P211 contained in it. Consequently, we can read values for b1 and b2 in block P1 and then

use those values in P211. Note that we *cannot* use them in that part of the main program that is not inside P21.

3. Variables w1 and w2, having been declared in P211, are local to P211 and cannot appear outside of it. In fact, w1 and w2 exist only when P211 is invoked. As soon as P211 completes its processing, w1 and w2 disappear, to be re-created only when P211 is invoked again.

4. The variable named emuk is introduced in Figure 13.13 to emphasize the difference between global and local variables. Note that emuk is declared in P2 and in P211. These are two different emuks. The one declared in P2 is recognized in all of P2 and P21 except for the block P211. The one declared in P211 is recognized only in P211 and nowhere else. Thus, the assignment

```
emuk := 0.0
```

in block P211 refers inevitably to the local emuk and has no effect on the global emuk, whose value remains 24.0. No sensible programmer would use the same name for two different items. However, it is helpful to know and understand the rule governing the scope of such duplicate names for the following reason: There are cases where we may be building a program in which we wish to incorporate a subprogram obtained from some external source. Since the names used in that subprogram are generally not within our control, we could end up with the kind of name duplication seen for emuk in Figure 13.13. Pascal's mechanisms for protecting local names makes it possible for such situations to be handled consistently.

13.7.2 Recognition of Blocks in a Program

Another simple organizational rule governs the relationships among the blocks in a program: Although blocks can be nested to any level, a block may invoke only those blocks immediately "below" it. In Figure 13.13, for example, the main program may invoke P21 but not P211. Block P21 may invoke only P211, and P211, sad to say, may invoke no one.

13.7.3 Why Use Parameters?

Take a look at the two little programs in Figure 13.14. It is obvious that they both perform the same computations. It is also clear (now that we have discussed the scope of variables) that both programs will produce the same results when given the same input values. Since that is the case, why complicate the subprogram definition by including a formal parameter list? All that seems to do is to obligate us to include an actual parameter list when we invoke the subprogram. Why not simplify things and write our programs as in Figure 13.14's second version, without parameter lists?

```
PROGRAM h1  ;
VAR
    vside1, vside2, vsum : REAL  ;
    PROCEDURE  vctradd (v1, v2 : REAL ; VAR rslt : REAL)  ;
    BEGIN
        rslt := SQRT(SQR(v1)+SQR(v2))
    END ;
BEGIN
    READLN (vside1, vside2)  ;
    WHILE  NOT EOF  DO
    BEGIN
        vctradd(vside1, vside2, vsum)  ;
        WRITELN (vside1, vside2, vsum)  ;
        READLN (vside1, vside2)
    END ;
    WRITELN ('END OF RUN.')
END .
```

(a) Subprogram organization with a parameter list

```
PROGRAM  h2  ;
VAR
    vside1, vside2, vsum : REAL  ;
    PROCEDURE  vctradd  ;
    BEGIN
        vsum := SQRT(SQR(vside1) + SQR(vside2))
    END ;
BEGIN
    READLN (vside1, vside2)  ;
    WHILE  NOT EOF  DO
        BEGIN
            vctradd  ;
            WRITELN (vside1, vside2, vsum)  ;
            READLN (vside1, vside2)
        END ;
    WRITELN ('END OF RUN.')
END .
```

(b) Subprogram organization without a parameter list

Figure 13.14————————————————————————————

Alternative Subprogram Organizations

The advantages of one organizational approach versus the other depend on the particular circumstances. Use of a parameter list admittedly can complicate both the definition and invocation of a subprogram. However, it makes that subprogram more flexible since we can invoke it with different actual parameters each time. Moreover, the use of a parameter list gives the programmer direct control over those variables whose values can or cannot be changed by an invoked subprogram. (Recall that a variable whose value is to be used but not changed by a subprogram is easily protected by specifying it as a value parameter.) Such protection is not available from Pascal without the parameter mechanism. When we eliminate the parameter list, we simplify the statements in exchange for a more rigid subprogram which will operate only on the global variables named in its processing statements. Thus, in Figure 13.14's second version, `vctradd` will compute the vector sum only of the two variables `vside1` and `vside2`.

If the computations performed by a subprogram are extensive and/or complicated, and the processing is expected to be useful above and beyond the context of a single program or application, there is good reason to design that subprogram with a parameter list. Then the statement can be lifted and placed in any program that needs them without having to change anything. (Pascal's extensive collection of built-in functions and procedures is an obvious example in which this policy is applied.) On the other hand, processing that is specific to a particular collection of variables in a particular program lends itself to organization as a subprogram without a parameter list. For example, if we have a program that repeatedly reads and processes sets of values for the same variables, the input and initial examination of the data are likely activities for a subprogram without parameters.

The criteria for using or avoiding a parameter list are not clear cut. Consequently, it is impossible to draw up a set of well-defined rules for all occasions. Instead, the programmer is well advised to examine each situation and make his or her choice accordingly.

13.8 RECURSIVE SUBPROGRAMS

When we set up syntax diagrams for Pascal's language components, we found it convenient, on occasion, to use recursive definitions. The consistency of such definitions was established in Chapter 2, where we saw that we can construct a recursive definition as long as we have a way of describing the object without using that same object in the description.

Recursion also can be applied to certain computational processes. A recursive process is one that uses itself to carry out the intended activities. For example, let us take a look at the process for computing n!, the factorial value for the positive integer n. One way to describe this computation is to say

$$n! = n(n - 1)(n - 2)(n - 3).....(3)(2)(1)$$

Another way to specify this computation is to describe it recursively:

$$n! = n(n-1)!; \qquad 1! = 1$$

This says that we can compute n! by first computing (n–1)!. More significantly for our discussion here, it implies further that we can compute (n–1)! by first computing (n–2)!. (n–2)!, in turn, can be produced from (n–3)!, and so on, until we have reached a number small enough (i.e., 1) so that further reduction is not needed. Then, we can work our way back up again through the values until we obtain the result we want.

For example, suppose n is 5. Then,

$$5! = 5(4!) \; ;$$
$$4! = 4(3!) \; ;$$
$$3! = 3(2!) \; ;$$
$$2! = 2(1!) = 2(1) = 2.$$

Now, having reached a stopping point and obtained a factorial value, we can use that value as a basis for completing the computations:

$$3! = 3(2) = 6 \; ;$$
$$4! = 4(6) = 24 \; ;$$
$$5! = 5(24) = 120.$$

Why go through all this intricacy? It is good that you asked. There are many instances where the representation of a process in recursive form is simpler or more "natural" than an alternative expression. (The recursive form for factorials does not offer a particularly dramatic simplification; however, it is a useful vehicle for introducing recursive forms and their implementation.)

13.8.1 Recursive Processes as Subprograms

Just as a recursive syntax definition must include a logical "escape hatch," it is necessary for a recursive algorithm to include a control mechanism that limits the level of recursion in some orderly way. In our factorial example, this "logical brake," so to speak, is applied by preventing a factorial calculation of any number less than 1. Consequently, when the algorithm is represented as a subprogram, the control mechanism must be stated explicitly so that every situation is handled properly.

We can see how this looks by implementing the recursive factorial algorithm as a Pascal function [as shown in Figure 13.15(a). A nonrecursive version is included in Figure 13.15(b).] There are two controls at work here: The first of these prevents any factorial computations at all if the argument's value is negative. Should such a situation occur, the computations are bypassed and the function returns a value of zero to indicate an erroneous (i.e., meaningless) invocation. Incidentally, the need for this mechanism can be avoided if we were to define a data type (let us name it positiveinteger) as follows:

```
TYPE
    positiveinteger = 0..MAXINT
```

Then, if the FUNCTION statement were to say

```
FUNCTION factr (num : positiveinteger) : positiveinteger
```

the check for an appropriate value would be built in automatically.

The second control mechanism limits the recursive computation to a minimum value of 2: After initializing the function value of 1 (which is the value for 0! or 1!), further processing is allowed only as long as the argument exceeds 1.

```
FUNCTION   factr (num : INTEGER) : INTEGER ;
BEGIN
    IF   num < 0   THEN
        factr := 0
    ELSE
        BEGIN
            factr := 1 ;
            IF   num >= 2   THEN
                factr := num * factr(num-1)
        END
END
```

(a) Recursive subprogram

```
FUNCTION   factr (num : INTEGER) : INTEGER ;
VAR
    i : INTEGER ;
BEGIN
    IF   num < 0   THEN
        factr := 0
    ELSE
        BEGIN
            factr := 1 ;
            FOR i := num DOWNTO 2 DO
                factr := i * factr
        END
END
```

(b) Conventional (nonrecursive) subprogram

Figure 13.15

Subprograms for Factorial Computation

13.8.2 Operation of Recursive Subprograms

The concept described earlier, i.e., working down through a series of recursive invocations and then working back up in reverse order, applies directly in recursive subprograms. Its success is based on the idea that each time a subprogram invokes itself, that subprogram is activated anew. This means that, at any time, there may be several such activations for a subprogram, one for each invocation, each with its own set of argument values and data areas for computed results. Each activation is temporarily suspended somewhere between its beginning and its conclusion. The only activation that is running is the one triggered by the most recent invocation. If it invokes itself again, a new activation is triggered, and the invoking one is suspended. Sooner or later (if the process is implemented properly), a subprogram will invoke itself, and this last invocation will run to its conclusion without further invocations. As a result, it will be deactivated (not suspended), its designated storage areas will "disappear," and its result(s) will be delivered to the activation that invoked it. That activation now can continue and, when it concludes, the same type of deactivation/ return will occur, thereby allowing the previous invocation to conclude. In this way, the cycle eventually reaches the top level (i.e., the invocation from the main program that started the recursion in the first place) and the process is completed.

Now we shall apply this mechanism to our factorial example by following the course of events for an argument of 5. Let us say that vnum is suitably declared and the initial invocation of factr occurs in the statement

```
vnum := factr(5)
```

As a result, factr is activated. Let us call this activation level 1. Looking at the subprogram in Figure 13.15(a), we see that the initial IF test fails, so that factr is initialized to 1. Since the argument given to this activation is >= 2 (it is 5), the second IF test passes, and factr invokes itself. This means that activation level 1 is suspended and a new activation, level 2, is running. This new activation has been given an argument of 4 (i.e., one less than the previous argument). Note that activation level 1 has been suspended in the midst of a computation. When it resumes control later on, it will receive a value which will then be multiplied by 5 and the result will be assigned to vnum.

Now activation level 2 starts, fails the first IF test, initializes its function value (a separate one, remember), passes the second IF test, and proceeds. In doing so, it invokes itself, so now we have activation 3, operating on an argument of 3 (one less than the argument given to the previous invocation). The same thing happens again: Activation 3 invokes itself, triggering activation 4 with an argument of 2. This activation invokes itself, so that it is activation 5 that is running (with an argument of 1), and the previous four activations are suspended, each waiting to receive a value so that it can conclude.

Activation 5, because of its argument, will not pass the second IF test. Consequently, it will *not* produce another invocation; instead it concludes, reactivating level 4 and returning a value of 1 to it. This allows level 4 to conclude by performing the multiplication and producing a function value (2) which is delivered to the newly rekindled activation 3. This level now can conclude and, in doing so, delivers a value of 6 to the level that invoked it, and so on, until level 1 is the only one left. It takes the 24 given to it by the recently departed level 2, multiplies it by 5, assigns the result to vnum, and that is that.

13.8.3 Pascal's Support of Recursion

Another look at Figure 13.15(a) shows that, aside from the fact that factr invokes itself, there is nothing special in the statements to earmark the subprogram as being recursive. Nothing was omitted; as far as Pascal is concerned, *all subprograms are inherently recursive*. If the programmer chooses not to write a recursive subprogram, fine. However, if recursion is used, it is up to the programmer to make sure that the subprogram can stop chasing itself when it is time for it to stop chasing itself.

Problems

1. Each of the following statements is a legal or illegal attempt to identify some kind of Pascal subprogram. For each one that is legal, indicate the number of required parameters and their respective data types. In addition, indicate the data type of the result for each FUNCTION statement. Show what is wrong with the illegal statements:

    (a) FUNCTION physmark(veloc : REAL ; n1, n2 : INTEGER) : REAL

    (b) FUNCTION findout(visc, diam, dens, veloc : REAL) : BOOLEAN

    (c) PROCEDURE trichar (c1 , c2, c3 : CHAR ; n1 : INTEGER) : REAL

    (d) FUNCTION last3 (c1 : CHAR ; r1 : REAL ; n1 : INTEGER)

    (e) PROCEDURE farwt (r1, r2, : REAL ; VAR r3, VAR r4, VAR r5 : REAL)

2. Consider the following declaration section:

```
. . . . . . . . . . . . . . . . . . .
VAR
    hival, lowval, range  :  INTEGER  ;
FUNCTION  produce (value, limit ; INTEGER) : INTEGER  ;
CONST
    factor := 3  ;
VAR
    i : INTEGER  ;
BEGIN
    produce := 0  ;
    FOR  i := 1 TO limit  DO
    produce := produce + factor*(value-1)
END
. . . . . . . . . . . . . . . . . . .
```

(a) What assumptions does the function make about `limit`?
Show the result(s) displayed by each of the independent sequences given below:

(b) range := produce (3,6) ;
WRITELN (range)

(c) lowval := 5 ;
range := 8 + produce (lowval, hival) ;
WRITELN (range)

(d) lowval := 5 ;
hival ;= 8 ;
lowval := lowval – highval * produce (highval, lowval) ;
WRITELN (lowval)

(e) lowval := 2 ;
hival := lowval + produce (lowval, 2) ;
range := produce (hival, lowval) – produce (lowval, hival) ;
WRITELN ('LOWVAL: ',lowval) ;
WRITELN ('HIVAL: ',hival) ;
WRITELN ('RANGE: ',range)

3. Consider the following function:

```
FUNCTION  vcomp  (pr1, pr2, pr3 : REAL) : REAL  ;
CONST
    critval = 230.0  ;
VAR
    tval : REAL  ;
BEGIN
    tval := SQRT (SQR(pr1)-SQR(pr2)+SQR(pr3))   ;
```

```
IF   tval >= critval   THEN   vcomp := critval
                       ELSE   vcomp := tval
END
```

Assuming values of 3.6 for trn, 8.0 for bKs, 1.0 for adl, and 11.5 for sPl, show the output values (if output is possible) resulting from each of the following independent fragments:

(a) adl := adl * vcomp(trn, trn, trn) ;
     WRITELN adl)

(b) adl := adl + adl*2*vcomp(trn+bKs+sPl) ;
     WRITELN (adl)

(c) adl := trn*vcomp(4.1*trn, adl, bsK) ;
     WRITELN (adl)

(d) bKs := bKs - vcomp(38.7, 6.6-trn, sPl+1) ;
     WRITELN (bKs)

(e) adl := SQR(vcomp(1.0,trn,sPl) ;
     WRITELN (adl)

(f) vcomp(bKs, 3.3-trn, adl) ;
     WRITELN (vcomp)

(g) adl := vcomp(bKs, -trn, 3.2) + 1.1*vcomp
     (3.2, -trn, bKs) ; WRITELN (adl)

(h) sPl := adl + 2.0*vcomp ;
     WRITELN (sPl)

(i) sPl := vcomp(bKs, vcomp(2.0, sPl, bKs), trn) ;
     WRITELN (sPl)

4. Write a function named extremes that operates on two integer values to produce the ratio of the larger to the smaller value, rounded to the nearest integer.

5. Rewrite the function in Problem 4 as a procedure. In addition to the result specified in that problem, the procedure is to produce the ratio of the smaller to the larger value, expressed as a percentage to the nearest tenth of a percent.

6. Generalize the function in Figure 13.4(a) so that it handles integer exponents that are either positive or negative.

7. Write a simple driver suitable for developing and testing the function prepared in Problem 6.

8. Generalize the function in Problem 6 so that it handles real as well as integer exponents.

9. Write a program that reads and processes an arbitrary number of input sets. Each input set consists of six real values: $x1$, $y1$, $x2$, $y2$, $x3$, and $y3$. Each pair of values represents a point on a rectangular coordinate system (as described in Section 13.2.2). The three

points are to be processed as follows: After displaying the first two points (i.e., the first four input values) on an output line, the program is to display another line showing the slope and intercept of the straight line formed by these two points. This is followed by a third line that shows the third point and one of these three messages:

LIES ON THE LINE BETWEEN THE FIRST TWO POINTS
LIES ON THE LINE OUTSIDE THE FIRST TWO POINTS
DOES NOT LIE ON THE LINE FORMED BY THE FIRST TWO POINTS

Leave two blank lines between output sets. (*Caution:* It will be up to you to decide when a point is on the line and when it is "not quite" on the line.)

10. Modify the program in Problem 9 so that each input set now consists of the first two points (i.e., the ones defining the straight line) followed by *one or more* points, each of which is to be tested against the line. There is no indication as to how many points are to be tested against a given line, but there will be at least one. Thus, the output for each line (i.e., for each input set) will consist of the two points defining that line, a second output line showing the slope and intercept (as before), and one or more additional output lines showing each additional point along with the appropriate message. As in the previous problem, leave two blank lines between the output sets.

11. In Example 13.3, we prepared a subprogram for computing the area of a triangle from three (X,Y) points (Figure 13.8). Implied in that subprogram is the assumption that the points do not lie on the same straight line, so that there is a triangle there with some area to it. For this problem, generalize that subprogram so that, if the three points do not lie on a single line, the subprogram delivers the area. If not, the subprogram delivers an area of 0.0.

12. Write a program in which an input set consists of four real (X,Y) points (i.e., eight values). This time, the program is to use the first three points to form a triangle. (There is no guarantee that these points do not lie on a single line.) The first line of output (for each input set) is to show the three points and the area formed by the triangle (or zero if there is only a single straight line). This is followed by a second output line that shows the fourth point and one of the following messages:

LIES INSIDE THE TRIANGLE FORMED BY THE ABOVE THREE POINTS
LIES OUTSIDE THE TRIANGLE FORMED BY THE ABOVE THREE POINTS

LIES ON THE SINGLE LINE FORMED BY THE ABOVE THREE
POINTS
LIES OFF THE SINGLE LINE FORMED BY THE ABOVE THREE
POINTS

13. Simplify the main program in Example 13.3 (Figure 13.8) to whatever extent seems reasonable to you by converting appropriate parts of the input and output activities to separate subprograms.

14. Reorganize the program for Example 8.1 (Figure 8.2) so that the following (simpler) main program will produce the same results as the original version:

```
BEGIN
    FOR  pianosize := upright TO mislabel  DO
        numsold[pianosize] := 0  ;
    WRITELN ('ENTER STARTYR AND ENDYR.') ;
    READLN (startyr, endyr)  ;
    WHILE  NOT EOF  DO
        BEGIN
            WRITELN ('SUBMIT DATA FOR A PIANO.') ;
            READLN (serial, piano, pianowt, price,
                    yrofsale, custloc)  ;
            IF  (yrofsale >= startyr) AND (yrofsale <= endyr)  THEN
                BEGIN
                    pianosize := findit (piano)  ;
                    numsold[pianosize] := numsold[pianosize] + 1
                END
        END  ;
    display (startyr, endyr, numsold)   ;
    WRITELN ('END OF RUN.')
END.
```

15. Ivan's Candies, Ltd. ("candy-makers for the Czars") has two kinds of candies: Supreme, priced at $8.80 the kilo, and Oboy, priced at $12.40 the kilo. The manufacturer has agreed to mix these in any proportion so that a range of prices may be obtained. Write a subprogram named mixem that takes values for a desired weight (in kilograms) and a desired price (in dollars per kilogram) and computes the number of kilograms of each type required to achieve the specified price. An additional result, status, reports the outcome: status is 0 if the specified requirements are met; it is −1 if the desired price is impossibly low, in which case all of the weight is assigned to the Supreme type; status is 1 if the desired price is impossibly high, in which case all of the weight is assigned to the Oboy type.

16. Prepare a driver for the subprogram in Problem 15. Equip your driver

with appropriate values to produce results for an inexpensive mixture, an expensive mixture, an impossibly inexpensive request, and an impossibly expensive request.

17. Under ideal conditions, the gas velocity at the exhaust end of a nozzle can be obtained as a function of the inlet conditions from the equation

$$v2 = \sqrt{\left(\frac{2\,g\,k}{k-1}\right)RT\left[1-\left(\frac{p2}{p1}\right)\frac{k-1}{k}\right]+v1^2}$$

where $v1$ and $v2$ are velocities at the inlet and exit, respectively, g is the gravitational constant, k is a dimensionless thermodynamic ratio, T is the inlet temperature in degrees Rankine, $p1$ and $p2$ are inlet and outlet pressures, respectively (the units are immaterial as long as they are the same for both pressures), R is 1544/29 for air. Write a program that reads in sets of values consisting of $v1$, $p1$, $p2$, T, and k, and produces $v1$, T, $p2/p1$, and $v2$, with the latter expressed in both feet per second and miles per hour. The input value of $v1$ is always in miles per hour. Assume that the gas under consideration is always air, so R need not change. T is submitted in degrees Fahrenheit.
    (a) Prepare a general pseudocode description of your program. Indicate clearly those activities to be handled by subprograms.
    (b) Prepare a driver for each of the subprograms defined in (a).

18. Referring to Problem 17, assume that the value for k can be determined from the formula

    $$k = a0 + a1T + a2T^2$$

    where $a0$ is 1.4, $a1$ is −0.00014, and $a2$ is 0.0000000032 for air. Accordingly, rewrite the program so that input consists only of $v1$, $p1$, $p2$, and T. Everything else is unchanged. How does this affect the structure of your program?

19. Write a function named numofdays that computes the number of days between two twentieth century dates submitted as month1, day1, year1 and month2, day2, year2. Remember to take leap year into account.

20. Write a suitable driver for the subprogram prepared for Problem 19.

21. The public library at Fenwick's Foothold just purchased a computer, and they are ready to automate everything. As a start, they would like a program that computes (and displays) the fines charged for overdue books. For each book, a line of input is submitted consisting of:

    cardnum, the cardholder's number (a 6-digit integer);
    booknum, the book's identification (two letters followed by

four digits, followed by a period, followed by two
digits. For example: HJ0587.31);

bmnth, the month the book was borrows (1–12);

bday, the day the book was borrowed (1–31);

byr, the year the book was borrows (1900–2200).

After reading today's date, the program is to read and process the
input for the books being returned that day. Any number of books may
be returned on a given day, and any number of them may be overdue.
There is no limit to the number of books that an individual may
borrow, and any book in the Fenwick's Foothold library may be
borrowed for 18 days. The library promises to submit all of the
information about a particular borrower on consecutive lines, so that
once the program has completed processing the data for a borrower, it
is done with that individual. A fine of four cents for each extra day is
imposed on an overdue book. The library is open every day of the
year.

After reading today's date, the program is to read and process the
input for the books being returned that day. Any number of books may
be returned on a given day, and any number of them may be overdue.
There is no limit to the number of books that an individual may
borrow, and any book in the Fenwick's Foothold library may be
borrowed for 18 days. The library promises to submit all of the
information about a particular borrower on consecutive lines, so that
once the program has completed processing the data for a borrower, it
is done with that individual. A fine of four cents for each extra day is
imposed on an overdue book. The library is open every day of the
year.

    After producing a suitable set of headings, your program is to print
a line for each borrower showing the borrower's identification, the
number of books returned, the number overdue, and the total amount
of the fine. (If none of a borrower's books were overdue, there is no
need to show any output for that borrower.) After the last borrower's
input has been processed, the program is to leave two blank lines, and
then it is to display the number of borrowers returning overdue books
that day, the number of overdue books returned, and the total amount
of fines collected.

22.   Now that Fenwick's Foothold is computerizing their library, they
have found that other libraries are interested in buying their overdue
fines program (the one specified in Problem 21). There is a chance to
sell the program to the nearby village of Stodgy Swope, but a change is
needed. Stodgy Swope closes their library on Christmas, July fourth,
and National Small-but-Well-Run Library Day (March ninth). There
is no fine connected with any of these days. Modify the program in
Problem 21 to accommodate this change.

23. Good news travels at amazing speeds. Now, the town of Dubious Dunes wants Fenwick's Foothold's program too. Again, there are differences. First of all, books whose identifications begin with the letters A through M can be taken out for 16 days, and the others go for 19 days. Second, although every overdue day counts, holiday or not, the fines are imposed differently than in the two hamlets mentioned in the previous two problems: it is five cents a day for the first ten days, four cents a day for the next twenty days, and three cents a day thereafter. Modify the program specified in either Problem 21 or 22 to accommodate these requirements.

24. Modify the program in Example 13.1 by removing the VAR specification from the PROCEDURE statement and run that version of the program with the array

    7   3   5   6   4   8

    What happens? Why?

25. Write a program that computes and displays the area of regular polygons. There may be any number of episodes in a run, and each episode consists of the following: The program asks for numof-sides (the number of sides) and side-lgth (the length of a side). After receiving these two values (the first being an integer and the second being real), it displays the values, along with the resulting area. Limit your program to 20-sided polygons and assume that users will submit sensible input values.

26. Modify the program in Problem 25 so that it will not fall apart if a user submits outlandish requests (e.g., a two-sided polygon).

27. *Special Challenge:* Write a program that simulates a scoresheet for a game of bowling. At the start, the program asks the bowler to "roll the first ball." In response the bowler submits an integer value indicating the number of pins knocked down, and the "game" is underway. Every time the bowler submits such a value, the program comes back with a line of output showing how the game stands at that point. Here is an example showing the start of a game:

```
program:  HERE WE GO, ROLL THE FIRST BALL,
 bowler:  8<enter>
program:  8
          ROLL THE NEXT BALL,
 bowler:  2<enter>
program:  /
          ROLL THE NEXT BALL,
 bowler:  9<enter>
program:  19   9
```

```
            ROLL THE NEXT BALL.
 bowler:   0<enter>
 program:  19   28
            ROLL THE NEXT BALL.
 bowler:   10<enter>
 program:  19   28   X
 bowler:   7<enter>
 program:  19   28   X   7
 bowler:   2<enter>
 program:  19   28   47   56
            ROLL THE NEXT BALL.

            etc.
```

After the last ball is "rolled," the program is to display the entire scoresheet, followed by the message "GAME OVER." The program is to handle any number of games in succession.

28. Modify the program in Problem 27 so that it is prepared for outlandish numerical input values (like 12). When such a value is submitted, the program is to display an appropriate message and ask for a more reasonable value.

29. Here is a more intricate version of the bowling problem: Design the program to treat a succession of games as a group. That is, the program displays individual game scores as before. However, when it receives a special signal from the bowler (the nature of the signal is up to you), it assumes that the bowler has completed a series of games. In response, it displays the number of games bowled, the total number of pins knocked down, and the average score, rounded to the nearest pin. Then, it displays a message asking the bowler whether he or she wishes to start a new series or quit.

30. In Example 13.4 we computed the mean and standard deviation using a fixed (predefined) number of readings. It is possible to use a more general computational method for standard deviation where we do not have to know the mean in advance. Instead of subtracting each individual value from the mean, we can arrive at the same result as follows:

$$stdevacid = \frac{1}{16-1}\left[\ \sum_{i=1}^{16} acidity_i^2\ -\ \frac{1}{16}\left(\ \sum_{i=1}^{16} acidity_i\ \right)^2\ \right]$$

This time, $numofreadings$ is a variable whose value is not available until all of the $acidity$ values have been read. Note also that it is unnecessary to store all of the $acidity$ values. Instead, we can read each one, use it in the computations, and then replace it with the next one. Revise the program in Example 13.4 so that there is no particular limit on the number of readings associated with each test. The revised output for each test is to include the number of readings.

31. If we write the formula for the polynomial P(x) in the following form:

$$P(x) = A_0X^n + A_1X^{n-1} + A_2X^{n-2} + \ldots + A_{n-1} X + A_n$$

we can conveniently isolate a_n and factor out an x from the remaining terms, giving us

$$P(x) = A_n = X(A_0X^{n-1} + A_1X^{n-2} + \ldots + A_{n-1})$$

Note that the expression inside the parentheses is another polynomial and has one term less (and is one degree lower) than the original one. Given this fine start, write a recursive function named `Poly` with `degree`, `xvar`, and `coefficients` as the formal parameters. Limit the maximum value of `degree` to 8. Support `Poly` with a suitable main program.

32. If n is an integer, and a and b are real numbers, the expansion of can be written as

$$(a + b)^n = a^n + na^{n-1}b + \frac{n (n - 1)a^{n-2}b^2}{2!} + \frac{n(n-1)(n-2)}{3!}a^{n-3}b^3 + \cdots + b^n$$

$$= c_1a^n + c_2a^{n-1}b + c_3a^{n-2}b^2 + c_4a^{n-3}b^3 + \cdots + c_{n+1}b^n$$

where $c_1 = 1$

$c_2 = n$

$$c_3 = \frac{n(n-1)}{2!}$$

$$c_4 = \frac{n(n-1)(n-2)}{3!}$$

etc.

(a) Write a formula for T_i, the ith term in a binomial expansion given i and n.

(b) Express the formula in (a) in recursive form.

(c) Implement a recursive function named `binum` from (b). Support it with a suitable main program.

33. Using the function from Problem 32 as a basis, write a program that reads integers n and i and computes and displays the first i coefficients of the binomial expansion.

34. Write an interactive version of the program for Problem 33.

Files

Our primary mode of operation thus far has been interactive: We have constructed programs whose input items were typed in response to explicit requests for them. Intervention by the user has been a necessary part of this process. Otherwise, the interactive program would be sitting there indefinitely, through snow and wind, waiting for somebody (or something) to supply the data to get it going again.

There are many circumstances in which there is no particular advantage in handling the processing this way. Instead, it would be more desirable to set up a program preparing input ahead of time so that it can be read and processed automatically, without the user's intervention. Similarly, we may want to produce output that can be retained in machine-readable form for use as input later on.

To equip programs with these capabilities, we shall use UCSD Pascal's facilities for defining and handling files other than the standard ones (such as INPUT and OUTPUT) that the system defines automatically. This chapter discusses the properties of such user-defined files, their role in the p-System, and techniques for manipulating them.

14.1 FILE ORGANIZATION

In Chapter 10 we saw that the use of READLN in the form

READLN (item,item,...,item)

persuaded Pascal to treat it as if we had said

READLN (INPUT,item,item,...,item)

INPUT, we learned, is one of several predefined interactive files, and an interactive file, in turn, is a special kind of textfile that enables a program to stop and wait for data from the user. Since we have accumulated some experience with textfiles in the course of our input/output activities, we shall start expanding our processing capabilities with programmer-defined textfiles.

14.1.1 Internal and External Files

INPUT and OUTPUT are examples of *internal files* defined within Pascal by Pascal itself. Other internal files may be defined by the programmer. We distinguish these files from *external files*. An external file, in this context, is a collection of data organized under (and managed by) the p-System's filer. For example, each of our Pascal source programs, after being prepared and entered via the p-System's screen editor, was stored as an external textfile named by us or defaulted to SYSTEM.WRK.TEXT. Although the files were prepared for eventual use within Pascal's environment, there is no apparent hint of that intention in the file's construction. The connection between an external file and Pascal is established in a separate process by associating the external file with an internal file. As we shall see a little later, this is done by means of Pascal's RESET procedure.

14.1.2 Preparation of Textfiles

By now we are old hands at preparing textfiles. The only change introduced here is the nature of the information that we shall place in such a file. Unlike our previous textfiles, whose contents have represented Pascal programs, these files will contain data to be processed by Pascal programs.

We shall prepare a textfile containing data to be used with the program in Example 14.1, a modification of Example 13.4. The program will be discussed later in this chapter. Right now, we shall concentrate on the external datafile to be processed by that program:

1. Bring up the p-System on drive #4 and clear the workfile if necessary. (Remember, this requires an F command to summon the filer and an N command to the filer.) Install your program diskette (we shall continue to call it MYVOL) in drive #5.
2. With the p-System at its executive level, issue an E command to bring in the screen editor. The display will inform you that there is no workfile. (This is not news.)
3. Type < return > to indicate your intention to start a new textfile. The editor will display an empty screen (except for its command line, of course).
4. An I command to the editor readies it for new text. Recall from Example 13.4 that each set of input for that program consists of an integer value for a test number, followed by 16 real values representing acidity readings. Here are the values we shall use:

```
322<return>
3.8 3.9 4.1 3.7 3.9 3.9 4.0 4.1 3.7 3.6 3.8 3.8 3.9 4.1 3.8 4.0<return>
344<return>
5.1 4.8 4.9 4.8 5.0 4.6 5.2 5.5 4.9 4.9 5.0 5.1 4.7 5.3 5.2 5.4<return>
351<return>
7.0 6.9 6.9 6.8 6.7 6.8 7.0 7.0 7.1 7.0 7.2 6.7 6.8 6.8 7.0 7.1<cntrl>C
```

5. Type the values as indicated above. The < c n t r l >C ends the text, and the editor is ready for the next command.

6. A Q command to the editor brings the menu of choices for handling the new text: We can Update (i.e., store it in the workfile), Write it to some other file, Exit from the editor without writing the file, or Return to the editor.

7. Issue a W command indicating your intent to store the data in a file other than the workfile. When the system asks you to name the file to contain your data, use the name MYVOL:DATA1401.TEXT. As a result, the data will be stored on your disk as MYVOL:DATA1401.TEXT.

8. Verify the results from the previous steps by calling the filer and using an L command to list your diskette's directory. When the filer asks you to name the volume whose directory you wish to see, MYVOL: (followed by < return >) will produce the desired display. Once you see MYVOL:DATA1401.text in that directory, you know your datafile is safely tucked away for future use.

14.1.3 Declaration of Files

As far as Pascal is concerned, an internal file is a named data structure like an array. Specifically, a file consists of a series of data values, one after the other. There is no inherent limit to the size of a file. In fact, the size may change as the file is processed. (Many people find it convenient to think of a file as a stream of data.) The organizational integrity of a file is unrelated to its size. Thus, it is possible to have an empty file whose name is recognized by the program.

A file (we shall be speaking here of internal files) is declared as part of Pascal's VAR declaration. Figure 14.1 shows the syntax, relating it back to the general categorization of Figure 5.7. Of specific concern to us right now is the FILE OF CHAR declaration because this is the way to describe a textfile. For example, if we wanted to declare an internal textfile named chem_file, we could say

```
VAR
  chem_file  :  FILE OF CHAR
```

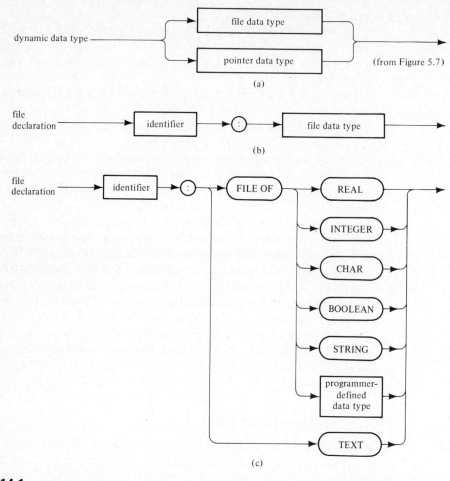

Figure 14.1

File Declaration Syntax

In fact, the many uses of textfiles prompted the inclusion of a separate form for declaring them. The declaration

```
VAR
   chem_file  :  TEXT
```

has the same effect as the previous one. In either case, Pascal is "made aware" of the existence of a textfile named `chem_file`.

14.2 PROCESSING OF TEXTFILES

Since external textfiles have the same organizational characteristics as internal ones. the READ, READLN, WRITE, and WRITELN procedures are applicable in much the same way as before. However, it is up to the programmer to establish the association between the internal file and the p-System external file from which input actually will be read or to which output actually will be written.

14.2.1 Opening a File

Declaring a file informs the program of its existence. *Opening* a file makes that file available for use by performing two keeping activities:

1. It establishes the required association between the external file (to or from which data will be transmitted) and the internal file to which the program will refer. For instance, suppose we declare the textfile chem_file so that, later in the program, we can say

    ```
    READLN (chem_file, testid)
    ```

    In response to this request, we want the program to read the next value from external file MYVOL:DATA1401.TEXT. In order for that to happen, we have to inform Pascal of this connection. Without explaining it now, we shall introduce the idea by saying that the connection is made by specifying

    ```
    RESET (chem_file, 'MYVOL:DATA1401.TEXT')
    ```

    (Note that the external file name is expressed as a string. If we were to specify just the file name, it would not get past the Pascal compiler.) At first glance, it might seem simpler just to declare the internal file with the same name as the external file with which it is to be associated. However, the system is oblivious to such a happy coincidence. We still would need a RESET to define the association.

2. The file opening activity also sets the file at its beginning. (We can think of this activity as being roughly analogous to placing the tone arm of a phonograph at the beginning of a record.) In the case of an internal file (textfile or otherwise), only a certain part of the file is available to the program at any given time. Access to that part of the file is said to be provided by a *window*, and the information thus available is said to be the *window variable*. (The window variable has the same name as the internal file.) The amount of information in the window depends on the way the file is organized; this is a concern when

handling files other than textfiles. If the program is to work on any information from the file, that information must appear in the window first. Moreover, textfiles are *sequential in that information is available in the window only in the order in which it is stored*. Consequently, it is necessary to provide a starting point for many file-related processes by setting the window at the beginning of the file, and placing the file's initial data in the window variable. This also is performed by RESET.

RESET takes two forms. The one we used before, i.e.,

    RESET (internalfilename, 'externalfilename')

performs both activities described before. In a way, RESET performs an initialization, so that it is best placed at the beginning of a program's block, together with the other initializations.

The relation between an internal and external file does not have to be fixed at the time the program is compiled. Instead of specifying the external file name as a string constant (as we did with 'MYVOL:DATA1401 .TEXT'), we can defer the specification of the external file until the program runs. One way to do this is to declare a string variable, read the external file name into it, and use that variable as the second argument in RESET. This approach is illustrated by the following fragment:

```
VAR
    chem_file  :  TEXT ;
    whichfile    :  STRING
      .
      .
      .
    WRITELN (OUTPUT,'WHAT IS THE NAME OF THE EXTERNAL FILE?') ;
    READLN (INPUT, whichfile) ;
    RESET (chem_file,whichfile)
```

RESET's shorter form, i.e.,

```
RESET (internalfilename)
```

performs only the second activity, assuming the relationship with an external file to have been established in an earlier RESET. This is useful in resetting the window back to the beginning of a file. (There are numerous processes whose activities make it an unavoidable necessity to read a file more than once.)

14.2.2 Reading External Textfiles

As pointed out earlier, READ and READLN are used for all textfiles, interactive or otherwise, and we can apply them to external textfiles without difficulty. The only major difference stems from the fact that the data in noninteractive files are available at the time the input operation is executed. This affects the way end of file is handled: For noninteractive files, a READ or READLN transfers data values to their respective destinations from the window. Then the window "moves" on to new data. This means that the value of EOF(filename) is FALSE until the window "moves" *beyond* the end of file. For interactive files, there are no values in the window variable because the user has to supply them on the spot. Consequently, the process is reversed: A READ or READLN "moves" the window to pick up new input, and *then* the values are transferred to their destinations. As a result, the value of EOF(filename) becomes true as soon as the end of file is read. This means that if a line in an interactive file is followed by an end-of-file indicator (i.e., <cntrl>C), EOF becomes true as soon as that line is read. It does not matter whether the line has a separate <eol> or not. Consequently, if EOF takes the program out of a processing loop, it will not get a chance to work on any data in that last line.

On the other hand, if a line in a noninteractive file is followed by an end-of-file indicator, EOF does not become TRUE until that line has been read and the program has tried (internally) to fill the window from the *next* line (which is not there). We shall be able to see this difference more precisely after developing Example 14.1 in the next section.

14.2.3 Example 14.1

We shall perform exactly the same processing as in Example 13.4. The only change will be in the way the input is delivered: Instead of submitting it interactively in response to the program's displayed requests, we shall read the data from the external file MYVOL:DATA1401.TEXT prepared earlier. We can consider this to be a *batch process*.

The procedures mstdev and update are not affected since they do not "know" how the data arrive. Consequently, we shall just indicate their positions in the overall program. Our main program needs to declare the internal file chem_file and establish its connection to MYVOL:DATA1401.TEXT. In addition, we shall remove the interactive requests for data. Input operations will be left as they were in Example 13.4. That is, we shall expect testid on a separate line, followed by 16 readings on a second line. The relevant parts of the resulting program are shown in Figure 14.2.

When the main program is compared with the one for Example 13.4

```
PROGRAM ex1401   ;
CONST
   numofreads = 16  ;
TYPE
   testgroup = ARRAY [1..numofreads] OF REAL   ;
VAR
   chem_file  :  TEXT ;
   acidity  :  testgroup  ;
   avgacidity, stdevacid, maxmean, minmean   :   REAL   ;
   testid, numoftests, maxtest, mintest, i   :   INTEGER   ;

      description of mstdev procedure

      description of update procedure

{                    THE MAIN PROGRAM                      }
BEGIN
  RESET(chem_file,'MYVOL:DATA1401.TEXT')  ;
  numoftests := 0 ;    maxmean := -200.0 ;  minmean := 200.0 ; sw := TRUE ;
  WHILE  sw  DO
    BEGIN
      READLN (chem_file,testid)  ;
      FOR i := 1 TO numofreads  DO
        READ (chem_file,acidity[i])   ;
      READLN(chem_file) ;
      mstdev (acidity, avgacidity, stdevacid) ;
      update (avgacidity, testid, maxmean, minmean, maxtest, mintest) ;
      numoftests := numoftests + 1  ;
      WRITELN ;
      WRITELN ('TEST NO.: ',testid) ;
      WRITELN ('MEAN ACIDITY: ,avgacidity:7:3,' STD DEV.: ',
                                 stdevacid:7:3) ;
      WRITELN ;
      IF  EOF(chem_file)  THEN sw := FALSE
    END ;
  WRITELN ;   WRITELN ;
  WRITELN ('SUMMARY:') ;
  WRITELN ('NO. OF TESTS THIS RUN: ',numoftests)   ;
  WRITELN ('TEST NUMBER  ',maxtest,' HAD A HIGH MEAN OF   ',maxmean:7:3)   ;
  WRITELN ('TEST NUMBER  ',mintest,' HAD A LOW MEAN OF   ',minmean:7:3)   ;
  WRITELN ('END OF RUN.')
END.
```

Figure 14.2————————————————————————————————

Program for Example 14.1

(Figure 13.11), we see only one significant difference: The interactive version has an additional READLN before each new set of input values. Correspondingly, the user is asked to type ⟨return⟩ if he or she intends to submit more data or ⟨cntrl⟩C if not. This lets the program read an end-of-file indicator without any accompanying data. As a result, the program gets to process *all* the data submitted by the user. The batch version does not need this extra ingredient: While the program picked up the final values for acidity, the internal window "moved" beyond the end-of-file indicator, and EOF(chem_file) became TRUE.

Although Example 14.1 is straightforward enough, there are additional things that can be learned from it when it is available for actual use on our processor. Consequently, it will be a good idea for you to type the program from Figure 14.2 and store it in a file named MYVOL:EX1401.TEXT. Subsequent references to a file with this name will imply the program for Example 14.1. (As an additional aid, a sample run for this program, using the data shown in Section 14.1.2, is given in Figure 14.3.)

14.2.4 Writing Files

WRITE and WRITELN are applicable to all textfiles. The underlying mechanism is based on a textfile's sequential structure in that the window is assumed to be at the end of the file. Consequently, when we send output to a textfile, we are *appending* data to that file. This notion certainly is not new to us: Every time we've written on the screen or the printer, we've added a new line (or a new value) rather than inserting it between existing

```
TEST NO.: 322
MEAN ACIDITY:    3.881 STD DEV.:    0.152


TEST NO.: 344
MEAN ACIDITY:    5.025 STD DEV.:    0.252


TEST NO.: 351
MEAN ACIDITY:    6.925 STD DEV.:    0.148


SUMMARY:
NUMBER OF TESTS THIS RUN: 3
TEST NO. 351 HAD A HIGH MEAN OF    6.925
TEST NO. 322 HAD A LOW MEAN OF    3.881
END OF RUN.
```

Figure 14.3

Sample Run for Example 14.1

ones. We shall apply this concept by using WRITE and WRITELN to add data to newly created files.

14.2.5 Closing Files

When a file is *closed*, it becomes unavailable for use. The most common reason for closing a file is that the program is through with it. The termination of a Pascal program brings with it an internal process that automatically closes all of the files used in that program. In many instances, this automatic action produces results that we would have requested anyway. (For example, external files are retained, but they are "disconnected" from associated internal files.) However, there are other situations where it is necessary for the programmer to exercise explicit control over when and how particular files are closed. Pascal provides the CLOSE procedure for this purpose. Once some further concepts of file creation are introduced, we shall discuss CLOSE's uses. This will be done in the next section.

14.2.6 Creation of New Files

The input textfile MYVOL:DATA1401.TEXT was prepared by hand: We typed the values, edited them as necessary, and associated the data collection with the filename using the p-System's file manager. It also is possible to prepare a p-System file as part of a UCSD Pascal program's activities. A file created in this manner is like any other file. It can be stored for later use as input, or for any other purpose. This section describes techniques for creating and using such files.

The REWRITE **Procedure**   We can create a new p-System external file by associating it with an internal file declared in the usual way. The association is established via the REWRITE procedure. For instance, the sequence

```
VAR
   chemout_file  :   TEXT
     .
     .
     .
   REWRITE (chemout_file,'MYVOL:OUT1402.TEXT')
```

defines the internal file chemout_file and informs UCSD Pascal to direct the p-System's filer to create an external file named OUT1402.TEXT on a volume named MYVOL. As a result, the system creates an empty file named MYVOL:OUT1402.TEXT. Then, whenever the program performs a WRITE or WRITELN on file chemout_file, the output values are appended to the new file.

When all of the program's output has been written, the programmer may keep the file or throw it away. UCSD Pascal assumes that our need for the file was temporary unless we say otherwise. We can specify our intent to keep the file by means of the CLOSE procedure, as the next section explains.

Retaining a Newly Produced File   Although UCSD Pascal closes files automatically, the associated processing is not always what we want. Retaining a newly created file (i.e., one defined with a REWRITE) is a case in point. If we want to keep it, we must close it ourselves with the LOCK option. For the internal file chemout_file, the procedure call would say

```
CLOSE (chemout_file, LOCK)
```

in which case the program would direct the p-System's filer to keep the associated external file (MYVOL:OUT1402.TEXT) on the diskette named MYVOL. (LOCK is one of several alternative options that may be used with CLOSE, but they are not of immediate concern.)

14.2.7 Example 14.2

We can illustrate the file creation process conveniently by modifying Example 14.2. In addition to producing the previous results, the expanded version also will deliver output to a new internal file named chemout_file. A line will be written for each test, and it will contain the test number (a three-digit integer), each of the 16 acidity readings, and the mean value. The resulting external file (named OUT1402.TEXT) is to reside on a diskette whose volume name is MYVOL. Consequently, the full name of the file will be MYVOL:OUT1402.TEXT.

The program's basic processing remains as it was. We need only attend to the new file. This requires:

1.   Declaration of chemout_file.
2.   A call to REWRITE to create MYVOL.OUT1402.TEXT and associate it with chemout_file.
3.   The WRITE and WRITELN statements to transmit output to chemout_file.
4.   A CLOSE statement to retain MYVOL:OUT1402.TEXT.

The changes are incorporated in the revised program shown in Figure 14.4. To observe the effect of the changes, make sure there is no workfile. If your computer has high capacity disk units, it is likely that your p-System and Pascal compiler both will be on the same diskette (installed in drive #4) and your program diskette (MYVOL) will be in drive #5. Alternatively, if you are using single-sided diskettes, your p-System will be on the diskette in drive #4 (as before) but your Pascal compiler will share the other diskette (the one in drive #5) with MYVOL. With the diskettes properly positioned:

1. Bring up the p-System, and ask for the filer with an F command.
2. Transfer the file containing the program for Example 14.1 (MYVOL:EX1401.TEXT) to MYVOL:EX1402.TEXT. This way, instead of retyping the entire program, we can prepare the revised version by modifying the original one. Check your directory to make sure the file was copied.
3. Leave the filer (by issuing a Q command) and call in the screen editor (E). In response to its plea that there is no workfile, type the name of the file you just prepared (MYVOL:EX1402.TEXT) followed by ⟨return⟩. This will make the newly copied file available so that you can modify it.
4. Make the changes to the file so that it now represents the program shown in Figure 14.4. (Recall that the two procedures mstdev and update are given in Example 13.4.) Conclude with ⟨cntrl⟩C.
5. Store the revised program back in MYVOL:EX1402.TEXT by quitting the editor and issuing a W command. Return the p-System to its executive level.
6. Issue a C command to bring in the Pascal compiler. The system will ask you to name the file whose contents are to be compiled. This, of course, is MYVOL:EX1402.TEXT. Then, it will ask you to name the file in which the compiled code is to be stored. We shall use the name MYVOL:EX1402.CODE.
7. When compilation is complete, the system will have returned to its executive level. Type "X" to indicate that you want to execute a .program. The system will ask you to name the file containing the code. That file, produced during the previous step, is MYVOL:EX1402 .CODE. Once you specify that file's name, processing will begin.
8. When the program concludes, bring the filer back.
9. List MYVOL's directory by issuing an L command to the filer and then specifying MYVOL: in response to the filer's request for a volume name.

This establishes the existence of OUT1402.TEXT as an entry in MYVOL's directory. If you want to look at the file's contents (to make sure the output actually got there), you can copy the file (by a Transfer command) to PRINTER:, or you can make it the workfile and display it by calling the screen editor.

```
PROGRAM ex1402  ;
CONST
    numofreads = 16  ;
TYPE
    testgroup = ARRAY [1..numofreads] OF REAL  ;
VAR
    chem_file, chemout_file  :  TEXT  ;
    acidity  :  testgroup  ;
    avgacidity, stdevacid, maxmean, minmean  :  REAL  ;
    testid, numoftests, maxtest, mintest, i  :  INTEGER  ;

            description of mstdev procedure

            description of update procedure

{                     THE MAIN PROGRAM                              }
BEGIN
    REWRITE(chemout_file,'MYVOL:OUT1402.TEXT')  ;
    RESET(chem_file,'DATA1401.TEXT')  ;
    numoftests := 0 ;  maxmean := -200.0 ;  minmean := 200.0 ;  sw := TRUE  ;
    WHILE  sw  DO
    BEGIN
        READLN (chem_file,testid)  ;
        FOR i := 1 TO numofreads  DO
            READ (chem_file,acidity[i])  ;
```

Figure 14.4 ———— Program for Example 14.2

```
WRITELN ;    WRITELN ;
WRITELN ('SUMMARY:') ;
WRITELN ('NO. OF TESTS THIS RUN: ',numoftests) ;
WRITELN ('TEST NUMBER ',maxtest,' HAD A HIGH MEAN OF ',maxmean:7:3) ;
WRITELN ('TEST NUMBER ',mintest,' HAD A LOW MEAN OF ',minmean:7:3) ;
CLOSE (chemout_file,LOCK) ;
WRITELN ('END OF RUN.')
END.

READLN(chem_file) ;
mstdev (acidity, avgacidity, stdevacid) ;
update (avgacidity, testid, maxmean, minmean, maxtest, mintest) ;
numoftests := numoftests + 1 ;
WRITELN ;
WRITELN ('TEST NO.: ',testid) ;
WRITELN ('MEAN ACIDITY: ',avgacidity:7:3,' STD DEV.: ',
                          stdevacid:7:3) ;
WRITELN ;
WRITE (chemout_file, testid:3) ;
FOR i := 1 TO numofreads DO
   WRITE (chemout_file, acidity[i]:3:1) ;
WRITE (chemout_file, avgacidity:7:3) ;
WRITELN (chemout_file) ;
IF EOF(chem_file) THEN sw := FALSE
END ;
```

Figure 14.4 Program for Example 14.2 (Continued)

14.2.8 More about REWRITE and CLOSE

Creation of new files is part of a broader set of services performed by the REWRITE procedure. The basic activity behind REWRITE is that it creates an empty (temporary) file having the same name as REWRITE's first argument. Pascal will accept a call to REWRITE with only one argument. (That argument must be an internal file name declared as such.) In response, it makes a copy of that file and works with it. The way we close the file will determine whether or not the temporary copy replaces the original one. As part of REWRITE's activity, the window is set up at the beginning of the temporary file.

When we produced the new file MYVOL:OUT1402.TEXT, we illustrated UCSD Pascal's acceptance of a second argument for REWRITE, namely, the identification of an external file. In the specific case of Example 14.2, the program, having determined that the file MYVOL:OUT1402 .TEXT did not exist, created it. (That was the "copy.") If the specified external file *does* exist, REWRITE makes a copy of it for use during processing. Since that copy is empty, this is a way of clearing a file.

We have already seen that we can use the LOCK option with the CLOSE procedure to retain a newly created file. Here is what happens when CLOSE is used with other options on an internal file associated with an existing external file. Since we are used to the names from earlier examples, we shall assume chemout_file to be an internal file associated with the existing external file MYVOL:OUT1402.TEXT:

1. CLOSE (chemout_file,NORMAL) leaves the original version untouched and destroys the copy.
2. CLOSE (chemout_file,LOCK) keeps the (formerly) temporary copy and discards the original.
3. CLOSE (chemout_file,PURGE) deletes the external file name (MYVOL:OUT1402.TEXT in this case) from the disk's directory. As a result, the original external file and its copy are discarded.

A fourth option, CLOSE (chemout_file,CRUNCH), relates to special input/output operations not considered here.

14.2.9 Datafiles

Not all files have to be textfiles. Recall (Figure 14.1) that files may consist of different data values. For example, the declaration

```
VAR
   mydata  :  FILE OF INTEGER
```

is a legitimate one. (It sets up an internal *datafile* named my data consisting of a sequence of integer values.) When information is written on such a file, it is represented using the computer's internal data formats and not as human-readable characters. Consequently, its storage is more compact, and its input or output proceeds more rapidly than that of a textfile. Operations other than READ, WRITE, READLN, and WRITELN are used to perform input/output on such files.

The requirement to restrict membership in such a file to a single data type limits its utility in this form (i.e., with INTEGER, REAL, STRING or BOOLEAN as its sole components). Instead, a much more common practice is to combine data types in any desired combination to form a *record*, and then define that structure as a new data type. This is how we shall use datafiles. The pertinent discussion is presented in the next section.

14.3 RECORDS AND RECORD PROCESSING

As Chapter 5 indicated, the RECORD construction gives the Pascal programmer an opportunity to deal with collections of data consisting of any combination of types. In this section we shall use that facility as a convenient and powerful vehicle for constructing data files.

14.3.1 Declaration of Records

Records are defined as specific data types using Pascal's TYPE declaration. For example, referring to Example 14.2, suppose we wanted to construct a collection of chemical test data so that each member of this collection consisted of an integer test number, 16 real test readings, and mean and standard deviation values (both real). This construction can be defined as follows:

```
CONST
   numofreads = 16 ;
TYPE
   test_rec = RECORD
                 testnum : INTEGER ;
                 hydro : ARRAY[1..numofreads] OF REAL ;
                 mean_acidity : REAL ;
                 std_acidity : REAL
              END
```

testnum, etc. are the *field names* that make up this structure. As is true with any other TYPE declaration, this is only bookkeeping. There are no records yet, nor is there a mechanism for recognizing them. This situation changes when we declare a variable of type `test_rec`, e.g.,

```
VAR
    chem_rslt : test_rec
```

Now we have a variable named `chem_rslt` associated with sufficient storage to accommodate values denoted by the field names listed in the `TYPE` declaration.

14.3.2 Internal Manipulation of Records

Each item in a record variable can be manipulated like any other single-valued variable. (We cannot place values in all of a record's items with a single assignment.) When we process a record's items, we must make sure that we identify each item unambiguously. For instance, assuming the `test_rec` data type defined before, we are well within our rights to declare

```
VAR
    chem_rslt, food_rslt, paint_rslt : test_rec
```

As a result of this declaration, it would appear that there are three different items named `testnum`, three named `mean_acidity`, etc. This is true, but the replicate names can be distinguished from each other by attaching the proper record name. Thus, the statement

```
food_rslt.testnum := 409
```

leaves no doubt as to which `testnum` we mean.

When a series of computations are to be done on items from the same record variable, we can avoid having to specify the record name repeatedly. This is done using the `WITH...DO` statement whose syntax is shown in Figure 14.5. For example, the statement

```
WITH  chem_rslt  DO
    BEGIN
        testnum := 409 ;
        FOR  i := 1 TO numofreads  DO
            hydro[i] := 1.0 ;
        mean_acidity := 1.0 ;
        std_acidity := 0.0
    END
```

refers specifically to `chem_rslt.testnum`, `chem_rslt.hydro`, `chem_rslt.mean_acidity`, and `chem_rslt. std_acidity`.

Semantics: The identifier must refer to a record data type of variable.

Figure 14.5

Syntax for the WITH Statement

Entire records may be compared with each other in UCSD Pascal as long as their respective constructions are identical and the type of comparison is either = or < >. Thus,

```
IF  chem_rslt = food_rslt   THEN...
```

is acceptable, but

```
IF  chem_rslt <= food_rslt   THEN...
```

is not.

14.3.3 Files of Records

A collection of records can be defined as a datafile by an ordinary file declaration. Thus,

```
VAR
   food_file : FILE OF test_rec
```

defines an internal file in which each record is to consist of the items described in test_rec's TYPE definition. Since this is not a textfile, it cannot be edited by the p-System's screen editor, nor can its values be transmitted via READ, READLN, WRITE, or WRITELN. Records for such files are built internally to begin with (instead of being typed in and edited), and they are transmitted by the special procedures GET and PUT, as explained in the next section. When it is not necessary for the user to view the data directly, it is advantageous to use datafiles (rather than textfiles) because the former are more compact and their transmission is more rapid.

14.3.4 Input/Output of Datafiles

RESET and REWRITE operate on datafiles as they do on textfiles. Thus, the previous discussion of these procedures applies here as well. Since all of the records in a given datafile have the same basic organization (more complex alternatives are possible, but they are beyond the scope of this book), their transmission is simplified by dealing with entire records rather than individual values. A datafile record is read by calling the GET procedure:

```
GET(internalfilename)
```

Whenever a datafile's record is read, its values become available in the file's window variable, whose name is internalfilename. For example, if food_file is a previously prepared datafile consisting of records of type test_rec, the statement

```
GET(food_file)
```

places food_file's next record in the window variable ^food_file. As a result, ^food_file contains the integer value ^food_file.testnum, 16 real values ^food_file.hydro[1] through ^food_file.hydro[16], and real values ^food_file.mean_acidity and ^food_file.std_acidity. These values may be assigned to other variables, written as part of another datafile (using PUT), or written as part of a textfile (using WRITE or WRITELN). Similarly, we can read data from a textfile (including an interactive file), prepare a datafile record by assigning values to a window variable, and then send the record off to the datafile with a PUT. This latter process is illustrated in the next section.

14.3.5 Example 14.3

We are going to use the textfile chem_file from Example 14.1 to prepare a datafile named test_file. As before, chem_file will be read from the external file MYVOL:DATA1401.TEXT. The new output file (test_file) will be sent to the external file MYVOL:OUT1403.DATA. Each of test_file's records will contain the test number, the 16 acidity readings, the mean, and the standard deviation.

As was the case in the previous two examples, we do not need to change any of the computations. The main program now will include a TYPE declaration for test_rec (and the corresponding file declaration for test_file), and the internal processing to prepare the record for the window variable ^test_file. The resulting program is shown in Figure 14.6. (One of the problems at the end of the chapter asks you to simplify the program.)

14.4 RANDOM ACCESS

The input/output operations we have been using thus far have enabled us to read the next data item (or record) in a file or to append data to the end of an output file. This method of handling input or output data is termed *sequen-*

```pascal
PROGRAM ex1403 ;
CONST
    numofreads = 16 ;
TYPE
    testgroup = ARRAY [1..numofreads] OF REAL ;
    testrec = RECORD
                  testnum : INTEGER ;
                  acidity : testgroup ;
                  mean_acidity, std_acidity : REAL
              END ;

VAR
    chem_file : TEXT ;
    test_file : FILE OF testrec ;
    acidity   : testgroup ;
    avgacidity, stdevacid, maxmean, minmean : REAL ;
    testid, numoftests, maxtest, mintest, i : INTEGER ;

    description of mstdev procedure

    description of update procedure

{                    THE MAIN PROGRAM                    }
BEGIN
    RESET(chem_file,'DATA1401.TEXT') ;
    REWRITE(test_file,'MYVOL:OUT1403.DATA') ;
    numoftests := 0 ; maxmean := -200.0 ; minmean := 200.0 ; sw := TRUE ;
    WRITELN ('INSTALL MYVOL ON UNIT 5 AND HIT <ENTER>,') ;
    READLN ;
    WHILE sw DO
        BEGIN
            READLN (chem_file,testid) ;
            FOR i := 1 TO numofreads DO
```

```
       READ (chem_file,acidity[i])    ;
       READLN(chem_file) ;
       mstdev (acidity, avgacidity, stdevacid) ;
       update (avgacidity, testid, maxmean, minmean, maxtest, mintest) ;
       numoftests := numoftests + 1 ;
       WRITE_N ;
       WRITE_N ('TEST NO.: ',testid) ;
       WRITE_N ('MEAN ACIDITY: ,avgacidity:7:3,' STD DEV.: ',
                              stdevacid:7:3) ;

       WRITE_N ;
       {BUILD THE OUTPUT FILE RECORD}
       WITH test_file) DO
         BEGIN
           testnum := testid ;
           FOR i := 1 TO numofreads  DO
              hydro[i] := acidity[i] ;
           mean_acidity := avgacidity ;
           std_acidity := stdevacid
         END ;
       PUT(test_file) ;
       IF EOF(chem_file)   THEN sw := FALSE

     END ;   WRITELN ;
     WRITELN ('SUMMARY:') ;
     WRITELN ('NO. OF TESTS THIS RUN:  ',numoftests) ;
     WRITELN ('TEST NUMBER  ',maxtest,' HAD A HIGH MEAN OF  ',maxmean:7:3) ;
     WRITELN ('TEST NUMBER  ',mintest,' HAD A LOW MEAN OF  ',minmean:7:3) ;
     CLOSE (test_file,LOCK) ;
     WRITELN ('END OF RUN.')
END.
```

Figure 14.6   Program for Example 14.3

tial access. As the name implies, there is an inherent restriction with regard to the availability of a file's contents: Access to a particular portion of a file is determined by its physical position relative to the window. Thus, if we want to read a certain record whose position is 23 records beyond the window, we must work our way toward it, record by record; if the record at the window already is beyond the record we want (and we are using sequential access), we cannot backtrack through the file to get to it. Instead, we must RESET the window back to the beginning of the file so that we can work our way forward toward the desired record.

For many applications, the restrictions imposed by sequential access do not represent any disadvantage. However, there are times when it would be useful to be able to process a file's record in some arbitrary order. This is particularly true when the processing is to be performed interactively and we would like to ask for any record in a file without having to go through a collection of other records. For example, when a doctor or nurse walks over to one of the terminals in a hospital and requests the data for a particular patient to be displayed, he or she wants *those* data now and not data on other patients. The ability to obtain data in such arbitrary order is called *random access.*

14.4.1 Techniques for Random Access

UCSD Pascal enables the programmer to use random access under certain well-defined conditions. Of course, the storage medium on which the file resides must be physically and organizationally capable of supporting random access; otherwise the whole thing does not make any sense. The most common type of equipment with random access capabilities is the *magnetic disk.* (By magnetic disk we refer generically to both the so-called "hard" disk and flexible diskette or "floppy disk.") Accordingly, the ensuing discussion will assume that a file used for random access resides on a magnetic disk.

Nothing special has to be done to a p-System file to make it suitable for random access. However, it cannot be a textfile. Since we shall not concern ourselves with the manipulation of codefiles (except to produce them and execute them), we shall focus our attention on datafiles. (We already know how to handle these from Section 14.2.9.)

When we use random access in UCSD Pascal, we obtain the record we want immediately by *knowing its position in the file in relation to the first record.* (When a file is used this way, some people like to describe it as a *relative record file.*) The organizational rule is simple: A file's first record is at position 0, the second record is at position 1, and so on.

The process of obtaining a desired record consists of two distinct stages:

1. We position the window at the appropriate position in the file by using UCSD Pascal's SEEK procedure.
2. We bring the record into the window variable by using UCSD Pascal's GET procedure.

Once we have made the record available in this manner, we can process it in any way we choose (as long as we do not change its size or organization). When processing has been completed, we can "rewrite" the record into its former position by using the PUT procedure. The new version of the record thus replaces the previous version, and we can obtain any other record (or the same record, for that matter) by performing another SEEK followed by a GET. It is important to understand that random access will not work unless both stages of the process are carried out. Specifically, *you must not perform two SEEKS in succession without a GET or PUT between them.* Otherwise, you lose control over the window's contents.

The SEEK procedure is invoked as follows:

SEEK (filename,position)

where the first argument gives the internal file name and the second indicates which record is wanted. As you would expect, the position is indicated by an integer that must have a value of zero or greater. If this value is less than zero or if it exceeds the position of the file's last record, the next GET or PUT will set EOF to TRUE for that file. The second argument's value can be in the form of a constant or (more likely) a variable name or an expression.

14.4.2 Example 14.4

To illustrate the use of random access, we shall construct a little program that processes a file's records interactively by applying transactions that change certain values in these records. As it happens, this program was needed anyway, because the Consolidated Floogle Company (formerly the Amalgamated Fleegle Company) wants to improve the way it handles its inventory. The company carries nine different parts identified by respective part numbers 1 through 9. This is most fortunate since we can use the part number to indicate a record's position. Each record contains information about one of the parts as indicated in Table 14.1. That same table also shows the values in the file at some particular time.

To keep our attention on the random access, we shall simplify the transactions to be handled in the program. (Not to worry; you will get your chance to complicate them in the problems at the end of the chapter.) The program will ask for a part number. When that part number has been read,

Table 14.1 File information for Example 14.4

Record Format:
  Part number (1 through 9)
  Number of units on hand (integer)
  Number of units back-ordered (integer)
  Unit price (real)
  Part name (up to 12 characters long)

pnum	current	back	price	pname
1	34	0	4.55	schmichik
2	517	0	23.80	widgetron
3	86	114	18.50	magglebox
4	0	20	77.77	bloomchik
5	7	0	125.50	fmevver
6	314	0	8.80	dablabber
7	43	0	41.00	boozle
8	1724	0	2.81	ingletron
9	113	0	225.50	snemovac

Semantics: UCSD Pascal does not allow a FILE OF FILE declaration.

the program will use it to determine the position of the corresponding record (information for part 1 is stored in record 0, part 2 in record 1, etc.), SEEK that record, and then GET it. Once the record is available, the program prompts for a value indicating the number of parts received and that number (if it is greater than zero) is added to the current inventory. The number of units back-ordered also is adjusted as necessary to record the effect of the newly received parts. Then, the user is asked for the number of units ordered. If the order can be filled completely from inventory, the inventory is depleted by that amount; if not, the number of units back-ordered is increased by the amount of the order. Since this completes the set of available transactions for that part number, its record is PUT in the file, replacing the previous version, and the user is asked for another part number. This cycle continues (with part numbers being submitted in random sequence) until the user terminates the program.

For illustrative purposes, Figure 14.7 shows the Pascal statements for an interactive program designed to prepare a file that can be used with Example 14.4. I suggest that you generate such a file by preparing this program and running it with the data from Table 14.1. The program for Example 14.4 is shown in Figure 14.8.

```
{*********************************************************}
{**                                                    **}
{**                  CHAPTER 14 EXAMPLE 4              **}
{**                                                    **}
{**   THIS INTERACTIVE PROGRAM PROCESSES ORDERS AND RECEIPTS OF  **}
{**   GOODS AGAINST A FILE OF INVENTORY DATA. THE ORDERS/RECEIPTS **}
{**   MAY BE SUBMITTED IN RANDOM ORDER.                **}
{**                                                    **}
{*********************************************************}
PROGRAM   ex1404
TYPE
   inv_rec = RECORD
             Pnum : INTEGER ;        {** PART NUMBER (1-9) **}
             current : INTEGER ;     {** NO. OF UNITS ON HAND **}
             back : INTEGER ;        {** NO. OF UNITS BACK ORDERED **}
             price : REAL ;          {** UNIT PRICE **}
             pname : STRING[12]      {** PART NAME **}
           END ;

VAR
   prt_file : TEXT ;
   wrhs : FILE OF inv_rec ;
   part, newparts, order : INTEGER ;
   sw : BOOLEAN ;
```

Figure 14.7

319

```
{******************************************************************}
{**** THIS PROGRAM BUILDS A DATAFILE NAMES #5:FLOOGLE THAT ****}
{**** CONTAINS INVENTORY DATA TO BE USED AS INPUT FOR THE ****}
{**** PROGRAM IN EXAMPLE 4 OF CHAPTER 14. EACH OF THE 9 ****}
{**** RECORDS IN THE FILE CONTAINS A PART NUMBER, NO. OF ****}
{**** UNITS ON HAND, NO. OF UNITS BACK ORDERED, A PRICE, ****}
{**** AND A PART NAME (12 CHARACTERS OR LESS). ****}
{******************************************************************}

PROGRAM bldinv ;
TYPE
   inv_rec = RECORD
                 pnum : INTEGER ;
                 current : INTEGER ;
                 back : INTEGER ;
                 price : REAL ;
                 pname : STRING[12]
             END ;
VAR
   part, onhand, backorder : INTEGER ;
   howmuch : REAL ;
   part_id : STRING[12] ;
   inv_file : FILE OF inv_rec ;
   pr_file : TEXT ;
   sw : BOOLEAN
BEGIN
   REWRITE (inv_file, '#5:floogles') ;
   REWRITE (pr_file, 'PRINTER:') ;
   WRITELN ('WE ARE READY TO BUILD THE FLOOGLE INVENTORY FILE.') ;
   WRITELN ('TYPE THE PART NO., NO. OF UNITS ON HAND, NO. BACK ORDERED,') ;
   WRITELN ('PRICE, AND PART NAME.') ;
   WRITELN ('LEAVE A BLANK AFTER EACH INPUT VALUE EXCEPT THE PRICE, THAT IS,') ;
   WRITELN ('TYPE THE PART NAME''S FIRST LETTER IMMEDIATELY AFTER THE PRICE.') ;
   READLN (part, onhand, backorder, howmuch, part_id) ;
```

320

```
WRITELN (pr_file,'                    CONSOLIDATED FLOOGLE COMPANY') ;
WRITELN (pr_file,'                           INVENTORY FILE') ;
WRITELN (pr_file) ;       WRITELN (pr_file) ;
WRITELN (pr_file)          PART NO.,'   ON HAND',,'     BACK',
                                PART') ;
WRITELN (pr_file),'                        ORDERED',,'               ',
                        PRICE',,'
             NAME') ;

sw := TRUE ;
WHILE  sw  DO
   BEGIN
   WITH inv_file^ DO
      BEGIN
      pnum := part ;      current := onhand ;        back := backorder ;
      price := howmuch ;        pname := part_id
      END ;
   PUT (inv_file)
   WRITELN (pr_file, part:10,onhand:12,backorder:12,howmuch:15:2,part_id:20) ;
   WRITELN ('TYPE <ENTER> TO CONTINUE OR <CNTRL>C TO QUIT,') ;
   READLN ;
   IF EOF
      THEN
         sw := FALSE
      ELSE
         BEGIN
         WRITELN ('TYPE NEXT PART NO., NO. ON HAND, BACK ORDERED, PRICE,',
                  ' AND PART NAME,') ;
         READLN (part, onhand, backorder, howmuch, part_id)
         END
   END ;
WRITELN ;   WRITELN ('END OF RUN.') ;      CLOSE (inv_file, LOCK)
END.
```

Figure 14.8

```
{ ****************************************** }
{ ****THIS PROCEDURE PRINTS THE INVENTORY FILE  *** }
{ ****************************************** }
PROCEDURE printem ;
BEGIN
RESET (wrhs, '#5:floogles') ;
WRITELN (prt_file,'                    CONSOLIDATED FLOOGLE COMPANY') ;
WRITELN (prt_file,'                          INVENTORY FILE') ;
WRITELN (prt_file) ;      WRITELN (prt_file) ;
WRITELN (prt_file,'      PART NO., ',' ON HAND',',      BACK',',  ,
                  :PRICE',',      PART') ;  ,
WRITELN (prt_file,                             ',' ORDERED',',
                                ',' NAME') ;

WHILE NOT EOF(wrhs)      DO
   BEGIN  WITH  wrhs^  DO
      WRITELN (prt_file,pnum:10,current:12,back:12,
                  price:15:2,pname:20) ;

      GET (wrhs)
   END ;
WRITELN (prt_file) ;     WRITELN (prt_file)
END ;

BEGIN
REWRITE (prt_file,'PRINTER:') ;
WRITELN (prt_file,'FLOOGLE FILE BEFORE PROCESSING.') ;
printem ;
CLOSE (wrhs,LOCK) ;   RESET (wrhs,'#5:floogles') ;
WRITELN ('TYPE A PART NUMBER (1-9), THEN <ENTER>,') ;
READLN (part) ;
sw := TRUE ;
WHILE sw DO
```

```
BEGIN
  WITH wrhs^ DO
    BEGIN
      SEEK (wrhs,Part-1) ;  GET (wrhs) ;
      WRITELN ('      #',Pnum:1,':',current:12,back:12,
                price:15:2,Pname:20) ;
      WRITELN ('TYPE THE NO. OF UNITS RECEIVED, THEN <ENTER>.') ;
      READLN (newParts) ;
      IF newParts > 0
        THEN
          BEGIN
            current := current + newParts ;
            IF newParts < back
              THEN
                back := back - newParts
              ELSE
                back := 0
          END ;
      WRITELN ('      #',Pnum:1,':',current:12,back:12,
                price:15:2,Pname:20) ;
      WRITELN ('TYPE NO. OF UNITS ORDERED.') ;
      READLN (order) ;
      IF order > current
        THEN
          BEGIN
            back := back + order - current ; current := 0
          END
        ELSE
          current := current - order ;
```

Figure 14.8 _____ (Continued)

```
WRITELN ('        #',Pnum:1,':',current:12,back,12,
         price:15:2,Pname:20) ;
   SEEK (wrhs,part-1) ; PUT (wrhs)
END ;
WRITELN ('TYPE <ENTER> TO CONTINUE OR <CNTRL>C TO QUIT.') ; READLN ;
IF EOF
   THEN
      sw := FALSE
   ELSE
      BEGIN
         WRITELN ('TYPE A PART NO., THEN <ENTER>.') ; READLN (part)
      END

END
WRITELN;           WRITELN ;   CLOSE (wrhs, LOCK) ;
WRITELN (prt_file, 'FLOOGLE FILE AFTER PROCESSING.') ;
Printem ;          CLOSE (wrhs,LOCK) ;    WRITELN ('END OF RUN.')
END.
```

Figure 14.8 _____ (Continued)

Problems

1. Modify Example 14.2 so that, before it shows the computed results for each test, it displays a line with the test number and the 16 readings.

2. Produce a version of Example 13.3 in which the input values are read from an internal textfile named `lake_file`. Run your program using the data given below. (Prepare these data as an external file named MYVOL:P1402.TEXT.)

```
117.0 86.5     123.5 81.1     127.2 92.0LAKE LACKALOOK
31.4 22.8      36.6 23.4      38.8 18.9LAKE LOOKALIKE
45.5 56.7      49.6 61.1      52.2 53.3LAKE LACKALOCK
71.5 19.8      73.4 15.7      72.8 24.6LAKE LACKALICK
204.4 6.7      209.9 18.5     211.3 8.7LAKE LOCALLOX
```

3. The Nineveh Ice Cream Company ("A Whale of a Treat") makes ice cream in eight incredible flavors: Chocomarsh, Vanillatron, Zoonegeberry, Colonial Mist, Cumulus, Barcarolle, Broccoli, and HehHeh. These delights are sold in Nineveh's three retail stores. At the end of each month, the home office receives a sales report from each store showing, for each flavor, the number of liters sold and the number of ice cream cones sold. (Nineveh has a special interest in ice cream cones.) From this information, the office prepares a textfile in which the first line shows the month and year (e.g., 6 1983), and each subsequent line shows the store number (1, 2, or 3), the number of liters sold (to the nearest liter), the number of ice cream cones sold (to the nearest cone), and the name of the flavor. (The ice cream sold as cones is part of the total liters.) Thus, the line

```
2     3140      12473CUMULUS
```

shows that store number 2 sold 3140 liters of Cumulus ice cream, including 12473 cones. Now, all the company needs is a program to operate on such a file. Write a program that shows the total sales (in liters) and the total number of cones sold for each flavor (one line for each flavor). In addition, the program is to show the total sales and total number of cones for each store regardless of flavor (one line per store). A final line of output shows the grand totals.

We have managed (at great expense and personal risk) to acquire Nineveh's textfile for June, 1983, and it appears below. As is evident, the lines are in no particular order.

```
6     1983
1     2178      9888CHOCOMARSH
```

1	2234	5676VANILLATRON
1	5443	13887COLONIAL MIST
1	3223	4452BARCAROLLE
1	4568	10095ZOONEGEBERRY
1	1088	2220CUMULUS
1	2121	2500BROCCOLI
1	6644	23888HEHHEH
2	3140	12473CUMULUS
2	3385	12500CHOCOMARSH
2	4665	22875VANILLATRON
2	3854	10006ZOONEGEBERRY
2	1172	766COLONIAL MIST
2	5766	12448BARCAROLLE
2	6979	34554HEHHEH
2	6176	344BROCCOLI
3	8860	96554HEHHEH
3	3424	6578COLONIAL MIST
3	4176	9767BARCAROLLE
3	998	1085ZOONEGEBERRY
3	2898	4658VANILLATRON
3	5433	5789CHOCOMARSH
3	6497	13884CUMULUS
3	7250	2548BROCCOLI

4. Modify the program in Problem 3 so that its output appears in the following order: The eight lines showing total sales by flavor are to be arranged in descending order (highest sales first). The three lines showing sales by store are to appear in descending order (highest sales first).

5. Modify the program in Problem 3 or 4 so that each line also includes a dollar amount for sales. The sales price is the same for all flavors in all stores (a typical value is $2.88 per liter), and it is entered interactively in response to a request from the program. (It is a good idea to display the price on the first line of output, along with the month.)

6. Modify the program in Problem 5 so that, in addition to displaying the results described before, it produces a datafile named ice_file in which each of the eight records contains the month, year, and flavor; liters sold, cones sold, and dollar amount of sales for each store; and total liters sold, cones sold, and dollar amount for that flavor. (Thus, each record would have 15 items.) Store the output in external file MYVOL:P1406.DATA.

7. Simplify the main program in Example 14.3 (For instance, are testid and ^test_file.testnum both necessary?) Input and output requirements are unchanged.

8. Modify the program in Example 13.1 so that the unsorted arrays are read from the textfile i n _ f i l e. Each line of i n _ f i l e consists of an (integer) array number followed by the six integer values. In addition to displaying the sorted arrays, the program is to produce a datafile named o u t d _ f i l e in which each record consists of the array number, the six values in descending order, and the mean value. Here are some test data:

304	6	7	4	18	5	9
226	8	4	−2	3	9	5
343	21	20	18	17	16	12
497	−41	−28	−17	−8	−6	−2
568	76	44	32	−76	−44	−32

The output file is to be stored in MYVOL:P1408.DATA.

9. Modify the program in Problem 8 so that the first record in o u t d _ f i l e is the one with the lowest mean value, the second is the one with the second lowest mean, etc. Design the program so that the number of arrays to be processed is not fixed, but does not exceed 10.

10. *Special Challenge:* Expand the program in Problem 8 as follows: After all the data for i n _ f i l e have been processed, the program asks for additional array data to be submitted interactively. Each additional array (along with its array number) is processed as before, and the results (in addition to being displayed) are appended to o u t d _ f i l e. The user signals the end of the run by typing ⟨c n t r l⟩C.

11. Modify the program in Example 14.4 so that the user can end the run by typing "Q". In addition, change the interactive input so that the user simply types ⟨r e t u r n⟩ (instead of 0 and a space) to indicate that zero parts were ordered or received.

12. Modify the program in Example 14.4 or in Problem 11 so that when the user specifies a part number, the program displays the information currently stored for that part.

13. Modify the program in Problem 12 so that the information displayed on the video screen also is printed. (If you have a parallel printer, the p-System recognizes it as device 6: or PRINTER:; if you have a serial printer, the p-System recognizes it as device 8: or REMOUT:.) After all transactions have been completed, the program is to print an additional summary. For each part number, the summary is to show the number of units received, the number of units ordered, the current status of the inventory (i.e., the number of units on hand and the number back-ordered), and the dollar value of the current inventory.

14. As a final gesture to Consolidated Floogle, expand the program in the previous problem so that it includes a module that can be activated prior to each request for a part number. (You might ask the user if he

or she wants a file summary.) If the module is activated, it prints a nice table showing the contents of each record. Use a scheme that makes it convenient to activate or bypass this service.

15. John's Airline runs exactly 24 flights a day seven days a week. Twelve of the flights (Flights 414 through 425) go from Burnt Toast, Nebraska to Sweatband, New Mexico. The other 12 flights (Flights 514 through 525) go from Sweatband, New Mexico to Burnt Toast, Nebraska. Reservations can be made only on the day of the flight, not before and (John decided this himself) not after. John's Airline flies the sleek Smedley Cruncheroo airplane, with a seating capacity of 24, all fourth class. Accordingly, there is one fare (58 dollars) which may change from time to time. However, a passenger may order a meal (catered by John's Aunt Hyacinth) when he or she reserves a seat. The meal costs $10.00 extra.

Write a program that handles a day's transactions for the airline. That is, when the program starts up, the reservation file is initialized. Then, reservations are taken in random order. A special signal can be entered to indicate that a particular flight has departed. Similarly, another special signal can be entered to indicate that the last flight has departed (i.e., the business day is over). When this latter signal is received, the program is to produce a summary report where, for each flight, it shows the number of seats sold, the number of meals sold, the revenue from the seats, the revenue from the meal, and the total revenue. Up, up and away.

Chapter 15

Sets

Our dealings with arrays, records, and files have shown the convenience that can be gained from treating data values as organized groups and collections. Another useful type of data organization is the set. Unlike the array, whose elements are ordered and usually fixed in number (for a given situation), the set accommodates more flexible constructions in which the number of members may vary arbitrarily, and their order may or may not be important.

Pascal's SET organization is designed to convey this flexibility. We can define sets by declaring them and specifying the criteria that make a data value eligible for membership. (The basic rules for doing this were introduced in Section 5.3.1, and you may want to check back there for a quick review.) Once declared, a set variable can be processed in a variety of ways, all of which treat the set as a unit of information. This chapter discusses these facilities and illustrates their use.

15.1 DECLARATION OF SETS

Declaration of a set variable (first defined in Figure 5.7) is described diagrammatically in Figure 15.1. While there is a generous allowance for the number of elements in a set (UCSD Pascal accepts up to 4080 of them), their values all must differ from each other, and they all must be of the same data type. (Recall from Chapter 5 that this underlying data type is called the *base type*.) Since the base type may be any simple type except REAL, this means that Pascal extends an open invitation to create a set for any coherent collection of items whose processing is made more convenient by this kind of organization.

For example, suppose we define a data type named weeks as follows:

```
TYPE
    weeks = 1..52
```

weeks now can serve as the base type for another data type. The declaration

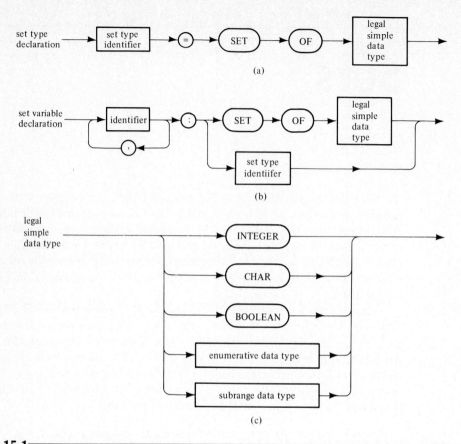

Figure 15.1

Declaration of Sets

```
TYPE
    season = SET OF weeks
```

defines a set type named s e as on such that each declared variable of this type can be a collection of anywhere from 0 to 52 values. We can have any kind of s e as on we want. For example,

```
VAR
    theater_season, hockey_season, mating_season,
    papaya_season, symphony_season, slack_season : season
```

gives us six different kinds of seasons. (No doubt you can think of many more.) The values that these variables may take on are drawn from those defined for the data type weeks. 49 is such a value, and to denote its use as a member of a set, we enclose it in square brackets. Based on our TYPE declarations, any value from [1] to [52] is a legitimate constant. For example, the assignment

```
papaya_season := [31]
```

tells Pascal that the set papaya_season is to consist of the single value 31. (This is a mighty short papaya season.) A more optimistic assignment might be

```
papaya_season := [31, 32, 33, 34, 35, 36]
```

which gives us a nice six-week season. Since these values are consecutive, we can say the same thing using Pascal's subrange notation:

```
papaya_season :- [31..36]
```

If the crop fails and there is no papaya season (ay, que cosa, can this happen?) we can describe the sad event by saying

```
papaya_season := []
```

15.2 MANIPULATION OF SETS

Pascal accepts several types of set operations. Although they are specified by some of the same operator symbols (e.g., +, *) used to describe arithmetic processing, Pascal has no difficulty in determining how to interpret the appearance of a particular operator. Ambiguity is avoided by Pascal's rule that allows sets and set constants to be the only legal operands in set expressions.

    To start the discussion of Pascal's set operations, we shall assume the following declarations:

```
TYPE
    weeks = 1..52 ;
    season = SET OF weeks ;
VAR
    theater_season, hockey_season, hunting_season,
    symphony_season, dance_season, opera_season,
    football_season, baseball_season, rock_season,
    drama_season, home_season, away_season,
    busy_season  :  season
```

15.2.1 Set Assignment

We have already seen the operation of set assignment for constant values (with our papaya_season). The same process can be applied to a variable as well. For example, the sequence

```
opera_season := [21..26] ;
dance_season := opera season
```

produces a situation in which the six-week opera and dance seasons coincide. (Who are these schedulers, anyway?)

15.2.2 Set Addition (Union)

Larger set memberships can be constructed by combining sets via the + operator. For instance, if we define the symphony season by saying

```
symphony_season := [33..52, 1..16]
```

the statement

```
rock_season := symphony_season + [17..20, 22]
```

specifies rock_season as consisting of all the weeks in symphony_season as well as weeks 17 through 20, and week 22. The sequence

```
drama_season := [37, 40..43, 48..50, 2, 6, 7] ;
dance_season := [41..46] ;
theater_season := drama_season + dance_season
```

assigns the set [37, 40..46, 48..50, 2, 6, 7] to theater_season. This is the set of elements found in either drama_season or dance_season or both. Each constant value appears only once, and the order is immaterial.

15.2.3 Set Differences

The – operator forms sets whose elements constitute the difference between two sets. For instance, the sequence

```
football_season := [33..48] ;
home_season := [34, 35, 38, 41, 43, 44, 46, 47] ;
away_season := football_season - home_season
```

assigns the set [33, 36, 37, 39, 40, 42, 45, 48] to away_season. These are all the elements in football_season that are not in home_season.

15.2.4 Set Multiplication (Intersection)

The * operator uses the elements common to two specified sets to form a third set. Thus, if we specify the following sets:

```
football_season := [33,48] ;
baseball_season := [13,,39] ;
rock_season := [21,,26, 30, 32,,34, 36, 37, 40,,44]
```

the statement

```
busy_season := football_season * baseball_season * rock_season
```

assigns the set [32..34, 36, 37] to busy_season. (These are the five elements found in all of the sets specified in the expression.)

15.3 DECISION OPERATIONS WITH SETS

The IF statement can be used to set up decision rules based on comparisons involving entire sets. Several types of comparisons can be specified, with all of them sharing the same basic property: The outcome is either TRUE or FALSE.

15.3.1 Searching Sets

Pascal's IN operation searches a specified set to determine whether a particular element is present in that set. The element (which itself is *not* a set) must be of the same type as that serving as the set's base type. For instance, let us assume the following fragment:

```
CONST
    end_goodnum = 1 ;
TYPE
    ticket = 1,,4000 ;
    winners = SET OF ticket ;
VAR
    entrant : INTEGER ;
    number, good_num : ticket ;
    lucky_list : winners ;
    sw : BOOLEAN
    ,
    ,
    ,
    sw := TRUE ;
    lucky_list := [] ;
    WHILE  sw  DO
```

```
BEGIN
  READ (good_num) ;
  IF  good_num <> end_goodnum
    THEN  lucky_list := lucky-list + [good_num]
    ELSE  sw := FALSE
END
```

ticket is defined as a subrange integer data type whose values may range from 1 to 4000. This becomes the base type for a set type named winners. So far we have no variables, just bookkeeping. The variables number and good_num, both of type ticket, may assume single values in the range 1 to 4000. Since lucky_list is a set variable with ticket as its base type, it may assume combinations of values in this range. So much for the declarations.

lucky_list is intended to contain the list of winning numbers in some lottery or sweepstakes. That list is filled by reading each of those numbers (good_num) in and adding it to the set. Accordingly, lucky_list is initialized to empty, and the winning values are read by means of a loop controlled by a terminating value of 1 (which we have given the name end_goodnum. Now the stage is set for the rest of the processing.

If we want to set up a loop in which each entry ticket is brought in to see whether its number is a winner, we are in an excellent position to take advantage of the IN operation:

```
READLN (entrant, number) ;
IF  number IN lucky_list
  THEN  WRITELN ('NUMBER ',number,' IS A WINNER, HOO HA!')
  ELSE  WRITELN ('NUMBER ',number,' DOES NOT WIN, ALAS,')
```

Notice that sets or set elements cannot be read or written. When we read a winning number, we read good_num, not [good_num].

15.3.2 Comparing Sets with Each Other

Sets having the same base type can be compared with each other using one of four relational operators:

1. The = comparison produces an outcome of TRUE if the two sets being compared contain the same elements (or are both empty). As pointed out earlier, the order is not important. Thus, the comparison

    [17, 21, 22, 23, 24, 8] = [23, 21, 22, 24, 8, 17]

    would result in a value of TRUE.

2. The <> comparison produces an outcome of TRUE if the two sets being compared differ in their content. (This is, for example, a convenient way to determine whether a set has anything in it.)

3. The >= comparison produces an outcome of TRUE if the first set contains all of the second set's elements. Thus, if result is declared as BOOLEAN, the statement

```
result := [18, 23, 6] >= [23, 6, 41, 18, 55]
```

will place a value of FALSE in result, but the statement

```
result := [23, 61, 41, 18, 55] >= [18, 23, 61]
```

will assign the value TRUE to result.

4. The <= comparison produces a value of TRUE if all of the elements in the first set are contained in the second set. Thus, the expression

['A'..'F','a..f','*'] <= ['a..h','*','D','F','A..C','E']

is TRUE.

15.3.3 Example 15.1

Hotshot Enterprises, eager to enjoy the benefits of modern business practices and methodologies, arranged for their staff to go to Lake Lackalooka-like for an Intensive Interdisciplinary Dynamic Management Seminar Workshop Conference. They have not reported on the outcome of that historic IIDMSWC (as we in the Management Dynamics set refer to it), but there is strong evidence that the group liked Lake Lackalookalike. Shortly after their return to the home base in Cranepool's Cavity, Hotshot announced a new addition to their business ventures: They have purchased a Luxury Sport Condominium on the Lake and are ready to lease its use, one week at a time, to qualified clients. Imagine.

In response to a request from Hotshot, we shall write a program to help keep track of the bookings for Hotshot Knolls (as they like to call it). Each client requesting to lease the condominium is given an i.d. number, and each request consists of this i.d. number and a week number (1 through 52; weeks 8 and 9 are reserved for maintenance and refurbishing). The program is to respond by indicating whether the reservation is accepted (i.e., the Knolls are available) or whether that week had been taken earlier. After the final request (for that run), the program is to display a list of the weeks that have been booked.

Organization of this program pivots around a set data type called a schedule whose values are drawn from the base type weeknum. Two

```
PROGRAM ex1501 ;
TYPE
  weeknum = 1..52 ;
  schedule = SET OF weeknum ;
VAR
  available, booked : schedule ;
  when : weeknum ;
  idnum, i, j : INTEGER ;
  sw : BOOLEAN ;
BEGIN
  available := [1..7, 10..52] ;
  booked := [] ;
  sw := TRUE ;
  WRITELN ('HI THERE. WELCOME TO HOTSHOT KNOLLS. THE EXCITEMENT BEGINS!') ;
  WRITELN ;
  WHILE sw DO
    BEGIN
      WRITELN ('TYPE IN I.D., DESIRED WEEK NO. (1-52), AND <RETURN>.') ;
      READLN (idnum, when) ;
      IF when IN available
        THEN
          BEGIN
            WRITELN ('WEEK ',when,' IS YOURS. CONGRATULATIONS!') ;
            booked := booked + [when] ;
            available := available - [when]
          END
```

336

```
        ELSE
            WRITELN ('WEEK ',when,' IS ALREADY BOOKED, SORRY,') ;
        WRITELN ('TYPE <RETURN> TO CONTINUE OR <CNTRL>-C TO QUIT,') ;
        READLN ;
        IF  EOF  THEN sw := FALSE
    END ;
WRITELN ;  WRITELN ;  WRITELN ('BOOKED WEEKS AT THE KNOLLS:') ;
WRITELN ;  i := 1 ;   j := 1 ;
WHILE i <= 52 DO
    BEGIN
        IF i IN booked
            THEN
                BEGIN
                    WRITE (i:4) ;                {*****************************************}
                    IF j = 10                    {THESE STATEMENTS FORMAT THE DISPLAY}
                        THEN                      {SO THAT TEN VALUES APPEAR ON EACH  }
                            BEGIN                 {LINE (EXCEPT, POSSIBLY, FOR THE    }
                                WRITELN ;         {LAST ONE,                          }
                                j := 1            {*****************************************}
                            END
                        ELSE
                            j := j + 1

                END ;
        i := i + 1
    END ;
WRITELN ;  WRITELN ('END OF RUN,')
END.
```

Figure 15.2 ───────── Program for Example 15.1

```
HI THERE, WELCOME TO HOTSHOT KNOLLS, THE EXCITEMENT BEGINS!

TYPE IN I.D., DESIRED WEEK NO.(1-52), AND <ENTER>.
222 6
WEEK 6 IS YOURS, CONGRATULATIONS!
TYPE <RETURN> TO CONTINUE OR <CNTRL>C TO QUIT.

3131 7
WEEK 7 IS YOURS, CONGRATULATIONS!
TYPE <RETURN> TO CONTINUE OR <CNTRL>C TO QUIT.

TYPE IN I.D., DESIRED WEEK NO.(1-52), AND <ENTER>.
4217 8
WEEK 8 IS ALREADY BOOKED, SORRY.
TYPE <RETURN> TO CONTINUE OR <CNTRL>C TO QUIT.

614 51
WEEK 51 IS YOURS, CONGRATULATIONS!
TYPE <RETURN> TO CONTINUE OR <CNTRL>C TO QUIT.

TYPE IN I.D., DESIRED WEEK NO.(1-52), AND <ENTER>.
7841 6
WEEK 6 IS ALREADY BOOKED, SORRY.
TYPE <RETURN> TO CONTINUE OR <CNTRL>C TO QUIT.

BOOKED WEEKS AT THE KNOLLS:

   6   7  51
END OF RUN.
```

Figure 15.3

Sample Run for Example 15.1

```
PROGRAM ex1501          {revised}

    {the TYPE and VAR declarations are exactly as before}

  PROCEDURE  addnum ;
  BEGIN
    IF  when IN available
      THEN
        BEGIN
          WRITELN ('WEEK ',when,' IS YOURS, CONGRATULATIONS!') ;
          booked := booked + [when] ;
          available := available - [when]
        END
      ELSE
        WRITELN ('WEEK ',when,' IS BOOKED, SORRY.')
  END ;
```

Figure 15.4

Revision of Example 15.1 Showing Set-processing Subprogram

```
BEGIN

    {initialization of available, booked, and sw as before}
    {hearty message still appears as in the initial version}

WHILE  sw  DO
  BEGIN
    WRITELN ('TYPE IN I.D., DESIRED WEEK NO.(1-52), and <RETURN>.') ;
    READLN (idnum, when) ;
    addnum ;
    WRITELN ('TYPE <RETURN> TO CONTINUE OR <CNTRL>C TO QUIT.') ;
    READLN ;

        {the rest is the same}
```

Figure 15.4 ———————————————————————————————

Revision of Example 15.1 (Continued)

schedules, available and booked, will keep track of the open and reserved week numbers, respectively. Consequently, when processing begins, available is initialized to its maximum number of elements, representing the situation in which all the weeks are available. Conversely, booked is initialized to the empty set to signify that nothing is booked. Then, as each request is brought in, a simple check (with the IN operation) determines whether to process it (i.e., move that week from available to booked) or to turn it down.

To display the results at the end of the run, we have to work our way around Pascal's refusal to read or write set data. Instead, we relate the set values to the base type and display the latter values. The program is shown in Figure 15.2, and a modest sample run is shown in Figure 15.3.

Sets can be processed by subprograms, so that we can exploit the organizational advantages of program modularity. To illustrate, Figure 15.4 shows Example 15.1's program reorganized so that the processing of each request is handled by a procedure named addnum. The use of the program, and its results, are unaffected by the reorganization.

Problems

1. Assume the following declarations and assignments:

```
TYPE
    letter = 'A'..'Z' ;
    ltrgroup = SET OF letter ;
```

```
VAR
    alphabet, alpha1, alpha2, alpha3 : ltrgroup
    .
    .
    .
    alphabet := ['A'..'Z']
```

Write the statement(s) to produce the results specified below. You may use any of the declared variables for intermediate purposes.

(a) Assign the consonants to alpha1.

(b) Assign the letters I through N to alpha1 and alpha2 and the rest to alpha3.

(c) Show the value of alpha3 after the following sequence:

```
alpha1 := alphabet - ['B'..'G','T'..'Z'] ;
alpha2 := alphabet - alpha1 + ['J'] ;
alpha3 := alphabet * alpha1 + ['R'] - ['K'..'M']
```

2. This question is for those of you with some formal musical background. Assume the following declarations and assignments:

```
TYPE
    tone = (c, csharp, d, dsharp, e, f, fsharp, g,
            gsharp, a, asharp, b) ;
    notes = SET OF tone ;
VAR
    row, cluster, scale, tune, chord3, chord4 : notes
    .
    .
    .
    row := [c..b]
```

(a) Assign to scale the notes of the B major scale.

(b) Assign to tune the notes not in the A major scale.

(c) Assign to scale the notes in the harmonic E minor scale.

(d) Assign to chord3 the notes in the F-sharp major triad.

(e) Assign to chord4 the notes in the D7 chord.

(f) Assign to cluster the notes in the E7 and A7 chords.

(g) Assign to cluster the notes that are neither in Dm7 or G7.

The following problems pertain to Example 15.1 Each of them specifies a modification or extension to that program and so may be treated singly or in combination.

3. Reorganize the program in Example 15.1 so that, if a particular client submits a request for a week that is already taken, he or she can submit another request without having to resubmit the i.d. number.

4. Revise the program in Example 15.1 to take care of the following deficiency: In its original version, the program will continue to take requests (and turn them down) when all the weeks are booked. In the revised version, the program is to display a special message and terminate when the last available week is booked.

5. Revise the program (we still are talking about Example 15.1 or any of its modifications) so that when a client submits his or her i.d. number, the program displays a list of the available weeks.

6. A small extension to the version of Problem 5 is to include a feature that allows a client to decide not to book a week after looking at the list of available weeks. In response, the program is to issue a polite message thanking the client for his or her interest and inviting him or her to come back next year.

7. Revise the program so that it can take care of special clients who want to book several consecutive weeks. In this version, the client is asked to submit his or her i.d. number and the number of consecutive weeks desired. If the number is 1, the program proceeds as before. If it is greater than 1, the program checks the available weeks to determine whether the request can be filled. If it can, the program displays the available groups of weeks and asks the client to select. (Remember to break up the ranges as necessary. For example, if the client wants to book for two weeks, and weeks 14 through 19 are available, the program must display this information as five separate choices, i.e., 14–15, 15–16, 16–17, 17–18, and 18–19.)

8. Revise the program so that the summary information includes a line showing the number of weeks booked in each quarter (1..13, 14..26, etc.) and a second line showing the total number of weeks booked.

Chapter 16

Dynamic Data Structures

Data structures such as arrays are said to be *static* because their size is defined when they are declared, and Pascal reserves storage for them as part of the compilation process. That storage is a permanent part of the program regardless of the number of elements actually used. If we use an array in a situation where the entire array may not always be occupied, we are compelled to carry the entire array. Moreover, if different parts of the array are occupied at different times, we have the additional task of keeping track of the array's pertinent sections.

When there are large differences between the full size of an array and the fraction currently in use, the situation often becomes intolerably cumbersome. Such circumstances are by no means exotic; the Pascal compiler is an example of a program whose operation on small computer systems would be much less assured if it had to rely on static data structures.

An effective way to handle situations with unpredictably extensive data requirements is to use *dynamic data structures*. Dynamic structures may assume a wide variety of forms; however, they share one common property: Storage for dynamic data structures is not allocated until the program is executing and explicitly asks for such storage. Moreover, storage usually is requested (and allocated) in small increments, so that there is a close relationship between the storage actually needed and that made available.

From what warehouse is this storage allocated? After all, the processor has a certain amount of storage, and that is what it has. Why should it make a difference whether the storage is allocated when the program is compiled or whether the allocation is deferred until the running program asks for it? We can only introduce some of the reasons here, but the discussion will point up some of the major benefits of dynamic data structures. Further insight can be developed through use and experimentation.

After taking care of its essential storage requirements, the p-System makes the remaining storage available to Pascal. Supporting this generosity are software facilities that keep track of how much is available, where it is located, and how the situation changes with each allocation. The available storage is not "promised" to any particular data items. Instead, it is totally uncommitted and, therefore, it may be assigned to fulfill whatever request the program may make. Working in conjunction with the allocating mechanism is another facility that enables the program to "return" storage when it is through with it. (In harmony with the exciting world of jet-set travel, where people "deplane," such returned storage is "deallocated.") Deallocation means that the storage is added to the pool of available storage for possible reallocation later in the same program execution. As a result, the program can be designed with any number of dynamic data structures, each with its own unpredictable storage requirements.

From the foregoing description, the allocation of storage would appear to be a haphazard way of doing business. When we declare an array, the storage reserved for that purpose is a cohesive unit of consecutive locations. If word_list is a one-dimensional array and we refer to word_list[4], the program "knows" exactly where it is because of its relation to word_list[1]. That relationship will exist for the entire life of the program. With dynamic structures, however, there cannot be such a relationship because no one (not the programmer, nor the program, nor the p-System) "knows" what will be needed when. The program, of course, contains the requests for storage, together with descriptions of the conditions under which such requests can be made. The frequency with which those conditions are met depends on the situation that develops during a particular run. Consequently, we must reconcile this apparent chaos with the fundamental need to know where everything is (and *what* everything is).

This knowledge is established and maintained by using a type of data item called a *pointer*. As the name implies, a pointer (the data item, not the doggie) tells us where something is. The something, which may be a velocity, a price, a weight, or any other value (or collection of values) we might want to represent, is made available to a program by tying it to a pointer. We always know where the pointer is because it is declared like any other static variable. Consequently, the pointer exists throughout the program's execution, and we can use it as a figurative hook (or Velcro, if you prefer) to grasp a dynamically allocated item. (We shall start with this fundamental notion of static pointers; a little later, we shall see that the pointers themselves can be dynamically allocated if we make the proper arrangements.)

If we say that nose is the name of a pointer, and density is the name of a variable for which storage is to be allocated dynamically, we can describe the basic dynamic allocation mechanism simply and clearly.

When we want a newly allocated piece of storage for density, we make the following request:

"Please find an appropriate amount of available storage and let me use it for density. When you decide which one it is, store its *location* in nose. Thank you. {Have a good day.}"

Once the storage is allocated, we still do not know where it is. (Neither does the program or the system.) As a result, we cannot say, "Store a 12.24 in density via a normal assignment." However, we do know how to find density's whereabouts because we made the arrangements. Consequently, we can gain access to density by referring to it as "the place that nose points to" (or "the place to which nose points" for those people vulnerable to any protruding prepositions).

This is the essence of Pascal's dynamic allocation mechanism. In subsequent sections we shall see exactly how these facilities are presented to the programmer and how to make them work for us.

16.1 POINTERS AND POINTEES

16.1.1 Declaration of Pointers

A pointer in Pascal is declared by giving it a name and defining the *data type* of the pointee (i.e., the item to which it will point). This does not mean that the pointer is inexorably tied to one variable. However, it is true that the pointer is *bound to* (can only be associated with) variables having the data type specified in its declaration.

The syntax for a pointer declaration is given in Figure 16.1. For instance, if we say

```
VAR
    nose : ^REAL
```

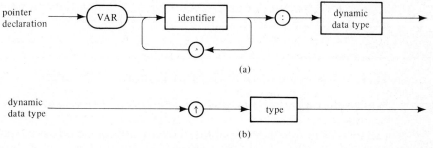

(a)

(b)

Figure 16.1

Construction of a Pointer Declaration

we reserve storage for a variable named nose whose value will represent the address of a real variable. (Although it is up to the programmer to make sure that nose's contents are consistent with its declaration, Pascal helps by making it difficult to violate this restriction.) The "up arrow" symbol is produced by the carat symbol (on the "6" key of many keyboards).

16.1.2 Allocation of Dynamic Variables

A dynamic variable is allocated by Pascal's NEW procedure. In its basic form, NEW is invoked with a single argument that names the pointer to be associated with the new variable. Thus, using the previous declaration,

```
NEW (nose)
```

allocates storage for a real variable and stores the address of that variable in nose. *The variable thus allocated has no name.* Access to the variable is gained only via its pointer. (If we want to associate a pointer with a particular variable name, that association exists in our heads but not in the program. We can show that association by noting it in a comment; as far as Pascal is concerned, the name is irrelevant.)

A pointer points only to one thing at a time. Consequently, the programmer must allocate storage carefully. For instance, the sequence

```
NEW (nose) ;
NEW (nose)
```

is legal. Pascal will allocate storage for a real value (assuming the earlier declaration for nose) and set its address in nose. Fine. Then, it will go ahead and repeat the allocation, moving the pointer to the new allocation. The result is that the first allocation is lost because there is no pointer to it. Furthermore, the storage is unavailable for other use because it has not been returned to the available pool. That takes a separate procedure, as we shall see. If we want to make such multiple allocations, the only way to do it is to arrange for separate pointers. Techniques for doing this, along with the fundamental benefits offered by those techniques, are discussed in Section 16.2.

16.1.3 Assignment of Values to Dynamic Variables

We can store a value in a dynamically allocated variable by assigning it or reading it in. These, of course, are the same mechanisms used for any variable. With dynamic variables, the only difference is that we must refer to the pointer. Pascal uses the form

pointername^

to specify a reference to a variable associated with *pointername*. For instance,

```
nose^ := 12.24
```

stores the value 12.24 in `nose`'s pointee. Similarly,

```
READLN (nose^)
```

stores the next input value (if it is a real number) in the variable associated with `nose`. `READ`, `WRITE`, and `WRITELN` also can be applied to dynamic variables.

Once a dynamic variable has been allocated, it can be processed like any other variable. For instance, the following sequence

```
VAR
    nose, finger : ^REAL ;            {nose --> density}
    NEW (nose) ;
    NEW (finger)
        .
        .
        .                             {finger --> density}
    READLN (nose^) ;
    finger^ := nose^
```

is legal. The result is that the value read into the variable pointed to by `nose` (i.e., the variable we choose to regard as `density` is copied into the variable pointed to by `finger`.

16.1.4 Assignment of Pointer Values

As explained earlier, part of the activity performed by the `NEW` procedure is to assign an address to a pointer. This is an automatic process, inseparable from the other work done by that procedure. In addition, it is possible for the program to assign an explicit value to a pointer. Of course, that value must be consistent with a pointer's usage, so that the only assignable value is that taken from another pointer. Since we have no direct knowledge of the actual values stored in pointers, we cannot read in such values (nor can they be written out).

This leaves us with the assignment operation. Thus, in the following sequence

```
VAR
    nose, finger : ^REAL ;
    NEW (nose) ;
    NEW (finger)
        .
        .
        .
```

```
READLN (nose^) ;
finger := nose
```

we end up with a situation where the variable associated with nose has a value in it, and both nose and finger point to that same unnamed variable.

16.1.5 A Name for Nowhere

Thus far, we have discussed the use of pointers to help us find dynamic variables. It also is necessary to have a way to denote the fact that a pointer points nowhere. This is handled by Pascal's built-in constant NIL. Thus, if we say

```
finger := NIL
```

we set the contents of the pointer finger to a particular value that is used consistently whenever NIL is mentioned. That means that we can test for it and use it as a basis for subsequent decisions.

16.1.6 Returning Dynamically Allocated Storage

When the programmer is through with some dynamically allocated storage and wishes to return it to the pool of available storage, he or she does so by invoking Pascal's DISPOSE procedure.

```
DISPOSE (pointername)
```

returns the variable *pointername*^ to unallocated storage and sets *pointername*^ to NIL. Consequently, the programmer must make sure that *pointername*^ is allocated before he or she refers to it. (*pointername* itself, of course, still is there, waiting for a pointee.)

16.2 LINKED LISTS

Now that we have become acquainted with Pascal's facilities for defining, allocating, and assigning dynamic data, we shall apply these features to the construction and processing of a powerful dynamic data structure, the linked list.

16.2.1 Properties of a Linked List

We can use dynamic data allocation to build data structures that expand and contract as needs dictate. Since we cannot count on consecutive elements being next to each other in storage, we have to construct explicit connections to join them. Such *links* are provided by pointers, and a collection of data joined by pointers is called a *linked list*. There are endless varieties of linked lists. Our concentration on the most basic type will enable us to become acquainted with its properties and develop insights into some of the more intricate possibilities.

The essential ingredients of a linked list are shown in Figure 16.2. Each element, usually called a *cell* or a *node*, consists of the data and a *forward pointer* that ties the cell to the next one in the list. As is true with any other data structure, it is up to the programmer to define the criteria for determining the cells' order. A list's first cell is called the *head*, and a separate *head pointer* points to it. This pointer generally is static since it is likely to be the only way to get hold of the list. The last cell, called the *tail*, is marked as such by having its forward pointer point nowhere. Since it is the only pointer in the list with this ephemeral destination, we have a convenient way of identifying the tail. (Some lists may be equipped with a separate tail pointer.)

A cell's contents are not subject to any particular restrictions. Nor is there any conceptual limit on the number of cells in a list. (Certain limitations may be imposed by a particular programming language, but those are not intrinsic to the data structure itself.) We shall keep things simple for our discussion by considering lists in which each cell may contain several values of arbitrarily different data types, but all cells in a list must be constructed identically.

16.2.2 Fundamental Operations on Linked Lists

Manipulation of a list requires three basic operations: insertion, deletion, and searching, the last being required to support the other two. Since the location of a cell bears no relation to that of its immediate (conceptual) neighbors, there is no movement of data when the list's structure changes. Instead, the pointer values are adjusted.

We shall use a simple list in which each cell consists of a forward

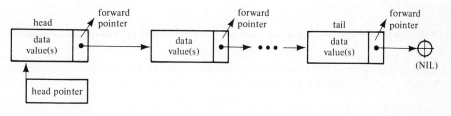

Figure 16.2

Components of a Simple Linked List

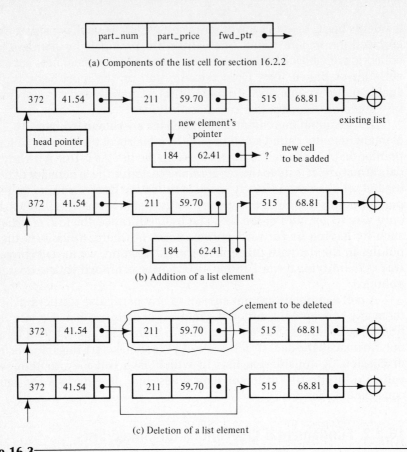

(a) Components of the list cell for section 16.2.2

(b) Addition of a list element

(c) Deletion of a list element

Figure 16.3

Basic List Operations

pointer, a part number, and a price. The assumption is that the list is to be in ascending order by price (i.e., the head contains the lowest priced item). This is shown in Figure 16.3(a).

As Figure 16.3(b) indicates, addition of a new cell to a list involves the following steps:

1. Allocating storage for the new cell and filling it with data
2. Finding where the new cell belongs
3. "Opening" the list to accommodate the new addition by adjusting the appropriate pointers

The addition (insertion) operation must include provisions for handling the special cases where the new cell is to be installed at the head or tail of the list. Another special case occurs when the list is empty and the element in question is the first one.

Deletion from a list can be viewed as the mirror image of insertion. It involves

1. Finding the element to be deleted
2. "Unhooking" the pointers from the unwanted cell and reconnecting the cells around it
3. Returning the newly deleted cell to available storage

This type of transaction is shown in Figure 16.3(c).

There are numerous ways to search a list for a cell containing a given value. The applicability of a particular technique depends on how the list is organized and on the kinds of supporting mechanisms with which the list is equipped. In our case, the search starts at the head of the list and systematically examines the specified data item in each cell until it finds what it is looking for or determines that the desired value is not there. With this type of list we have no choice: Its facilities make it impossible to start anywhere except the head; moreover, given a particular element, the only one we can reach is the next one.

16.2.3 Implementation of List Processing Operations

Now that we are acquainted with the basic properties of linked lists, we are ready to use Pascal's dynamic data facilities to define, build, and process such lists.

Construction of a List Element   Since there are virtually endless possibilities for the constituents of a list element, we need a flexible vehicle for its construction. Pascal's RECORD data type is well suited for this use, and we can apply it conveniently. To illustrate, let us say that we want each cell to consist of an integer named part_num, a real variable named part_price, and a forward pointer named fwd_ptr. Remember that fwd_ptr will point either to another list element (consisting, in turn, of a part_num, and a part_price, and a fwd_ptr) or it will point to NIL. With these requirements in mind, consider the following declarations:

```
TYPE
   part_cell = RECORD
                   part_num : INTEGER ;
                   part_price : REAL ;
                   fwd_ptr : list_pointer
               END ;
   list_pointer = ^part_cell
```

The newly defined part_cell data type describes the required list element. (Pascal is able to deal with the fact that list_pointer appears inside a declaration prior to its own definition.)

We shall not declare a variable of type `part_cell` because the resulting record would be static, and we want each cell to be allocated on demand. Consequently, we shall declare a pointer named `new_part` as follows:

```
VAR
    new_part : ^list_pointer
```

Now, whenever we want storage to be allocated for a list element, the invocation

```
NEW (new_part)
```

will get it for us, and `new_part` will point to it.

Assignment of Values to a List Element   The newly allocated cell is of little use as it is. Invocation of the NEW procedure obtained the storage, but it is an island accessible through its pointer. It has no values in it of interest to us, nor is the cell part of a list. This section takes care of providing values for a new cell, and the ensuing sections show how to bring that cell into the warmth and comfort of the linked list.

Once the cell is allocated, each constituent can be treated like an ordinary variable, as long as we remember that we must refer to it via its pointer. Thus, the statement

```
READLN (new_part^.part_num, new_part^.part_price)
```

reads two values and stores them in the indicated components of the newly allocated cell. Alternatively, we could have stored values by means of ordinary assignment statements. For instance,

```
new_part^.part_price := 386.79
```

is a legitimate assignment. That is all there is to it.

Initializing a List   As indicated earlier, a head pointer is a crucial component of a list structure. Let us define one for our example:

```
VAR
    hdptr : list_pointer
```

Initially, the head pointer has no pointee (the list has no members yet). Consequently, NIL is a reasonable value with which to initialize it. (Later, we shall use the value as a test to determine whether a list is empty.)

Now we can add the first element to the list. All that is required is to set the head pointer so that it points to the newly allocated cell:

```
hdptr := new_part
```

Remember that we do not use the up-arrow (^) here because we want to refer to the pointers and not the cell. Assuming all the TYPE and VAR declarations given before, let us review the processing needed to initialize the head pointer, allocate a cell, fill in its data values, and establish the cell as the sole member of the list:

```
hdptr := NIL ;
NEW (new_part) ;
READLN (new_part^.part_num, new_part^.part_price) ;
hdptr := new_part ;
new_part^.fwd_ptr := NIL    {the head also is the tail}
```

Searching a List   The most direct way to construct a search for a simple linked list is to set up a loop that starts at the head and works its way through the list. To help manage this process, we shall define another pointer named next. Initially, next will point to the head of the list. Then, as we go through each cycle and finish with a given cell, the value in that cell's forward pointer is assigned to next, thereby enabling the program to examine the next cell.

We shall illustrate the technique by setting up a loop that looks through a list of part_cells to find a part_price equal to a static real variable named testvalue. The value of part_num for the matching cell will be stored in testpart. If there is no match, testpart will be zero. Figure 16.4 shows Pascal statements. For the sake of brevity, only next, testvalue, testpart, and sw (a switch for loop control) are explicitly declared in the figure; the earlier declarations are assumed. Furthermore, we assume an existing list with hdptr pointing to its first cell.

Adding an Element to a List   There are two basic steps involved in adding an element to a list: Finding where it belongs and installing it there. The first step can be handled by a slight variation of the search described in Figure 16.4. This time, instead of looking for a matching price, we shall be interested in finding two adjacent (i.e., linked) cells such that the price value in the new cell falls between their respective price values. In addition, we shall be alert for special situations in which the new cell's price value compels us to install that cell as the new head or tail of the list. Further help will be sought from another pointer named prior. If a new

```
VAR
   .
   .
   .
   next : listpointer ;
   testvalue : REAL ;
   testpart : INTEGER ;
   sw : BOOLEAN
     .
     .
     .
      READLN (testvalue) ;
      next := hdptr ;    {next --> head of the list}
      testpart := 0 ;
      sw := TRUE ;
      WHILE   sw  DO
         IF   next^.part_price = testvalue
            THEN
                BEGIN
                    testpart := next^.part_num ;
                    sw := FALSE
                END
            ELSE
                IF   next^.fwd_ptr = NIL            {end of list?}
                THEN
                    sw := FALSE
                ELSE
                    next := next^.fwd_ptr
```

Figure 16.4 ───

Outline for a List Search to Find a Matching Value

cell is to be installed between two members of the current list, we shall arrange for prior and next to point to these two members. This process is outlined in Figure 16.5.

Deleting an Element from a List   The two basic steps in this operation consist of finding the element and removing it from the list. To find the cell, we can go back to the search technique outlined in Figure 16.4 and expand it to take care of the special situation where there is an attempt to remove a cell from an empty list. Actual deletion simply requires the adjustment of the preceding cell's forward pointer so that it points to the cell following the one to be deleted. A special case is one where the cell to be deleted turns out to be the head of the list.

We shall organize the deletion process as a procedure that handles the same list structure we have been using all along. The cell to be deleted is the one whose part_price matches test_value. We shall use next to point to the unfortunate cell (if it is in the list). ᴩʀɪᴏʀ will point to the cell preceding the one to be deleted. It will be ᴩʀɪᴏʀ's cell, of course, whose forward pointer has to be changed. An additional variable, the integer ʀᴇsᴜʟᴛ, will be used to report the subprogram's activity to an invoking program: A ʀᴇsᴜʟᴛ of 1 means that the requested deletion was performed; zero means that there was no such cell in the list; when ʀᴇsᴜʟᴛ is –1, it means that the list was empty. The resulting subprogram is shown in Figure 16.6. Declarations from a hypothetical invoking program are included to provide context.

```
{ASSUME DECLARATIONS FOR PART_CELL, LIST_POINTER, NEW_PART;   }
{ASSUME THAT A CELL HAS BEEN ALLOCATED AND NEW VALUES WERE    }
{ASSIGNED. THUS, NEW_PART POINTS TO THE NEW CELL TO BE ADDED. }
VAR
    hdptr, prior, next : list_pointer ;
    testvalue : REAL ;
    testpart : INTEGER ;
    sw1, sw2 : BOOLEAN
      .
      .
      .
    sw1 := TRUE ;
    prior := hdptr ;
    next := hdptr^.fwd_ptr ;
    WHILE  sw1  DO
       IF  hdptr = NIL            {IS LIST EMPTY?}
          THEN
             BEGIN
                hdptr := new_part ;        {INSTALL FIRST}
                new_part^.fwd_ptr := NIL ; {ELEMENT        }
                sw1 := FALSE
             END
       ELSE
          IF  new_part^.part_price < hdptr^.part_price
             THEN
                {INSTALL NEW CELL AS HEAD OF LIST}
                BEGIN
                   new_part^.fwd_ptr := hdptr ;
                   hdptr := new_part ;
                   sw1 := FALSE
                END
```

Figure 16.5

Process for Addition to a Linked List

```
        ELSE
          BEGIN
            sw2 := TRUE ;
            WHILE  sw2  DO
               IF  next = NIL
                  THEN
                     {INSTALL NEW CELL AS THE TAIL}
                     BEGIN
                        new_part^.fwd.ptr := NIL ;
                        next^.fwd_ptr := new_part ;
                        sw2 := FALSE ;
                        sw1 := FALSE
                     END
                  ELSE
                     IF (new_part^.part_price >
                         prior^.part_price)        AND
                        (new_part^.part_price <
                         next^.part_price)
                        THEN
                           {INSTALL NEW CELL BETWEEN}
                           {PRIOR AND NEXT          }
                           BEGIN
                              new_part^.fwd_ptr :=
                              prior^.fwd_ptr ;
                              prior^.fwd_ptr := new_part ;
                              sw1 := FALSE ;
                              sw2 := FALSE
                           END
                        ELSE
                           BEGIN     {SHIFT POINTER}
                              prior := next ;
                              next := next^.fwd_ptr
                           END
      END
```

Figure 16.5

Procedure for Addition to a Linked List (Continued)

```
{ASSUME THE FOLLOWING DECLARATIONS IN THE INVOKING PROGRAM:}
{TYPE                                                      }
{   part_cell = RECORD                                     }
{      part_num : INTEGER ;                                }
{      part_price : REAL ;                                 }
{      fwd_ptr : list_pointer                              }
{   END ;                                                  }
{   list_pointer = ^part_cell ;                            }
```

Figure 16.6

Procedure for Deletion from a List

```
{VAR                                                              }
{    testvalue : REAL ;                                           }
{    result : INTEGER ;                                           }
{    hdptr, prior, next : listpointer                            }

PROCEDURE  delete ;
VAR
    sw : BOOLEAN ;
BEGIN
    result := 0 ;
    IF  hdptr = NIL
        THEN
            result := -1                      {LIST IS EMPTY}
        ELSE
            BEGIN
                sw := TRUE ;
                next := hdptr ;
                prior := NIL ;
                WHILE  sw  DO
                    IF  next^.part_price = testvalue
                        THEN
                            BEGIN
                                sw := FALSE ;
                                result := 1            {SUCCESSFUL MATCH}
                            END
                        ELSE
                            IF  next^.fwd_ptr = NIL
                                THEN
                                    sw := FALSE          {NOT IN LIST}
                                ELSE
                                    BEGIN
                                        prior := next ;
                                        next := next^.fwd_ptr
                                    END ;
                {SEARCH COMPLETED}
                IF  result = 1
                    THEN
                        IF  prior := NIL        {DELETE HEAD OF LIST}
                            THEN
                                hdptr := hdptr^.fwd_ptr
                            ELSE
                                prior^.fwd.ptr := next^.fwd_ptr
            END
END
```

Figure 16.6
───

Procedure for Deletion from a List (Continued)

Problems

1. Using the part_cell structure, assume that we want to construct a list in which the cells are in order by increasing part_num. Write a procedure named add_cell that adds a new cell to the list. Assume that the new cell is allocated and that new_part points to it. Furthermore, when add cell is invoked, the new cell's values already are assigned. The existing list may be empty, or a cell with that part_num may already be in it.

2. Write a program named list_build that uses add_cell to construct a list of part_cells in order by increasing part number. Design your program so that it asks for a part number and price. When the user submits the values, the program adds the new cell to the list and displays the number of cells currently in the list. Run your program with the following data:

part number	price
121	38.71
86	40.40
218	36.05
271	41.70
250	65.37
321	59.50
308	72.14
265	68.00

3. Write a version of the program in Problem 2 that reads the data from a textfile.

4. Revise the program in either of the preceding two problems so that each cell includes a part name up to 12 letters long.

5. Using the data structure from Problem 1, write a procedure named price_change that finds a cell with a specified part_num and replaces its part_price value with a new one. There is no guarantee that the list contains a cell with the indicated part number.

6. Here is the grand finale for part_cell: Combine the appropriate components from previous problems and illustrations to write the following interactive program: Using part_num, part_price, and fwd_ptr, and starting with an empty list, the program asks the user whether he or she wishes to add to the list, delete from the list, change a price in the list, or quit. After the user indicates the desired activity, the program requests the appropriate data, reads the value(s), and reports what it did.

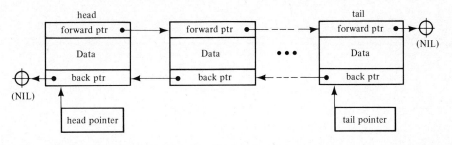

Figure 16.7

Basic Components of a Doubly-Linked List

7. Now we shall call on our newly acquired prowess with simple linked lists to build and process more intricate structures. One such structure is the *double linked* list in which each cell is equipped with two pointers: A *forward pointer* to the next cell (or to NIL) and a *backward pointer* (or *back pointer*) to the previous cell (or to NIL). The basic structure is depicted in Figure 16.7. As a starting point in our examination of double linked list structures, define a data type named aqua_cell whose constituents consist of a string of 12 letters or less named fish_name_, an integer named fish_ref, and two pointers named fwd_fish and bkwd_fish.

8. Using the data structure developed for the previous problem, write a program that builds a doubly linked list in which the cells are arranged in alphabetical order by fish_name. Design your program to operate interactively and run it with the following data:

fish name	ref
guppy	181
mollie	109
betta	265
oscar	347
swordtail	216
angelfish	452
tetra	146

(Loaded Question): Is there any advantage in setting up and maintaining a pointer that points to the center of the list?

9. Write a version of the program for the previous problem that reads the input from a textfile.

10. Expand the program of Problem 8 or 9 so that it will handle a series of intermixed additions and deletions.

Chapter 17

Modular Programs and Program Modules

One of the fundamental ideas that have helped the programming process move away from an art toward a more disciplined activity is that of modularity. Instead of constructing a program as a monolithic sequence of statements, programmers are encouraged to modularize a program by subdividing it into a number of interconnected components, each of which can be perceived as a "black box" designed to handle a particular aspect of the process. This notion of combining building blocks (each of which is known to work) to form an arbitrarily complex program is no different in concept from the traditional practice applied to the development of any engineered product.[*]

We introduced the subprogram as the crucial vehicle for modularization (Chapter 13), and we applied Pascal's features for writing subprograms by using them as building blocks in modular programs. Since Pascal's design explicitly supports modularization as a primary contributor to the development of clear, reliable programs, it is no surprise that the use of subprograms in Pascal is a simple, straightforward matter.

What is surprising, however, is that Pascal, in its standard versions, stops short of fully exploiting the properties of subprograms in the design and construction of modular programs. Frequently, such programs are prepared by attaching a collection of subprograms to a main program whose major duties consist of invoking the subprograms and coordinating their activities. Subprograms thus attached are called *external subpro-*

---

[*]This concept, along with its implications, is explored with unusual clarity in "An introduction to Engineered Software" by W.D. Gillett and S. V. Pollack (CBS College Publishing, New York, 1982.)

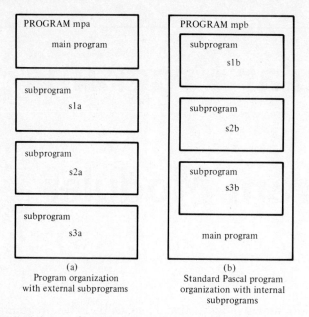

Figure 17.1

Alternative Program Organizations

grams. The general organization of such programs is shown in Figure 17.1, where it is contrasted with Pascal's standard construction, i.e., the one we have been using all along, in which a program consists of a main program and a collection of *internal subprograms*.

Although many standard Pascal programs are constructed in which the main program does little more than invoke its subprograms, the structural organization just introduced provides additional flexibility in the following important respects:

1. With external subprograms, it is a relatively simple matter to arrange for a subprogram to be used by several other subprograms (as well as by the main program, if that is desired). For instance, referring to Figure 17.1, s1a and s2a can invoke s3a (so can mpa), but that relationship does not apply to subprograms s1b, s2b, and s3b. As we know from our previous experience, mpb can invoke any of its subprograms, and that is it. This is not an insurmountable obstacle, but it means that the programmer using standard Pascal (which does not support external subprograms) sometimes has to introduce considerable complication just to overcome this restriction.

2. The ability to use external subprograms also implies that the subprograms may be independent entities not necessarily related to each other or to the main program. (Such mutual independence also is possible with internal subprograms, but its extent is considerably

more limited.) Some or all of the subprograms in such a structure may have been developed originally for other programs, or they may have been intended for general use without any specific program in mind.

3. External subprograms take on even more flexibility when they are supported by a facility that allows them to be compiled separately, i.e., independent of any program(s) to which they eventually may be attached. This means that programs can be put together from components, some or all of which already are in machine language form. As a result, such a program literally can be compiled piecemeal, thereby increasing the size of programs that can be run on a system of a given size.

For these and numerous other reasons, UCSD Pascal includes facilities that allow programs to be constructed from an arbitrary combination of internal and external subprograms. This chapter introduces these facilities and shows how they are used.

17.1 THE UNIT AND ITS PROPERTIES

In UCSD Pascal, an external subprogram generally is used by compiling it as a separate component and attaching the resulting p-Code to a main program. This process of independent compilation means that it is possible to prepare a collection of (previously compiled) subprograms, retain them in a *library*, and retrieve any or all of them for use with any main program that needs them.

To handle such compilations simply and conveniently, UCSD Pascal introduces the *unit* as a structural component in the programming environment. A unit is a sequence of Pascal statements that can be compiled by itself, but the resulting instructions cannot be executed without being connected to (*used by*) a program. A unit may consist of a single subprogram or a collection of subprograms. In either case, UCSD Pascal treats the unit as a single structure and compiles it into a functionally equivalent structural entity. It also is possible to string together a collection of units and submit them to UCSD Pascal as a structural grouping to be processed by a single compilation. The crucial point here is that the compiler can go through its entire processing on something that is not a complete program, with the result being available as an executable program component. This section examines the structure of a unit, after which we can deal with its preparation.

17.1.1 Construction of a Unit

A unit, like a program, begins with an identifying statement that defines the unit's name:

```
UNIT   unitname
```

When a programmer wants to use a unit as part of a program, the program using the unit is called the *host program*. The connection between the host and the unit is indicated by specifying the unit's name in a USES statement in the host program. (We shall look at that connection in Section 17.2.) The body of the unit consists of an *interface section* that describes the unit's contents and how they are used, an *implementation section* that contains the actual processing statements, and an optional *special coding section*. The unit concludes with END. Figure 17.2 gives the syntax diagram for a unit's construction.

The Interface Section As its name implies, a unit's interface section contains declarations that describe the way a host program communicates with the unit. Thus, if a unit consists of a collection of related subprograms to be made available for any host program, the unit's interface section will define how each subprogram is to be invoked. To underscore the fact that communication between the host program and the unit occurs through the interface section, your attention is called to the following fact:

> Since a unit's implementation section contains the processing statements for that unit, any changes in that section, of course, will make it necessary for the unit to be compiled again. However, if those changes do not affect the implementation section, the host program does not have to be recompiled. Read that again.

An interface section's general syntax is shown in Figure 17.3.

For instance, suppose we wanted to construct a unit named `pwrf` consisting of a function named `pwr_func` that raises a REAL number to an INTEGER power. The beginning of the unit could look like this:

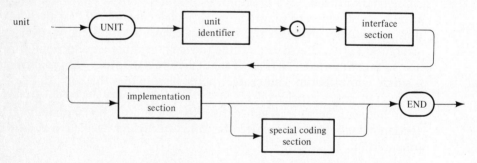

Semantics: The END is followed by a period if the unit is a single unit being compiled separately or if it is the last of a series of units being compiled together. A semicolon separates units when several are to be compiled together.

Figure 17.2

Syntax of a Unit

```
UNIT  pwrf ;
INTERFACE
FUNCTION  pwr_func(bval : REAL ; power : INTEGER) : REAL
```

The FUNCTION declaration provides the same kind of information as any other FUNCTION declaration; i.e., it indicates how the function is to be invoked. The UNIT statement indicates (to UCSD Pascal and all other concerned parties) that any host program wishing to invoke pwr_func can do so by using a unit named pwrf.

According to Figure 17.3, subprogram declarations represent only one

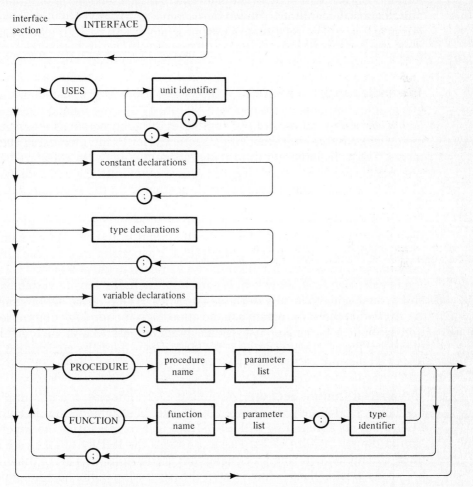

Semantics: The USES clause may appear *either* in the implementation section or the interface section.

Figure 17.3————————————————————————————

Syntax of a Unit's Interface Section

of several kinds of declarations that could be included in an interface section. The constants, data types, and variables declared in the interface section are *public* in that their appearance here makes them available to a host program. (It is up to the programmer to make sure that naming conflicts are prevented by avoiding the use of the same names in the host program.) Variables in the subprogram's parameter list, of course, are not declared separately. A parameter list still is a parameter list regardless of where it appears.

Note also (Figure 17.3) that the interface section may contain a USES declaration. This means that it is possible for a unit to use another unit. Our current concern will be with units whose interface sections are limited to subprogram declarations. Once you become familiar with a unit's basic construction and its relation to a host program, it will be a straightforward matter to design units that contain public declarations and use other units.

The Implementation Section   A unit's actual processing statements are given in the implementation section (Figure 17.4). Any named constants and/or variables that are not transmitted to the subprogram as arguments are declared in the implementation section prior to the processing statements. These declarations are *private* in that the items thus declared are unavailable outside the unit. If a unit uses another unit, the USES declaration may appear either in the interface section or in the implementation section.

To see these structural rules applied to an actual case, we shall write the implementation section for the unit started in the previous section. Given REAL parameter bval and INTEGER parameter power, the function pwr_func will return the value bval raised to the power power. The implementation unit, shown in Figure 17.5, includes private variables i and t, analogous to locally declared variables in an internal subprogram.

Note that the subprogram's name appears in the implementation section without a parameter list. (Some programmers like to include the parameter list as a bookkeeping aid. This is done simply by enclosing it in braces so that the UCSD Pascal compiler treats it as a comment.)

The Special Coding Section   As Figure 17.2 indicates, a unit's implementation section may be followed by a group of statements starting with BEGIN but not concluding with END. (END is there already as the conclusion of the unit itself.) UCSD Pascal provides the facility to take care of those situations requiring processing that is conceptually part of the unit but needs to take place before or after the processing in the host program. Accordingly, the special coding section may include *initialization statements* and/or *termination statements*. For example, a unit may be designed to perform certain operations on a set, and its initialization statements start

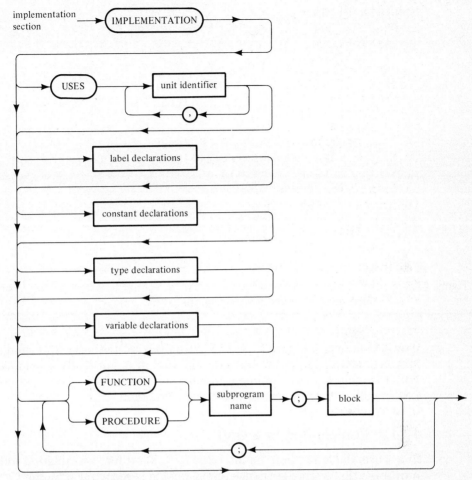

Semantics: The USES clause may appear *either* in the unit's interface section or implementation section.

Figure 17.4

Syntax for a Unit's Implementation Section

off with an empty set before the host program does anything. Similarly, a unit designed to perform certain file processes may include statements that close the files after the host program finishes its activities.

Figure 17.6 shows the syntactic details of the special coding section. Note that if this section contains only initialization statements, the asterisks are not needed.

Example 17.1   We shall combine the pieces from the previous sections to produce a complete unit for the function pwr_func. The unit, named

```
IMPLEMENTATION
  VAR
    t: REAL ;
    i : INTEGER ;
  FUNCTION pwr_func ;
  BEGIN
    t := 1 ;
    IF  power <> 0
      THEN
        BEGIN
          FOR  i := ABS(power) DOWNTO 1   DO
            t := t*bval ;
          IF  power < 0
            THEN
              t := 1.0/t
        END ;
    pwr_func := t
  END
```

Figure 17.5

Implementation Section for Example 17.1

pwrf, is shown in Figure 17.7. There is no special coding section, and the "parameter list" in the implementation section is not really a parameter list. It is included as a comment to help documentation. The concluding END is followed by a period, just as in a program.

17.1.2 Compilation of a Unit

In a sense, the term "unit" is intended to be short for "compilation unit," indicating that such a sequence of statements is recognized by the UCSD Pascal compiler as an entity to be processed by itself. Consequently, the compilation of a unit does not differ procedurally from that of a program:

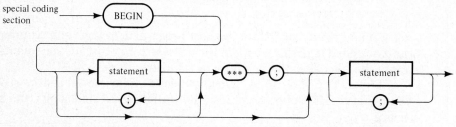

Semantics: Statements in a special coding section without the asterisks are treated as initialization statements.

Figure 17.6

A Unit's Special Coding Section

```
[**************************************************************]
[**                          PWRF                          **]
[**************************************************************]
[** THIS UNIT MAKES AVAILABLE A FUNCTION NAMED pwr_func    **]
[** THAT RAISES A POSITIVE REAL VALUE TO AN INTEGER        **]
[** POWER, THE EXPONENT MAY BE ZERO OR NEGATIVE,           **]
[**************************************************************]
UNIT  pwrf ;
{$L MYVOL:PWRLST}
INTERFACE
  FUNCTION  pwr_func(bval : REAL : power : INTEGER) : REAL ;
IMPLEMENTATION
  VAR
    t: REAL ;
    i : INTEGER ;
  FUNCTION pwr_func {(bval : REAL ; power : INTEGER) : REAL} ;
  BEGIN
    t := 1 ;
    IF  power <> 0
      THEN
        BEGIN
          FOR  i := ABS(power) DOWNTO 1  DO
            t := t+bval ;
          IF  power < 0
            THEN
              t := 1.0/t
        END ;
    pwr_func := t
  END
END.
```

Figure 17.7

Unit For External Function pwr_func

1. Prepare the unit as you would any other text, using the editor to type the statements. Conclude with <cntrl>C.
2. Q(uit) the editor (type "Q") and W(rite) the unit to a named textfile. To practice, type the unit from Figure 17.7 and store it in a file named MYVOL:PWR. When that process is complete, E(xit) to the p-System's executive command level.
3. C(ompile) the unit by typing "C" and naming the file you just wrote as the file to be compiled. (In Example 17.1 this would be MYVOL:PWR.) The p-System will ask you to name a file in which the compiled code is to be stored. Many programmers like to use the same file name for a program's (or a unit's) source and object code. Thus, for our example, that name would be MYVOL:PWR. The p-System automatically assumes the CODE suffix.

The unit, in object form, now is available in a codefile. For our Example 17.1, the situation is as follows: We have a unit named ᴘᴡ ʀ ꜰ that contains the function ᴘᴡ ʀ _ ꜰ ᴜ ɴ ᴄ. The unit's Pascal statements are stored in a textfile named MYVOL:PWR, and the unit's object code is stored in a codefile named MYVOL:PWR. (There is no problem with the names, of course, since the p-System will edit or compile only a textfile, and it will execute only a codefile.)

Now that the unit is available as a codefile, its instructions need no further processing. However, a host program still cannot use it. For that to happen, the unit's object code must be placed in a *library* to which the host program can refer. In concept, this is no different from the situation surrounding the use of UCSD Pascal's built-in subprograms. When we invoke a standard function (such as ꜱǫʀᴛ or ꜱ ɪ ɴ), that function's code, already in object form, is obtained from a standard library, stored in a codefile named SYSTEM.LIBRARY. Similarly, when a host program specifies that it uses a particular unit, the p-System expects to obtain that unit's code from a library containing one or more such units. In fact, it is possible to prepare a new version of SYSTEM.LIBRARY in which the library's standard contents are augmented by the unit(s) that we construct. However, we shall examine the more general mechanism in which we produce and use a separate library. This is done in the next section.

17.2 PREPARATION OF LIBRARIES

In the p-System, a library (or, more specifically, a *user library*) consists of one or more compiled units. Organizationally, the library is a codefile constructed from other codefiles.

The process of preparing such a library is handled by a utility program named LIBRARY. (The program may be named LIBRARIAN in some p-System implementations.) In general, the procedure involves the transfer (duplication) of code from one or more existing *input files* into an *output file* representing the new library. Each unit occupies a *slot* in that library. An input file may contain a single unit or it may be another library containing several units, any or all of which can be copied into the new library.

To see how the process operates, we shall create a library file named MYVOL:EX17 consisting of the unit named ᴘᴡ ʀ ꜰ copied from the codefile named MYVOL:PWR. The displays produced by the p-System may vary in some details from one implementation to another, but the overall procedure will be consistent. Consequently, this will give you an excellent picture of the library-building procedure.

The process is started by bringing the p-System to its executive command level and eX(ecuting) the LIBRARY program. The resulting initial display appears as in Figure 17.8. (The LIBRARY program may or may not

```
Library:
Output file?_
```

Figure 17.8

Initial Display of LIBRARY Utility Program

be on your p-System diskette, depending on your particular configuration. If it is not, it is likely to be on a diskette with other system utility programs. Place the diskette containing LIBRARY in drive #5 and eX(ecute) #5:LIBRARY. Once the initial display appears on your video screen, the LIBRARY program is available internally, and you can remove the diskette from which it was read, replacing it with your program diskette.) We are ready to prepare our one-unit library:

1. Type in the name of the file in which our library is to be stored, followed by <return>. For our example, the file is MYVOL:EX17. LIBRARY will ask for the name of an input file.
2. The code for the unit ₚwrf was compiled into a file named MYVOL:PWR. Accordingly, type that name (followed by <return>) so that LIBRARY can find the proper input file. (The .CODE suffix is assumed automatically since user libraries can be built only from codefiles.) LIBRARY will find MYVOL:PWR, and it will display its description, along with a command line:

```
Library: N(ew, 0-9(slot-to-slot,
E(very, S(elect, C(omp-unit,? _

Input file? MYVOL:PWR
  0 u PWRF            55
```

This tells us that the input file consists of a single slot (slot 0) containing a unit (u) named PWRF with length 55. That unit has not yet been copied to the output file. The command line gives us a choice of activities, with the question mark indicating that additional commands (i.e., an alternative command line) can be displayed by typing "?." Our current interest will be restricted to a few of these commands:

(a) The E(very) command allows us to copy every unit from the input file into the output file. Since our input file has only one unit, this command is overpowering, but it will do the job.

(b) The 0–9 (slot-to-slot) command allows us to choose a particular slot from the input file and copy it into a designated slot of the output file. In our case, we would specify that slot 0 from the input file (the only slot) is to be copied to slot 0 of the output file.

(c) The N(ew) command is used after a transfer to the output file has been completed and we want the next unit to be copied from a different input file. This makes it possible for a library to be built from a collection of units drawn from any number of codefiles. We shall not need this command for our example, but it is a good thing to know.

(d) The Q(uit) command, shown on the alternative command line, enables us to signal that our library is complete.

3. Type "0" to indicate your intention to copy the unit from slot 0 of the input file. (As stated earlier, we can do the same thing in this case simply by typing "E," but this will give us an opportunity to see how the slot-to-slot process works.) LIBRARY will ask us for slot 0's destination:

```
From slot #? 0_
```

Type <return> and LIBRARY will ask for the destination:

```
From slot #? 0        To slot #? _
```

Type "0" followed by <return> to indicate that the unit thus copied is to occupy slot 0 of the output file. LIBRARY will copy the unit as specified and display the results in the "output file" portion of the display:

```
Output file? MYVOL:EX17
Output file is 3 blocks long
  0 u PWRF          55
```

The cursor is repositioned on the command line, indicating that LIBRARY is ready for the next command. At this point we can copy another slot, ask for a new input file, etc.

4. Since our library (such as it is) is complete, we can type "Q" to quit. LIBRARY will ask if we want to include a copyright notice:

```
Notice? _
```

Well, of course we do. ᴘᴡʀf is a useful and attractive piece of merchandise, destined to produce seven fortunes. Accordingly, we can type in an appropriate notice, hit <return>, and the process is finished. The p-System returns to its executive command level and the final display appears as in Figure 17.9.

Now the unit is in the proper form and is squirreled away in a proper user library. Are we ready to use it? No. One more step is required, but it is a simple one: We must prepare a textfile in which the *names* of the available

```
Command: E(dit, R(un, F(ile, C(omp, L(ink, X(ecute, A(ssem,?  _
Notice? Copyright 1983 by Peerless Software Ltd.
Input file? MYVOL:PWR
  0 u PWRF           55


Output file? MYVOL:EX17
Output file is 3 blocks long
  0 u PWRF           55
```

Figure 17.9————————————————————————————————————

Final Display after Library Construction

user libraries are listed. Since there is only one user library (for our example), our textfile will have only one name in it. We shall name this file MYVOL:MYLIB. To prepare it, all we need to do is to bring in the p-System editor, type the single line MYVOL:MYLIB (followed by <return> and <cntrl>C, of course), and store the line in MYVOL:MYLIB. Now our unit is ready for use by any host program, and in the next section we shall write a main program to use it. Although this seems like a lot of bother to prepare one simple unit, remember that the same process, without further complication, can be applied to arbitrarily large collections of units.

17.3 USING A PRECOMPILED UNIT IN A HOST PROGRAM

Having gone through all that fuss to prepare a unit, its actual use by a host program is quite simple. We shall illustrate the process with an appropriate main program.

17.3.1 Preparation of the Host Program

Any subprogram contained in a unit is invoked just as though that subprogram were written as an internal procedure or as if the subprogram were one of UCSD Pascal's built-in subprograms. The only required references to the unit have nothing directly to do with the invocations:

1. The host program must include a USES declaration that names each unit to be used. For instance, if a program were to use pwrf, the declaration

    USES   pwrf

If several units are to be used, their names are listed in a single USES declaration, separated by commas. This declaration appears after the PROGRAM statement.

2. When a host program uses a unit whose code is stored in a user library, that library's name must appear in a pseudocomment with a $U directive to the UCSD Pascal compiler. This lets the compiler know that the unit named in the USES declaration will not be found in the standard system library. Instead, the compiler is directed to look in a user library (EX17 in our example).

That is all there is to it.

17.3.2 Example 17.2

The unit named pwrt, prepared as Example 17.1, will be used by a main program named EX1702. The program will contain internal procedures pwrc1 and pwrc2, each of which invokes the external function pwr_func several times in the process of performing its computations. The Pascal statements, given in Figure 17.10, are simple enough, as long as we keep the names straight:

1. pwrf is the name of the unit containing the external function pwr_func. It is the unit's name that must appear in the USES declaration.
2. EX17 is the name of the library in which the unit's object code is stored. It is the library's name that must appear in the {$U} directive.
3. pwr-func is the name of the external function itself. Thus, the function is invoked by that name.

```
[****************************************************************]
[**                        EX1702                            **]
[****************************************************************]
[** THIS PROGRAM PERFORMS SOME NUMERICAL COMPUTATIONS BY     **]
[** INVOKING INTERNAL PROCEDURES pwrc1 AND pwrc2. EACH       **]
[** PROCEDURE,  IN TURN, INVOKES A FUNCTION NAMED pwr_func   **]
[** TO PRODUCE ITS RESULTS. pwr_func IS AN EXTERNAL FUNC-    **]
[** TION MADE AVAILABLE VIA A UNIT NAMED pwrF STORED IN A    **]
[** USER LIBRARY NAMED SVP:EX12.                             **]
[****************************************************************]
PROGRAM ex1702 ;
{$L MYVOL:UNITLST}
{$U MYVOL:EX17}
USES  pwrf ;
VAR
  xval, yval, pval, qval, sval, tval : REAL ;
```

Figure 17.10

Main Program for Example 17.2

```
   exp1, exp2 : INTEGER ;
   sw : BOOLEAN ;
PROCEDURE pwrc1 (x1, x2 : REAL : e1, e2 : INTEGER ;
                 VAR z1 : REAL : VAR z2 : REAL) ;
BEGIN
   z1 := pwr_func(x1,e1) + pwr_func(x2,e2) ;
   z2 := pwr_func(x1,e2) + pwr_func(x2,e1)
END ;
PROCEDURE  pwrc2 (y1, y2 : REAL ; f1, f2 : INTEGER ;
                 VAR w1 : REAL ; VAR w2 : REAL) ;
BEGIN
   w1 := pwr_func(y1,f1)/pwr_func(y2,f2) ;
   w2 := pwr_func(y1,f2)/pwr_func(y2,f1)
END ;
BEGIN
   sw := TRUE :
   WRITELN ('TYPE VALUES FOR xval AND yval') ;
   READLN (xval, yval) ;
   WRITELN ('TYPE VALUES FOR exp1 AND exp2.') ;
   READLN (exp1, exp2) ;
   WHILE  sw  DO
     BEGIN
       pwrc1(xval, yval, exp1, exp2, pval, qval) ;
       pwrc2(xval, yval, exp1, exp2, sval, tval) ;
       WRITELN ('XVAL: ',xval:7:2,' YVAL: ',yval:7:2) ;
       WRITELN ('EXP1 :', exp1,' EXP2: ',exp2) ;
       WRITELN ('PVAL: ',pval:7:2,' QVAL: ',qval:7:2) ;
       sval := pwr_func(xval,exp1)/pwr_func(yval,exp2) ;
       tval := pwr_func(xval,exp2)/pwr_func(yval,exp1) ;
       WRITELN ('SVAL: ',sval:7:2,'   TVAL: ',tval:7:2) ;
       WRITELN ('TYPE <RETURN> TO CONTINUE OR <CNTRL>C TO QUIT.') ;
       READLN ;
       IF  EOF
         THEN
           sw := FALSE
         ELSE
           BEGIN
             WRITELN ('TYPE VALUES FOR xval, yval.') ;
             READLN (xval, yval) ;
             WRITELN ('TYPE VALUES FOR exp1, exp2.') ;
             READLN (exp1, exp2)
           END
     END ;
   WRITELN ('END OF RUN.')
END.
```

Figure 17.10

Main Program for Example 17.2 (Continued)

Remember one other thing: Any units used by a host program must be precompiled and in the user library before the host program can be compiled.

The host program is prepared and compiled in the usual manner. We shall use MYVOL:EX1702 as the name for the host program's textfile and codefile.

17.3.3 Execution of a Host Program

Now we are here, and the moment is at hand. The run, like the host's compilation, is simplicity itself: All we have to do is specify the name of the host's codefile and the name of the textfile in which the library is listed. For our example, the process begins by making sure that the p-System is at its executive command level. The dialogue then proceeds as follows (we are USER and it is SYSTEM):

```
SYSTEM:Command: E(dit, R(un, F(ile, C(omp, L(ink,
        X(ecute, A(ssem,?_
   USER:X
SYSTEM:Execute what file?_
   USER:MYVOL:EX1702 L=MYVOL:MYLIB<return>
```

The system responds by bringing in our program and starting the run, an example of which is shown in Figure 17.11.

Problems

1. Modify the unit from Example 17 so that it handles zero and negative as well as positive real numbers. Replace the file MYVOL:PWR with this revised version. Compile it into the codefile MYVOL:PWR and reconstruct the library MYVOL:EX17 using the revised codefile.

2. Prepare and compile a unit named sqratio that embodies a function named sqdiv that operates on two real arguments a1 and a2 to produce

    $$\frac{a1 - \sqrt{|a2|}}{a2 + \sqrt{|a1|}}$$

3. Prepare and compile a unit named strig that embodies a subprogram named tcomp. Given three real arguments b1, b2, and b3 in that

```
TYPE VALUES FOR xval AND yval,
2.2 2.3<RETURN>
TYPE VALUES FOR exp1 AND exp2,
2 3<RETURN>
XVAL:     2.20 YVAL:      2.30
EXP1: 2 EXP2: 3
PVAL:    17.01 QVAL:     15.94
SVAL:     0.40 TVAL:      2.01
TYPE <RETURN> TO CONTINUE OR <CNTRL>C TO QUIT,
<RETURN>
TYPE VALUES FOR xval, yval,
3.3 4.4<RETURN>
TYPE VALUES FOR exp1, exp2,
5 4<RETURN>
XVAL:     3.30 YVAL:      4.40
EXP1: 5 EXP2: 4
PVAL:   766.16 QVAL:   1767.75
SVAL:     1.04 TVAL:      0.07
TYPE <RETURN> TO CONTINUE OR <CNTRL>C TO QUIT,
<CNTRL>C
END OF RUN,
```

Figure 17.11

Sample Run for Example 17.2

order, tcomp computes the following:

$$b3 = \frac{b1 \text{ sine } b2}{b2 \text{ cosine } b1} \qquad b4 = \frac{b1 \text{ sine } b2}{b2 \text{ sine}(b1+b2)}$$

4. Write a program named c17p4 that reads an artitrary number of input value collections. Each collection of input values consists of the nonzero real values pval, ymas, gvar, and tprod. For each collection, the program is to display the four input values, each on its own line, followed by computed values for bmake, rback, and umax where

$$bmake = \frac{pval - \sqrt{|ymas|}}{ymas + \sqrt{|pval|}} + \frac{gvar - \sqrt{|tprod|}}{tprod + \sqrt{|gvar|}}$$

$$rback = \frac{gvar \text{ sine } pval}{pval \text{ cosine } gvar} \left[\frac{tprod - \sqrt{|ymas|}}{ymas + \sqrt{|tprod|}} \right]$$

$$umax = \frac{gvar \text{ sine } pval}{pval \text{ sine}(gvar + pval)} \left[\frac{ymas - \sqrt{|tprod|}}{tprod + \sqrt{|ymas|}} \right]$$

Use the units developed in Problems 2 and 3 as external components. Run c17p4 with the following test data:

collection no.	pval	ymas	gvar	tprod
1	0.5	1.4	2.0	1.5
2	0.6	0.8	−4.0	2.0
3	0.3	−0.6	0.5	4.4
4	1.2	1.8	3.2	− 0.8

5. Revise the program in Example 17.2 so that pwrc1 and pwrc2 are reorganized as separate units named pwrpr1 and pwrpr2. NOTE: Since each of these procedures invokes pwr_func, the reorganization will give us a situation in which a unit uses another unit. This means that a USES clause must appear in each of the two new units. In addition, pwrf's name still must appear in the main program's USES list even though pwr_func is not invoked directly from the main program. Moreover, pwrf's name must appear as the first unit named in that list because it is the one that is "lowest" (i.e., at the deepest nesting level) in the chain of usage. Compilation of pwrf must precede that of the two new units and the resulting codefile must be placed in a user library so that it is available as a point of reference. Then, after pwrpr1 and pwrpr2 are compiled, their codefiles can be added to that library as well. Run the reorganized program with the following values:

xval	yval	exp1	exp2
2.2	3.3	2	3
2.7	4.1	3	4
6.0	5.5	4	3
2.2	3.3	−2	−3

6. Reorganize the program in Problem 5 so that pwrpr1 and pwrpr2, though still separate units, are processed as a single compilation producing a single codefile. Run the reorganized program using the data given in Problem 5.

7. Reorganize the program for Problem 13 of Chapter 13 so that all of the subprograms are external.

8. Rewrite the program in Problem 21 of Chapter 13 so that the subprograms are made available as separate units.

9. Rewrite the program in Problem 27, 28, or 29 of Chapter 13 so that the subprograms are organized as separate units.

10. Reorganize the program in Problem 33 or 34 of Chapter 13 so that the subprogram is made available as a separate unit.

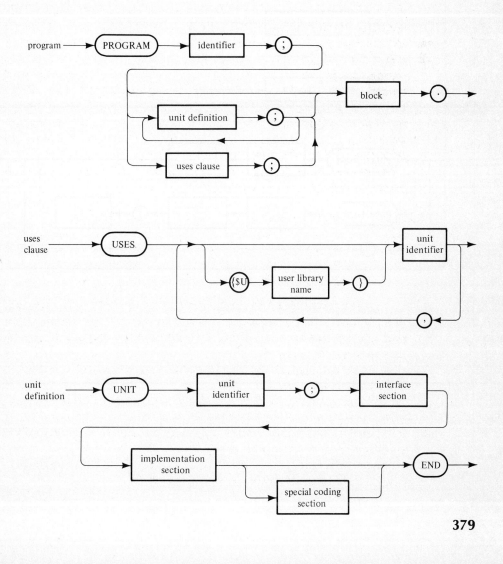

Railroad Diagrams for Pascal

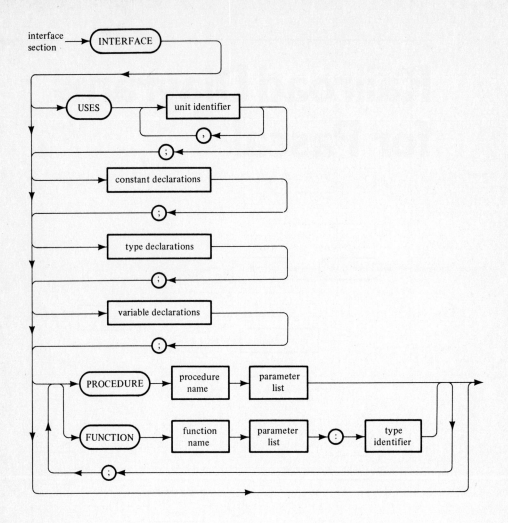

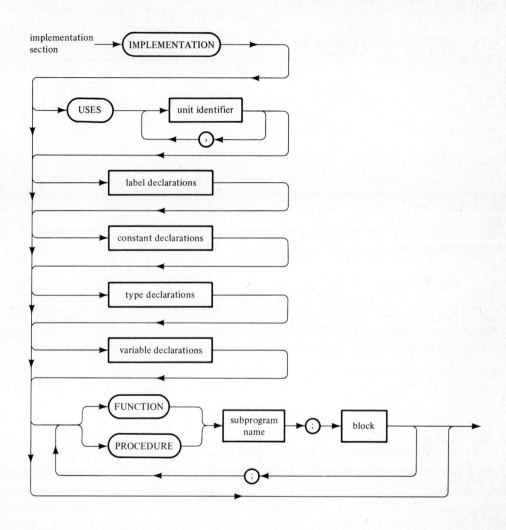

special coding section

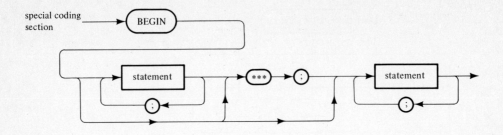

block

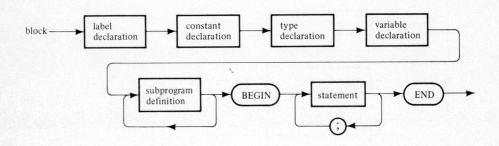

label declaration

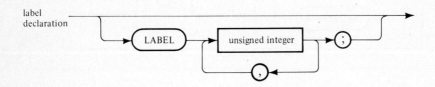

constant declaration

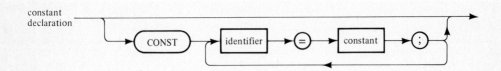

type
declaration

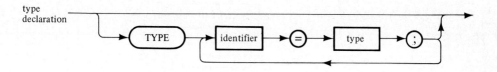

variable
declaration

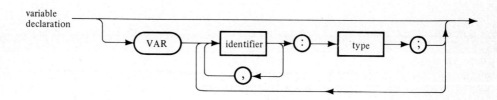

type

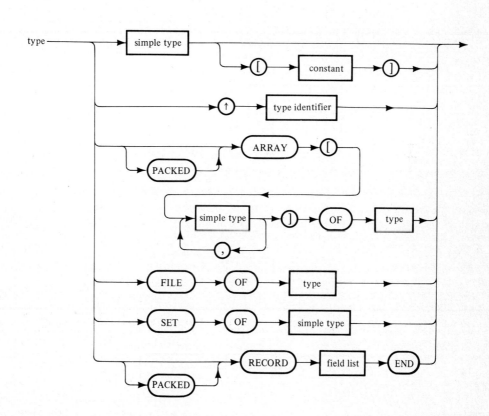

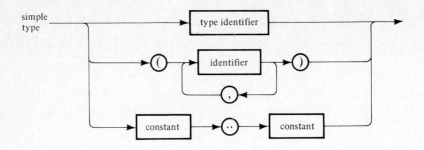

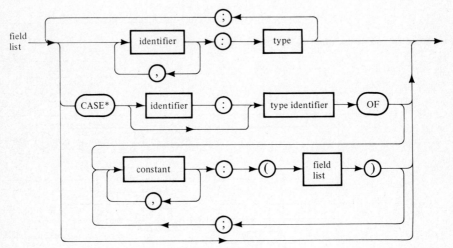

*Not covered in the text.

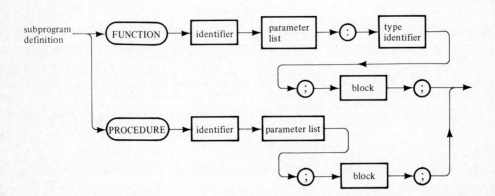

parameter
list

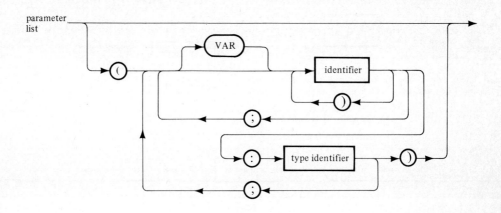

statement

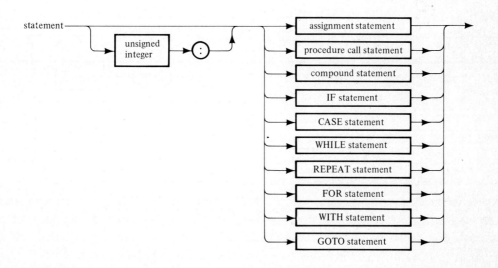

assignment
statement

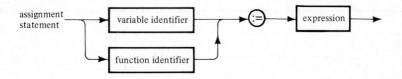

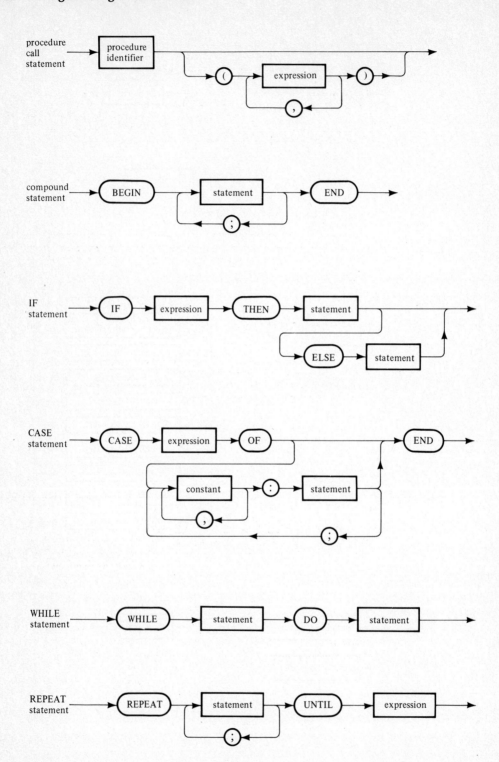

procedure
call
statement

compound
statement

IF
statement

CASE
statement

WHILE
statement

REPEAT
statement

FOR
statement

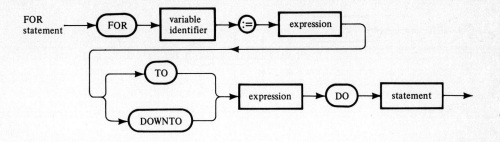

WITH
statement

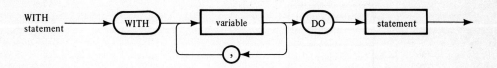

GOTO
statement

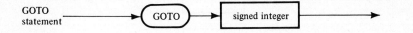

expression

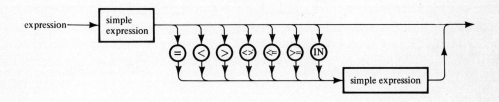

simple
expression

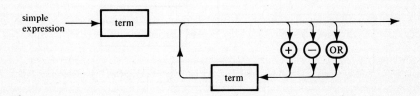

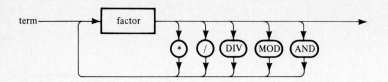

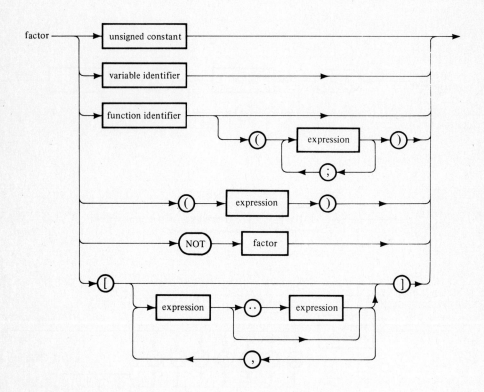

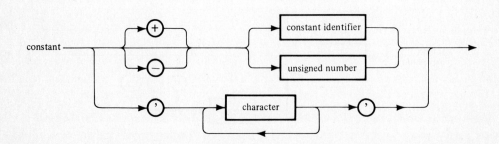

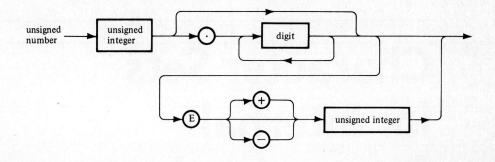

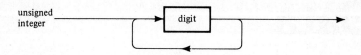

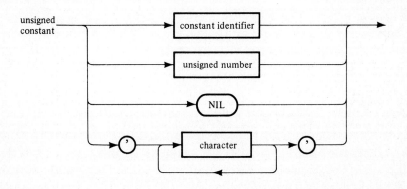

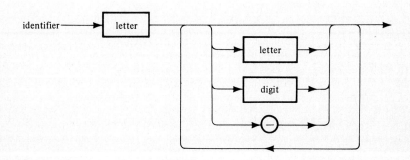

Character Sets for Internal Representation of Data

Table B.1 The ASCII Character Set

Symbol*	Internal Numerical Value	Symbol†	Internal Numerical Value	Symbol	Internal Numerical Value	Symbol‡	Internal Numerical Value
NLL	0	SP	32	@	64		96
SO-1	1	!	33	A	65	a	97
STX	2	"	34	B	66	b	98
ETX	3	#	35	C	67	c	99
EOT	4	$	36	D	68	d	100
ENQ	5	%	37	E	69	e	101
ACK	6	&	38	F	70	f	102
BEL	7	'	39	G	71	g	103
BS	8	(	40	H	72	h	104
HT	9	)	41	I	73	i	105
LF	10	*	42	J	74	j	106
VT	11	+	43	K	75	k	107
FF	12	,	44	L	76	l	108
CR	13	-	45	M	77	m	109
SO	14	.	46	N	78	n	110
SI	15	/	47	O	79	o	111
DLE	16	0	48	P	80	p	112
DC1	17	1	49	Q	81	q	113
DC2	18	2	50	R	82	r	114
DC3	19	3	51	S	83	s	115
DC4	20	4	52	T	84	t	116
NAK	21	5	53	U	85	u	117
SYN	22	6	54	V	86	v	118
ETB	23	7	55	W	87	w	119
CAN	24	8	56	X	88	x	120
EM	25	9	57	Y	89	y	121
SUB	26	:	58	Z	90	z	122
ESC	27	;	59	[	91	{	123
FS	28	<	60	\	92	¦	124
GS	29	=	61	]	93	}	125
RS	30	>	62	^	94	~	126
US	31	?	63	—	95	DEL*	127

*These are control symbols that are recognized by the processor but do not appear as visible characters when displayed or printed. ETX, for example, is the signal produced by <CTRL-C>.
†SP is a control character
‡DEL is a control character

Table B.2 The EBCDIC Character Set

Symbol	Internal Numerical Value	Symbol	Internal Numerical Value	Symbol	Internal Numerical Value	Symbol	Internal Numerical Value
blank	64	a	129	A	193	0	240
¢	74	b	130	B	194	1	241
.	75	c	131	C	195	2	242
<	76	d	132	D	196	3	243
(	77	e	133	E	197	4	244
+	78	f	134	F	198	5	245
I	79	g	135	G	199	6	246
&	80	h	136	H	200	7	247
!	90	i	137	I	201	8	248
$	91	j	138	J	209	9	249
*	92	k	145	K	210		
)	93	l	146	L	211		
;	94	m	147	M	212		
^	95	n	148	N	213		
−	96	o	149	O	214		
/	97	p	150	P	215		
,	107	q	151	Q	216		
%	108	r	152	R	217		
-	109	s	162	S	226		
>	110	t	163	T	227		
?	111	u	164	U	228		
:	122	v	165	V	229		
#	123	w	166	W	230		
@	124	x	167	X	231		
'	125	y	168	Y	232		
=	126	z	169	Z	233		
"	127	[	173				
		]	189				

*Other internal numerical values correspond to control characters.

Compiler Options

Information may be added to a UCSD Pascal program to exercise certain types of control over the activity of the compiler. The specifications are included as *pseudocomments* where general form is

{$ compile option} or (*$ compile option*)

Several compiler options may be specified in a size pseudocomment:

{$ option, option,. . .option} or (*$option, option,. . .option*)

However, when this is done, certain restrictions must be noted (see Table C.1 on the following page). To avoid complication, it is a good idea to use a separate pseudocomment for each desired compiler option.

Table C.1   UCSD Pascal Compiler Options*

Option	Result	Remarks
C string†	String is included in a special section of the codefile	Must be the last option in a pseudo-comment; cannot appear in the same pseudocomment with L string or T string options
L+	A listing of the Pascal program is stored in a file named SYSTEM .LST.TEXT	L− disables this option. The system default is L−
L string	A listing of the Pascal program is stored in the file named by string	Must be the last option in a pseudo-comment; cannot appear in the same pseudocomment with L string or T string options
N+	Pascal compiler produces output that can be converted to actual machine code instead of P-machine code	N− disables this option. The system default is N−
P+	Pascal compiler automatically paginates the program listing for 8½ inch paper	P+ is the system default. A {$P} pseudocomment anywhere in the program forces a new page
Q+	Suppresses compiler's output of intermediate progress (i.e., all the dots, etc.)	Q− allows transmission of intermediate compiler output of console. System default is Q−
R2	Real numbers are two words long regardless of default	
R4	Real numbers are four words long regardless of default	
T string	The string is shown at the top of each page of the listing	Must be the last option in a pseudo-comment; cannot appear in the same pseudocomment with C string or L string

*Consult your specific manual for possible additional options.
†Example: {$C Copyright 1983 by Schmugelski and Daughters}

How to Set Up a UCSD Pascal Program for Printing

The following provides a framework for directing your program's output to the p-System's parallel printer (instead of the video display):

```
PROGRAM name ;

VAR
    filename : TEXT ;
        ............
    other declarations
        ............
    volumename : STRING ;
        ............
BEGIN
    volumename := '#6:' ;    (*or volumename := 'printer:' *)
    REWRITE (filename, volumename) ;
        ............
        other statements
        ............
    WRITELN (filename, outlist) ; (*or WRITE (filename, outlist)*)
            ............
    CLOSE (filename) ;
            ............
END.
```

filename and *volumename* are programmer-defined names. (For a serial printer use `volumename := '#8:'` or `volumename := 'remout:'#`.)

Glossary

algorithm   A finite, precise sequence of steps that describes how to do something.

argument   A value delivered to a subprogram for processing.

array   A data structure whose members (elements) all are of the same data type and are stored adjacent to each other. Each element is identified by a unique subscript.

ASCII   The abbreviation for American Standard Code for Information Interchange. A system in which each of 256 distinguishable symbols is represented by a unique combination of eight 1s and 0s. See Table B.1.

bit   The indivisible element of computer storage. Each bit can represent a 1 or a 0. (Bit is an acronym for Binary digit.)

block   The body of a Pascal program or subprogram.

bootload   The process of reading the p-System (or any operating system) into storage and readying it for use. "Boot" is short for "bootstrapping" to reflect the idea that the process starts with a little program whose job is to bring in a larger program, etc.

built-in function   A function (like SQRT or EOF) that is a permanent part of the Pascal language.

byte   The amount of storage (eight bits) required to represent a single character of information.

<Ctrl>   The control key.

call   An explicit program statement requesting the use of a procedure. See *invocation*.

cell   A member of a linked list.

character   An item of information (e.g., a letter, numerical digit, punctuation mark) represented by a single symbol. A character occupies one byte of storage.

codefile   A p-System file containing all or part of a program in executable form.

command   A specific request for some service to be rendered by an operating system component.

compiler   A program that analyzes source program statements in a high-level language and produces a functionally equivalent sequence of object instructions in a machine language.

compound statement   A group of Pascal statements, bracketed by BEGIN....END and treated structurally as a single conceptual activity.

concatenation   Production of longer character strings by combining shorter ones.

CPU   The central processing unit (the processor) is the part of a computing system that contains the circuits that analyze machine instructions and perform the computations specified by them.

cursor   An electronic pointer, built into the video display unit, that enables the user (and the CPU) to keep track of movements around the screen.

data structure   A particular arrangement of information in which the contents, the organizational relations among the components, and the permissible operations are constrained by a set of rules peculiar to that data structure. (Arrays and linked lists are examples of data structures.)

default   A processing action that is built into a program for use when an explicit specification for that action is not supplied by the user.

driver   A minimally equipped program whose sole purpose is to provide a processing vehicle for invoking a subprogram.

dynamic storage   Storage assigned to data values on demand while a program is executing. Such storage, when not needed, can be returned to a pool of unallocated storage for reassignment later in the same program. See *static storage*.

EBCDIC   The abbreviation for Extended Binary Coded Decimal Interchange Code. A system (differing from ASCII) in which each of 256 distinguishable symbols is represented by a unique combination of 1s and 0s. See Table B.2.

echo   A printout or display of data values just read in.

editor   A software package that enables its users to manipulate computer-stored text interactively.

end-of-file (EOF)   A special signal (character) placed immediately after the final data item in a file. The Pascal function EOF tests for the presence of this signal.

end-of-line (EOL)   A special signal (character) that is placed after the final character of information on a line. The Pascal function EOL tests for the presence of this signal.

end-of-text   (‹ETX›)   A special signal used in the p-System to indicate the conclusion of numerous different interactive processes. ‹ETX› is produced by typing ‹Ctrl-C›.

enumerative data type   A programmer-defined data type in which each value is drawn from a finite repertoire of discrete, mutually exclusive values.

file   An arbitrary collection of information identified by a unique name that incorporates the collection into a system library.

file manager (filer)   That software component of an operating system that provides services for creating, storing, retrieving, processing and destroying files.

function   A Pascal subprogram that operates on an arbitrary number of arguments to return a single result.

hardware   The physical components in a computer system.

index   A variable used to keep track of a changing event (such as a counter in a loop) or of the location of an element in a collection of elements (such as a subscript for an array element).

instruction   The unit of activity recognized by a processor; a member of the processor's machine language.

interactive processing   A mode of computer operation where the currently active program is designed to stop at one or more points to enable the user to enter information that could affect that program's subsequent course of action.

interpreter   A program designed to analyze each statement in another program submitted to it and to perform the activities requested by that statement. P-code programs are "executed" in this manner.

invocation   Activation of a subprogram by referring to its name and supplying it with an appropriate list of arguments on which to operate. A function is invoked as part of an expression, and a Pascal procedure is invoked in a separate statement.

linked list (list)   A data structure in which each component (cell) may be anywhere in storage. Each cell is explicitly connected to the next one in the list by a pointer.

loop   A sequence of statements or instructions designed to perform a given process repeatedly and supported by a control mechanism that determines whether the loop will be allowed to execute another time.

machine language   The collection of instruction types comprising the elementary activities that a particular processor is designed to perform.

main storage   The memory component of a computer system used to store instructions and data.

menu   An interactive display showing the choice of commands available for a given system in a given mode of operations.

microprocessor   A central processing unit (often contained on a single physical chip) in which microelectronic technology is exploited to produce machines that are compact and economical. Most personal computers are based on microprocessors.

mode   The set of prevailing circumstances that will determine what a computer system will do when it encounters a particular item of data.

object program   The sequence of machine-language instructions produced by a compiler from a source program. An object program may or may not be directly executable.

operating system   A collection of programs designed to allocate and manage the hardware, software, and data resources available in a computer system.

ordinal date type   See *enumerative data type.*

p-Code   The "machine language" into which p-System source programs are compiled.

p-Machine   The hypothetical processor imposed by the p-System on the actual hardware. p-Code is the machine language for the p-Machine.

parameter   A specification in a subprogram description, placed there to represent an argument to be supplied when the subprogram actually is invoked.

pointer   An item of information indicating the address of another item of information.

procedure   A subprogram with no constraints on the number of arguments that may be supplied to it or the number of results that it may deliver. A procedure is invoked by a separate statement.

program   A sequence of statements or instructions describing an algorithm in terms that ultimately will be recognized by a computer system.

promptline   A display, issued by an interactive program at a predesigned stopping point, that informs the user of the choice of program-related actions he or she may take at that point.

record   A data structure consisting of an arbitrary collection of data items with arbitrarily diverse data types.

reserved word   A symbol (such as BEGIN) that is a permanent part of Pascal's vocabulary.

return   A process whereby a subprogram, upon completion of its processing, turns control of the processor back to the program (or subprogram) that invoked it.

set   A data structure consisting of zero or more elements of a given data type. Sets can grow or shrink dynamically, but each element must have a unique value.

source program   A sequence of statements written in a programming language different from the processor's machine language. A source program requires additional processing (e.g., by a compiler or interpreter) to produce an executable equivalent.

statement   The unit of expression (i.e., a single conceptual activity) in a high-level language.

static storage   Main storage that is assigned to a specific data item at the time the program is compiled. The association thus established remains in force throughout the program's execution. See *dynamic storage.*

string   A data structure consisting of a sequence of zero or more characters. The length of a string may change dynamically.

subprogram   A sequence of statements organized so that their combined processing can be activated by a single request (invocation) from any place in a program.

subrange   A contiguous sequence of values extracted from an available repertoire of discrete values. (For example 1..24 defines a subrange of 24 values from the repertoire of expressible positive and negative integers.)

subroutine   See *procedure.*

subscript   A combination of one or more identifiers used to distinguish an array element from all others in that array.

textfile   A p-System file consisting of an arbitrarily long sequence of characters. Textfiles are the only kinds of files that can be processed by the editor.

unit   A sequence of (Pascal) statements that can be compiled separately but cannot be executed without being attached to a program. Generally, a unit contains one or more subprograms.

word   A unit of main storage consisting of one or more bytes.

workfile   The central file in the p-System around which numerous system processes are organized. For example, the editor is designed to edit the workfile, the compilers are designed to process the workfile, and so on.

Index